Adventures in Social Research

Adventures in Social Research

Data Analysis Using SPSS™
for Windows 95/98®

Earl Babbie

Fred Halley

Jeanne Zaino

 PINE FORGE PRESS
Excellence and Innovation for Teaching

For Information:

 Pine Forge Press
A Sage Publications Company
2455 Teller Road
Thousand Oaks, California 91320
E-mail: sales@pfp.sagepub.com

Sage Publications Ltd.
6 Bonhill Street
London EC2A 4PU
United Kingdom

Sage Publications India Pvt. Ltd.
M-32 Market
Greater Kailash I
New Delhi 110 048 India

Printed in the United States of America

ISBN 0-7619-8676-6

SPSS® is a registered trademark of SPSS, Inc., Chicago, Illinois.

The authors and publisher have taken care in the preparation of this book, but make no expressed or implied warranty of any kind and assume no responsibility for errors or omissions. No liability is assumed for incidental or consequential damages in connection with or rising out of the use of the information or programs contained herein.

This book is printed on acid-free paper.

00 01 02 03 04 05 10 9 8 7 6 5 4 3 2 1

Publisher:	Stephen D. Rutter
Assistant to the Publisher:	Ann Makarias
Typsetter:	Ruth Cottrell Books

About the Authors

Earl Babbie was born in Detroit, Michigan, in 1938, although he chose to return to Vermont three months later, growing up there and in New Hampshire. In 1956, he set off for Harvard Yard, where he spent the next four years learning more than he initially planned. After three years with the U.S. Marine Corps, mostly in Asia, he began graduate studies at the University of California, Berkeley. He received his Ph.D. from Berkeley in 1969. He taught sociology at the University of Hawaii from 1968 through 1979, took time off from teaching and research to write full-time for eight years, and then joined the faculty at Chapman University in southern California in 1987. Although an author of research articles and monographs, he is best known for the many texts he has written, which have been widely adopted in colleges throughout the United States and the world. He has been married to his wife, Sheila, for more than 30 years, and they have a son, Aaron, who would make any parent proud.

Fred Halley left his home state of New Jersey for Ohio where he earned his bachelors degree at Ashland College and his masters degree at Western Reserve University in 1964. After teaching for a year, he began doctoral studies at the University of Missouri. As a graduate student, he became interested in using data processing machinery for social research. As a graduate student, he performed data analysis for several large surveys. After receiving his Ph.D. in 1970, he joined the Sociology Department at SUNY Brockport where he taught research methods, statistics, and data analysis until 1999. In addition to his teaching, he directed the sociology department's Data Analysis Laboratory for 13 years. He has presented more than 40 teaching workshops and demonstrations. His leadership in developing instructional computer applications for teaching sociology has been recognized by awards from the American Sociological Association and EDUCOM. Currently, he is designing software systems evaluation research with Socware, Inc. in Brockport, NY. He has been married to his wife, Judy, for more than 35 years, and they have two sons, a granddaughter and grandson who bring them great joy.

Jeanne S. Zaino earned a bachelors degree in political science at the University of Connecticut, Storrs. Upon graduation, she remained at UConn to work as a research assistant at the Roper Center for Public Opinion Research, where she received a masters degree in survey research. She went on to earn a masters degree in political science from the University of Massachusetts, Amherst, where she is currently completing work on her Ph.D. In addition to her teaching responsibilities, while at UMass she worked as a research assistant at the Massachusetts Institute of Social and Economic Research. She recently relocated to New York where she is teaching research methods, computer-based data analysis, American government, and world politics at Purchase College, State University of New York and Iona College, New Rochelle while she finishes research for her doctoral dissertation. She and her husband Jeff are the proud parents of a two-year-old son, Maxim.

About the Publisher

Pine Forge Press is a new educational publisher, dedicated to publishing innovative books and software throughout the social sciences. On this and any other of our publications, we welcome your comments and suggestions.

Please write to
Pine Forge Press
A Sage Publications Company
31 St. James Avenue, Suite 510
Boston, MA 02116
617-753-7512
E-mail: sdr@pfp.sagepub.com
Visit our World Wide Web site, your direct link to a multitude of online resources:
www.pineforge.com

Brief Contents

Detailed Contents

Part V   Multivariate Analysis / 307

A Theory of Involvement
Charles Y. Glock, Benjamin B. Ringer, and Earl R.
Babbie

The Social Bases of Abortion Attitudes
Elizabeth Adell Cook, Ted G. Jelen, and Clyde Wilcox

*Ideal Family Size as an Intervening Variable between
Religion and Attitudes towards Abortion*
Mario Renzi

*Religion, Ideal Family Size, and Abortion: Extending
Renzi's Hypothesis*
William V. D'Antonio and Steven Stack

Preface

This workbook is offered with a number of aims in mind. To begin, we want to provide a practical and hands-on introduction to the logic of social science research, particularly survey research. Moreover, we want to give readers an accessible book that guides them step-by-step through the process of data analysis using current GSS data and the latest versions of SPSS. Most importantly, we want to involve readers directly in the practice of social research, allow them to experience the excitement and wonder of this enterprise, and inspire them to pursue their own adventure in social research.

As we pursue these goals, however, there are a number of agendas in the background. For example, students and other readers who complete the book will have learned a very useful, employable skill. Increasingly, job applicants are asked about their facility with various computer programs: word processing, spreadsheets, and data analysis. As of this writing, SPSS is still clearly the most popular professional program available for social science data analysis, hence our choice of it as a vehicle for teaching social research.

A Focus on Developing Professional and Intellectual Skills

What sets this book apart from others that teach SPSS or similar programs is that we cast that particular skill within the context of social research as a logical enterprise. Thus, in addition to learning to use SPSS, students are learning the intellectual "skills" of conceptualization, measurement, and association. Whereas those who know only SPSS can assist in data analysis, our intention is that readers of this book will also be able to think for themselves, mapping out analytic paths into the understanding of social data. As they polish these intellectual skills, they should be able to progress to higher levels of research and to the administration of research enterprises.

More generally, we aim to train students who will use computers rather than be used by them. It is our experience that when students first confront computers in school, they tend to fall into two groups: those who recognize computers as powerful instruments for pursuing their goals in life, or at least as the grandest of toys; and those who are intimidated by computers and seek the earliest possible refuge from them. Our intention is to reveal the former possibility to students and to coax them into that relationship with computers.

Educators are being challenged increasingly to demonstrate the practical value of instruction, in the social sciences no less than in other fields. Too often, the overreaction to this demand results in superficial vocational courses that offer no intellectual meaning or courses hastily contrived as a home for current

xxii   Adventures in Social Research

buzzwords, whose popularity is often short-lived. We are excited to be able to offer an educational experience that is genuinely practical for students and that also represents an intellectual adventure.

Those who have taught methods or statistics courses typically find themselves with a daunting task—to ignite their often involuntary students with the fire of enthusiasm they themselves feel for the detective work of social research at its best. In this book, we seek to engage students' curiosity by setting them about the task of understanding issues that are already points of interest for them: topics such as abortion, religion, politics, poverty, gender roles, health care, sexual attitudes, mass media, gun control, child rearing, and others. For many of our readers, we imagine that mathematical analysis still smacks of trains leaving Point A and Point B at different speeds, and so on. Now, they are going to learn that some facility with the logic and mathematics of social research can let them focus the light of understanding on some of the dark turbulence of opinion and hysteria. We do not tell students about opinions on abortion as much as we show them how to find out for themselves. We think that will get students to Point C ahead of either of the trains.

A Focus on Active and Collaborative Learning

As we are teaching students to learn for themselves, this book offers a good example of what educators have taken to calling "active learning." We have set up all of our demonstrations so that students should be executing the same SPSS operations we are discussing at any given point. Although we may give them the "answers" to assure them that they are on the right track, we leave them on their own often enough to require that they do the work rather than simply read about it.

Finally, the culture of personal computers has been one of "collaborative learning" from its very beginning. More than people in any other field of activity, perhaps, computer users have always delighted in sharing what they know with others. There is probably no better context within which to ask for help: Those who know the answer are quick to respond, and those who do not often turn their attention to finding an answer, delighting in the challenge.

Because this book is self-contained, even introductory students can walk through the chapters and exercises on their own, without outside assistance. However, we imagine that students will often want to work together as they progress through this book. That has been our experience in student testing and in earlier courses we have taught involving computers. We suggest that you encourage cooperation among students; we are certain they will learn more that way and will enjoy the course more. In fact, those who are initially intimidated by computers should especially be encouraged to find buddies with whom to work.

Intended for Readers from a Variety of Social Science Disciplines

This book is intended for use in any social science course that either introduces or focuses exclusively on social research methods, social statistics, data analysis, or survey research. It can be easily combined with or used as a supplement to most standard social science textbooks including, but not limited to, those in fields as varied as communication science, criminal justice, health studies, political science, public policy, social work, and sociology.

As far as possible we have designed this book to be "self-writing" and "open-ended" to insure that it is relevant to students and professionals with varying interests across numerous subjects. Throughout the text we encourage readers to focus on issues and questions that are relevant to their particular area of interest. After walking through the demonstrations that introduce the fundamentals of the data analysis process, readers are given a chance to apply what they have learned. In many of the lab exercises, they are encouraged to design their own hypotheses, choose their own variables, and interpret the results. Moreover, we encourage both readers and instructors to apply the principles, techniques, and methods discussed to other data sets that are relevant to their fields.

Intended for Readers at a Variety of Levels

We have designed and structured this book to support readers at a variety of levels. This includes both those students who are taking their first course in social research as well as more advanced students (including graduate students) who either want to hone their social research, statistical, and data analysis skills, or those who merely want to become acquainted or reacquainted with the latest versions of SPSS for Windows. More advanced students who come at this book full speed may choose to either work through the text from beginning to end or skip around and focus on particular chapters and sections.

It is important to note, however, that because this book is "self-contained" and guides the student-analyst step-by-step through the demonstrations and exercises, no previous experience with social research, statistics, computers, Windows, or SPSS is required. Those who have never taken a research methods, statistics, or computer-based course will find that they can easily make it through this book.

The Book and the Disk: What Is Included?

The book contains everything necessary, except for SPSS itself. We have included two data sets containing a total of more than 85 variables from the 1998 General Social Survey, which can be analyzed by most versions of SPSS, including the Student Version. As you will see, the variables cover a fairly broad terrain although we have provided for analysis in some depth in a few instances. In addition to working their way through the demonstrations and exercises presented in the book, students will be able to find original lines of inquiry that grow out of their own interests and insights.

SPSS 9.0 for Windows

This book will illustrate the use of SPSS, using Version 9.0 for Windows 95 and 98. Whereas the text focuses specifically on SPSS 9.0, it can also be easily used with earlier versions including SPSS 7.0 and higher. Regardless of the version you are using, throughout the text we will refer to the program simply as "SPSS for Windows."

Using Adventures with SPSS 10.0

It is important to note that as we were going to press with this edition of *Adventures*, SPSS 10.0 became available. In Release 10.0, SPSS uses an improved Data Editor and a new method for establishing and modifying variables. The Define Variable menu item has been replaced with a Variable View screen in the Data Editor that displays the variable information in a row and column format. When you click Variable View, you can define or redefine variables by adding or altering variable information. Complete instructions for using the new Variable View are contained in SPSS 10.0's Help screen. Simply click:

Help → Contents → Data Management → Using the Data Editor → Defining Variables

SPSS 10.0 will provide simple instructions for defining variables. In addition to simple instructions, a Show Me button takes users step-by-step through the variable definition process.

Since the variables on the enclosed data disk are already defined as SPSS variables, students may start using SPSS immediately. With the exception of data definition, readers can be assured that the current edition is generally compatible with SPSS 10.0 in almost every respect. Instructions for using the statistical procedures and their output are the same.

Accessing the GSS Data Files

Using the General Social Survey data on your disk is easy. After starting SPSS for Windows, click the following sequence

File → Open

to display the Open File window. Click on the **Look in** field and select the drive that contains your disk. Next, move the mouse to the **Files of type** dialog box and click on the suffix for SPSS for Windows data files, **SPSS(*.sav)**. Now you should see the names of the General Social Survey system files, DEMO.SAV and EXER.SAV, in the list of files. Both of these files contain more than 40 variables from the 1998 GSS. The DEMO.SAV file is used primarily in the demonstrations in the body of each chapter, whereas the EXER.SAV file is used for the "SPSS Lab Exercises" at the end of each chapter (Chapters 5–20). Select either **DEMO.SAV** or **EXER.SAV** by placing the mouse on it and **double-clicking**, or highlight the file name and click the **Open** button near the lower right corner of the Open File window. In a few seconds, SPSS will display the GSS data in its data window. Specific instructions on using SPSS with these data are provided in later chapters.

SPSS for Windows comes with extensive help screens. They are almost like having a coach built in to your computer! Begin with the menu farthest to the right. You can click **Help** or hit **ALT-H** to see the options available to you. Topics will usually be your most useful choice. This will give you four options. Contents and Index present you with two ways of zeroing in on the topic of interest to you. Find will search for the specific terms or keywords you indicate, whereas Ask Me allows you to search for information using complete sentences or questions. You should experiment with these several options to discover what works best for you.

Organization and Content

The chapters are arranged in an order that roughly parallels the organization of most introductory social science research methods texts. Parts I and II (Chapters 1–5) include an overview of the essentials of social research, an introduction to SPSS for Windows, and a description of the 1998 GSS. Parts III through V (Chapters 6–20) introduce data analysis, beginning with univariate analysis, then bivariate analysis, and finally multivariate analysis, respectively. Part VI (Chapters 21–22) focuses on primary research and additional avenues for secondary research.

Part I includes three chapters that help prepare students for social research. Our goal in these chapters is to give students an introduction to some of the fundamental elements of social scientific research, particularly those they will encounter later in the text. Chapter 1 discusses the main purposes of the text and introduces students to some of the historical background behind computerized social research, data analysis, and statistical software packages. In Chapters 2 and 3 we introduce students to the logic of social research by focusing on theory, research, and measurement.

Part II is designed to help students "get started" using the GSS data and SPSS. Chapter 4 describes the GSS and the data sets included with this book, whereas Chapter 5 introduces students to SPSS by guiding them through the steps involved in launching the program, opening their data sets, and exploring the variables contained on the disk which accompanies this book.

Data analysis begins in Part III with univariate analysis. In Chapter 6 we introduce frequency distributions, descriptive statistics, recoding, and saving and printing data. Chapter 7 focuses on the graphic presentation of univariate data by covering the commands for creating simple bar charts and line graphs. Whereas the bulk of the discussion of bivariate analyses is reserved for Part IV, in Chapter 8 we give students a preview by showing them how they can use Crosstabs to examine the structure of attitudes in more depth. Chapter 9 introduces several techniques for creating composite measures, whereas in Chapter 10 students are given a chance to strike out on their own and apply the methods and techniques discussed in Part III to other topics.

Part IV focuses primarily on bivariate analysis. In Chapters 11 through 13 we limit our discussion to the analysis of percentage tables, whereas in Chapters 14 and 15 we introduce other methods for examining the extent to which two variables are related to one another. Chapter 14 focuses on some common measures of association, including lambda, gamma, Pearson's r, and simple regression, whereas Chapter 15 introduces tests of statistical significance, such as chi-square, *t*-tests, and ANOVA. Once again, in Chapter 16, students are given a chance to apply the bivariate techniques and methods discussed in Part IV to other topics and issues.

Our discussion of data analysis concludes in Part V with a discussion of multivariate analyses. Chapter 17 focuses primarily on multiple causation. Chapter 18 picks up on some of the loose threads of our bivariate analyses and pursues them further, whereas Chapter 19 guides students through the steps involved in creating composite measures to predict opinions. Finally, in Chapter 20 students are given a chance to apply the methods and techniques discussed in Part V to other topics and issues.

The final section is composed of two chapters that explore some further opportunities for social research. Because students often express an interest in collecting their own data, Chapter 21 focuses on primary research. We introduce students to the steps involved in designing and administering a survey, defining and entering data in SPSS, and writing a research report. This chapter is supplemented by Appendix B and on-line E-Appendicies C, D, and E, which give students additional information regarding preparing a research proposal, designing and administering a survey, constructing a sample questionnaire, and writing a research report. Chapter 22 suggests other avenues for pursuing secondary social research by focusing on the unabridged GSS, additional data sources, and other statistical software packages which students may find useful.

In addition to Apendix B and E-Appendices C, D, and E, which primarily supplement Chapter 21, we have also included three other appendices. E-Appendix F includes a comprehensive list of all the SPSS Commands introduced in the text. Appendix A contains answers to selected SPSS Lab Exercises. E-Appendix G includes five recommended readings that relate to topics and issues covered in the text. Finally, we have updated and expanded the Reference and Index/Glossary sections.

Structure of Each Chapter

Each chapter includes explanations of basic research principles, techniques, and specific instructions regarding how to use SPSS, demonstrations, a brief Conclusion, a list of Main Points, Key Terms, SPSS Commands Introduced in the Chapter, Review Questions, and SPSS Lab Exercises. Students are expected to follow along with the demonstrations in the body of each chapter. They are aided in this process by both the text, which walks them step-by-step through the process of data analysis, and screens that help them understand what they should be seeing on their own monitors. The Review Questions at the end of each chapter are designed to test the students' knowledge of the material presented in the text. Because they do not require SPSS, they can be assigned as either classwork or homework assignments. In the SPSS Lab Exercises students are given a chance to apply what they learned in the explanatory sections and demonstrations. These exercises generally follow a fill-in-the-blank format for presenting, analyzing, and summarizing results. Instructors may wish to assign these exercises as lab assignments to be completed either in lab or as homework, provided students have access to SPSS.

Whereas the book is designed to guide students through the process of computerized data analysis from beginning to end, we encourage instructors, and particularly more advanced readers, to skip around and focus on chapters and sections of interest to them. We designed the book with the understanding that students at various levels may find different demonstrations, techniques, discussions, and methods of varying interest. Consequently, all of the chapters are self-contained and both students and instructors should feel comfortable picking and choosing among topics, issues, and material of particular interest. Instructors and students who choose to take this approach may want to refer to the Detailed Table of Contents, Introductions to each part, chapter Conclusions, and Main Points to get a better sense of what sections and chapters they want to focus on.

Software Support and Service

If you or your students should run into any problems using this package, there are several sources of support that should serve your needs. Frequently, college and university computing centers have student assistants who are very helpful to new computer users. In fact, most academic computing centers employ a user services coordinator who can help faculty plan student use of the school's computers and provide aid when problems arise.

There are at least two sources of SPSS assistance available via the Internet. The first is a home page (www.spss.com) maintained by SPSS, Inc. In addition to providing answers to frequently asked questions, it provides variety tips and white papers on important issues in data analysis. Specific questions may be submitted to consultants via e-mail from the homepage. SPSS requests that a legitimate license or serial number be submitted with questions for questions to receive a response.

A second source of help on the Internet is a listserve for SPSS users maintained at the University of Georgia (spssx-l@uga.cc.uga.edu). It provides a forum where SPSS users can ask questions of other SPSS users. SPSS programmers and statisticians informally monitor the listserve and frequently offer their expertise in answering users' problems. The listserve is primarily intended to meet the needs of academics and professionals using SPSS as part of their work. This virtual community is very good at identifying questions that come from students rather than professionals. Students posting questions are warned that if detected, they may be severely flamed (admonished) for attempting to take a shortcut in completing their assignments!

If you cannot find local help to solve a problem, you can call Fred Halley at Socware, Inc., in Brockport, New York, at (716) 352-1986. If you get the answering machine, please leave a time and phone number where you can be reached. As a last resort, you can call SPSS, Inc., in Chicago for technical support at (312) 329-2400. Be forewarned that SPSS cannot give assistance with pedagogical or substantive problems and that you may have a long wait in a telephone queue for your turn to talk to a technical support person. It has been our experience that our best help comes from local resources.

Acknowledgments

In conclusion, we would like to acknowledge a number of people who have been instrumental in making this book a reality. First and foremost, Steve Rutter and Sherith Pankratz of Pine Forge Press have been full partners from start to finish. They are able to bring full measures of enthusiasm, commitment, and ingenuity to every book on which they work, and it is a joy for us to play together in that environment, even if we expressed our joy by whining and complaining at times. Our thanks also go to many others at Pine Forge Press and Sage Publications who aided us in numerous ways, including Steve Lawrence, Ann Makarias, Astrid Virding, and Karen Wiley. We owe special thanks to Ruth Cottrell for all her work in producing the book.

We would also like to thank the many reviewers who helped us along the way:

Kim Alexander, Southern Methodist University
Shelly Arsneault, Western Kentucky University
Philip Broyles, Shippensburg University
James A. Danowski, University of Illinois at Chicago
Shenyang Guo, Case Western Reserve University
Lawrence K. Hong, California State University, Los Angeles
Satoshi Kanazawa, University of Illinois at Urbana
Greer Litton, University of Tennessee, Knoxville
Randall MacIntosh, California Technical Institute
Thomas O'Rourke, University of Illinois at Urbana-Champaign
Marilyn Potts, California State University, Long Beach
Jennifer L. S. Teller, Kent State University
Tim Thornton, SUNY College at Brockport
Steve Wilson, California State University, Long Beach
Roger Wojtkiewicz, Louisiana State University

We reserve our final acknowledgment for our students, to whom this book is dedicated. We recognize that we have often asked them to think and do things they sometimes felt were beyond their abilities. We have admired their courage for trying anyway, and we have shared their growth.

Part I Preparing for Social Research

In the opening chapters, we introduce you to computerized data analysis and the logic of social science research.

Chapter 1 discusses the book's two main purposes and gives you some of the historical background that lies behind computerized social research.

In Chapter 2, you will discover that social research (like other forms of scientific inquiry) is based on two pillars: logic and observation. You will see how theory (the logic component) informs our investigations, making sense out of our observations, and sometimes offers predictions about what we will find. The other aspect of research, on which we will focus in this book, is the collection and analysis of data, such as those collected in a survey.

Chapter 3 delves more deeply into one central component of scientific inquiry: measurement. We look at some of the criteria for measurement quality and start examining the kinds of measurements represented by the data at hand.

Chapter 1   Introduction

Social research is the detective work of big questions. Whereas a conventional detective tries to find out who committed a specific crime, the social researcher looks for the causes of crime in general. The logic of social scientific investigation extends beyond crime to include all aspects of social life, such as careers, marriage and family, voting, health, prejudice, and poverty. In fact, anything that is likely to concern you as an individual is the subject of social science research.

Overview

The purpose of this book is to lead you through a series of investigative adventures in social research. We can't predict exactly where these adventures will lead, because you are going to be the detective. Our purpose is to show you some simple tools (and some that are truly amazing) that you can use in social investigations. We'll also provide you with a body of data, collected in a national survey, that is so rich you will have the opportunity to undertake investigations that no one else has ever pursued.

If you have access to a microcomputer that uses the Windows 95 or 98 operating system and SPSS for Windows (Version 7.0 or higher), this book and the computer disk that comes with it contain everything you need for a wide range of social investigations. This tool is designed specifically for exploring data. If you are already comfortable with computers, you can jump right in, and very quickly you will find yourself in the midst of a fascinating computer game. Instead of fighting off alien attacks or escaping from dank dungeons, you'll be pitting your abilities and imagination against real life, but you'll be looking at a side of life that you may not now be aware of.

This tool is also well-designed for the creation of college term papers. Throughout the book, we suggest ways to present the data you discover in the context of a typical term paper in the social sciences. Whereas most students are limited in their term papers to reporting what other investigators have learned about society, you will be able to offer your own insights and discoveries.

Finally, the data sets included here are being analyzed by professional social scientists today. Moreover, the analytical tools that we've provided for you are as powerful as those used by many professional researchers. Frankly, there's no reason you can't use these materials for original research worthy of publication in a research journal. All it takes is curiosity, imagination, practice, and a healthy obsession with knowing the answers to things. In our experience, what sets professional researchers apart from others is that they have much greater curiosity about the world around them, are able to bring powerful imagination to bear on understanding it, are willing to put in the time required of effective investigation, and are passionately driven to understand it.

Why Use a Computer?

Social and behavioral scientists' use of data-processing machinery has evolved to its present state over a period of more than 50 years. In the late 1800s, as the various disciplines which now make up the "social sciences" were developing, becoming more professional and arguably "scientific," many students of the budding social and behavioral sciences found that there was a greater need to record, organize, and analyze observations of social phenomena. Data analysis needs quickly became so great that it was too time-consuming, if not impossible, to keep track of data in ledgers or on index cards.

In 1885, Herman Hollerith, an employee of the U.S. Census Bureau, developed the punch card, a prototype of the now obsolete IBM card, to help meet the data analysis needs of the Census Bureau at a time when the U.S. population was growing and changing rapidly. By the 1930s, social scientists had adapted the new technology for more sophisticated research purposes. (In 1896, by the way, Herman Hollerith established the Tabulating Machine Company, later renamed International Business Machines: IBM.)

In the early 1960s, the electromechanical data tabulation machinery was replaced by electronic computers. Although by today's standards the early computers had small capacity and were expensive and very prone to break-downs, they greatly enhanced social scientists' ability to organize and analyze data. Tasks that took days or weeks using data tabulation equipment took only a few hours on computers.

In addition to the development of electronic computers, or hardware, social scientists' use of computing was also advanced by the development of computer programs, or software. In 1962, the computer programming language FORTRAN (an acronym for formula translation) was developed. FORTRAN made it possible for social scientists to write programs for data analysis that could be used on different kinds of computers. Prior to FOR-TRAN, programming could be accomplished only by manually rewiring accounting machinery or by using machine languages limited to specific computers.

In the 1960s, social scientists used programs written by themselves and by colleagues, graduate students, and programmers in university computing centers. Most information about programs was gained informally through professional grapevines. These programs greatly expanded the research capabilities of social scientists, but there was no standardization of programs or of the format of the data to be analyzed by them. Searching for and using a statistical program could be a harrowing and time-consuming experience. Most of the programs were transported on punch cards, and if one card got out of order, the program might not run; worse yet, it might run and produce inaccurate results.

By 1970, the data analysis problems of social and behavioral scientists were well recognized. To answer these needs, social scientist-programmers (most notably at the University of Chicago and the University of Michigan) developed the concept of a program package. In addition to statistical calculations, these program packages allowed researchers to modify or recode data, to create indexes and scales, and to employ many other techniques you will learn in this workbook.

Today, the two statistical packages most widely used by social scientists are *SPSS* (the Statistical Package for the Social Sciences) and *SAS* (the Statistical Analysis System).[1] Until the mid-1980s, these large, generalized statistical packages were available only for large mainframe computers. The advent of personal computers created a revolution in the way social science data analysis was done. By the mid-1980s, personal computers became powerful enough to run statistical packages and cheap enough for individuals to purchase them. This made it feasible for statistical package producers to rewrite their packages for personal computers. Although personal computers do not have the storage capacity to work with extremely large amounts of data, they are very appropriate for moderate data analysis needs.

We have selected SPSS for your use in these exercises for three reasons. First, early versions of SPSS date back to 1968. The package is well-known, and there is hardly a social scientist who has earned a graduate degree in the past 20 years who has not had some contact with SPSS. Second, SPSS takes you through all the basic issues of using a statistical package. This knowledge will give you a head start if you learn some other package later. Finally, SPSS comes in several versions. *The SPSS Mainframe Version* is the largest and most powerful and can analyze millions of cases with thousands of variables. It is available for all of the major mainframe computers, such as IBM, Honeywell, and Digital. Two recent versions of SPSS are available for IBM-compatible computers with Windows 95 or Windows 98. The *SPSS Professional Version*, like a car, is sold as a basic package. Then, if the buyer wishes, it can be "souped up" with powerful statistical accessories, all of which are beyond the scope of this book. A scaled-down version, called the *SPSS Student Version*, is also available for use with Windows. Unlike the

---

1. While the letters "SPSS" originally stood for the "Statistical Package for the Social Sciences" (and the package is still most commonly referred to this way), SPSS Inc. recently "updated the meaning of the letters to more accurately reflect the company and its products. Today, SPSS stands for 'Statistical Product and Service Solutions'" (http://www.spss.com/corpinfo/faqs/htm). Please keep in mind that because the World Wide Web is constantly changing, this web site and others referenced in the text may no longer be accessible.

Professional Version, it is limited to 50 variables and 1,500 cases, and it can't be upgraded. The SPSS Student Version has fewer statistical procedures than the Professional Version, but it has most of the procedures that will ever be needed by an undergraduate social science major or a master's-level graduate student. A "Grad Pack," which is essentially the same as the Professional Version, is available through college bookstores. You can learn more about SPSS by visiting their web site at www.spss.com.

A WORD OF CAUTION: Throughout the book we suggest various web sites that you may find useful. Keep in mind, however, that the World Wide Web is constantly changing. For this reason some web sites referred to in the text may no longer be available; things can change overnight. If particular web sites are no longer available, you can use one of the many search engines that are available and use key words to locate the information you are looking for. Your instructor should be able to help you if necessary.

Conclusion

This book has two educational aims. First, we want to share with you the excitement of social scientific research. You are going to learn that a table of numerical data, which may seem pretty boring on the face of it, can hold within it the answers to many questions about why people think and act the way they do. Finding those answers requires that you learn some skills of logical inquiry.

Second, we will show you how to use a computer program that is very popular among social scientists. SPSS is the tool you will use to unlock the mysteries of society, just as a biologist might use a microscope or an astronomer a telescope.

You may have seen prepared foods with the instruction: Just add water and heat. Well, the package in your hands is something like that, but the instructions read: Just add you, and let's get cooking.

Main Points

- The main purpose of this text is to introduce you to the logic and practice of social scientific research by showing you some simple tools you can use to analyze real-life data.

- Social and behavioral scientists' use of data-processing machinery has evolved over many years, from the early punch cards and IBM cards to the statistical packages used today.

- SPSS is a widely used state-of-the-art statistical software program that will take you through all the basics of using any sophisticated statistical package.

- SPSS comes in several versions. While this textbook is designed specifically for use with both the Professional and Student Versions of SPSS 9.0 for Windows, the data can also be read using SPSS Versions 7.0 or higher for Windows.

Key Terms

SPSS   SPSS Professional Version

SAS   SPSS Student Version

SPSS Mainframe Version

Review Questions

1. Describe the historical development of social scientists' use of data-processing machinery beginning with the development of tabulating machines that used punch (IBM) cards.

2. What are the two most widely used statistical packages today?

3. What revolutionized the way social scientific data analysis was done in the mid-1980s?

4. Which of the three versions of SPSS described is the least powerful in terms of the number of cases and variables it can handle?

5. Which version of SPSS is the most powerful in this regard?

6. What version (or versions) of SPSS are you using?

7. Name two tasks a statistical package such as SPSS can be used for.

Chapter 2   **Theory and Research**

This book addresses primarily the techniques of social science data analysis. Thus, we're going to be spending most of our time analyzing data and reaching conclusions about the people who answered questions in the General Social Survey, which is described in more detail in Chapter 4. Data analysis, however, doesn't occur in a vacuum. Scientific inquiry is a matter of both observing and reasoning. Consequently, before getting into the techniques of data analysis, let's take a minute to consider some of the central components of social science research. We will start this chapter by looking at the role of theory in conjunction with research. Then, in the next chapter, we will turn our attention to another fundamental aspect of scientific inquiry—measurement. While these chapters are not designed to give you an in-depth understanding of every aspect of the social research process, they will give you the background necessary to master the techniques of data analysis presented in this textbook.[1]

Concepts and Variables

Given the variety of topics examined in social science research, there is no single, established set of procedures that is always followed in social scientific inquiry. Nevertheless, data analysis almost always has a bigger purpose than the simple manipulation of numbers. Our larger aim is to learn something of general value about human social behavior. This commitment lies in the realm of theory.

Social scientific inquiry involves a bringing together of *concepts* and data: ideas and observations about human social life. Ultimately, we seek to establish a correspondence between what we observe and our conceptual understanding of the way things are. Some of the social scientific concepts

---

1. If you are thinking about designing social scientific research (particularly for the first time) or just want to learn more about the process and practice of scientific inquiry, you may find the discussion in Chapter 21, Appendix B, and E-Appendices C, D, and E a useful starting point. E-Appendices C–E are located on-line at http://www.pineforge.com. You may also want to browse through the Reference section for citations to other texts that focus on the nature of social scientific inquiry, designing a research project, and other aspects of the social research process.

with which you are familiar might include social class, deviance, political orientations, prejudice, and alienation.

Many concepts, such as those just mentioned, distinguish variations among people. Gender, for example, distinguishes men and women. Social class might distinguish upper class, middle class, and working class. When social scientists actually measure concepts that capture variations among people, we shift terminology from concepts to *variables*. As an idea, then, gender is a concept; when actually measured, in a questionnaire, for example, it becomes a variable for analysis.

Explanatory social inquiry is a matter of discovering which attributes of different variables are causally associated with one another. Are men or women the more religious? Which ethnic groups are the most liberal and which the most conservative? These are the kinds of questions that social scientists address.

Theory and Hypotheses: Religiosity

A *theory* is a statement or set of statements pertaining to the relationships among variables. Because one of the subjects we are going to examine in this textbook is religiosity, we will begin with an example of a theory deriving from the sociology of religion. In 1967 Glock, Ringer, and Babbie developed what they call the deprivation theory of church involvement. Having asked why some church members participated more in their churches than others, the researchers' analyses led them to conclude that those who were deprived of gratification in the secular society would be more likely to be active in church life than were those who enjoyed the rewards of secular society.

In accordance with the deprivation theory, therefore, it was to be expected that poor people would be more active in the church than rich people, given that the former would be denied many secular gratifications enjoyed by the latter. Or, in a male-dominated society, it was suggested that because women are denied gratifications enjoyed by men, women would be more likely to participate actively in the church. Similarly, in a youth-oriented society, the theory would suggest that older people would be more active in church than the young. A theory, therefore, is a set of logical explanations about patterns of human social life: patterns among the variables that describe people. In this example, the variables are church involvement, wealth, gender, and age. The theory explains why these variables are related to one another in a particular way.

Looked at only a little differently, the theory offers expectations about the ways variables would be found to relate to one another in life. In scientific language, these are called *hypotheses*. A hypothesis is a statement of expectation derived from a theory that proposes a relationship between two or more variables. Specifically, a hypothesis is a tentative statement which proposes that variation in one variable (the *independent variable*) causes or leads to variation in the other variable (the *dependent variable*). For example, one hypothesis to be derived from the deprivation theory is that women will be more involved in church than will men. You will note that this hypothesis proposes a relationship between two variables: gender (independent variable) and church involvement (dependent variable). After developing a hypothesis, a researcher may decide to design and conduct a scientific study to test whether there is a relationship such as the one proposed between gender and church involvement.

It is important to recognize that relationships such as the one predicted in this hypothesis are *probabilistic*. The hypothesis says that women, as a group, will have a higher average level of church involvement than men will as a group. This does not mean that all women are more involved than any men. It does mean, for example, that if we asked men and women whether they attend church every week, a higher percentage of women than of men would say yes, even though some men would say yes and some women would say no. That is the nature of probabilistic relationships.

Sometimes, theories and the hypotheses derived from them are the result of largely intellectual procedures: thinking about and reasoning what should be the relationships among some set of variables. At other times, researchers build theories later to explain the relationships they've already observed in their analysis of data. In the case of church involvement, discussed above, the data analysis occurred first, and the researchers then faced the task of making sense out of the several relationships they had uncovered.

Stepping back a pace for a larger perspective on the process of social scientific inquiry, we find an alternation between the two approaches just described. Understandings and expectations are reached; they are tested through the collection and analysis of data; the findings arrived at in the data analysis are then subjected to further evaluation and understanding, producing a modified theory. Often, the phase that involves moving from theoretical understandings and the derivation of specific hypotheses to the collection and analysis of data is called *deduction*, and the process that proceeds from data back to theory is called *induction*. More simply, deduction can be seen as reasoning from general understandings to specific expectations, whereas induction can be seen as reasoning from specific observations to general explanations. Both deduction and induction are essential parts of any scientific inquiry.

Now, let's examine some of the theoretical work that informs two of the other subjects we are going to analyze together in this book: political orientations and attitudes toward abortion.

Political Orientations

One of the more familiar variables in social science is political orientation, which typically ranges from liberal to conservative. It lies at the heart of much voting behavior, and it relates to a number of nonpolitical variables as well, which you are going to discover for yourself shortly.

There are several *dimensions* of political orientations, and it will be useful to distinguish them here. Three commonly examined dimensions are (1) social attitudes, (2) economic attitudes, and (3) foreign policy attitudes. Let's examine each dimension briefly.

Some specific social attitudes and related behaviors might include abortion, premarital sex, and capital punishment. Let's see where liberals and conservatives would generally stand on these issues:

Issue	*Liberals*	*Conservatives*
abortion	permissive	restrictive
premarital sex	permissive	restrictive
capital punishment	opposed	in favor

In terms of economic issues, liberals are more supportive than are conservatives of government programs such as unemployment insurance, welfare, and Medicare, and of government economic regulation, such as progressive taxation (the rich taxed at higher rates), minimum wage laws, and regulation of industry. By the same token, liberals are likely to be more supportive of labor unions than are conservatives.

Attitudes Toward Abortion

Abortion is a social issue that has figured importantly in religious and political debates for years. The General Social Survey contains several variables dealing with attitudes toward abortion. Each asks whether a woman should be allowed to get an abortion for a variety of reasons. The following list shows these reasons, along with the abbreviated variable names you'll be using for them in your analyses later on.

ABDEFECT	because there is a strong chance of a serious defect
ABNOMORE	because a family wants no more children
ABHLTH	because the woman's health would be seriously endangered
ABPOOR	because a family is too poor to afford more children
ABRAPE	because the pregnancy resulted from rape
ABSINGLE	because the woman is unmarried
ABANY	because the woman wants it, for any reason

Before we begin examining answers to the abortion attitude questions (in Chapter 8), it is worth taking a moment to reflect on their logical implications. Which of these items do you suppose would receive the least support? That is, which will have the smallest percentage of respondents agreeing with it? Think about that before continuing.

Logically, we should expect the smallest percentage to support ABANY, because it contains all the others. For example, those who would support abortion in the case of rape might not support it for other reasons, such as the family's poverty. Those who support ABANY, however, would have to agree with both of those more specific items.

Three of the items tap into reasons that would seem to excuse the pregnant woman from responsibility:

ABDEFECT	because there is a strong chance of a serious defect
ABHLTH	because the woman's health would be seriously endangered
ABRAPE	because the pregnancy resulted from rape

We might expect the highest percentages to agree with these items. We'll come back to this issue later to find out whether our expectations are correct.

When we analyze this topic with data, we will discover useful ways of measuring overall attitudes toward abortion. Once we've done that, we'll be in a position to find out why some people are generally supportive and others generally opposed.

Conclusion

By now, you should have gained an initial appreciation of the relationship between theory and research in the social sciences. This examination will continue throughout the book. While our most direct attention will focus on the skills of analyzing data, we will always want to make logical sense out of what we learn from our manipulations of the numbers.

Measurement is a fundamental topic that bridges theory and research. We turn our attention to that topic next.

Main Points

- The primary goal of all social scientific research is to develop theories that help us explain, make sense of, and understand human social behavior.
- A theory is a general statement or set of statements that describes and explains how variables are related to one another.
- A hypothesis is a tentative statement of expectation derived from a theory.
- A hypothesis proposes a relationship between two or more variables (the independent and dependent) that can be tested by researchers employing scientific methods.
- When a social scientist proceeds from theory to hypotheses development, data collection, and data analysis, the process is called deduction.
- When a social scientist moves from data collection to data analysis and then induces a general theory based on those observations, the process is called induction.
- Theoretical work informs all of the subjects we are going to analyze in this book and, indeed, all questions and issues of relevance to social scientists.

Key Terms

Concepts   Dependent variable
Variables   Probabilistic
Theory   Deduction
Hypotheses   Induction
Independent variable   Dimensions

Review Questions

1. What is the primary goal of social scientific research?

2. Name two social scientific concepts.

3. What is the relationship between theory and hypotheses?

4. Does a hypothesis propose a relationship between dimensions or variables?

5. Construct a hypothesis derived from the depravation theory of church involvement (select an independent variable other than gender).

6. Identify the independent variable in the hypothesis you formulated in response to Question 5 above.

7. Identify the dependent variable in the hypothesis you formulated in response to Question 5 above.

8. Consider the following hypothesis: People who earn more than $50,000 a year are more likely to vote Republican than people who earn less than $50,000 a year. Does this mean that all people who earn more than $50,000 a year vote Republican? Why or why not?

9. A researcher formulates a hypothesis based on the "magic bullet theory" and then selects independent and dependent variables to test this hypothesis. What process is the researcher engaged in?

10. A researcher studies the spread of AIDS in the United States and then, based on his or her findings, develops a theory to explain why the rate of exposure and infection to the disease is higher among certain racial and ethnic groups than among others. What process is the researcher engaged in?

Chapter 3   The Logic of Measurement

Measurement is one of the most fundamental elements of science. In the case of social research, the task typically is one of characterizing individuals in terms of the issues under study. Thus, a study of voting will characterize respondents in terms of the candidate for whom they plan to vote. A study of abortion attitudes will describe people in terms of their attitudes on that topic.

Validity Problems

Validity is a term used casually in everyday language, but it has a precise meaning in social research. It describes an indicator of a concept. Most simply, an indicator is said to be valid if it really measures what it is intended to measure, and it is invalid if it doesn't.

As a simple example, let's consider political orientations, ranging from very liberal to very conservative. For an example of a clearly valid measure of this concept, here's the way the General Social Survey asked about it.

POLVIEWS: We hear a lot of talk these days about liberals and conservatives. I'm going to show you a seven-point scale on which political views that people might hold are arranged from extremely liberal to extremely conservative. Where would you place yourself on this scale?

1. Extremely liberal

2. Liberal

3. Slightly liberal

4. Moderate, middle-of-the-road

5. Slightly conservative

6. Conservative

7. Extremely conservative

At the opposite extreme, a simple question about respondent gender obviously would not be a valid measure of political orientations. It has nothing to do with politics. But now let's consider another questionnaire item that does not come from the General Social Survey. This item lies somewhere in between these two extremes of validity with regard to measuring political orientations.

Which of these two political parties do you most identify with?

1. Democratic Party
2. Republican Party
3. Neither

This second item is another reasonable measure of political orientation. Moreover, it is related to the first, because Democrats are, on the whole, more liberal than Republicans. On the other hand, there are conservative Democrats and liberal Republicans. If our purpose is to tap into the liberal-conservative dimension, the initial item that asks directly about political orientations is obviously a more valid indicator of the concept than is the item about political party.

This particular example offers us a clear choice as to the most valid indicator of the concept at hand, but matters are not always that clear-cut. If we were measuring levels of prejudice, for example, we could not simply ask, How prejudiced are you? because no one is likely to admit to being prejudiced. As we search for workable indicators of a concept such as prejudice, the matter of validity becomes something to which we must pay careful attention.

Validity is also a problem whenever you are conducting *secondary analysis* or reanalyzing someone else's data as you will be doing in this book. Even if you can think of a survey question that would have captured your concept perfectly, the original researchers might not have asked it. Hence, you often need to use ingenuity in constructing measures that nevertheless tap the quality in which you are interested. In the case of political orientations, for example, you might combine the responses to several questions: asking for attitudes about civil liberties, past voting behavior, political party identification, and so forth. We'll return to the use of multiple indicators shortly.

In large part, the question of validity is settled on prima facie grounds: We judge an indicator to be relatively valid or invalid on the face of it. It was on this basis that you had no trouble seeing that asking directly about political orientations was a valid indicator of that concept, whereas asking a person's gender was definitely not a valid measure of political orientations. Later in the book, we'll explore some simple methodological techniques that are also used to test the validity of measures.

Reliability Problems

Reliability is a different but equally important quality of measurements. Reliability refers to the quality of a measuring instrument that would cause it to report the same value in successive observations of a given case (provided the phenomenon being measured has not changed). For instance, if you step on a bathroom scale five times in a row, and each time it gives you a different weight, the scale has a reliability problem. Conversely, if you step on a bathroom scale five times in a row and the scale gives you the same weight each time (even if the weight is wrong), the scale is reliable. In the context of survey research, reliability also refers to the question of whether we can trust the answers that people give us even when their misstatements are honest ones.

Years ago, one of us was asked to assist on a survey of teenage drivers in California. Over researcher objections, the client insisted on asking the question, How many miles have you driven? and providing a space for the teenager to write in his or her response. Perhaps you can recognize the problem in this question by attempting to answer it yourself. Unless you have never driven an automobile, we doubt that you can report how many miles you have driven with any accuracy. In the survey mentioned, some teenagers reported driving hundreds of thousands of miles.

A better technique in that situation, by the way, would be to provide respondents with a set of categories reflecting realistically the number of miles respondents are likely to have driven: fewer than 1,000 miles; 1,000 to 4,999 miles; 5,000 to 9,999 miles; and so on. Such a set of categories gives respondents a framework within which to place their own situations. Even though they still may not know exactly how much they had driven, there would be a fair likelihood that the categories they chose would actually contain their correct answers. The success of this technique, of course, would depend on our having a good idea in advance of what constitutes reasonable categories, determined by previous research, perhaps. As an alternative, we might ask respondents to volunteer the number of miles they have driven but limit the time period to something they are likely to remember. Thus, we might ask how many miles they drove during the preceding week or month, for example.

Conceptually, the test of reliability is whether respondents would give the same answers repeatedly if the measurement could be made in such a way that (a) their situations had not changed (hadn't driven any more miles), and (b) they couldn't remember the answer they gave before.

Perhaps the difference between validity and reliability can be seen most clearly in reference to a simple bathroom scale. As we noted earlier, if you step on a scale repeatedly (scales don't remember) and it gives you a different weight each time, then the scale has a reliability problem. On the other hand, if the scale tells you that you weigh 125 pounds every time you step on it, it's pretty reliable, but if you actually weigh 225, the scale has a problem in the validity department; it doesn't indicate your weight accurately.

Both validity and reliability are important in the analysis of data. If you are interested in learning why some people have deeply held religious beliefs and others do not, then asking people how often they attend church would be problematic. This question doesn't really provide a valid measure of the concept that interests you, and anything you learn will explain the causes of church attendance, not religious belief. And suppose you asked people how many times they had attended church in the past year, any answers you received would probably not be reliable, so anything you might think you learned about the causes of church attendance might be only a function of the errors people made in answering the question. (It would be better to give them categories from which to choose.) You would have no assurance that another study would yield the same result.

Multiple Indicators

Often, the solution to the problems discussed above lies in the creation of *composite measures* using *multiple indicators.* As a simple example, to measure the degree to which a sample of Christian church members held the beliefs associated with Christianity, you might ask them questions about several issues, each dealing with a particular belief, such as the following:

- belief in God
- belief that Jesus was divine
- belief in the existence of the devil
- belief in an afterlife: heaven and hell
- belief in the literal truth of the Bible

The several answers given to these questions could be used to create an overall measure of religious belief among the respondents. In the simplest procedure, you could give respondents 1 point for each belief to which they agreed, allowing you to score them from 0 to 5 on the index. Notice that this is the same logic by which you may earn 1 point for each correct answer on an exam, with the total score being taken as an indication of how well you know the material.

Some social science concepts are implicitly multidimensional. Consider the concept of social class, for example. Typically, this term is used in reference to a combination of education, income, occupation, and sometimes dimensions such as social class identification and prestige. This would be measured for data analysis through the use of multiple indicators.

When it becomes appropriate in the analyses we are going to undertake together below, we'll show you how to create and use some simple composite measures.

Levels of Measurement

As we convert the concepts in our minds into empirical measurements in the form of variables, we sometimes have options as to their level of statistical sophistication. Specifically, there are a number of different possibilities regarding the relationships among the attributes comprising a variable. Let's look at those alternatives.

Nominal Variables

Some variables simply distinguish different kinds of people. Gender is a good example of this; it simply distinguishes men from women. Political party distinguishes Democrats from Republicans and from other parties. Religious affiliation distinguishes Protestants, Catholics, Jews, and so forth. We refer to these measurements as nominal, in that term's sense of naming. *Nominal variables* simply name the different attributes constituting them.

The attributes comprising a nominal variable (e.g., gender, composed of male and female) are simply different. Republicans and Democrats are simply different from each other, as are Protestants and Catholics. In other cases, however, we can say more about the attributes making up variables.

Ordinal Variables

Many social scientific variables go a step beyond simply naming the different attributes comprising a variable. *Ordinal variables* arrange those attributes in some order: from low to high, from more to less, and so on. Whereas the nominal variable religious affiliation classifies people into different religious groups, religiosity might order them in groups, such as very religious, somewhat religious, and not at all religious. And where the nominal variable political party identification simply distinguishes different groups (e.g., Democrats and Republicans), an ordinal measure of political philosophy might rank order the very liberal, the somewhat liberal, the middle-of-the-road, the somewhat conservative, and the very conservative. Ordinal variables share the nominal variable quality of distinguishing differences among people, and they add the quality of *rank ordering* those differences.

At the same time, it is not meaningful to talk about the distances separating the attributes that make up an ordinal variable. For example, we have no basis for talking about the amount of liberalism separating the very liberal from the somewhat liberal or the somewhat liberal from the middle-of-the-road. We can say that the first group in each comparison is more liberal than the second, but we can't say how much.

Ratio Variables

Some variables allow us to speak more precisely about the distances between the attributes comprising a variable. Consider age for a moment. The distance between 10 years old and 20 years old is exactly the same as that between 60 years old and 70 years old. Thus, it makes sense to talk about the distance between two ages (i.e., they are 10 years apart).

Moreover, *ratio variables* such as age have the additional quality of containing a genuine zero point, in this case no years old. This quality is what allows us to examine ratios among the categories constituting such variables. Thus, we can say that a 20-year-old is twice as old as a 10-year-old. By comparison, notice that we would have no grounds for saying one person is twice as religious as another.

Ratio variables, then, share all the qualities associated with nominal and ordinal variables, but they have additional qualities not applicable to the lower-level measures. Other examples of ratio measures include income, years of schooling, and hours worked per week.

Interval Variables

Rarer in social research are variables that have the quality of standard intervals of measurement but lack a genuine zero point, or ***interval variables***. One example is intelligence quotient (IQ). Although IQ is calculated in such a way as to allow for a score of zero, that would not indicate a complete lack of intelligence, because the person would at least have been able to take the test.

Moving outside the social sciences, consider temperature. The Celsius and Fahrenheit measures of temperature both have 0° marks, but neither represents a total lack of heat, given that it is possible to have temperatures below zero. The Kelvin scale, by contrast, is based on an absolute zero, which does represent a total lack of heat (measured in terms of molecular motion).

For most statistics used by social scientists, interval and ratio scales may be considered the same. When we start using SPSS, we'll see that its creators have lumped interval and ratio variables into a single category called *scale*. Although these variables may be combined for practical purposes, the distinction between them helps us understand why a negative income might be interpreted as debt and a negative age is impossible!

Measurement and Information

Knowing a variable's level of measurement is important for selecting an appropriate statistic. Variables of different levels of measurement contain different amounts of information. The only information we have about nominal variables is the number of cases that share a common attribute. With ordinal variables, in addition to knowing how many cases fall in a category, we know a greater than/less than relationship between the cases. Variables measured at the interval level have their points equidistant from one another. With equidistant points, we know how much greater than or less than cases are from each other. Finally, with ratio variables, we have all the characteristics of nominal, ordinal, and interval variables, plus the knowledge that zero is not arbitrary but means an absence of the phenomena.

The statistics that SPSS has been programmed to compute are designed to make maximum use of the information preserved in a level of measurement. Using the mode on a sample of GPAs ignores information used by the mean. Conversely, using the mean for a sample of religious preferences assumes information (equidistant points) not contained in a nominal measure. Responsible use of statistics requires selecting a statistic that matches the data's level of measurement. We'll talk about this more later. Right now, we want you to know that being able to identify a variable's level of measurement is essential for selecting the right statistical tool. We don't want to see you using a screwdriver when you need a hammer!

Measurement Options

Sometimes you will have options regarding the levels of measurement to be created in variables. For instance, although age can qualify as a ratio variable, it can be measured as ordinal (e.g., young, middle-aged, old) or even as nominal (baby-boomer, not baby-boomer).

The significance of these levels of measurement will become more apparent when we begin to analyze the variables in our data set. As you'll discover, some analytic techniques are appropriate to nominal variables, some to ordinal variables, and some to ratio variables. On one hand, you will need to know a variable's level of measurement in order to determine which analytic techniques are appropriate. On the other hand, where you have options for measurement, your choice of measurement level may be determined by the techniques you want to employ.

Conclusion

Measurement is a fundamental aspect of social science research. It may be seen as the transition from concepts to variables—from sometimes ambiguous mental images to precise, empirical measures. Whereas we often speak casually about such concepts as prejudice, social class, and liberalism in everyday conversation, social scientists must be more precise in their uses of these terms.

Chapters 2 and 3 have given you a brief overview of two important issues in social scientific inquiry that are directly relevant to our primary focus—computerized statistical analysis. The chapters that follow will build on this discussion of theory and measurement and show you the concrete techniques you need to engage in data analysis. Those of you who are interested in designing and conducting your own research, or who just want to learn more about the process and practice of social research, may want to consult Chapter 21, Appendix B, and E-Appendices C, D, and E located at http://www.pineforge.com. In addition, the Reference section lists books that discuss in greater detail these and other issues relevant to social scientific research.

Main Points

- Measurement is a vital component of social scientific research.
- In designing and evaluating measurements, social scientists must pay particular attention to the problems of validity and reliability.
- A common remedy for problems of validity and reliability is the construction of composite measures using multiple indicators.
- Level of measurement signifies the different amount and type of information obtained about a variable and is essential for selecting appropriate statistical tools.
- The four levels of measurement are: nominal, ordinal, ratio, and interval.
- Variables of different levels of measurement contain different amounts of information.

Key Terms

Validity	Nominal variables
Secondary analysis	Ordinal variables
Reliability	Ratio variables
Composite measures	Interval variables
Multiple indicators	Scale

Review Questions

1. A researcher sets out to measure drug use on U.S. college campuses by asking a representative sample of undergraduates whether they are currently receiving federal grants or loans. What is the problem with this measure?

2. A researcher asks a representative sample of baby-boomers how much alcohol they consumed during their college years and leaves a space for them to write in their response in terms of the actual number of drinks. Four weeks later, the researcher administers the same questionnaire to the same respondents. However, this time more than half of the respondents report consuming much less alcohol during their college years than they did just a month earlier. What is the problem with this measure?

3. Multiple indicators are useful in dealing with what types of problems?

4. Name one reason why it is important to know or to be able to identify a variable's level of measurement.

5. Ordinal variables have all the qualities of variables at which other level of measurement?

6. Ratio variables have all the qualities of variables at which other levels of measurement?

7. If you were using SPSS to define the levels of measurement of variables at the ratio and/or interval levels, which of the following terms would you use: "interval," "scale," or "multiple"?

Identify the level of measurement of each of the following variables:

8. A researcher measures respondents' attitudes toward premarital sex by asking the following question: "If a man and woman have sexual relations before marriage, do you think it is always wrong, almost always wrong, wrong only sometimes, or not wrong at all?"

9. A researcher measures the amount of television viewing by asking the following question: "On the average day, how many hours do you personally watch television?" Respondents are then asked to fill in the actual number of hours in the space provided.

10. A researcher measures marital status by asking respondents whether they are currently married, widowed, divorced, separated, or never married.

Part II Getting Started

In the following two chapters we introduce you to the data you will be using throughout the text and show you how to use SPSS to load and access the data. Chapter 4 describes the real-life data that accompany this textbook. The data come from the 1998 General Social Survey, which was conducted among a national sample of American adults.

The computer program we will be using, SPSS, is introduced in Chapter 5. This chapter provides you with some initial familiarization with the version of the program you will be using, and you will see how it differs from the others that are available. You will also learn how to launch an SPSS session and open a file so you can begin exploring your data sets. By the time you have gone through these two chapters, you should be amply prepared to undertake your adventure in social research.

Chapter 4   Description of Your Data Sets

The data we provide for your use here are real. They come from the responses of 2,832 adult Americans selected as a representative sample of the nation in 1998. These data are a major resource for professional social scientists and are the basis of many published books and articles.

The ***General Social Survey (GSS)*** is conducted regularly by the ***National Opinion Research Center (NORC)*** in Chicago, with financial support from the National Science Foundation and private sources. The purpose of the GSS program is to provide the nation's social scientists with accurate data for analysis. This activity was the brainchild of Jim Davis, one of the most visionary social scientists alive during your lifetime. The GSS, which began in 1972, was conducted annually until 1994 when it became biennial.[1]

Sampling

The data provided by the GSS are representative of American adults. This means that anything we learn about the 2,832 people sampled can be taken as an accurate reflection of what all (noninstitutionalized, English-speaking) American adults (18 years of age or older) would have said if we could have interviewed them all. This is the case because of a technique known as ***multistage probability sampling***.

The researchers began by selecting a random sample of cities and counties across the country, having grouped them in such a way as to ensure that those selected would reflect all the variations in cities and counties in the nation. At the second stage of sampling, the researchers selected a random sample of city blocks or equivalent units in rural areas within each of the selected cities and counties.

---

1. For more information about the GSS, see Davis and Smith 1992 or Davis, Smith, and Marsden 1998. You may also want to visit one of two NORC web sites devoted to the GSS at: http://www.norc.uchicago.edu/gss/homepage.htm or http://www.icpsr.umich.edu/GSS99/. The NORC is a nonprofit corporation affiliated with the University of Chicago, which conducts the GSS. You can also access more information about the GSS by visiting the Roper Center web site at http://www.ropercenter.uconn.edu/. The Roper Center is a nonprofit corporation for public opinion research affiliated with the University of Connecticut, which provides access to the GSS.

The researchers then visited each of the selected blocks and chose specific households at random on each block. Finally, when interviewers visited each of the selected households, they determined the number of adults living in the household and selected one of them at random as the respondent.

This complex and sophisticated sampling process makes it possible for the responses of 2,832 individuals to provide an accurate reflection of the feelings of all adult Americans. Similar techniques are used by the U.S. Census Bureau for the purpose of government planning and by polling firms that predict voting behavior with relative accuracy.

We have reduced the size of the samples to 1,500 cases each, so that the data can be analyzed with the Student Version of SPSS for Windows. Whereas the professional version of SPSS for Windows is virtually unlimited by the size of the computer on which it is installed, the student version is limited to 1,500 cases and 50 variables. The disk included with this book contains two files named *DEMO.SAV* (for DEMOnstration) and *EXER.SAV* (for EXERcise), respectively. As noted, each file contains a subsample of 1,500 cases from the 1998 General Social Survey's 2,832 cases. DEMO.SAV contains 41 variables, while EXER.SAV contains 44 variables. Consequently, both files may be used with either the Student or Professional Versions of SPSS for Windows. Because both files come from the same sample and the identification numbers have been preserved, anyone using the Professional Version of SPSS can merge the files.

The data you have at hand, then, can be taken as an accurate reflection of the characteristics, attitudes, and behaviors of Americans 18 and older in 1998. This statement needs to be qualified slightly, however. When you analyze the data and learn that 45.5 percent of the sample said that they supported a woman's unrestricted right to have an abortion for any reason, you are safe in assuming that about 45.5 percent of the entire U.S. adult population feels that way. Because the data are based on a sample rather than on asking everyone, however, we need to anticipate some degree of sampling error. You can think of *sampling error* as the extent to which the responses of those sampled, in this case using multistage probability sampling, differ from the responses of the larger population (English-speaking persons 18 years of age or older living in noninstitutionalized arrangements within the United States in 1998). As a general rule, the greater the sampling error, the less representative the sample. It would not be strange, based on the example given, to discover that 43 percent or 47 percent of the total adult population (rather than exactly 45.5 percent) support a woman's unrestricted right to have an abortion for any reason. It is inconceivable, however, that as few as 10 percent or as many as 90 percent held the opinion in question.

As a rough guideline, you can assume that the sampling error in this data set is plus or minus only a few percentage points. In Chapter 15, we'll see how to calculate the actual sampling error for specific pieces of data.

Even granting the possibility of sampling error, however, our best estimate of what's true among the total U.S. population is what we learned from the probability sample. Thus, if you were to bet on the percentage of the total U.S. population who supported a woman's unrestricted right to an abortion, you should put your money on 45.5 percent. You would be better off, however, to bet that it was, say, between 42.5 percent and 48.5 percent.[2]

Data Collection

The GSS data were collected in face-to-face household interviews. Once the sample households were selected, professional interviewers were dispatched to call on each one. The interviewers asked each of the questions and wrote down the respondents' answers. Each interview took approximately 90 minutes.

To maximize the amount of information that can be collected in this massive interviewing project, NORC asked some questions in only a random subsample of the households, asking other questions in the other households. Some questions were asked of all respondents. When we begin analyzing the GSS data, you will notice that some data items have a substantial number of respondents marked *missing data.* For the most part, this refers to respondents who were not asked that particular question.

Although only a subsample was asked some of the questions, you can still take the responses as representative of the U.S. adult population except that the degree of sampling error, mentioned above, is larger.[3]

The Codebook

The two data sets on your disk contain the questionnaire items that follow. We attempted to choose variables that are both interesting and relevant to students who are working across various social science disciplines in areas as diverse as communications, criminal justice, health studies, political science, public administration, social work, and sociology. You might review the lists now to make a note of issues that are of particular interest to you. Before long, you'll be getting much more familiar with them. As you analyze survey data, it is important to know exactly how questions were asked if you are to understand the meaning of the answers given in response.

Each item on the list has an abbreviated *variable name*, the full wording used in the NORC interview (item wording), *values* (sometimes called *numeric values* or *codes*), *value labels* (excluding missing values and responses coded as "Don't know"), and the variables level of measurement.

2. For a detailed description of the sample design see Davis, Smith, and Marsden 1998, Appendix A or http://www.icpsr.umich.edu/GSS99/.

3. For more information about how the data was collected see Davis, Smith, and Marsden 1998, Appendices B and C or http://www.icpsr.umich.edu/GSS99/.

Subsample 1: DEMO.SAV

DEMO.SAV will be used and referred to primarily in the demonstrations in the body of the chapters. These examples are basically demonstrations that you can "follow along with" on your own computer. This subsample contains 1,500 cases and 41 variables drawn from the 1998 GSS. The items are arranged according to the following subject categories: Abortion, Children, Family, Politics, Religion, Social-Political Opinions, and Sexual Attitudes. It is important to note that this list is composed of 32 variables. It does not include the identification variable or any additional demographic variables (nine in all including the ID variable) that are contained in both files and thus listed separately at the end of the chapter.

Subject Category   Question
Variable Name   [Level of Measurement]
            Value   Labels

Abortion

Please tell me whether or not you think it should be possible for a pregnant woman to obtain a legal abortion if:

1)   ABANY   the woman wants it for any reason?
            [Nominal]

            1   Yes
            2   No

2)   ABDEFECT   there is a chance of serious defect in the baby?
            [Nominal]

            1   Yes
            2   No

3)   ABHLTH   the woman's own health is seriously endangered by the pregnancy?
            [Nominal]

            1   Yes
            2   No

4)   ABNOMORE   she is married and does not want any more children?
            [Nominal]

            1   Yes
            2   No

5) ABPOOR   the family has a very low income and cannot afford any more children?

[Nominal]

1   Yes
2   No

6) ABRAPE   she became pregnant as a result of rape?

[Nominal]

1   Yes
2   No

7) ABSINGLE   she is not married and does not want to marry the man?

[Nominal]

1   Yes
2   No

Children

8) CHLDIDEL   What do you think is the ideal number of children for a family to have?

[Interval/Ratio [I/R]][1]

0   None

1   One

2   Two

3   Three

4   Four

5   Five

6   Six

7   7 or more

8   As many as you want

1. As we noted in the previous chapter, SPSS refers to "interval" and "ratio" data as "scale," as opposed to distinguishing between the two. In order to simplify reference, we will use "I/R" to refer to both interval and ratio data.

If you had to choose, which thing on this list would you pick as the most important for a child to learn to prepare him or her for life?

9) OBEY   To obey
[Ordinal]

     1   Most important

     2   2nd important

     3   3rd important

     4   4th important

     5   Least important

10) POPULAR   To be well-liked or popular
[Ordinal]

     1   Most important

     2   2nd important

     3   3rd important

     4   4th important

     5   Least important

11) THNKSELF   To think for himself or herself
[Ordinal]

     1   Most important

     2   2nd important

     3   3rd important

     4   4th important

     5   Least important

12) WORKHARD   To work hard
[Ordinal]

     1   Most important

     2   2nd important

     3   3rd important

     4   4th important

     5   Least important

13) HELPOTH   To help others when they need help
[Ordinal]

     1   Most important

     2   2nd important

3   3rd important

4   4th important

5   Least important

Family

14) MARITAL   Are you currently married, widowed, divorced, separated, or have you never been married?
[Nominal]

1   Married

2   Widowed

3   Divorced

4   Separated

5   Never married

15) DIVORCE   Have you ever been divorced or legally separated?
[Nominal]

1   Yes

2   No

16) CHILDS   How many children have you ever had? Please count all that were born alive at any time (including any you had from a previous marriage).
[I/R]

0   None

1   One

2   Two

3   Three

4   Four

5   Five

6   Six

7   Seven

8   Eight or more

17) SIBS   How many brothers and sisters did you have? Please count all those born alive, but no longer living, as well as those alive now. Also include stepbrothers and stepsisters, and children adopted by your parents.
[I/R]

0   None

1   One

2   Two

3   Three

4   Four

5   Five

6   Six

7   Seven or more

Politics

18) PARTYID   Generally speaking, do you usually think of yourself as a
                  Republican, Democrat, Independent, or what?
                  [Ordinal]

          0   Strong Democrat

          1   Not very strong Democrat

          2   Independent, close to Democrat

          3   Independent (neither)

          4   Independent, close to Republican

          5   Not very strong Republican

          6   Strong Republican

          7   Other party, refused to say

19) POLVIEWS   We hear a lot of talk these days about liberals and conser-
                  vatives. I'm going to show you a 7-point scale on which
                  the political views that people might hold are arranged
                  from extremely liberal point 1 to extremely conservative
                  point 7. Where would you place yourself on this scale?
                  [Ordinal]

          1   Extremely liberal

          2   Liberal

          3   Slightly liberal

          4   Moderate

          5   Slightly conservative

          6   Conservative

          7   Extremely conservative

Religion

20) ATTEND   How often do you attend religious services?
[Ordinal]

    0   Never

    1   Less than once a year

    2   Once a year

    3   Several times a year

    4   Once a month

    5   2–3 times a month

    6   Nearly every week

    7   Every week

    8   More than once a week

21) POSTLIFE   Do you believe there is a life after death?
[Nominal]

    1   Yes

    2   No

22) PRAY   About how often do you pray?
[Ordinal]

    1   Several times a day

    2   Once a day

    3   Several times a week

    4   Once a week

    5   Less than once a week

    6   Never

23) RELIG   What is your religious preference? Is it Protestant, Catholic, Jewish, some other religion, or no religion?
[Nominal]

    1   Protestant

    2   Catholic

    3   Jewish

    4   None

    5   Other (specify)

    6   Buddhism

7	Hinduism
8	Other Eastern
9	Moslem/Islam
10	Orthodox-Christian
11	Christian
12	Native American
13	Inter-denominational

Social-Political Opinions

24) CAPPUN   Do you favor or oppose the death penalty for persons convicted of murder?
[Nominal]

1   Favor

2   Oppose

25) GETAHEAD   Some people say that people get ahead by their own hard work; others say that lucky breaks or help from other people are more important. Which do you think is most important?
[Ordinal]

1   Hard work

2   Both equally

3   Luck or help

4   Other

26) GUNLAW   Would you favor or oppose a law which would require a person to obtain a police permit before he or she could buy a gun?
[Nominal]

1   Favor

2   Oppose

Note: For the following three questions, interviewers were instructed to use the term Black or African-American, depending on the customary usage in their area.

27) RACDIF4   On the average (Blacks/African-Americans) have worse jobs, income, and housing than white people. Do you think this difference is because most (Blacks/African-

Americans) just don't have the motivation or will power to pull themselves out of poverty?

[Nominal]

1   Yes

2   No

28) RACMAR   Do you think there should be laws against marriages between (Blacks/African-Americans) and Whites?

[Nominal]

1   Yes

2   No

29) RACPUSH   Here are some opinions other people have expressed in connection with (Black/African-American)–White relations. Which statement on the card comes closest to how you, yourself feel? (Blacks/African-Americans) shouldn't push themselves where they're not wanted.

[Ordinal]

1   Agree strongly

2   Agree slightly

3   Disagree slightly

4   Disagree strongly

Sexual Attitudes

30) HOMOSEX   What about sexual relations between two adults of the same sex? Do you think it is always wrong, almost always wrong, wrong only sometimes, or not wrong at all?

[Ordinal]

1   Always wrong

2   Almost always wrong

3   Sometimes wrong

4   Not wrong at all

5   Other

31) XMOVIE   Have you seen an X-rated movie in the last year?

[Nominal]

1   Yes

2   No

32) PREMARSX   There's been a lot of discussion about the way morals and attitudes about sex are changing in this country. If a man and woman have sexual relations before marriage, do you think it is always wrong, almost always wrong, wrong only sometimes, or not wrong at all?
[Ordinal]

1   Always wrong

2   Almost always wrong

3   Sometimes wrong

4   Not wrong at all

5   Other

Subsample 2: EXER.SAV

EXER.SAV will be used primarily in the exercises at the end of the chapters. This file contains 1,500 cases and 44 variables drawn from the 1998 GSS. The 35 items below are arranged according to the following subject categories: Sex Roles, Police, Health and Health Insurance, Mass Media, National Government Spending Priorities, Teen Sex, Affirmative Action, and Equalization. Once again, this list does not include the nine variables that are contained in both the DEMO.SAV and EXER.SAV files. These variables are listed in a separate section at the end of the chapter subtitled "ID and Demographic Variables Contained in Both Files."

Subject Category
Variable Name   Question
                     [Level of Measurement]

                     Value   Labels
Sex Roles

Now I'm going to read several statements. As I read each one, please tell me whether you strongly agree, agree, disagree, or strongly disagree with it. For example, here is the statement.

1)   FECHLD   A working mother can establish just as warm and secure a relationship with her children as a mother who doesn't work.
[Ordinal]

1   Strongly agree

2   Agree

3   Disagree

4   Strongly disagree

2) FEHELP   It is more important for a wife to help her husband's career than to have one herself.

[Ordinal]

1   Strongly agree

2   Agree

3   Disagree

4   Strongly disagree

3) FEPRESCH   A preschool child is likely to suffer if his or her mother works.

[Ordinal]

1   Strongly agree

2   Agree

3   Disagree

4   Strongly disagree

4) FEFAM   It is much better for everyone involved if the man is the achiever outside the home and the woman takes care of the home and family.

[Ordinal]

1   Strongly agree

2   Agree

3   Disagree

4   Strongly disagree

Police

5) POLHITOK   Are there any situations you can imagine in which you would approve of a policeman striking an adult male citizen?

[Nominal]

1   Yes

2   No

3   Don't know

If YES or Not Sure: Would you approve of a policeman striking a citizen who:

6) POLABUSE   Had said vulgar and obscene things to the policeman?

[Nominal]

1   Yes

2   No

7) POLMURDR   Was being questioned as a suspect in a murder case?
                [Nominal]

    1   Yes

    2   No

8) POLESCAP   Was attempting to escape from custody?
                [Nominal]

    1   Yes

    2   No

9) POLATTAK   Was attacking the policeman with his fists?
                [Nominal]

    1   Yes

    2   No

Health and Health Insurance

10) HEALTH   Would you say your own health, in general, is excellent,
                good, fair, or poor?
                [Ordinal]

    1   Excellent

    2   Good

    3   Fair

    4   Poor

11) HLTHINSR   First, are you, yourself covered by health insurance, a gov-
                ernmental plan like Medicare or Medicaid, or some other
                plan that pays for your medical care?
                [Nominal]

    1   Yes covered

    2   No not covered

IF YES:

There are many different types of health care plans. I'd like to know which
type of plan is most like yours. Please tell me if your plan has any of the following features:

12) DOCLIST   Is there a book, directory, or list of doctors whom you
                must use?
                [Nominal]

    1   Yes

    2   No

13) ANYDOC   Can you choose any doctor you like in your community or elsewhere, perhaps paying part of the bill?
[Nominal]

1   Yes

2   No

14) SWITHLTH   Have you ever switched your plan or the medical care provider within your plan due to dissatisfaction with a prior plan?
[Nominal]

1   Yes

2   No

3   Can't switch

15) USEDMNTL   Since you joined this plan, have you sought medical care for problems with your emotions, nerves, or mental health?
[Nominal]

1   Yes

2   No

IF YES:

16) MNTLDENY   Were you denied services under your plan's benefit package?
[Nominal]

1   Yes

2   No

Mass Media

17) NEWS   How often do you read the newspaper—everyday, a few times a week, once a week, less than once a week, or never?
[Ordinal]

1   Everyday

2   Few times a week

3   Once a week

4   Less than once a week

5   Never

18) TVHOURS   On the average day, about how many hours do you personally watch television?

[I/R]

Responses in actual hours

I am going to name some institutions in this country. As far as the people running these institutions are concerned, would you say you have a great deal of confidence, only some confidence, or hardly any confidence in them?

19) CONPRESS   Press?

[Ordinal]

1   A great deal

2   Only some

3   Hardly any

20) CONTV   TV?

[Ordinal]

1   A great deal

2   Only some

3   Hardly any

National Government Spending Priorities

We are faced with many problems in this country, none of which can be solved easily or inexpensively. I'm going to name some of these problems, and for each one I'd like you to tell me whether you think we're spending too much money on it, too little money, or about the right amount. Are we spending too much money, too little money, or about the right amount on

21) NATHEAL   Improving and protecting the nation's health?

[Ordinal]

1   Too little

2   About right

3   Too much

22) NATCITY   Solving the problems of the big cities?

[Ordinal]

1   Too little

2   About right

3   Too much

23) NATCRIME   Halting the rising crime rate?
[Ordinal]

1   Too little

2   About right

3   Too much

24) NATDRUG   Dealing with drug addiction?
[Ordinal]

1   Too little

2   About right

3   Too much

25) NATEDUC   Improving the nation's education system?
[Ordinal]

1   Too little

2   About right

3   Too much

26) NATRACE   Improving the conditions of Blacks?
[Ordinal]

1   Too little

2   About right

3   Too much

27) NATFARE   Welfare?
[Ordinal]

1   Too little

2   About right

3   Too much

Teen Sex

28) PILLOK   Do you strongly agree, agree, disagree, or strongly disagree that methods of birth control should be available to
teenagers between the ages of 14 and 16 if their parents do
not approve?
[Ordinal]

1   Strongly agree

2   Agree

3   Disagree

4   Strongly disagree

29) SEXEDUC   Would you be for or against sex education in the public schools?
[Ordinal]

1   Favor

2   Oppose

3   Depends

30) TEENSEX   What if they are in their early teens, say 14 to 16 years old? In that case do you think sex relations before marriage are always wrong, almost always wrong, wrong only sometimes, or not wrong at all?
[Ordinal]

1   Always wrong

2   Almost always wrong

3   Sometimes wrong

4   Not wrong at all

5   Other

Affirmative Action

31) AFFRMACT   Some people say that because of past discrimination, Blacks should be given preference in hiring and promotion. Others say that such preference in hiring and promotion of Blacks is wrong because it discriminates against Whites. What about your opinion—are you for or against preferential hiring and promotion of Blacks?

IF FAVOR: Do you favor preference in hiring and promotion strongly or not strongly?

IF OPPOSE: Do you oppose preference in hiring and promotion strongly or not strongly?
[Ordinal]

1   Strongly support preference

2   Support preference

3   Oppose preference

4   Strongly oppose preference

32) WRKWAYUP   Do you agree strongly, agree somewhat, neither agree nor disagree, disagree somewhat, or strongly disagree with the following statement: Irish, Italians, Jewish and many other minorities overcame prejudice and worked their way up. Blacks should do the same without special favors.
[Ordinal]

1   Agree strongly

2   Agree somewhat

3   Neither agree nor disagree

4   Disagree somewhat

5   Disagree strongly

33) RACWORK   Are the people who work where you work all White, mostly White, about half and half, mostly Black, or all Black?
[Ordinal]

1   All White

2   Mostly White

3   Half White-Black

4   Mostly Black

5   All Black

6   Work alone

8   Don't work

34) DISCAFF   What do you think the chances are these days that a White person won't get a job or promotion while an equally or less qualified Black person gets one instead? Is this very likely, somewhat likely, or not very likely to happen these days?
[Ordinal]

1   Very likely

2   Somewhat likely

3   Not very likely

Equalization

35) EQWLTH   Some people think that the government in Washington ought to reduce the income differences between the rich and the poor, perhaps by raising the taxes of wealthy families or by giving income assistance to the poor. Others

think that the government should not concern itself with reducing the income difference between the rich and the poor. Here is a card with a scale from 1 to 7. Think of a score of 1 as meaning that the government ought to reduce the income differences between rich and poor, and a score of 7 as meaning that the government should not concern itself with reducing income differences. What score comes closest to the way you feel.

[I/R]

1   Government should reduce differences

2

3

4

5

6

7   No government action

ID and Demographic Variables Contained in Both Files

Both of the files on your disk contain the following nine identification and demographic variables. In other words, you will find the variables ID and AGE, as well as all the other variables listed below, in both the DEMO.SAV and EXER.SAV files.

Variable Name	Question [Level of Measurement] Value Labels
1) ID	Respondent Identification Number [assigned by the inter-viewers] [I/R]
2) AGE	What is your date of birth? [I/R] This was recoded into age in years.
3) CLASS	If you were asked to use one of the four names for your social class, which would you say you belong to: the

lower class, the working class, the middle class, or the upper class?

[Ordinal]

1   Lower class

2   Working class

3   Middle class

4   Upper class

5   No class

4) EDUC   What is the highest grade in elementary school or high school that you finished and got credit for? [If high school graduate] Did you complete one or more years of college for credit not including schooling such as business college, technical or vocational school? [If yes] How many years did you complete?

[I/R]

0   No formal schooling

1   1st grade

2   2nd grade

3   3rd grade

4   4th grade

5   5th grade

6   6th grade

7   7th grade

8   8th grade

9   9th grade

10   10th grade

11   11th grade

12   12th grade

13   1 year of college

14   2 years of college

15   3 years of college

16   4 years of college

17   5 years of college

18	6 years of college
19	7 years of college
20	8 years of college

5) INCOME98   In which of these groups did your total family income, for all sources, fall last year, before taxes, that is?
[Ordinal]

1	Under $1,000
2	$ 1,000 to 2,999
3	$ 3,000 to 3,999
4	$ 4,000 to 4,999
5	$ 5,000 to 5,999
6	$ 6,000 to 6,999
7	$ 7,000 to 7,999
8	$ 8,000 to 9,999
9	$10,000 to 12,499
10	$12,500 to 14,999
11	$15,000 to 17,499
12	$17,500 to 19,999
13	$20,000 to 22,499
14	$22,500 to 24,999
15	$25,000 to 29,999
16	$30,000 to 34,999
17	$35,000 to 39,999
18	$40,000 to 49,999
19	$50,000 to 59,999
20	$60,000 to 74,999
21	$75,000 to 89,999
22	$90,000 to 109,999
23	$110,000 or over

6) SEI   Hodge-Siegel-Rossi socioeconomic ratings for respondents' occupations.[4]

[I/R]

7) RACE   What race do you consider yourself?

[Nominal]

1   White

2   Black

3   Other

8) RINCOM98   In which of these groups did your earnings from [occupation from a previous question] fall for last year? That is, before taxes or other deductions?

[Ordinal]

Coded the same as INCOME98

9) SEX   Coded by the interviewers, based on observation.

[Nominal]

1   Male

2   Female

Conclusion

By now you should be familiar with the GSS and the two subsamples you will be working with. The data you will be using are real and can be taken as an accurate reflection of the attitudes, opinions, beliefs, characteristics, and behaviors of adult Americans in 1998. In the next chapter we are going to get started using SPSS. Once you have learned how to launch an SPSS session and access the files contained on your disk, you will be ready to begin exploring your data. With the help of SPSS and some simple tools, we think you will find that the possibilities for discovery can be both rich and rewarding.

Main Points

- The GSS is a national survey of adult Americans that has been conducted more or less annually since 1972.
- The 1998 data are based on a sample of 2,832 adult Americans and can be taken as an accurate reflection of the opinions, attitudes, behaviors, and

---

4. See E-Appendix E at http://www.pineforge.com for a listing of occupational titles and their prestige scores. For more information on the Hodge-Siegel-Rossi occupational prestige score see Davis, Smith, and Marsden 1998. See also Nakao and Treas (1994) for an in-depth discussion of the updated occupational prestige and socioeconomic scores.

characteristics of all adult Americans (18 years of age or older, noninstitu-tionalized, English-speaking) in 1998.

■ The data were collected in face-to-face household interviews averaging approximately 90 minutes each.

■ The disk included with this book contains two subsamples of data from the 1998 GSS named DEMO.SAV and EXER.SAV, respectively.

■ To insure that the files can be used with both the student and professional ver-sions of SPSS for Windows, we reduced the size of the subsamples; DEMO.SAV contains 1,500 cases and 41 variables, whereas EXER.SAV con-tains 1,500 cases and 44 variables.

Key Terms

General Social Survey (GSS)
National Opinion Research Center (NORC)
Multistage probability sampling
DEMO.SAV
EXER.SAV

Sampling error
Missing data
Variable name
Value (numeric values or codes)
Value labels

Review Questions

1. What is the GSS?

2. When was the data discussed in this chapter collected?

3. Describe how the 2,832 respondents were selected?

4. What is this method of sampling called?

5. If the data show that 55 percent of respondents favor capital punishment, what would be your best estimate in terms of the percentage(s) of adult Americans who feel this way as well?

6. Is it possible, based on this example, that as few as 10 to 15 percent of adult Americans favor capital punishment? Why or why not?

7. When social scientists refer to "sampling error," what are they referring to?

8. Would you agree that as a general rule, the smaller the sampling error, the less likely it is that the data are representative of the population?

9. What method was used to collect the data for the GSS?

10. List the abbreviated variable names for three items that deal with the issue of health insurance from the file labeled EXER.SAV.

Chapter 5 Using SPSS

Like most data analysis programs, SPSS is capable of computing many different statistical procedures with different kinds of data. This makes SPSS a very powerful and useful tool, but because of its generalization, we need to specify what we want it to do for us.

In many ways, SPSS is a vehicle for discovering differences and relationships in data, the same way a car is a vehicle for discovering places we have not yet visited. The car does not know where we want to go or what we wish to see. We, rather than the car, plan the trip and set the direction. Similarly, when we use SPSS, we choose the data we wish to explore and select the statistical procedures we wish to use. Sitting at our computer keyboards, we are in SPSS's driver's seat.

We tell SPSS where to go and what to do in our social research adventure with SPSS commands. These commands instruct SPSS where to find our data, ways in which we want to modify the data, and the statistical procedures we want to use. While there are several ways to issue commands to SPSS, you usually rely on the mouse connected to your computer. By clicking or double-clicking the button on the left side of your mouse, you will be able to tell SPSS what you want it to do.

Demonstration 5.1: Starting an SPSS Session

SPSS for Windows has probably already been installed for you by computer center personnel, lab assistants, or your instructor. You need to learn which of the machines available to you are equipped with the system. Your instructor will probably help you get started, but we think you will find it pretty simple.

Once you have run Windows 95 or 98, you will probably find yourself looking at something like this:

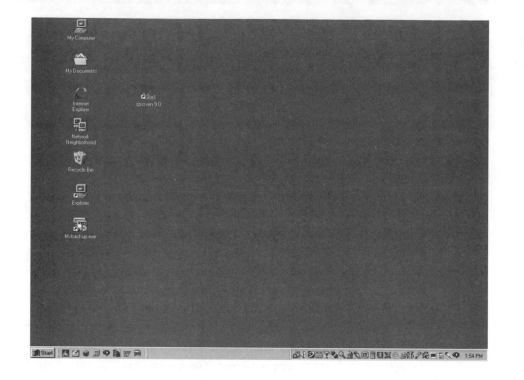

At this point you have some options.

Option 1

Perhaps the easiest way to start an SPSS session is to move your cursor to the ***SPSSwin icon*** and double-click it. It will take SPSS a little while to respond, with the length of time depending on the kind of computer you are using.

Option 2

If you do not find the SPSSwin icon on the desktop, as shown in the screen above, don't panic. There are other ways of launching SPSS. A second option is to click the **Start** button in the lower left corner of your screen. Move the cursor up the list to **Programs**, and look for SPSS among the programs resident on this computer. When you find **SPSS**, move your cursor to highlight it and then click on it.[1]

If neither of these alternatives works, you can panic if you like. Better yet, ask your instructor for assistance.

After launching SPSS, you may see a ***dialog box*** asking "What would you like to do?" For now, click on **Cancel** and this box will disappear. SPSS will finish loading and you should see something like what is shown in the following screen.

---

1. A third option is to click the **Start** button and move your cursor up the list to **Documents**. At this point you should be able to see if DEMO.SAV, EXER.SAV, or a similar data set is listed as a recently used document. If so, move your cursor to highlight the document name and click. This will load both SPSS and the data file. A fourth option is to click on the **My Computer** icon on your desktop. Once you locate the file, you can double-click on the file name to load both SPSS and the data file.

After each new SPSS command is introduced, you will see a summary of the command in a box like the one below (SPSS Command 5.1):

SPSS COMMAND 5.1: Starting an SPSS Session

Once you are in Windows you have two major options:

Option 1:

Double-click **SPSS icon** →
Click **Cancel**

Option 2:

Click **Start** → **Programs** → **SPSS** →
Click **Cancel**

The box contains a brief description of the command, as well as a summary of how to accomplish the procedure. You will also find a list of the new SPSS commands introduced in each chapter at the end of the chapter. In addition, E-Appendix F on-line contains a comprehensive list of all the SPSS commands introduced in the text.

Demonstration 5.2: Data Editor—Operating SPSS and Getting Help

Once SPSS opens, you will notice that most of the screen is taken up by the SPSS *Data Editor*. You can find that name at the very top of the screen. This matrix is designed to hold data for analysis. If you wished, you could enter data directly into the matrix now and analyze it. Instead, however, we are going to load the GSS data set into the matrix in a moment.

Right beneath the window's title is a set of menus called a *menubar*, running from File on the left to Help on the right. You are going to become very familiar with these menus, because they are the control system or the primary means through which you will operate SPSS.

As a preview, click on the word **File** on the menubar and the *drop-down menu* will appear. Notice how some commands in the drop-down menu appear black, whereas others are faint gray. Whenever you see a list like this, you can execute the black commands (by clicking on them), but the gray ones are not currently available to you. Right now, for example, you could Open a data set, but you can't Save it because there's nothing to be saved at this time.

Click on the word **File** again, and the list disappears. Do that to get rid of the File menu now, and we'll come back to it shortly.

New	▶
Open...	Ctrl+O
Database Capture	▶
Read Text Data	
Save	Ctrl+S
Save As...	
Display Data Info...	
Apply Data Dictionary...	
Print...	Ctrl+P
Stop Processor	Ctrl+.
Recent File List	
Exit	

At the far right-hand side of the menubar you will see the SPSS Help menu, something that you may want to take note of in case you need to use it later. As you are now aware, SPSS is a powerful state-of-the-art statistical package that allows users to accomplish numerous tasks and procedures. While this textbook will introduce you to a variety of SPSS commands, options, and procedures, we cannot hope to cover all of the program's capabilities. Consequently, if you find that you want to use SPSS to perform a procedure that is not covered in the text or if you have a question or problem that hasn't been addressed in the book, you may want to consult the Help feature. All you have to do is click on the word **Help** and a drop-down menu containing several options will appear.

For instance, one of the options available in the Help menu is Topics. You can access Topics by clicking on **Help** and then **Topics**. The Help Topics: SPSS for Windows dialog box gives you several options for getting assistance on a specific topic, issue, or procedure. Another Help feature that you may find useful is the SPSS on-line tutorial that gives a comprehensive overview of SPSS basics. You can access the tutorial by clicking **Help** and then selecting **Tutorial** in the drop-down menu.

These are just some of the many Help features available on SPSS. There are many other options that you may find useful as you continue moving through the text and using SPSS for your own research.

SPSS COMMAND 5.2: Accessing the Help Feature

Click **Help** → Click the help option you wish to access . . .

In addition to the menubar, a second common way to communicate with SPSS is through the use of the *toolbar*. The toolbar is the line of buttons or "tools" running from left to right directly below the menubar. While you can use the menubar and drop-down menus to perform most tasks, sometimes it is easier to just click a button on the toolbar.

You can find out what tasks each button on the toolbar performs by placing your cursor on the button and waiting a moment until a brief description of the tool pops up on the screen. For instance, if you place your cursor on the button toward the left end of the toolbar which contains a picture of a disk, you will soon see the words "save file" pop up on the screen. This, of course, lets us know that we can use this tool to save a file.

If you want to take a moment to explore what other tools are available on the toolbar, you can do that now. Otherwise we will move ahead.

Demonstration 5.3: Windows Options— Minimizing and Reducing

Before continuing with SPSS, let's examine a couple of Windows options that will be useful to you. Notice that there are three small buttons in the upper right corner of the screen. Click the **leftmost button**, the one with heavy underscore on it.

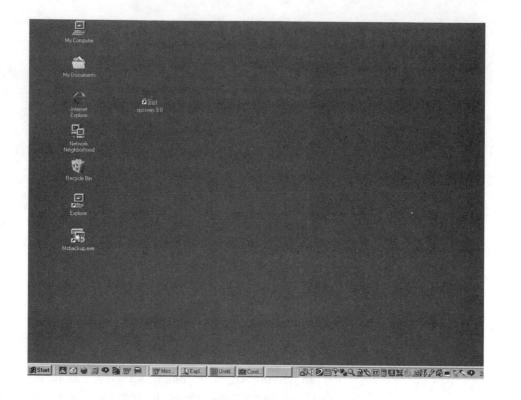

Notice that the window has disappeared! Not to worry. Look now at the task bar at the bottom of the screen and locate a button titled **Untitled—SPSS for Windows Data Editor**. Click it.

Aha! The window didn't exactly disappear; Windows says it was mini-mized. That's certainly not an overstatement. This feature will be very useful to you once you have several documents on the screen at once. The minimize option lets you move windows out of the way without actually closing them.

Now click the **middle button** and notice how the window shrinks. If you click on the **window's title bar and hold your mouse button down**, you can drag the window around the screen. Sometimes this is a useful alternative to minimizing a window. Click the **middle button** again, and the window once more fills the screen.

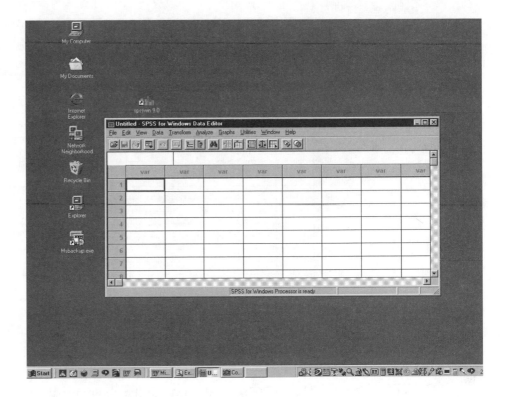

The **rightmost button**, with an **X**, will close the window altogether. If you click it now, you will have to relaunch SPSS to get back here. You choose. We'll wait if you want to shut things down and reopen them.

Demonstration 5.4: Entering Data in the Data Editor— A Preview

You should now be looking at the SPSS Data Editor window again. As we indicated earlier, this is the window that contains the data for SPSS to analyze, although right now it is empty. If you wanted, you could begin entering data for analysis. In fact, if you decide to conduct your own survey later on, this is how you would enter those data. As a quick preview of this feature, type a **1** and press the **Enter** key on your keyboard.

You have now created the world's smallest data set: with one piece of information about one person. The 1 on the left of the matrix represents Person 1. If you entered another number as you did just above, you would have brought Person 2 into existence with one piece of information. Why don't you do that now—enter a **2** for that person.

The var00001 at the head of the column in the matrix represents the specific information we are storing about each person. It might represent his or her gender, for example. Moreover, a value of 1.00 might mean male and a value of 2.00 might mean female. Therefore, we would have indicated that Person 1 is a man, Person 2 a woman.

This is the basic structure of the data sets analyzed by SPSS. The good news for you is that we've already prepared large data sets for your use, so you won't have to keep entering data like this. However, if you are interested in using SPSS to create your own data file, you may want to consult Chapter 21 and E-Appendix E on-line, which take you through this process step-by-step.

Before loading our GSS data, we want to close the small data set that we just created. To do that simply click **File** and then click **Exit**. At this point SPSS will ask you if you want to "save the contents of data editor to Untitled," which is just a fancy way of asking if you want to save the "world's smallest data set" which we just created. Because we are not interested in saving this data set, click **No**. If we wanted to save the data, we would click **Yes** and follow the instructions in the dialog box.

To move to the next section you will need to *relaunch SPSS* (if you have forgotten how to do this, refer back to "SPSS Command 5.1").

Demonstration 5.5: Loading a Data Set

Now that you have successfully relaunched SPSS, we are going to load one of the GSS data sets provided with this book. This is easily done in SPSS for Windows. Insert the 3.5″ disk that came with this book in the disk drive. Click the word **File** and its menu will open up below it. The second command in that menu is the one we want: Open. Click on **Open**, and a new window will open to assist us in selecting the data set we want.

```
▦ Untitled - SPSS for Windows Data Editor
File  Edit  View  Data  Transform  Analyze  Graphs  Utilities  Window  Help
```

Open File   ? ☒

Look in: [💾] 3½ Floppy (A:)   [▼] [🔼] [⊘] [🗋] [⊟] [▦]

▦ demo.sav
▦ exer.sav

File name: demo.sav   Open

Files of type: SPSS (*.sav)   [▼]   Paste

                                                    Cancel

This command will present you with the Open File window. Click on the **Look in** field and select the drive that contains your disk (usually it will be the **A:** drive). Next, move the mouse to the **Files of type** dialog box and click on the suffix for SPSS for Windows data files, **SPSS(*.sav)**. Now you should see names of the files on your disk. Select **DEMO.SAV** by placing the mouse on it and clicking. Click the **Open** button near the lower right corner of the Open File window. In a few seconds, SPSS will display the GSS data in its data window. Specific instructions on using SPSS with these data are provided in later chapters.

SPSS COMMAND 5.3: Opening a Data File

Click **File** → **Open** →
Click on the **Look in field** → Select the drive that contains your disk →
Files of Type → click on **SPSS (*.sav)** →
Click the name of the data file → **Open**

	id	abany	abdefect	abhlth	abnomore	abpoor	abrape	absingle	age	attend	cappun	childs	chldidel	class	d
1	2	0	0	0	0	0	0	0	27	5	2	0	2	2	
2	4	2	1	1	2	2	1	2	21	3	2	0	2	2	
3	6	2	1	1	8	1	1	8	33	4	1	1	2	2	
4	10	1	1	1	1	1	1	1	45	6	1	0	3	3	
5	12	1	1	1	1	1	1	1	41	5	8	1	-1	3	
6	13	1	1	1	1	1	1	1	32	4	1	2	2	1	
7	14	1	1	1	1	1	1	1	48	1	1	1	-1	3	
8	15	0	0	0	0	0	0	0	20	0	1	0	2	3	
9	16	2	8	8	2	2	8	2	43	7	8	5	-1	2	
10	19	1	8	1	1	1	1	1	43	4	2	0	-1	2	
11	20	2	2	1	2	2	1	2	28	2	1	1	-1	3	
12	25	0	0	0	0	0	0	0	81	7	1	8	4	3	
13	26	2	1	1	2	2	1	2	65	5	1	3	2	2	
14	30	1	1	1	1	1	1	1	61	2	1	2	-1	3	
15	33	8	8	8	8	8	8	8	51	6	8	3	-1	3	
16	34	1	1	1	1	1	1	1	56	7	1	4	4	3	
17	35	0	0	0	0	0	0	0	41	3	1	0	9	3	
18	38	0	0	0	0	0	0	0	31	2	1	2	4	3	
19	39	2	2	1	2	2	1	2	25	3	2	4	8	1	
20	41	2	2	1	2	2	2	2	50	7	1	4	-1	4	
21	42	8	8	8	8	8	8	8	81	6	8	8	9	4	

Demonstration 5.6: Exploring Your Data Set

Now you should be looking at the data in the DEMO.SAV file. This is the GSS data we will be using for the demonstrations in the body of each chapter. You will notice that there are variable names across the top of the matrix and numbers in the cells. Each row represents a person or ***respondent*** to the survey (what is often referred to as a ***case***). Based on our discussion in Chapter 4, we already know that this data set has 1,500 rows or 1,500 respondents/cases. Each column represents a variable, indicated by the variable name at the top of the column. This data set contains 41 columns, or 41 variables.

You can get a brief description of each abbreviated variable name by placing your cursor on the variable name at the top of the columns and waiting for a moment until the description pops up on the screen. For instance, if you place the cursor on the variable name ATTEND, a brief description of the variable that reads "How often R [respondent] attends religious services" will magically appear on your screen.

Now turn your attention to respondent number 1 (the ***record numbers*** run down the left side of the matrix. Do not confuse them with the "ID" numbers) and the variable MARITAL. You will notice that respondent number 1 has a 5 in the column for MARITAL. This variable reflects respondents' marital statuses. As you may recall from the list of variables in Chapter 4, a 5 (the ***numeric value*** or ***code***) on MARITAL means the respondent has never been married (the ***value label***). If you didn't recall this, don't worry. There are several ways you can use SPSS to access the information.

Option 1: Variables Window

One option is to click on the **Utilities** menu and select **Variables**. The following screen is what you should be looking at after that command.

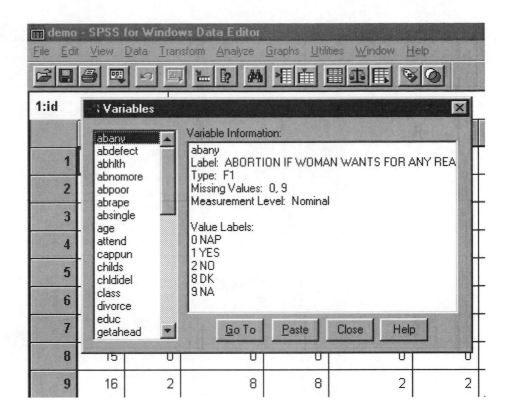

As you can see, the Variables window has two main parts. On the left is a list of the variables contained in our data set. On the right side is some information about the highlighted variable **ABANY**, including the information we are looking for—numeric values and value labels. This box tells us that for the variable ABANY, a "1" (value) means "yes" (label), a "2" (value) means "no" (label), and so on. Consequently, if you didn't recall what a value of "5" on MARITAL means, you can easily access the information by scrolling down through the list of variables until you see MARITAL.[2] Now click on **MARITAL**, and this is what you should see.

---

2. In addition to scrolling, there are several other ways to move through the list of variables on the left side. For instance, you can click on the **up** and **down arrows** on the right-hand side of the variables list. You can also use the arrow keys on your keyboard or type the first letter of the variable's name. The highlight will then move to the first variable that begins with that letter in your data set.

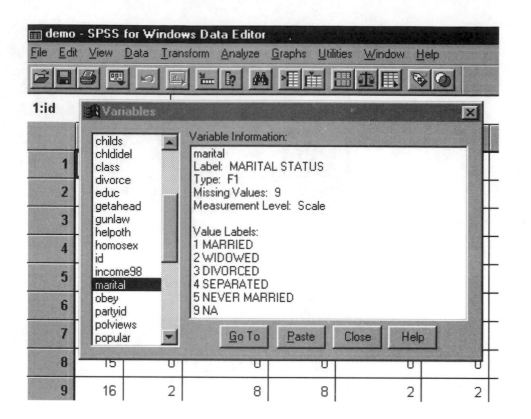

The box on the right side tells us that anyone with a code of 1 is married, anyone with a 2 is widowed, and so forth. You might want to take a minute to explore some of the other variables in the data set, because it will be useful for you to be familiar with them later on.

SPSS COMMAND 5.4 (1): Finding Information on Variables

> Option 1: Variables Window
> Click **Utilities** → **Variables**

When you get bored with the Variables window, there are a couple of ways to leave it. First, you can click the **Close** button at the bottom of the window. Or you can click the small button with the **X** in the upper right corner of the window. Either will produce the same result.

Option 2: Toggling Between Numeric Values and Value Labels

Another way to find out what a numeric value (such as a "5" on MARITAL) means is to click on **View** in the menubar. Then click on **Value Labels** in the drop-down menu. This command tells SPSS to change the numeric values in the data matrix into descriptive value labels. You will see, for instance, that the numeric value "5" under MARITAL for respondent 1 has been replaced by a descriptive value label indicating that the respondent has never been married.

demo - SPSS for Windows Data Editor

File Edit View Data Transform Analyze Graphs Utilities Window Help

1:id

	id	abany	abdefect	abhlth	abnomore	abpoor	abrape	absingle	age	attend	cappun	childs	chldidel	class
1	2	NAP	NAP	NAP	NAP	NAP	NAP	NAP	27	2-3X A M	OPPOS	0	2	WORKI
2	4	NO	YES	YES	NO	NO	YES	NO	21	SEVRL T	OPPOS	0	2	WORKI
3	6	NO	YES	YES	DK	YES	YES	DK	33	ONCE A	FAVOR	1	2	WORKI
4	10	YES	YES	YES	YES	YES	YES	YES	45	NRLY E	FAVOR	0	3	MIDDL
5	12	YES	YES	YES	YES	YES	YES	YES	41	2-3X A M	DK	1	-1	MIDDL
6	13	YES	YES	YES	YES	YES	YES	YES	32	ONCE A	FAVOR	2	2	LOWE
7	14	YES	YES	YES	YES	YES	YES	YES	48	LT ONC	FAVOR	1	-1	MIDDL
8	15	NAP	NAP	NAP	NAP	NAP	NAP	NAP	20	NEVER	FAVOR	0	2	MIDDL
9	16	NO	DK	DK	NO	NO	DK	NO	43	EVERY	DK	5	-1	WORKI
10	19	YES	DK	YES	YES	YES	YES	YES	43	ONCE A	OPPOS	0	-1	WORKI
11	20	NO	NO	YES	NO	NO	YES	NO	28	ONCE A	FAVOR	1	-1	MIDDL
12	25	NAP	NAP	NAP	NAP	NAP	NAP	NAP	81	EVERY	FAVOR	EIGHT O	4	MIDDL
13	26	NO	YES	YES	NO	NO	YES	NO	65	2-3X A M	FAVOR	3	2	WORKI
14	30	YES	YES	YES	YES	YES	YES	YES	61	ONCE A	FAVOR	2	-1	MIDDL
15	33	DK	DK	DK	DK	DK	DK	DK	51	NRLY E	DK	3	-1	MIDDL
16	34	YES	YES	YES	YES	YES	YES	YES	56	EVERY	FAVOR	4	4	MIDDL
17	35	NAP	NAP	NAP	NAP	NAP	NAP	NAP	41	SEVRL T	FAVOR	0	DK,NA	MIDDL
18	38	NAP	NAP	NAP	NAP	NAP	NAP	NAP	31	ONCE A	FAVOR	2	4	MIDDL
19	39	NO	NO	YES	NO	NO	YES	NO	25	SEVRL T	OPPOS	4	AS MANY	LOWE
20	41	NO	NO	YES	NO	NO	NO	NO	50	EVERY	FAVOR	4	-1	UPPER
21	42	DK	DK	DK	DK	DK	DK	DK	81	NRLY E	DK	EIGHT O	DK,NA	UPPER

SPSS for Windows Processor is ready

To display numeric values in the data matrix once again, all you have to do is click on **View.** You will now see a check mark next to Value Labels in the drop-down menu. Click on **Value Labels** and the check mark will disappear. You should now see the numeric values in the data matrix once again. This process of switching back and forth between numeric values and value labels is known as *toggling*.

SPSS COMMAND 5.4 (2): Finding Information on Variables

> Option 2: Toggling
> Click **View → Value Labels**

Option 3: "Value Labels" Tool

A third way to discover what a numeric value refers to is to click on the button in the toolbar which looks like a price tag, the **Value Labels** tool (second from the right side of the toolbar). You will notice that the numeric values in the data matrix have now magically changed into value labels. To change the value labels back into numeric values, all you have to do is click on the **Value Labels** tool once again.

SPSS COMMAND 5.4 (3): Finding Information on Variables

> Option 3: Value Labels Tool
> Click **Value Labels** tool

Now that you are back in the Data Editor window and the numeric values are showing, you might want to browse through more of the data. You can accomplish this by clicking the **two arrows at the bottom, right-hand side of the matrix**. Why not experiment with this? The two scroll bars on the bottom and right-hand side of the matrix will let you move through the list of respondents. While you are exploring the data set, try to use one of the three options just discussed to find the marital status of respondent 10 and the sex of respondent 20.

While exploring the data you may notice that you can move the *active cell* (the cell in the data matrix with the thick black lines around it) by using the arrow keys on your keyboard. Or you can use your mouse to place the active cell by pointing and clicking on the cell you want to move to. One note of caution, however. When moving the active cell, make sure you are very careful *not* to make any keystrokes on the keyboard because you may accidentally change or alter the existing data set.

Demonstration 5.7: Ending Your SPSS Session

When you've finished for this session, open the **File** menu by clicking it. At the very bottom, you'll see the command **Exit**. Clicking this will instruct the computer to terminate the SPSS session and return you to the Windows desktop.

Before executing your command, however, the computer may ask if you want to save contents of data editor. Recall that we've loaded the file DEMO.SAV into that window. Because the data set is already saved, we can safely click the **No** button now. If you had entered your own data or changed the existing data set, you definitely would have wanted to save the data and the computer would have asked you to name the new data set.

SPSS COMMAND 5.5: Ending Your SPSS Session

Click **File → Exit**

Conclusion

So, in this first encounter, you've learned how to launch SPSS for Windows, load a data set, and explore in it. In the next chapter, we'll revisit some of the variables in the data set and see how SPSS lets us explore more deeply than we've done in this first incursion.

Main Points

- Because SPSS is generalized, we use SPSS commands to tell it what to do.
- To issue commands to SPSS, you usually click or double-click on the button on the left side of your mouse.

- There are two main options for starting an SPSS session.
- The **SPSS Data Editor** is a matrix designed to hold data for analysis.
- The menubar, drop-down menus, toolbars, and dialog boxes are the primary means by which you operate SPSS.
- If you are using several documents at once, you may want to take advantage of Windows minimizing and reducing options.
- You can use SPSS to either enter data or load an existing data set, such as the data provided on the disk that came with this book.
- Once you have loaded your data set, you can explore the data and find out what values refer to by looking in the **Variables** window, toggling, or using the **Value Labels** tool.
- Once you finish your SPSS session, you can easily exit by selecting **File** and **Exit**. If you entered data or changed an existing data set, do not forget to save it.

Key Terms

SPSSwin icon	Toolbar	Numeric value or code
Dialog box	Respondent	Value label
Data Editor	Case	Toggling
Menubar	Record numbers	Active cell
Drop-down menu		

SPSS Commands Introduced in This Chapter

5.1   Starting an SPSS Session

> **Option 1:**
>
> Double-click **SPSS** icon →
> Click **Cancel**
>
> **Option 2:**
>
> Click **Start** → **Programs** → **SPSS** →
> Click **Cancel**

5.2   Accessing the Help Feature

> Click **Help** → Click the help option you wish to access . . .

5.3   Opening a Data File

> Click **File** → **Open** →
> Click on the **Look in field** → Select the drive that contains your disk →
> **Files of Type** → click on **SPSS (*.sav)** →
> Click the name of the data file → **Open**

5.4   Finding Information on Variables

> Option 1: Variables Window
> Click **Utilities** → **Variables**
>
> Option 2: Toggling
> Click **View** → **Value Labels**
>
> Option 3: Value Labels Tool
> Click **Value Labels** tool

5.5   Ending Your SPSS Session

> Click **File** → **Exit**

Review Questions

1. What is the primary means through which we operate SPSS?

2. If you have a question or problem, what on-line feature(s) does SPSS provide to offer you assistance?

3. If you are using several documents at once, what Windows' option might you want to take advantage of?

4. In SPSS, are the cases/respondents arranged in rows or columns?

5. In SPSS, are the variables arranged in rows or columns?

6. If you don't recall what a value of a particular variable in your data set means, what three SPSS commands can you use to find this information?

7. What does "toggling" refer to?

8. If you use SPSS to enter your own data or change an existing data set, what one thing should you do before ending your SPSS session?

NAME _____

CLASS _____

INSTRUCTOR _____

DATE _____

To complete the following exercises you need to start an SPSS session and load the data file EXER.SAV *(found on the disk that came with this book). You can find answers to selected Questions (1–3) in Appendix A.*

1. Using the variable AFFRMACT, note the numeric value for each of the following respondents (listed by case number). Then open the Variables window and note the appropriate label for each value listed below:

                                       Value   Label

Respondent #89 _____

Respondent #556 _____

Respondent #1065 _____

2. Use the Toggle command to find the following variable information. What is the race (variable RACE) of each of the following respondents (listed by case number)?

                                         Value   Label

Respondent #18 _____

Respondent #765 _____

Respondent #1386 _____

3. Use the Value Labels tool to find the following variable information. Do the following respondents have confidence in the press (variable CONPRESS)?

                                         Value   Label

Respondent #63 _____

Respondent #190 _____

                              Value   Label
        Respondent #1499_____

    4. Select any variable from the EXER.SAV file that interests you except
        AFFRMACT, RACE, or CONPRESS. Then use SPSS to find the following
        variable information:

        a. What is the abbreviated variable name?_____

        b. What is the variables level of measurement?_____

        c. List the values and labels associated with the variable?

                              Value   Label

        d. Choose three respondents and list how they responded to the variable/
            question item you chose (list case number, values, and value labels).

                              Value   Label

        Respondent #_____

        Respondent #_____

        Respondent #_____

    5. Use the SPSS Help feature Tutorial (Click on **Help** → **Tutorial** → **Tutorials** →
        Open → **Overview** → **Open**) to run through the following SPSS Tutorials:
        Windows and menus, **Toolbars**, and **Dialog boxes**.

Part III Univariate Analysis

We are going to begin our data analyses with some basic measurements of variables. In the body of the chapters, we are going to pay special attention to three concepts: religiosity, political orientations, and attitudes toward abortion. In the exercises at the end of each chapter, you will have a chance to explore other issues, such as sex roles, law enforcement, health insurance, mass media, national government spending priorities, teen sex, and affirmative action. We've chosen these topics on the basis of general interest and the possibilities they hold for analysis.

In Part III, we are going to begin with univariate analysis, the analysis of one variable at a time. This is a basic act of measurement. In Chapter 6, for example, we are going to examine the different ways we might measure the religiosity of the respondents to the GSS, distinguishing the religious from the nonreligious and noting variations in between. In so doing, we are going to learn how to instruct SPSS to create frequency distributions, produce descriptive statistics, modify variables with recodes, and save and print our output.

In Chapter 7 we look at differences in political orientations and show you how to present your data in graphic form by reviewing commands for creating simple bar charts and line graphs.

In Chapter 8 we turn our attention from univariate to bivariate analysis, or the analysis of two variables at a time. Whereas the bulk of our discussion of bivariate analysis is reserved for Part IV, in Chapter 8 we give you a preview of sorts by showing you how you can use crosstabs to examine the structure of attitudes toward abortion.

In Chapter 9 we build on our discussion in the previous chapter by focusing on the way social researchers combine several responses into more sophisticated measures of the concepts under study. You'll learn a couple of techniques for doing that.

Finally, Chapter 10 suggests a number of other topics you might be interested in exploring: desired family size, child training attitudes, sexual behavior, and prejudice. We'll give you some guidance in approaching these topics, but our main purpose is to give you opportunities to strike out on your own and experience some of the open-endedness of social research.

Chapter 6   Describing Your Data: Religiosity

In this chapter we are going to begin analyzing data. You'll need to launch the SPSS program as described earlier. Double-click the **SPSSwin** icon to get things going.

Demonstration 6.1: Opening a Frequently Used Data File

After you launch SPSS, you may see the dialog box asking "What would you like to do?" If so, you have a few options. One shortcut when opening a frequently used file is to make sure the button next to the SPSS icon, labeled **Open an existing file**, is selected. (This is the last option displayed.) If it is not, simply click on that button. Since SPSS keeps track of files that have been used recently, you should see the DEMO.SAV file listed in the box. You can access the file by simply highlighting **DEMO.SAV** and then clicking **OK**.

If you do not see this dialog box or if the DEMO.SAV file is not listed, don't worry. You can also open the file by following the instructions for opening a data file discussed in the last chapter (SPSS Command 5.3).[1] Better yet, once you have launched an SPSS session, simply click **File** to open the File menu and then select **DEMO.SAV** from the list of files presented.

---

1. If you prefer that the "What would you like to do?" box not be displayed every time you open SPSS, click **Don't show this dialog in the future** at the bottom left-hand corner of the dialog box.

New	▶
Open...	Ctrl+O
Database Capture	▶
Read Text Data	
Save	Ctrl+S
Save As...	
Display Data Info...	
Apply Data Dictionary...	
Print...	Ctrl+P
Stop Processor	Ctrl+.
1 A:\Interview1.sav	
2 A:\exer.sav	
3 A:\demo.sav	
4 E:\PINE FORGE\...\Example.sav	
5 E:\SOC200\...\alldepts.sav	
Exit	

SPSS COMMAND 6.1:   Shortcut for Opening a Frequently Used Data File

Option 1:

In "What would you like to do?" dialog box
Click **Open an existing file** → Highlight **file name** → click **OK**

Option 2:

Click **File** → Select **file name** from the list presented ...

Demonstration 6.2: Setting Options

Before we begin analyzing data, we want to make a few changes in the way SPSS displays information. This will make it easier for us to tell SPSS what we want it to do when, for instance running Frequencies, recoding Variables, and so on. To set options, simply click on **Edit** (located on the left-hand side of the menubar). Now choose **Options** and the Options window will open. You will see a series of tabs along the top of the window. Select **General** (if it is not already visible).

In the upper right-hand corner of the screen you will now see the Variable Lists option. In that box choose **Display names** and **Alphabetical**. Now click on **OK** at the bottom of the window. You may get a message telling you that this option will take effect the next time a data file is opened. If so, simply click **OK** once again. This tells SPSS to display abbreviated variable names (as opposed to variable labels) alphabetically whenever it is listing variables. This will make it easier for us to select variables when we are in the process of data analysis.

SPSS COMMAND 6.2:   Displaying Abbreviated Variable Names Alphabetically

Click **Edit** → **Options** → **General** tab → **Display names** → **Alphabetical** → **OK** → **OK**

A second change we want to make deals with the way SPSS displays output (such as frequency distributions). By following the commands listed below, you can insure that SPSS will display both the value and label for each variable you select for analysis, as well as the abbreviated variable names and labels. Simply choose **Edit** and **Options** once again. This time click on the **Output Labels** tab located along the top of the Options window.

At the bottom left-hand corner of this tab, under where it says Pivot Table Labeling, you will see two rectangles labeled Variables in labels shown as: and Variable values in labels shown as:. Click on the **down arrow** next to the first rectangle (Variables in labels shown as:) and choose the third option, **Names and Labels**. Now click on the **down arrow** next to the second rectangle (Variable values in labels shown as:) and select **Values and Labels**. When you are done, click **OK**. If you get a message saying that the option will take effect the next time a data file is opened, click **OK**. After you have made these changes you will be returned to the Data Editor window.

SPSS COMMAND 6.3:   Setting Options—Output Labels

Click **Edit** → **Options** → **Output Labels** tab →
Click **down arrow** next to "Variables in labels shown as:" →
     Names and Labels →
Click **down arrow** next to "Variable values in labels shown as:" →
     Values and Labels →
Click **OK** → **OK**

The options are now set. If you received a message saying that the options will take effect the next time a data file is opened, you will need to end your SPSS session momentarily. You can do this by clicking **File** and **Exit**. Now relaunch SPSS once again and open the **DEMO.SAV** file. This will give you another chance to practice using the shortcut method of opening a frequently used data file.

Demonstration 6.3: Frequency Distributions

Now that you have launched SPSS and loaded the data set, we are ready to begin looking at some aspects of religious behavior. We will do this by first asking SPSS to construct a *frequency distribution*. A frequency distribution is a numeric display of the number of times (frequency) and the relative percentage of times each value of a variable occurred in a given sample. We instruct SPSS to run a frequency distribution by selecting **Analyze** from the menubar, and then choosing **Descriptive Statistics** and **Frequencies...** in the drop-down menus. Once you've completed these steps, you should be looking at the following screen:

Four of the variables in this data set have to do with religiosity:

RELIG   respondent's religious preference

ATTEND   how often the respondent attends religious services

POSTLIFE   belief in life after death

PRAY   how often the respondent prays

Let's start by looking first at the distribution of religious preferences among the sample. This is easily accomplished as follows. First, use the scroll bar on the right-hand side of the list of variable names to move down until RELIG is visible. You may notice that it is fairly easy to find RELIG because the abbreviated variable names are being displayed in alphabetical order (as opposed to the variable labels which can be cumbersome to sift through). This is a result of our first task in this chapter, setting the options so SPSS shows abbreviated variables names alphabetically. Locate the variable **RELIG**, highlight it, and click on the **arrow** to the right of the list. This will transfer the variable name to the field labeled Variable(s):.[2]

---

2. After the variable name has been transferred to the Variable(s): field and is highlighted, you can view the variable's value labels by clicking on the **right mouse button** and selecting **Variable information** (the second of two options that appears on the screen). To see the complete list of all the value labels, simply click on the **down arrow**.

Once you've moved the name RELIG, click the **OK** button. This will set SPSS off on its assigned task. Depending on the kind of computer you are using, this operation may take a few seconds to complete. Eventually, a new window called the *SPSS Viewer* will be brought to the front of the screen, and you should see the following:

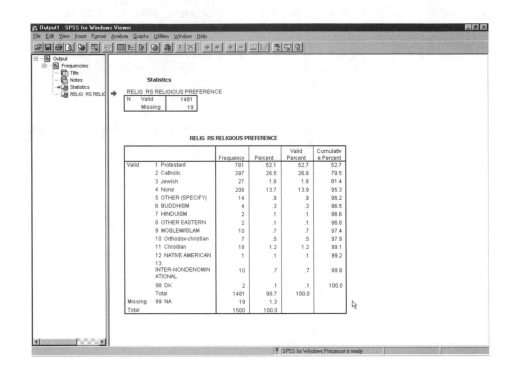

If you don't see both of the tables above in their entirety, don't worry. It's probably because your monitor is not capable of showing as much information as ours. To see all the information, scroll down using the scroll bar on the right-hand side of your screen.

SPSS COMMAND 6.4:   Running Frequency Distributions

> Click **Analyze** → **Descriptive Statistics** → **Frequencies...** →
> Click on **name of the variable** →
> Click on **arrow pointing right** (toward Variable field) → **OK**

The SPSS Viewer—Output

You should now be looking at the SPSS Viewer. You can see that this window is divided into two main parts, or "panes." The left pane, often called the *Outline* or *Output Navigator*, contains a complete list of everything we have instructed SPSS to do in this session. This is useful because if you use SPSS for several hours to run a large amount of analysis, you can use this feature to navigate through your output. If, for instance, you want to find a specific table, all you have to do is find and select the name of the table in the Output Navigator and wait a moment. The table will then appear in the *Viewer*

Document (the pane on the right side of the screen). The Viewer Document is the pane where charts, tables, and other text output (such as Frequencies for the variable RELIG) are displayed.

There are many ways to move through the Viewer. You can place your mouse on the arrow keys on the right-hand side and lower part of the screen and then click or scroll through the window. Or you can use the arrow keys or Page Up and Page Down keys on your keyboard.[3]

Don't forget, you can also hide the SPSS Viewer by using the minimizing and reducing options discussed in Chapter 5. If you minimize the Viewer and then want to restore it, all you have to do is click on the **SPSS Output icon** in the task bar toward the bottom of your screen.

Reading Frequency Distributions

Now that we are more familiar with the SPSS Viewer, lets take a few minutes to analyze the output for the variable RELIG which is located in the Viewer Document.

The small box titled Statistics tells us that of the 1,500 respondents in our subsample of the 1998 GSS, 1,481 gave valid answers to this question, whereas the remaining 19 have missing data. The larger box below marked RELIG RS contains the data we were really looking for.

Let's go through this table piece by piece. As we requested when we changed the options earlier, the first line identifies the variable, presenting both its abbreviated variable name and its full name. Variable names are limited to eight characters and are the key to identifying variables in SPSS commands. Sometimes, it is possible to express the name of a variable clearly in eight or fewer characters (e.g., SEX, RACE), and sometimes the task requires some ingenuity (e.g., RINCOM98 for the respondent's annual income).

The leftmost column in the table lists the numeric values and value labels (recall that we asked SPSS to display both when we changed the options) of the several categories constituting the variable RELIG. These include (1) Protestant, (2) Catholic, (3) Jewish, (4) None, (5) Other, and so on. As we discussed in Chapter 5, the *numeric values* (sometimes called *numeric codes*) are the actual numbers used to code the data when they were entered. The *value labels* are short descriptions of the response categories; they remind us of the meaning of the numeric values or codes. As you'll see later on, you can change both kinds of labels if you want.

The column headed Frequency simply tells how many of the 1,500 respondents said they identified with the various religious groups. We see, for example, that the majority of 781 said they were Protestant, 397 said they

---

3. You may also want to experiment with SPSS's Zoom feature. Simply click on the **Print Preview** icon (the magnifying glass) on the left side of your menubar and you will be able to choose either *Zoom In* or *Zoom Out* in the box presented. Once you have activated the Zoom feature, your cursor will change into a magnifying glass, and you can click directly on the output you want to zoom in (or zoom out) on. When you are done experimenting with this option select **Close** in the Print Preview window and your cursor will become an arrow once again.

were Catholic, and so forth. Note that in this context, None means that some respondents said they had no religious identification; it does not mean that they didn't answer. Near the bottom of the table, we see that two people answered Don't know and 19 people failed to answer.

The next column tells us what percentage of the whole sample each of the religious groups represents. Thus, 52.1 percent are Protestant, for example, calculated by dividing the 781 Protestants by the total sample, 1,500.

Usually, you will want to work with the *valid percentage*, presented in the next column. As you can see, this percentage is based on the elimination of those who gave no answer, so the first number here means that 52.7 percent of those giving an answer said they were Protestant.

The final column presents the *cumulative percentage*, adding the individual percentages of the previous column as you move down the list. Sometimes this will be useful to you. In this case, for example, you might note that 79.5 percent of those giving an answer were Christians, combining the Protestants and Catholics.

Frequency Distribution: Running Two or More Variables at One Time

Now that we've examined the method and logic of this procedure, let's use it more extensively. As you may have already figured out, SPSS doesn't limit us to one variable at a time. (If you tried that out on your own before we said you could, you get two points for being adventurous. Hey, this is supposed to be fun as well as useful.)

So, return to the Frequencies window with:

Analyze → Descriptive Statistics → Frequencies

If you are doing this all in one session, you may find that **RELIG** is still in the Variable(s): field. If so, you should click it, and once it's highlighted, notice that the arrow between the two fields changes direction. By clicking on the **arrow** (which should now be pointing left), you can return RELIG to its original location. A second option for moving the RELIG variable back to its original location is to simply click the **Reset** button located toward the right side of the window. Choose whichever option appeals to you, and then take a moment to move the RELIG variable back to its original position.

Now, let's get the other religious variables. One at a time, click and transfer **ATTEND**, **POSTLIFE**, and **PRAY**. When all three are in the Variables(s): field, click the **OK** button.

After a few seconds of cogitation, SPSS will present you with the Viewer window again. You should now be looking at the results of our latest analysis. If necessary, move up or down through the Viewer until you get to the beginning of our newest data. Your screen should look like this:

Statistics

		ATTEND HOW OFTEN R ATTENDS RELIGIOUS SERVICES	POSTLIFE BELIEF IN LIFE AFTER DEATH	PRAY HOW OFTEN DOES R PRAY
N	Valid	1476	1249	744
	Missing	24	251	756

ATTEND HOW OFTEN R ATTENDS RELIGIOUS SERVICES

		Frequency	Percent	Valid Percent	Cumulative Percent
Valid	0 NEVER	282	18.8	19.1	19.1
	1 LT ONCE A YEAR	159	10.6	10.8	29.9
	2 ONCE A YEAR	158	10.5	10.7	40.6
	3 SEVRL TIMES A YR	167	11.1	11.3	51.9
	4 ONCE A MONTH	110	7.3	7.5	59.3
	5 2-3X A MONTH	120	8.0	8.1	67.5
	6 NRLY EVERY WEEK	82	5.5	5.6	73.0
	7 EVERY WEEK	278	18.5	18.8	91.9
	8 MORE THN ONCE WK	120	8.0	8.1	100.0
	Total	1476	98.4	100.0	
Missing	9 DK,NA	24	1.6		
Total		1500	100.0		

POSTLIFE BELIEF IN LIFE AFTER DEATH

		Frequency	Percent	Valid Percent	Cumulative Percent
Valid	1 YES	905	60.3	72.5	72.5

SPSS COMMAND 6.5:   Running Frequency Distributions with Two or More Variables

> Click **Analyze → Descriptive Statistics → Frequencies... →**
> Click on **name of variable** → click on **arrow pointing right** →
>   **repeat this step** until all variables have been moved into the
>   variable field → **OK**

Take a few minutes to study the new table. The structure of the table is the same as the one we saw earlier for religious preference. This one presents the distribution of answers to the question concerning the frequency of attendance at religious services. Notice that the respondents were given several categories to choose from, ranging from Never to More than once a week. The final category combines those who answered ***Don't know*** (***DK***) with those who gave ***No answer*** (***NA***).

Notice that church attendance is an ordinal variable. The different frequencies of church attendance can be arranged in order, but the distances between categories vary. Had the questionnaire asked, How many times did you attend church last year? the resulting data would have constituted a ratio variable. The problem with that measurement strategy, however, is one of reliability: We couldn't bank on all the respondents recalling exactly how many times they had attended church.

The most common response in the distribution is Never. Just under one-fifth of respondents, or 19.1 percent, gave that answer. The most common answer is referred to as the *mode*. This is followed very closely by 18.8 percent of the respondents who reported attending church every week. If we combine the respondents who report attending religious services weekly with the category immediately below them, more than once a week, we might report that 26.9 percent of our sample reports attending religious services at least once a week. If we added those who report attending nearly every week, we see that approximately 32.5 percent attend church about weekly.

Combining adjacent values of a variable in this fashion is called *collapsing categories*. It is commonly done when the number of categories is large and/or some of the values have relatively few cases. In this instance, we might collapse categories further, for example:

About weekly	33%
1–3 times a month	16%
Seldom	33%
Never	19%

Compare this abbreviated table with the original, and be sure you understand how this one was created. Notice that we have rounded off the percentages here, dropping the decimal points. As a result, you can see that the combined percentages are slightly more than 100 percent. Typically, data such as these do not warrant the precision implied in the use of decimal points, because the answers given are themselves approximations for many of the respondents. Later in this chapter, we'll show you how to tell SPSS to combine categories in this fashion. That will be especially important when we want to use those variables in more complex analyses.

Now let's look at the other two religious variables. Use the scroll bar of the Output window to move to **POSTLIFE**.

POSTLIFE BELIEF IN LIFE AFTER DEATH

		Frequency	Percent	Valid Percent	Cumulativ e Percent
Valid	1 YES	905	60.3	72.5	72.5
	2 NO	204	13.6	16.3	88.8
	8 DK	140	9.3	11.2	100.0
	Total	1249	83.3	100.0	
Missing	0 NAP	237	15.8		
	9 NA	14	.9		
	Total	251	16.7		
Total		1500	100.0		

As you can see, there are significantly fewer attributes making up this variable: Yes or No. Notice that 237 respondents are coded *NAP* (*not applicable*). This means that 237 people were not asked this question.

To collect data on a large number of topics, the GSS asks only subsets of the sample for some of the questions. Thus, you might be asked whether you believed in an afterlife but not asked your opinions on abortion. Someone else might be asked about abortion but not about the afterlife. Still other respondents would be asked about both.

Notice that almost three out of four American adults believe in an afterlife. Is that higher or lower than you would have predicted? Part of the fun of analyses like these is the discovery of aspects of our society that you might not have known about. We'll have numerous opportunities for that throughout the remainder of the book.

Let's look at the final religious variable, PRAY, now.

PRAY HOW OFTEN DOES R PRAY

		Frequency	Percent	Valid Percent	Cumulativ e Percent
Valid	1 SEVERAL TIMES A DAY	183	12.2	24.6	24.6
	2 ONCE A DAY	232	15.5	31.2	55.8
	3 SEVERAL TIMES A WEEK	103	6.9	13.8	69.6
	4 ONCE A WEEK	52	3.5	7.0	76.6
	5 LT ONCE A WEEK	155	10.3	20.8	97.4
	6 NEVER	17	1.1	2.3	99.7
	8 DK	2	.1	.3	100.0
	Total	744	49.6	100.0	
Missing	0 NAP	745	49.7		
	9 NA	11	.7		
	Total	756	50.4		
Total		1500	100.0		

This completes our introduction to frequency distributions. Now that you understand the logic of variables and the values that constitute them, and know how to examine them with SPSS, you may want to spend some time looking at other variables in the data set. You can see them by using the steps we've just gone through.

Descriptive Statistics—Basic Measures of Central Tendency and Dispersion

If you followed our closing suggestion above that you run Frequencies for all variables, you may have noticed some oddities. You will have discovered, for example, that 0.3 percent of the sample is 18 years of age, 1.3 percent is 19, 1.3 percent is 20, and so forth. This display of AGE is not very useful for analysis, primarily because age is presented here as a *continuous variable* (in contrast to *discrete* or *categorical variables*).

In Chapter 3 we noted that social scientists often distinguish between variables at the nominal, ordinal, interval, and ratio levels of measurement. In addition, it is also fairly common to distinguish between continuous and discrete or categorical variables.

Continuous variables are variables whose values can be infinitely subdivided, such as AGE or EDUC in our data set, whereas discrete or categorical variables are variables whose values are completely separate from one another, such as RACE or SEX.

The Frequencies procedure we just reviewed is generally preferred when you are dealing with discrete or categorical variables. If you are dealing with a continuous variable, such as AGE, you will want to use the *descriptives procedure*, which we are going to discuss shortly. Before we do that, we want to take a moment to review which basic measures of central tendency and dispersion are appropriate for variables at different levels of measurement. Consequently, while we previously referred to AGE as an Interval-Ratio [I/R] variable (see Chapter 4), it is also appropriate to refer to it as a continuous variable. Similarly, whereas we previously referred to SEX as a nominal variable, it is appropriate to refer to it as a discrete or categorical variable as well.[4]

As we noted in Chapter 3, a variable's level of measurement is one of the primary considerations in deciding which statistics you want to use for which variable. In other words, certain measures are appropriate for variables at certain levels of measurement.

The following tables are designed to give you a quick overview of which basic measures of central tendency and dispersion are generally considered appropriate for different types of variables (Table 6.1) and variables at different levels of measurement (Table 6.2).

Table 6.1　Basic Descriptive Statistics Appropriate for Different Types of Variables

Type of Variable	Measures of Central Tendency			Measures of Dispersion	
	Mode	Median	Mean	Range	Variance & Standard Deviation
Nominal/ Categorical	√	√			
Continuous		√	√	√	√

Table 6.2　Basic Descriptive Statistics Appropriate for Different Levels of Measurement

Levels of Measurement	Measures of Central Tendency			Measures of Dispersion	
	Mode	Median	Mean	Range	Variance & Standard Deviation
Nominal	√				
Ordinal	—	√		√	
I/R	—	√	√	√	√

---

4. One note of caution: While it is fairly common to equate nominal/ordinal variables with discrete/categorical variables and interval/ratio variables with continuous variables, we need to be careful because, for example, all interval/ratio variables are not continuous (i.e., the number of books a student owns).

A check mark [√] indicates that the measure is generally considered both appropriate and useful, whereas a dash [—] indicates that the measure is permissible but not generally considered very useful. We can see from Table 6.2, for example, that the mode is appropriate for variables at the nominal level, whereas the median, range, and perhaps the mode are appropriate for variables at the ordinal level, and every measure listed is generally appropriate for ratio and interval level data.

You are probably already familiar with the three *measures of central tendency* listed above. As we noted in the previous section, the *mode* refers to the most common value (answer or response) in a given distribution. The *median* is the middle category in a distribution, and the *mean* (which is sometimes imprecisely called the *average*) is the sum of the values of all the cases divided by the total number of cases.

You may already be familiar with the *measures of dispersion* as well. In this section we are going to focus on two: the range and standard deviation. While variance is also listed in the tables, we will not discuss this measure until later in the text. The *range* indicates the distance separating the lowest and highest values in a distribution, whereas the *standard deviation* indicates the extent to which the values are clustered around the mean or spread away from it.

Demonstration 6.4: The Descriptives Procedure— Calculating Descriptive Statistics for Continuous Variables

We can instruct SPSS to calculate descriptive statistics such as those mentioned above fairly easily. In this section we are going to focus on how you can use the Descriptives command to calculate the mean, range, and/or standard deviation. As we noted, the descriptives procedure is generally preferred to the frequencies procedure for continuous, interval, or ratio variables. We will review how to instruct SPSS to calculate the other measures discussed in Tables 6.1 and 6.2 in the next section.

If we wanted to use SPSS to calculate the mean, range, and standard deviation for AGE (appropriate because it is a continuous variable) we could do that simply by clicking **Analyze** in the menubar. Next, select **Descriptive Statistics** and then **Descriptives...** from the drop-down menus. You should now be looking at the Descriptives window, as shown below:

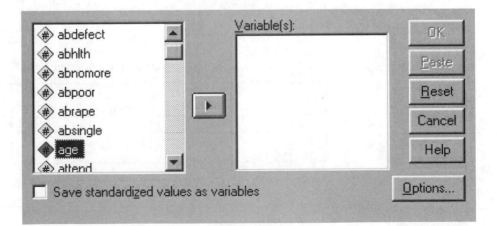

Highlight the variable **AGE** on the list of variables in the box on the left-hand side, then click on the **arrow** pointing right (toward the Variable(s): field). Once you have done that, AGE will appear in the Variable(s): field. Now select **Options...** at the bottom of the window. This opens the Options window, which lets you specify what statistics you want SPSS to calculate.

The **Mean**, **Standard Deviation**, **Minimum**, and **Maximum** options may already be selected. If not, select those by pointing and clicking in the small box next to those options. When you do this you will notice that a check mark appears in the box. Notice that you can also ask SPSS to calculate the range by clicking on the button next to the Range option. While we are not going to ask SPSS to do that now because we can easily calculate the Range on our own, keep that in mind as a future option. Now that you have specified which statistics you want SPSS to calculate for the variable AGE, click **Continue** and you will be back in the Descriptives window. Then, to run Descriptives, simply click **OK**.

Descriptive Statistics

	N	Minimum	Maximum	Mean	Std. Deviation
AGE AGE OF RESPONDENT	1500	18	89	45.78	17.21
Valid N (listwise)	1500				

We can see that the mean age of respondents in this study is 45.78. As we already know, this was calculated by adding the individual ages reported by the 1,500 respondents and dividing that total by 1,500.

Skipping a column, we see that the minimum age reported was 18 and the maximum was 89. The distance between these two values is the Range, in this case 71 years (89 − 18).

The standard deviation tells us the extent to which the individual ages are clustered around the mean or spread out away from it. It also tells us how far we would need to go above and below the mean to include approximately two-thirds of all of the cases. In this instance, two-thirds of the 1,500 respondents have ages between 28.57 and 62.99: (45.78 − 17.21) and (45.78 + 17.21), respectively. Later, we'll discover other uses for the standard deviation.

SPSS COMMAND 6.6:   The Descriptives Procedure—Calculating Descriptive Statistics for Continuous Variables (Mean, Range, and/or Standard Deviation)

Click **Analyze** → **Descriptive Statistics** → **Descriptives...** →
Highlight the **variable name** → click on the **arrow** pointing right →
Click **Options...** → Choose options by clicking on the **button** next to the appropriate measure(s) →
Click **Continue** → **OK**

You may want to practice using the Descriptives command by choosing another continuous variable from the subsample and calculating the mean, range, and/or standard deviation following the procedures listed above.

Demonstration 6.5: The Frequencies Procedures— Calculating Descriptive Statistics for Discrete/Categorical Variables

We want to turn to another command to calculate the other measures listed in Tables 6.1 and 6.2. One option, with which you are already somewhat familiar, is to open the Frequencies window and choose the **Statistics** option. The Statistics box that appears allows us to instruct SPSS to calculate all the measures of central tendency and dispersion we listed in Tables 6.1 and 6.2. One note of caution, however. As we noted earlier, the frequencies procedure is generally preferred for discrete or categorical variables, whereas the Descriptives command is useful for continuous variables. Consequently, if you are working with interval and ratio level data, you will generally want to use the Descriptives command as opposed to the frequencies procedure, even though you can instruct SPSS to produce the mean, range, and standard deviation using either procedure.

To produce descriptive statistics using the Frequencies command, simply choose **Analyze**, **Descriptive Statistics**, and **Frequencies...** as we did earlier. If there are any variables listed in the Variable(s): field, click **Reset**. We will use a simple example to describe the commands and then you can practice using other variables. If, for example, you want to calculate the mode for the variable SEX (appropriate because it is nominal), all you have to do is highlight **SEX** and move it into the Variable(s): field by clicking on the **arrow** pointing right. Now choose **Statistics** at the bottom of the window.

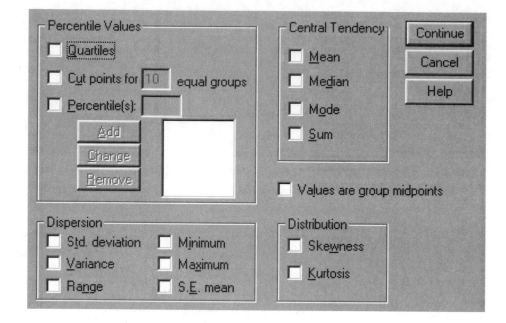

When the Statistics window opens you will see the measures of central tendency listed in the box in the upper right-hand corner and the measures of dispersion listed in the box in the lower left-hand corner. To select an option, simply click on the button next to the appropriate measure. For our simple example then, all we have to do is click on the button next to **Mode** (upper right-hand corner). After you have made your selection(s), click **Continue**. You will now be back in the Frequencies box and you can select **OK**.

Statistics

SEX RESPONDENTS SEX

N	Valid	1500
	Missing	0
Mode		2

SEX RESPONDENTS SEX

		Frequency	Percent	Valid Percent	Cumulative Percent
Valid	1 MALE	661	44.1	44.1	44.1
	2 FEMALE	839	55.9	55.9	100.0
	Total	1500	100.0	100.0	

You should now see your output displayed in the **Viewer**. Remember, the output should include both the mode and frequencies for the variable SEX. By just looking at the frequencies you should be able to say quite easily what the mode (the most frequent response or value given) is for this variable. You can check to make sure you are right by comparing your answer with the one given by SPSS. By glancing through our output, we find that the mode in this instance is "2" because there are more females (numeric value 2) than males (numeric value 1) in our data set.

SPSS COMMAND 6.7:   The Frequencies Procedure—Calculating Descriptive Statistics for Discrete/Categorical Variables

> Click **Analyze** → **Descriptive Statistics** → **Frequencies...** →
>
> Highlight the **variable name** → Click on the **arrow** pointing right → **Statistics** →
>
> Choose options by clicking on the **button(s)** next to the appropriate measure(s) →
>
> Click **Continue** → **OK**

You may want to practice this command by choosing another discrete or categorical variable from the DEMO.SAV file, determining the appropriate measures for the variable, and following the procedure listed above.

Demonstration 6.6: Modifying Variables with Recode

You'll recall from earlier in this chapter that we found that the variable ATTEND had so many categories that it was a bit difficult to handle. To simplify matters, we combined some adjacent answer categories.

Now we are going to see how SPSS can be instructed to do that using the *Recode* command. On the data screen, under the **Transform** menu, select **Recode**. (If you do not see a Transform menu, you are probably looking at the Output window. Go to the Data Editor window by clicking on the SPSS icon in the task bar at the bottom of the screen which is labeled **DEMO–SPSS for Windows Data Editor**.) SPSS now asks if you want to replace the existing values of the variables with the new, recoded ones. Select **Into Different Variables...**, because we are going to assign a new name to the recoded variable.[5] SPSS now presents you with the following screen, in which to describe the recoding you want.

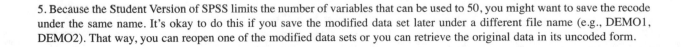

---

5. Because the Student Version of SPSS limits the number of variables that can be used to 50, you might want to save the recode under the same name. It's okay to do this if you save the modified data set later under a different file name (e.g., DEMO1, DEMO2). That way, you can reopen one of the modified data sets or you can retrieve the original data in its uncoded form.

In the variable list at left, find and select **ATTEND**. Use the **arrow** to the right of the list to move the variable name to the field in the middle of the window. Notice that you need to tell SPSS what you would like to name the new, recoded variable. You can accomplish this easily in the section of the window called Output Variable.

Let's name the recoded variable CHATT (for CHurch ATTendance). Type **CHATT** into the space provided for the Output Variable Name and then label the variable (perhaps *Recoded Church Attendance*). When you are done click the **Change** button. As you can see in the middle field, SPSS will now modify the entry to read ATTEND → CHATT.

Thus far, we have created a new variable, but we haven't entered any data into it. We initiate this final step by clicking the **Old and New Values...** button. Now SPSS presents you with the following window:

The left side of this window provides us with several options for specifying the old values we want to recode. The first, which SPSS has selected as a default, lets us specify a single value on the old variable such as 8 (More than once a week). A more efficient option, for our present purposes, is found farther down the list, letting us specify a range of values. (To find the numerical codes assigned to ATTEND, you can return to Variables under the Utilities menu.)

In our manual collapsing of categories on this variable earlier, you'll recall that we combined the values 6 (Nearly every week), 7 (Every week), and 8 (More than once a week). We can accomplish the same thing now by clicking the first **Range:** button and entering **6** and **8** in the two boxes.

At the top of the right side of the window, notice a space for you to enter the new value for this combination of responses. Let's recode it **1**. Enter that number in the box provided, as shown below:

Once you've added the recode value, notice that the **Add** button just below it is activated. Where it was previously grayed out, it is now a clear black and available for use. Click it.

This action causes the expression 6 through 8 → 1 to appear in the field. We've given SPSS part of its instructions. Now let's continue.

Click **Range** again, and now, let's combine values **4** (Once a month) and **5** (Two to three times a month). Give this new combined category the value of **2**. Click **Add** to add it to the list of recodes.

Now combine categories **1** (Less than once a year), 2 (Once a year), and **3** (Several times a year). Recode the new category as **3** and **Add** it to the list.

Finally, let's recode 0 (Never) as **4**. On the left side of the window, use the **Value** button to accomplish this. Enter **0** there, and enter **4** as the new value. Click on **Add**.

To tidy up our recoding, we could have SPSS maintain the missing data values of the original variable. We would accomplish this by clicking **System-or user-missing** as an **old value (on the left side)** and as the **new value (on the right side)**, and then clicking on **Add**. Although it is a good practice to consciously recode every category, in this case it is not necessary. Any cases that were not covered by the range of the old values would be undefined and treated as missing values.

Your Recode window should now look like this:

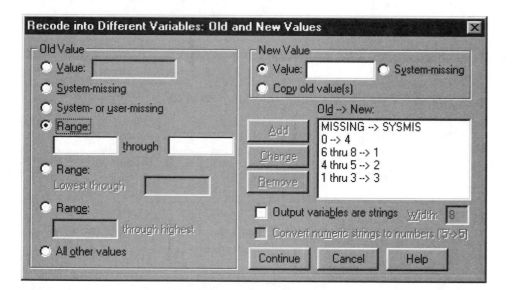

As we wrap up, we should repeat that there are no hard-and-fast rules for choosing which categories to combine in a recoding process like this. There are, however, two rules-of-thumb to guide you: one logical, the other empirical.

First, there is sometimes a logical basis for choosing cutting points at which to divide the resulting categories. In recoding AGE, for example, it is often smart to make one break at 21 years (the traditional definition of adulthood) and another at 65 (the traditional age of retirement). In the case of church attendance, our first combined category observes the Christian norm of weekly church attendance.

The second guideline is based on the advantage of having sufficient numbers of cases in each of the combined categories, because a very small category will hamper subsequent analyses. Ideally, each of the combined categories would have roughly the same number of cases.

How do you suppose we'd continue the recoding process? Click **Continue**, you say? Hey, you may be a natural at this. Do that.

This takes you back to the Recode into Different Variables window. Now that you've completed your specification of the recoding of this variable, all that remains is to click **OK** at the bottom of the window. SPSS may take a few seconds now to accomplish the recoding you've specified.

Go to the Data Editor window again. (You need to minimize the Output Navigator window and enlarge the Data Editor window.) To see your new variable, scroll across the columns of the window until you discover CHATT in the last column used thus far.[6] Notice the values listed in the column. Person number 1 has a value of 2.00 on the new variable.

Now find ATTEND. Notice that person 1 has a 5 in ATTEND. That's correct because everyone with a 1, 2, or 3 in the original variable was recoded as 3 in the new one. You can check a few more people if you want to verify that the coding was accomplished as we instructed. This is a good idea, by the way, to ensure that you haven't made a mistake. (Presumably SPSS doesn't make mistakes.)

Scroll across the columns again until you find **CHATT**. Click the variable name at the top of the column and see how SPSS selects the whole column. With **CHATT** selected, from the **Data** menu, select **Define Variable...**. That should present you with the following window:

Variable Name: chatt

Variable Description
  Type: Numeric8.2
  Variable Label:
  Missing Values: None
  Alignment: Right

Change Settings
  [Type...]   [Missing Values...]
  [Labels..]   [Column Format...]

Measurement
  ● Scale   ○ Ordinal   ○ Nominal

  [OK]   [Cancel]   [Help]

---

6. If you've used the same variable name, look at ATTEND.

Below the variable name, you'll see a summary of the characteristics currently in effect for this variable. The first line tells us the variable type. In the example above, Numeric 8.2 means that codes on this variable are set up as numbers that are 8 digits wide with two digits to the right of the decimal point, so that 1 would be stored as 1.00. Because the decimal points are of no use to us in this situation, let's get rid of them. They only make our output harder to read.

Click on **Type...** .

This window shows all the possibilities available to you. For our purposes, however, we want a numeric variable with zero decimal places. Substitute **0** for the 2 in the Decimal Places field. Then click on **Continue**.

The Define Variable window also allows us to assign value labels to the recoded, numerical codes for CHATT, so we don't have to remember what a 1 or a 2 represents on the recoded variable.

Click on **Labels...** .

Now SPSS is asking us to give names to the numerical values of the new variable. To start, enter **1** in the Value field. Recall that this value represents people who originally scored 6 (Nearly every week), 7 (Every week), and 8 (More than once a week). Let's call this new, combined category "**About weekly**." Enter that description in the Value Label field and click on **Add**.

Now, enter the remaining value labels as indicated below:

```
Define Labels: chatt                                    [X]

Variable Label: [                                    ]        Continue

 Value Labels
 Value:  [              ]                                     Cancel

 Value Label: [                                    ]           Help

   Add        1 = "About weekly"
              2 = "About monthly"
   Change     3 = "Seldom"
              4 = "Never"
   Remove

                              k
```

Once your screen looks like this, click **Continue**.

Finally, the Define Variables window allows you to select the appropriate level of measurement for your new variable CHATT.

Once you are done, you can click **OK** to indicate that you've indicated all the changes we want SPSS to make.

Let's review the results of our recoding process now. We can do this most easily through the use of the now-familiar Frequencies command. If you scroll down the variable list, you'll see that CHATT is now included in the list.

Statistics

CHATT

N	Valid	1476
	Missing	24

CHATT

		Frequency	Percent	Valid Percent	Cumulativ e Percent
Valid	1 About weekly	480	32.0	32.5	32.5
	2 About monthly	230	15.3	15.6	48.1
	3 Seldom	484	32.3	32.8	80.9
	4 Never	282	18.8	19.1	100.0
	Total	1476	98.4	100.0	
Missing	System	24	1.6		
Total		1500	100.0		

Notice how much more manageable the recoded variable is. Now we can use the recoded variable in our later analyses.

The value of recoding is especially evident in the case of continuous variables such as age and education. Because they have so many answer categories, they are totally unmanageable in some forms of analysis. Fortunately, we can recode continuous variables as easily as we just recoded ATTEND. In the case of AGE, for instance, we might establish categories Under 21, 21 to 35, and so on.

You can probably figure out how to do this, but we are going to take advantage of one additional feature in the recoding procedure.

Let's launch **Transform → Recode → Into Different Variables...** again. Notice that the Recode into Different Variables... window still has our recoding of ATTEND. Clear the boards by clicking **Reset** at the bottom of the window. Then, select **AGE** and move it to the Input Variable window.

Let's name the new variable **AGECAT** (to represent AGE CATegories). Once you've named and labeled the new variable, click on **Change** to insert the new name. Now you can click on **Old and New Values...** to tell SPSS how to recode.

In recoding AGE, we want to make use of the Range option again, but for our first recode, check the second one: the one that specifies **lowest through _____**. This will ensure that our youngest category will include the youngest respondents without our having to know what the youngest age is. Enter **20** in the box, specify the new value as **1**, and click on **Add**.

Beware! Although the lowest and highest specifications are handy, they must be used with care. If you look at the frequency distribution for EDUC, you will see that the two missing cases were coded 98. If we used 17 through highest, we would code two people we knew nothing about as being among the most highly educated.

Do what you have to do to create the remaining recode instructions indicated below:

Old Value
- ○ Value: [ ]
- ○ System-missing
- ○ System- or user-missing
- ○ Range:
  [ ] through [ ]
- ○ Range:
  Lowest through [ ]
- ○ Range:
  [ ] through highest
- ○ All other values

New Value
- ○ Value: [ ]   ○ System-missing
- ○ Copy old value(s)

Old --> New:

| Add |
| Change |
| Remove |

```
SYSMIS --> SYSMIS
Lowest thru 20 --> 1
21 thru 39 --> 2
40 thru 64 --> 3
65 thru Highest --> 4
```

☐ Output variables are strings Width: [8]
☐ Convert numeric strings to numbers (5'->5)

| Continue | Cancel | Help |

Click **Continue** to return to the main Recode window and then **OK** to make the recoding changes. Once again, you should be looking at the Data window, and you have a new variable in the rightmost column. Check it out.

To complete the process, let's tidy up the new variable. In the Data window, click the **AGECAT** column label to select the column. Now activate the **Data → Define Variable...** command. With **Type...**, set the decimal places to **0**. Select the appropriate **level of measurement**. And finally, with **Labels...**, establish the following labels for the new variable:

Variable Label: [Recoded Age Categories]

| Continue |
| Cancel |
| Help |

Value Labels
Value: [ ]
Value Label: [ ]

| Add |
| Change |
| Remove |

```
1 = "Under 21"
2 = "21-39"
3 = "40-64"
4 = "65 and older"
```

Once you've completed the recoding and labeling, check the results of your labors by running Frequencies on the new variable. Notice that CHATT is still in the list of variables to be analyzed. You can place CHATT in the list of abbreviated variable names by using one of the two methods we discussed previously (clicking **Reset** or highlighting **CHATT** and selecting the **left-**

pointing arrow). If you fail to do this, SPSS will simply calculate and report the frequencies on CHATT again.[7]

Statistics

AGECAT Recoded Age Categories

N	Valid	1500
	Missing	0

AGECAT Recoded Age Categories

		Frequency	Percent	Valid Percent	Cumulative Percent
Valid	1 Under 21	44	2.9	2.9	2.9
	2 21-39	585	39.0	39.0	41.9
	3 40-64	615	41.0	41.0	82.9
	4 65 and older	256	17.1	17.1	100.0
	Total	1500	100.0	100.0	

SPSS COMMAND 6.8:   Recoding a Variable

> Click **Transform** → **Recode** → **Into Different Variables...**→
>
> Select **name of variable to be recoded** → click **arrow** pointing right →
>
> In Output Variable window **name new variable** → Click **Change** →
>
> In Output Variable window **label new variable** →
>
> Click **Old and New Values...** →
>
> Choose option for specifying old values you want to recode (i.e.,**Range:, etc...**) → Enter **old values codes** → enter **new value recodes** → click **Add** [repeat this step until all old values are recoded]
>
> Click **Continue** → **OK** →
>
> Highlight **new variable name** in Data Editor →
>
> Click **Data** → **Define Variable...** → change characteristics of new Variable (i.e., **Type...** , **Labels...** , **Level of Measurement, etc...**) → Click **OK**

Demonstration 6.7: Saving and Printing Your Work

That's enough work for now. But before we stop, let's save the work we've done in this session so we won't have to repeat it all when we start up again.

---

7. If you have been going through this chapter in one SPSS session, you may also want to deselect Mode, which we selected earlier. This is easily done by choosing **Statistics**, deselecting **Mode** (by clicking on the button next to it), and then clicking **Continue**.

The recoding you've done so far is being held only in the computer's volatile memory. That means that if you leave SPSS right now, all the recoding changes will disappear. Because we will want to use the recoded variables CHATT and AGECAT, there's a simple procedure that will save us time at our next session.

Saving Your Output

Before we save our recoded variables, however, we will go through the instructions for saving the output that you've been accumulating in the Viewer window during this session. If you are writing a term paper that will use these results, you can probably copy portions of the output and paste it into your word-processing document. To save the Output window, first make sure it is the window frontmost on your screen, then select **Save As** under the **File** menu. SPSS will present you with the following window:

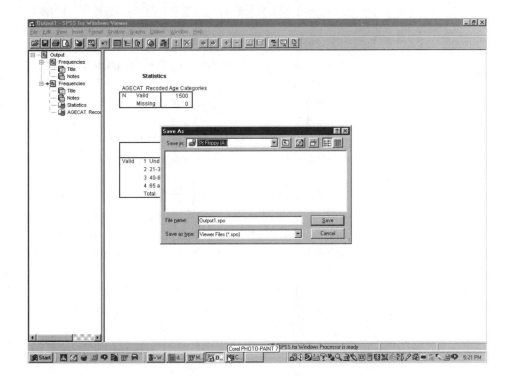

In this example, we've decided to save our output on the Drive A diskette under the name Output1 (which SPSS thoughtfully provided as a default name). As an alternative, you might like to use a name like Out1022 to indicate it was the output saved on October 22, or use some similar naming convention. Either way, insert your disk and change the file name if necessary, choose the appropriate drive in the "Save In" field, and then click **Save**.

SPSS COMMAND 6.9:   Saving Your Output (saving the contents of the SPSS Viewer)

> Click **File** → **Save As** → choose the appropriate drive →
> name your file → click **Save**

Printing Your Output

If you are interested in printing a copy of the output from the Viewer window, all you have to do is click **File** and **Print**. A window with information about your printer set-up will appear. Simply choose **OK** and your output will begin printing.

SPSS COMMAND 6.10:   Printing Your Output (printing the contents of the SPSS Viewer)

> Click **File** → **Print** → **OK**

Saving Changes to Your Data Set

Now, let's save the data file with the recodes we created so painstakingly. Keep in mind that whenever you save a file in SPSS (whether you are saving output or your data set), you are saving only what is visible in the active window. Consequently, to save your data set you need to make sure the Data Editor is the active window. Start by selecting the **Data Editor** window. You can do that by either clicking on **DEMO.SAV** in the task bar or choosing **Window** in the menubar and then selecting **DEMO.SAV** in the drop-down menu. Then, go to the **File** menu and select **Save** again. Now your recodes (CHATT and AGECAT) have been saved, and you can leave SPSS with the **File** → **Exit** command. The next time you start an SPSS session and load the data set, it will have all the new, recoded variables.

If you are using the student version and have written over the earlier forms of some variables, it's a good idea to save your changes using a new file name such as DEMO1, DEMO2, and so on. Then, if you want to use the unrecoded variables, you can always load the original data set for that purpose. To accomplish this, select **File** and **Save As** instead of Save. Then, in the **File Name** field, type in the **new name**. While Windows 95 and 98 do not limit you to an eight-character file name, it may be a good idea to restrict your file name to eight characters because some software still recognize only the first eight characters.

SPSS COMMAND 6.11:   Saving Changes Made to an Existing Data Set

> Click **File** → **Save**

Conclusion

We've now completed your first interaction with data. Even though this is barely the tip of the iceberg, you should have begun to get some sense of the possibilities that exist in a data set such as this. Many of the concepts with which social scientists deal are the subjects of opinions in everyday conversations. A data set such as the one you are using in this book is powerfully different from *opinion*. From time to time, you probably hear people make statements like these:

Almost no one goes to church anymore.

Americans are pretty conservative by and large.

Most people are opposed to abortion.

Sometimes, opinions like these are an accurate reflection of the state of affairs; sometimes, they are far from the truth. In ordinary conversation, the apparent validity of such assertions typically hinges on the force with which they are expressed and/or the purported wisdom of the speaker. Already in this book, you have discovered a better way of evaluating such assertions. In this chapter, you've learned some of the facts about religion in the United States today. The two chapters that follow will take you into the realms of politics and attitudes toward abortion.

Main Points

- In this chapter we began our discussion of univariate analysis by focusing on different ways to measure the religiosity of respondents to the 1998 GSS.

- Before embarking on our analysis, we reviewed a shortcut for opening a frequently used data file and learned to change the way SPSS displays information and output.

- The Frequencies procedure is most useful when you are working with discrete or categorical variables.

- The Frequencies command can be used to produce frequencies for one or more variables at a time.

- The descriptives procedure is usually preferred when you are working with continuous variables.

- After running the frequency and descriptives procedures, your output is displayed in the SPSS Viewer, which is composed of two "panes": the Output Navigator and the Viewer Document.

- Certain measures of central tendency and dispersion are appropriate for variables at different levels of measurement.

- There are a variety of ways to instruct SPSS to calculate measures of central tendency and dispersion. We reviewed two: the descriptives procedure and the frequencies procedure.

- Modifying variables by combining adjacent categories is particularly useful when you are dealing with a variable with many response categories.

- There are no "rules" for deciding which categories to combine when you are recoding. There are, however, two guidelines—one logical and the other empirical.

- When you are ready to end your SPSS session, you may want to save and/or print your output so you can use it later on.

- Before exiting SPSS, don't forget to save any changes you made to the existing data set.

Key Terms

Frequency distribution	NAP (Not applicable)
SPSS Viewer	Continuous variable
Outline	Discrete variables
Output Navigator	Categorical variables
Viewer Document	Measures of central tendency
Numeric values	Mode
Numeric codes	Median
Value labels	Mean
Valid percentage	Measures of dispersion
Cumulative percentage	Range
DK (Don't know)	Standard deviation
NA (No answer)	Recode
Collapsing categories	

SPSS Commands Introduced in This Chapter

6.1: Shortcut for Opening a Frequently Used Data File

> **Option 1:**
>
> In "What would you like to do?" dialog box
> Click **Open an existing file** → Highlight **file name** → click **OK**
>
> **Option 2:**
>
> Click **File** → Select **file name** from the list presented …

6.2: Display Abbreviated Variable Names Alphabetically

> Click **Edit** → **Options** → **General** tab → **Display names** →
> **Alphabetical** → **OK** → **OK**

6.3: Setting Options—Output Labels

> Click **Edit** → **Options** → **Output Labels** tab →
> Click **down arrow** next to "Variables in labels shown as:" →
> **Names and Labels** →
> Click **down arrow** next to "Variable values in labels shown as:" →
> **Values and Labels** →
> Click **OK** → **OK**

6.4:   Running Frequency Distributions

> Click **Analyze** → **Descriptive Statistics** → **Frequencies...** →
> Click on **name of the variable** →
> Click on **arrow pointing right** (toward Variable field) → **OK**

6.5:   Running Frequency Distributions with Two or More Variables

> Click **Analyze** → **Descriptive Statistics** → **Frequencies...** →
> Click on **name of variable** → click on **arrow pointing right** →
>   **repeat this step** until all variables have been moved into the
>   variable field → **OK**

6.6:   The Descriptives Procedure—Calculating Descriptive Statistics for Continuous
Variables

> Click **Analyze** → **Descriptive Statistics** → **Descriptives...** →
> Highlight the **variable name** → click on the **arrow** pointing right →
> Click **Options...** → Choose options by clicking on the **button** next
>   to the appropriate measure(s) →
> Click **Continue** → **OK**

6.7:   The Frequencies Procedure—Calculating Descriptive Statistics for
Discrete Categorical Variables

> Click **Analyze** → **Descriptive Statistics** → **Frequencies...** →
> Highlight the **variable name** → Click on the **arrow** pointing right →
>   **Statistics** →
> Choose options by clicking on the **button(s)** next to the appropriate
>   measure(s) →
> Click **Continue** → **OK**

6.8:   Recoding a Variable

> Click **Transform** → **Recode** → **Into Different Variables...** →
> Select **name of variable to be recoded** → click **arrow** pointing right →
> In Output Variable window **name new variable** → Click **Change** →
> In Output Variable window **label new variable** →
> Click **Old and New Values...** →
> Choose option for specifying old values you want to recode
>   (i.e., **Range:, etc...**) → Enter **old values codes** → enter **new
>   value recodes** → click **Add** [repeat this step until all old values
>   are recoded]
> Click **Continue** → **OK** →
> Highlight **new variable name** in Data Editor →
> Click **Data** → **Define Variable...** → change characteristics of new
>   Variable (i.e. **Type.... , Labels... , Level of Measurement,
>   etc...**) → Click **OK**

6.9:   Saving Your Output (saving the contents of the SPSS Viewer)

> Click **File** → **Save As** → choose the appropriate drive →
>   name your file → click **Save**

6.10:   Printing Your Output (printing the contents of the SPSS Viewer)

> Click **File** → **Print** → **OK**

6.11:   Saving Changes Made to an Existing Data Set

> Click **File** → **Save**

Review Questions

1. Analysis of one variable at a time is often referred to as what type of analysis?

2. What is a frequency distribution?

3. In a frequency distribution, what information does the column labeled "frequency" contain?

4. In a frequency distribution, what information does the column labeled "valid percent" contain?

5. What is a continuous variable?

6. Give an example of a continuous variable from the 1998 GSS.

7. What is a discrete or categorical variable?

8. Give an example of a discrete/categorical variable from the 1998 GSS.

9. Is a frequency distribution generally preferred for continuous or categorical variables? Why?

10. If you are working with interval or ratio data, would you generally use the frequency procedure or the descriptives procedure?

11. List the measures of central tendency and dispersion that are appropriate for variables at each of the following levels of measurement:

    A. Ordinal —

    B. Nominal —

    C. Interval/Ratio —

12. Calculate the mode, median, mean, and range for the following numbers: 7, 5, 2, 4, 4, 0, 1, 9, 6

13. Is the standard deviation a measure of central tendency or dispersion?

14. In general terms, what information does the standard deviation tell us?

15. Describe the two general guidelines you might want to keep in mind when you are deciding how to combine adjacent categories for recoding.

16. If you were going to recode the variable POLVIEWS, which measures political orientations ranging from very liberal to very conservative, how might you collapse (or combine) the following categories?

    1. Extremely liberal

    2. Liberal

    3. Slightly liberal

    4. Moderate, middle-of-the-road

    5. Slightly conservative

    6. Conservative

    7. Extremely conservative

17. After recoding a variable and going back to the **Data Editor** window, we recommend that you open the **Define Variable** dialog box because it allows you to accomplish what specific task(s)?

18. Explain why, for certain GSS variables, half or more of the responses may be labeled "missing."

NAME _____

CLASS _____

INSTRUCTOR _____

DATE _____

To complete the following exercises, you need to open the data file EXER.SAV. You can find answers to selected Questions (1–2, 5–7) in Appendix A.

Produce and analyze frequency distributions for the variables RACE and HEALTH. Then use your output to answer Questions 1 and 2.

1. (RACE)   The largest racial grouping of respondents to the 1998 GSS was _____, with _____%. The second largest grouping was _____, with _____%.

2. (HEALTH)   Most respondents to the 1998 GSS reported that they are in _____ health, with _____% of the sample. This was followed by _____% of respondents who reported being in _____ health. Only _____% of respondents reported being in poor health.

Choose two variables from the EXER.SAV file you are interested in. Produce and analyze frequency distributions for both variables and then summarize your frequency table in a few sentences in the space provided below (Questions 3 and 4).

3. Abbreviated Variable Name _____

     Summary of Frequency Table:

4. Abbreviated Variable Name _____

     Summary of Frequency Table:

Use the Descriptives command to examine the variables EDUC and TVHOURS.
Then use your output to answer Questions 5 and 6.

5. (EDUC) The mean education of respondents to the 1998 GSS is _____, and two-thirds of them have between _____ and _____ years of education.

6. (TVHOURS) Respondents to the 1998 GSS reported watching an average of _____ hours of television a day, with two-thirds of them watching between _____ and _____ hours of television per day.

7. Recode the variable EDUC, creating a new variable EDCAT with the following categories:

   ■ Less than high school graduate
   ■ High school graduate
   ■ Some college
   ■ College graduate
   ■ Graduate studies (beyond college)

   After you have completed your recoding:
   A) Run Frequencies on the variable EDCAT.
   B) Print your output.
   C) Save the recoded variable EDCAT so we can use it in its recoded form later on.

8. Recode the variable INCOME98. In the space provided below, list the name of the new recoded variable and specify how you are going to collapse the categories and why. When you are done with your recoding, run Frequencies and print your output.

Chapter 7 Presenting Your Data in Graphic Form: Political Orientations

Now let's turn our attention from religion to politics. Some people feel so strongly about politics that they joke about it being a "religion." The GSS data set has several items that reflect political issues. Two are key political items: POLVIEWS and PARTYID. These items will be the primary focus in this chapter. In the process of examining these variables, we are going to learn not only more about the political orientations of respondents to the 1998 GSS but also about how to use SPSS to produce and interpret data in graphic form. You will recall that in the last chapter we focused on a variety of ways of displaying univariate distributions (for example, frequency tables) and summarizing them (for instance, measures of central tendency and dispersion). In this chapter we are going to build on that discussion by focusing on two common and useful ways to present your data in graphic form: bar charts and line graphs.

Demonstration 7.1: Political Views: Liberalism Versus Conservatism (POLVIEWS)

We'll start our examination of political orientations with POLVIEWS. Let's see what that variable measures. Use the **Frequencies** command to find out.

Take a few minutes to examine this table. As you can see, POLVIEWS

POLVIEWS THINK OF SELF AS LIBERAL OR CONSERVATIVE

		Frequency	Percent	Valid Percent	Cumulative Percent
Valid	1 EXTREMELY LIBERAL	35	2.3	2.3	2.3
	2 LIBERAL	184	12.3	12.3	14.7
	3 SLIGHTLY LIBERAL	170	11.3	11.4	26.1
	4 MODERATE	537	35.8	36.0	62.0
	5 SLGHTLY CONSERVATIVE	226	15.1	15.1	77.2
	6 CONSERVATIVE	230	15.3	15.4	92.6
	7 EXTRMLY CONSERVATIVE	45	3.0	3.0	95.6
	8 DK	66	4.4	4.4	100.0
	Total	1493	99.5	100.0	
Missing	9 NA	7	.5		
Total		1500	100.0		

taps into basic political philosophy, ranging from Extremely liberal to Extremely conservative. As you might expect, most people are clustered near the center, with fewer numbers on either extreme.

Demonstration 7.2: Producing a Bar Chart— A Graphic View of POLVIEWS

Sometimes the information in a univariate analysis can be grasped more quickly if it is presented in graphic form rather than in a table of numbers. Without looking back at the table you just created, take a moment to think about the distribution of political orientations for respondents to the 1998 GSS. You may recall that most respondents were clustered near the center, but do you remember the relative sizes of the different groups? Was the "moderate" group a little bigger than the others or a lot bigger? Sometimes a graphic presentation of such data sticks in your mind more than a table of numbers.

SPSS gives us a variety of ways to present data graphically. In this section we are going to focus on one basic procedure to construct a simple *bar chart* for POLVIEWS. Bar charts display the same type of information as frequency tables (the number or percentage of cases in a category). The difference is that bar charts display this information graphically rather than in a table.

SPSS offers an easy method for producing a simple bar chart. Under the **Graphs** menu select **Bar...** and the Bar Charts dialog box will open. This box will give you an opportunity to select the kind of graph you would like: Simple, Clustered, or Stacked. Because we have only one variable, we want to choose the **Simple** type. Probably that's the one already selected, but you can click it again to be sure. Then, click the **Define** button.

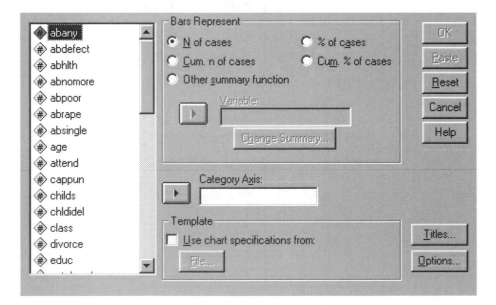

The next window allows you to further specify the kind of bar chart you would like, including a specification of the variable(s) to be graphed. As a start, let's find **POLVIEWS** in the list and click it. Then click the **arrow** beside the Category Axis: box. This lets SPSS know that you want to construct the bar chart with the categories of POLVIEWS (Extremely liberal, Liberal, Slightly liberal, and so on) on the *horizontal* (or "*x*") *axis*.

The Bars Represent box at the top of the window allows you to specify a format for the *vertical* (or "*y*") *axis* of the bar chart. In other words, you can choose to display "N of cases" (frequencies), "% of cases" (percentages), "Cum. n of cases" (cumulative frequencies) or "Cum. % of cases" (cumulative percentages). For now let's click on **% of cases**.

Next, click on the **Options...** button in the lower right-hand corner. After you do this, you will be presented with a screen that allows you to select how missing values will be treated. Because we are not interested in cases coded as "missing," make sure that the check mark next to the line that says Display groups defined by missing values is NOT showing. If the box has a check in it, simply click on the box to make the mark disappear and then select **Continue**. If the box is already blank, click **Continue**.

You should now be back in the Define Simple Bar: dialog box. Before we tell SPSS to produce the chart, we want to draw your attention to one option that you may find useful. The Titles... button, located in the lower right-hand corner, opens a dialog box that allows you to specify titles and footnotes to further define your chart. While we are not going to do that now, you may want to keep this option in mind, particularly if you are planning to prepare charts for a presentation, inclusion in a paper, report, publication, and so on.

Now that you are ready to instruct SPSS to produce the chart, click **OK**. It may take SPSS a few seconds to construct the bar graph to your specifications, but in a short time your chart will appear in the SPSS Viewer.

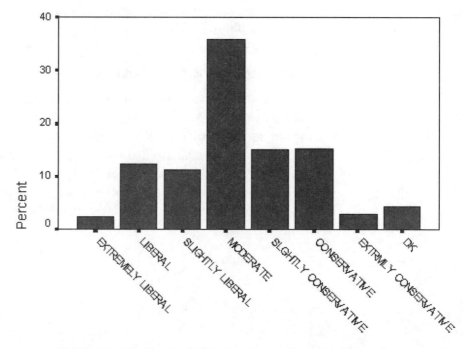

THINK OF SELF AS LIBERAL OR CONSERVATIVE

Now that you have had a chance to study your bar chart, you may want to make note of the fact that SPSS allows you to change its appearance. To do this, simply **double-click on the chart**. You should now see the Chart Editor, which provides you with a variety of options for changing and editing your chart. The Chart Editor can be very useful, particularly if you are planning to present, publish, or otherwise share your analysis. Consequently, you may want to keep this option in mind and explore it further when you have some extra time. To close the Chart Editor, simply click **File** and **Close**.

If you take a moment now to compare your bar chart to the frequency table you ran for POLVIEWS, it should become clear why graphic presentations are sometimes preferred to tables and why they can be more powerful. Viewing the data in graphic form makes it easy to see most people are "Middle-of-the-road," and very few people are extreme in their political views. Graphic presentations are useful because they often do a better job of communicating the relative sizes of the different groups than a table of numbers. Chances are, for instance, that after analyzing this chart, you will have a more vivid memory of the distribution of political views in the United States.

Moreover, it should also be clear that bar charts are essentially just the graphic or visual equivalent of a frequency distribution—equivalent in the sense that they convey essentially the same information in a different format.

SPSS COMMAND 7.1:   Producing a Simple Bar Chart

> Click **Graphs** → **Bar...** → **Simple** → **Define** →
>
> Highlight the **variable name** → Click **arrow** pointing to the "Category Axis:" box →
>
> Click on an option in the "Bars Represent" box →
>
> Click **Options...** → Make sure there is **not a check mark next to the "Display groups defined by missing values"** option → **Continue** → **OK**

Recoding POLVIEWS → POLREC

After studying the frequency table and bar graph for POLVIEWS, you may decide that you want to work with fewer categories. Let's do that now by recoding the variable to just three categories: Liberal, Moderate, and Conservative. Recall from the previous chapter that there are two steps involved in recoding the categories of a variable. First, we combine categories; then we assign names to identify the new groupings.

First, let's create a new variable, **POLREC**, by recoding POLVIEWS as follows:

1 through 3 → 1

4 → 2

5 through 7 → 3

Next, let's take care of the 66 people who did not know their political views. Since they were not able to express a political opinion, they are not useful in analyzing the relationship between political opinion and political party identification. We can eliminate them from our analysis by telling SPSS to treat them as "missing."

8 → System-missing

Then, using Define Variable..., assign new labels to the values of **POLREC**:

1 = Liberal

2 = Moderate

3 = Conservative

If you are having trouble remembering how to run a recode, you may want to refer back to the discussion in Chapter 6 and the commands for recoding a variable listed at the end of that chapter and on-line in E-Appendix F.

To see the results of our recoding, we repeat the **Frequencies** command with the new variable:

Bar Chart POLREC

POLREC Recoded polviews

		Frequency	Percent	Valid Percent	Cumulative Percent
Valid	1 Liberal	389	25.9	27.3	27.3
	2 Moderate	537	35.8	37.6	64.9
	3 Conservative	501	33.4	35.1	100.0
	Total	1427	95.1	100.0	
Missing	System	73	4.9		
Total		1500	100.0		

Now that we've recoded political orientations into a form we can use easily in our future analyses, we are going to turn to the other fundamental political measure—PARTYID. Before we do that, however, you may want to take a few minutes to practice the commands for producing a simple bar chart by instructing SPSS to create a **bar chart** for **POLREC**.

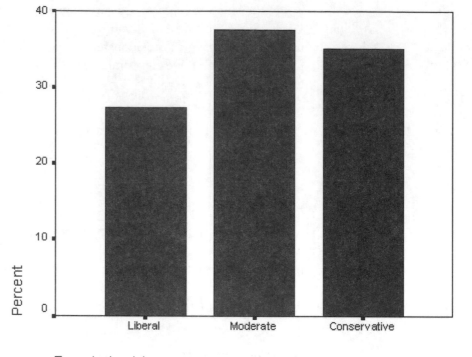

Recoded polviews

A quick look at both bar charts shows us that while collapsing categories produces groups of more nearly equal size, the amount of variation in POLVIEWS becomes obscured in the larger categories.

Demonstration 7.3: Political Party Affiliations (PARTYID)

Another basic indicator of a person's political orientation is found in the party with which he or she tends to identify. Let's turn now to the variable PARTYID. Get the **Frequencies** for that variable.

You should get the following result from SPSS.

Bar Chart PARTYID

PARTYID POLITICAL PARTY AFFILIATION

		Frequency	Percent	Valid Percent	Cumulativ e Percent
Valid	0 STRONG DEMOCRAT	189	12.6	12.6	12.6
	1 NOT STR DEMOCRAT	291	19.4	19.5	32.1
	2 IND,NEAR DEM	192	12.8	12.8	44.9
	3 INDEPENDENT	269	17.9	18.0	62.9
	4 IND,NEAR REP	130	8.7	8.7	71.6
	5 NOT STR REPUBLICAN	255	17.0	17.1	88.7
	6 STRONG REPUBLICAN	138	9.2	9.2	97.9
	7 OTHER PARTY	31	2.1	2.1	100.0
	Total	1495	99.7	100.0	
Missing	9 NA	5	.3		
Total		1500	100.0		

Now that you have run the Frequencies for **PARTYID**, instruct SPSS to create a **simple bar chart** for this variable as well. By following the commands listed in SPSS Command 7.1, you should get the following chart:

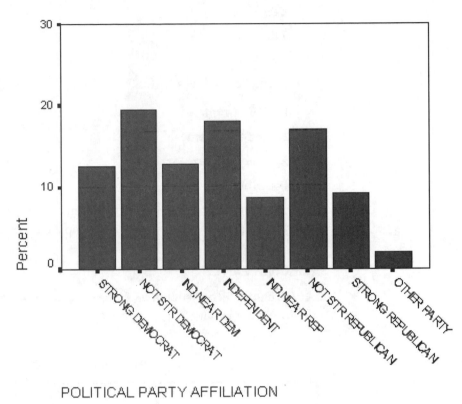

POLITICAL PARTY AFFILIATION

Recoding PARTYID → PARTY

Once again, you will notice that there are more answer categories here than we will be able to manage easily in our subsequent analyses, so let's consider recoding the variable. Let's call the recoded variable simply **PARTY**.

It makes sense to combine the first two categories: the "Strong" and "Not strong" Democrats. Similarly, we will want to combine the corresponding Republican categories (5 and 6). Two of the categories, however, need a little more discussion: the two Independent groups, who said, when pressed by interviewers, that they were "near" one of the two parties.

Should we combine those near the Democrats with that party, for example, or should we combine them with the other Independents? There are a number of methods for resolving this question. For now, however, we are going to choose the simplest method. As we continue our analyses, it will be useful if we have ample numbers of respondents in each category, so we will recode with an eye to creating roughly equal-sized groups. In this instance, that means combining the three Independent categories into one group. So, let's recode as follows:

0 through **1** → **1**

2 through **4** → **2**

5 through **6** → **3**

7 → **4**

Then, label **PARTY** as follows:

1 = Democrat

2 = Independent

3 = Republican

4 = Other

Enter and execute these commands now. Once you've done so, we'll be ready to create a frequency table and simple bar chart for the new variable.

Bar Chart PARTY

After running **Frequencies** and creating a **simple bar chart**, you should get the following results.

PARTY Recoded party ID

		Frequency	Percent	Valid Percent	Cumulativ e Percent
Valid	1 Democrat	480	32.0	32.1	32.1
	2 Independent	591	39.4	39.5	71.6
	3 Republican	393	26.2	26.3	97.9
	4 Other	31	2.1	2.1	100.0
	Total	1495	99.7	100.0	
Missing	System	5	.3		
Total		1500	100.0		

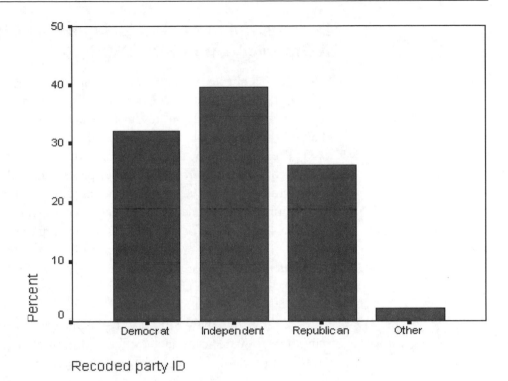

Now we have two basic measures of political orientations. There are other possibilities, however.

Political Attitudes

The GSS data set contains other variables that also tap into people's political orientations. For instance, GUNLAW measures how people feel about the registration of firearms. This has been a controversial issue in the United States for a number of years, involving, on one hand, Second Amendment guarantees of the right to bear arms, and on the other, high rates of violent crime, often involving firearms. CAPPUN measures whether respondents favor or oppose capital punishment, another topic that is associated with political attitudes.

As you can see, there is no lack of ways to explore people's political outlooks in the data set. We're going to focus on some of these items in later sections of the book. You should take some time now to explore some of them on your own. Take capital punishment, for example. How do you think the American people feel about this issue? Do you think most are in favor of it or most are opposed? This is your chance to find out for yourself.

If you have any interest in political matters, you should enjoy this exercise. You may have your own personal opinion about extramarital sex or homosexuality, but do you have any idea how the general population feels about such things? You have the definitive answers to those questions at your fingertips right now, using the GSS data set and your developing mastery of SPSS.

Demonstration 7.4: Producing a Line Chart— A Graphic View of RINCOM98

So far in this chapter we have focused on how to use SPSS to produce one type of graphic—bar charts. However, this is just one of many options available. Another common and useful type of graph is a *line chart*. Like bar charts, line graphs have two axes, the vertical (y axis) and the horizontal (x axis). The categories of the variable are displayed along the horizontal axis, while frequencies or percentages are displayed along the vertical axis. A single line running from the far left to the far right of the graph connects points representing the frequency or percentage of cases for each category or value.

Line charts are particularly useful in showing the overall shape or distribution of variables with a large number of values or categories. Consequently, while bar charts are generally used to display discrete or categorical variables, line charts are most often used to display the distribution of continuous variables.

To demonstrate how SPSS can be instructed to produce a line chart, we want to work with a continuous variable. Because the political items that we have been focusing on in this chapter are discrete, we need to turn our attention to another issue. For now, let's focus on RINCOM98 (respondents' personal income); a measure that you may suspect is at least peripherally related to political orientations and party identification.

To create a line chart, click on **Graphs** once again. This time, however, select **Line...** and the Line Charts dialog box will open, as shown below:

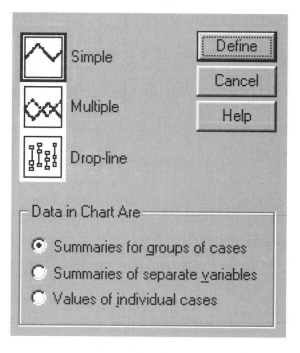

On the left side of the box you see three types of graphs listed: Simple, Multiple, and Drop-line. Because we are charting only one variable, we want to choose **Simple**, which is probably already highlighted, but you can click on it once again just to be sure. Now click on the **Define** button and the Define Simple Line: dialog box will open:

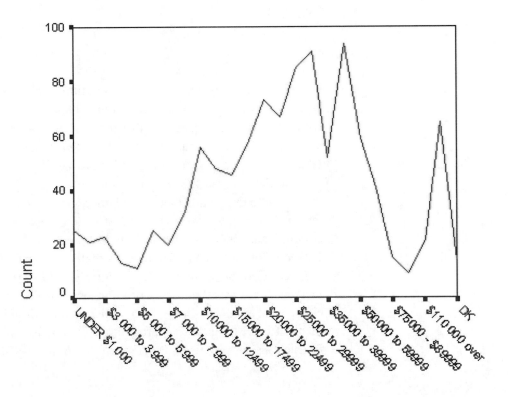

On the left side of the box you can see the list of variables. Scroll down the list until you find **RINCOM98** and highlight it. Now click on the **arrow** next to the Category Axis: box to transfer the variable name. This time choose **N of cases** as opposed to % of cases (it may already be selected) and then click on the **Options...** button to make sure that there is *not* a check mark next to the Display groups defined by missing values. After you have done that, click **Continue** and you will be back in the Define Simple Line: box. As in the Define Simple Bar: dialog box, the Titles... option can be used to add titles and footnotes to the chart. You can explore that option now or just click on **OK** if you are ready to produce your line chart. Once you do that, you should see the following line chart displayed in your Viewer:

Take some time to review your line chart. You can see how respondents' reported annual income ranged from those who received under $1,000 to those who received more than $110,000 in 1998. You may want to take note of the shape of the distribution and whether the sample is concentrated in a specific area or fairly evenly spread out.

SPSS COMMAND 7.2:   Producing a Simple Line Chart

> Click **Graphs** → **Line...** → **Simple** → **Define**
> Highlight the **variable name** → Click **arrow** pointing to the "Category Axis:" box →
> Click **Options...** → Make sure there is **no check mark next to the Display groups defined by missing values option** → Click **Continue** → **OK**

Once again, you can use the Chart Editor to change the appearance of your line graph.

Some Guidelines for Choosing a Chart or Graph

Table 7.1 summarizes the information just discussed regarding how to choose a chart depending on the type of variable you are working with. A check mark indicates that the chart is generally considered appropriate for the type of item indicated.

Table 7.1   Choosing a Bar or Line Chart

	Type of Variable	
	Discrete/Categorical	Continuous
Bar Chart	√	
Line Chart		√

Table 7.2 goes even further in describing the charts and graphs that are generally considered appropriate for variables at a particular level of measurement. A check mark indicates that the chart is generally considered appropriate for variables at a particular level of measurement. Before you review the table, however, a few words of caution are in order. Whereas Table 7.1 focused only on the two charts we reviewed in this chapter, Table 7.2 goes a step further in including charts that we did not review in this chapter. You will recall that in this chapter we reviewed instructions for creating only the two most common and easily constructed charts: bar and line charts. However, in Table 7.2 we mention two additional charts that you may find useful as you become more comfortable using SPSS: *pie charts* and *histograms.* This information is included only as a bonus of sorts for those of you who may find it helpful either now or in the future. And while we are not going to review the commands for creating these charts, please remember that you can easily access instructions for producing these charts by consulting SPSS's Help feature.

Table 7.2   Some Basic Graphic Presentations by Level of Measurement

	Level of Measurement		
	Nominal	**Ordinal**	**I/R**
Pie Charts	√		
Bar Charts*	√		
Histograms			√
Line Chart*			√

*The graphic presentations that are "starred" (*) and in bold/italics are the ones we reviewed in this chapter (bar and line charts).

Demonstration 7.5: Saving and Printing Your Charts

If you are interested in saving or printing any of your charts, keep in mind the fact that you can do so easily in the Viewer by selecting either **File** → **Save As** or by clicking **File** → **Print**.

SPSS COMMAND 7.3:   Saving a Chart/Graph (Bar, Line, etc…)

> Click **File** → **Save As…**

SPSS COMMAND 7.4:   Printing a Chart/Graph (Bar, Line, etc…)

> Click **File** → **Print**

Before ending your session, be sure to **Save** the new recoded variables POLREC and PARTY so we can use them in our analysis later on. If necessary, refer back to the commands for saving data discussed in Chapter 6. If you are using the Student Version of SPSS, please keep in mind the 50-variable limit and refer to the discussion in Chapter 6 regarding saving your work.

Conclusion

Politics is a favorite topic for many Americans, and it is a realm often marked by the expression of unsubstantiated opinions. Now you are able to begin examining the facts of political views. In later chapters, we'll move beyond describing political orientations and start explaining why people have the political views they have.

Main Points

- In this chapter we focused on two key political items: POLVIEWS and PARTYID.

- POLVIEWS taps into basic political philosophy, whereas PARTYID measures political party affiliation.

- We recoded both items to insure that they are in a form we can use easily in future analysis.

- We named the new recoded variables POLREC and PARTY.

- A graph or chart can sometimes communicate the relative sizes of different groups or the shape of the distribution of a variable more powerfully than can a table of numbers.

- You can use SPSS to produce two of the most common and useful types of charts: simple bar and line charts.

- Bar charts are the graphic equivalent of frequency tables.

- Bar charts are most often used with discrete or categorical variables.

- Line charts are most often used with continuous variables that have numerous categories or values.

Key Terms

Bar chart   Line chart
Horizontal ("x") axis   Pie chart
Vertical ("y") axis   Histogram

SPSS Commands Introduced in This Chapter

7.1:   Producing a Simple Bar Chart

Click **Graphs** → **Bar...** → **Simple** → **Define** →

Highlight the **variable name** → Click **arrow** pointing to the "Category Axis:" box →

Click on an option in the "Bars Represent" box →

Click **Options...** → Make sure there is **no check mark next to the "Display groups defined by missing values"** option → **Continue** → **OK**

7.2:   Producing a Simple Line Chart

Click **Graphs** → **Line...** → **Simple** → **Define**

Highlight the **variable name** → Click **arrow** pointing to the "Category Axis:" box →

Click **Options...** → Make sure there is **no check mark next to the "Display groups defined by missing values"** option → Click **Continue** → **OK**

7.3   Saving a Chart/Graph (Bar, Line, etc...)

> Click **File** → **Save As...**

7.4:   Printing a Chart/Graph (Bar, Line, etc...)

> Click **File** → **Print**

Review Questions

1. What does the variable POLVIEWS measure?

2. What does the variable PARTYID measure?

3. Name one reason we chose to recode POLVIEWS and PARTYID.

4. Does PARTY (recoded PARTYID) show that most respondents are Liberal, Moderate, or Conservative?

5. If you wanted to produce a chart of a discrete/categorical variable, would you generally want to create a bar or a line chart?

6. Bar charts are equivalent to what type of table?

7. If you wanted to produce a chart of a variable with many categories or values, would a bar or a line chart be a better option?

8. Why are graphic presentations of data useful?

9. Name one reason why you might make a bar chart for the variable POLREC (recoded POLVIEWS), as opposed to a line chart.

10. Name two measures of political attitudes contained on either DEMO.SAV or EXER.SAV.

11. Why is it sometimes useful to reduce the number of categories in a variable?

12. List the types of chart(s)/graph(s) that are generally recommended for variables at the following levels of measurement: nominal, ordinal, and I/R.

NAME _____

CLASS _____

INSTRUCTOR _____

DATE _____

To complete the following exercises, you need to load the data file EXER.SAV. You can find answers to Questions 1–4 in Appendix A. The file contains four items that deal with the mass media: NEWS (how often respondents read the newspaper); TVHOURS (how often respondents watch television); CONPRESS (confidence in press); CONTV (confidence in television). Questions 1–4 below are based on these items. Produce the appropriate graph (either simple bar or simple line chart) for each variable. When creating your graphs, choose percentages (% of cases) *as opposed to* Frequencies *in the* Bars/Line Represent(s) *box.*

Questions 1 and 2: Use the charts for NEWS and TVHOURS to complete the following sentences. Bear in mind that in some instances, more than one value may be appropriate for the lowest or highest points.

1. (NEWS)

   A. Appropriate chart type _____
      [bar/line]

   B. About _____% of respondents read the newspaper every day,
      whereas approximately _____% said they never read the newspaper.

2. (TVHOURS)

   A. Appropriate chart type _____
      [bar/line]

   B. Most respondents reported watching about _____ hours of television each
      day. The lowest point(s) on the chart, indicating the least common number of
      hours of television watching by respondents, was _____. The number
      of hours respondents spend watching television every day drops off consider-
      ably after approximately _____ hours.

Questions 3 and 4: After you have produced and analyzed the charts for CONPRESS and CONTV, briefly describe the distribution of each in the space provided below. You may want to note the largest and smallest categories for the items as well as any other interesting or pertinent information.

3. (CONPRESS)

    A. Appropriate chart type _____

                                  [bar/line]

    B. Description of chart:

4. (CONTV)

    A. Appropriate chart type _____

                                    [bar/line]

    B. Description of chart:

5. (RINCOM98) Create a new variable, RECRIN98, by recoding RINCOM98 and then assigning new labels to the values of RECRIN98. Keep in mind our discussions in Chapters 6 and 7 regarding how to combine categories (particularly the theoretical and empirical considerations discussed in Chapter 6).

    A. List how you are planning to recode RINCOM98 (i.e., which categories you are going to combine).

    B. Assign new labels to the values of RECRIN98.

After you have run your recoding, produce a chart of RECRIN98 and describe it briefly in the space below.

    C. Appropriate chart type _____

                                    [bar/line]

    D. Description of chart:

Chapter 8 Crosstabulating Abortion Responses: Moving from Univariate to Bivariate Analysis

Now that you have used *univariate analysis* to examine responses to a single item, we are ready to introduce you to *bivariate analysis*. While we will reserve the bulk of our discussion of bivariate analysis for Part IV, you can think of this as a preview of sorts. As the name suggests, bivariate analysis allows us to examine the relationship between two variables. Although there are several types of bivariate analysis, in this chapter we will explore just one, *crosstabulations*, or shortened to *crosstabs* by most social researchers. Some texts and statistical packages refer to crosstabulations as *bivariate distributions*, *contingency tables*, or *two-way frequency distributions*, but SPSS just refers to them as crosstabs.

When we examined the topic of abortion in Chapter 2, we discussed the different degrees of approval represented by the several questions and made some educated guesses as to which ones would receive the most (and least) support. Now that we have gained some proficiency in the use of SPSS to analyze data, we are going to check on how well we did in our predictions.

We will extend our analysis of this controversial issue using SPSS's crosstabs procedure. Crosstabs will allow us to gain a more in-depth understanding of the structure of abortion attitudes by cross-classifying respondents in terms of their answers to more than one question. This procedure is also the first step on the road toward one of the most exciting aspects of social scientific research—answering questions empirically and testing hypotheses. But before we begin running Crosstabs, we must familiarize ourselves with the variables we intend to include in our analysis.

Demonstration 8.1: Identifying the Seven Abortion Variables

To start the process, we will instruct SPSS to produce frequency tables for the abortion variables contained in the file DEMO.SAV. If you do not recall the names of the seven variables that measure abortion in this data set, there are several ways you can use SPSS to find this information.

One option is to click **Utilities** on the right-hand side of the menubar and then select **Variables...** from the drop-down menu. Once you do this, the

Variables box will open and you can scroll or click through the list of variables on the left side to identify the seven abortion items.

A second option is to select **Utilities** and then click on **File Info**. In a moment, information about the variables on your DEMO.SAV file should appear in the Output Navigator, as shown below:

```
Name                                                                    Position

ID        RESPONDENT ID NUMBER                                              1
          Measurement Level: Scale
          Column Width: Unknown  Alignment: Right
          Print Format: F4
          Write Format: F4

ABANY     ABORTION IF WOMAN WANTS FOR ANY REASON                            2
          Measurement Level: Nominal
          Column Width: Unknown  Alignment: Right
          Print Format: F1
          Write Format: F1
          Missing Values: 0, 9

          Value    Label

            0 M   NAP
            1     YES
            2     NO
            8     DK
            9 M   NA

ABDEFECT  STRONG CHANCE OF SERIOUS DEFECT                                   3
          Measurement Level: Nominal
          Column Width: Unknown  Alignment: Right
          Print Format: F1
          Write Format: F1
          Missing Values: 0, 9

          Value    Label

            0 M   NAP
            1     YES
            2     NO
```

Just **double click** in the Viewer window and you should be able to move through the viewer and access information for all the variables by using the **Page Up** and **Page Down** keys or the **arrow keys** on your keyboard.

SPSS COMMAND 8.1:   Identifying Variables

Option 1:

Click **Utilities → Variables...**

Option 2:

Click **Utilities → File Info...**

Demonstration 8.2: Running Frequencies for Several Variables at Once

Once you have identified the names of the seven abortion variables, you can easily instruct SPSS to run **Frequencies** for all the items at once. If the variables are clustered together (as the abortion items in our DEMO.SAV file are), you can simply *scroll* down the list of variables until all the *names are highlighted* and then click the right-pointing **arrow** to transfer them to the Variable(s): field.

If the variables are not clustered together, you can transfer them all at once by holding down the *shift* key on your keyboard as you click on the **name of the item**. After all the items have been highlighted, click on the right-pointing **arrow** to transfer them to the Variable(s): field.

You may want to experiment with both of these options. Ultimately, however, you want to transfer all seven abortion items to the Variable(s): field as shown below.

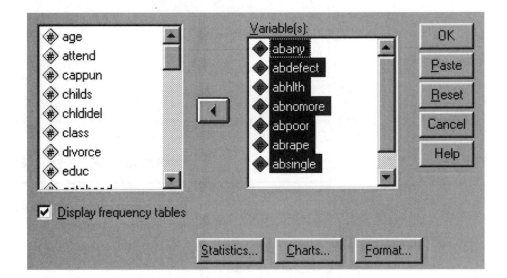

SPSS COMMAND 8.2:   Running Frequencies for Several Variables at Once

Option 1:

If the variables are clustered together

Click **Analyze → Descriptive Statistics → Frequencies... →**
Scroll down list of variable names until all appropriate **items are highlighted →**
Click on the **arrow** pointing toward the "Variable(s):" field → **OK**

Option 2:

If the variables are not clustered together

Click **Analyze → Descriptive Statistics → Frequencies... →**
Hold down the **Shift key** on your keyboard as you **click on the names of the variables →**
Click on the **arrow** pointing toward the "Variable(s):" field → **OK**

Once you have given SPSS the command that will result in the frequency distributions for the various abortion items, you should get the following results in your Output window. The tables, as shown below, indicate the different levels of support for abortion under various circumstances.

ABDEFECT STRONG CHANCE OF SERIOUS DEFECT

		Frequency	Percent	Valid Percent	Cumulative Percent
Valid	1 YES	740	49.3	75.5	75.5
	2 NO	190	12.7	19.4	94.9
	8 DK	50	3.3	5.1	100.0
	Total	980	65.3	100.0	
Missing	0 NAP	519	34.6		
	9 NA	1	.1		
	Total	520	34.7		
Total		1500	100.0		

ABHLTH WOMANS HEALTH SERIOUSLY ENDANGERED

		Frequency	Percent	Valid Percent	Cumulative Percent
Valid	1 YES	833	55.5	85.1	85.1
	2 NO	108	7.2	11.0	96.1
	8 DK	38	2.5	3.9	100.0
	Total	979	65.3	100.0	
Missing	0 NAP	519	34.6		
	9 NA	2	.1		
	Total	521	34.7		
Total		1500	100.0		

ABRAPE PREGNANT AS RESULT OF RAPE

		Frequency	Percent	Valid Percent	Cumulative Percent
Valid	1 YES	745	49.7	76.1	76.1
	2 NO	196	13.1	20.0	96.1
	8 DK	38	2.5	3.9	100.0
	Total	979	65.3	100.0	
Missing	0 NAP	519	34.6		
	9 NA	2	.1		
	Total	521	34.7		
Total		1500	100.0		

Items with the Highest Levels of Support

Although we don't have any basis for comparison yet, it would seem at first glance that very high percentages of the general public support a woman's right to an abortion in cases of the danger of birth defects (76 percent), threats to the woman's health (85 percent), and rape (76 percent). Now, let's see how these compare with other reasons.

Items with Less Support

Let's look at the three items we identified as probably enjoying less support. Here's what you should get in return.

ABNOMORE MARRIED--WANTS NO MORE CHILDREN

		Frequency	Percent	Valid Percent	Cumulative Percent
Valid	1 YES	382	25.5	39.1	39.1
	2 NO	543	36.2	55.6	94.7
	8 DK	52	3.5	5.3	100.0
	Total	977	65.1	100.0	
Missing	0 NAP	519	34.6		
	9 NA	4	.3		
	Total	523	34.9		
Total		1500	100.0		

ABPOOR LOW INCOME--CANT AFFORD MORE CHILDREN

		Frequency	Percent	Valid Percent	Cumulative Percent
Valid	1 YES	409	27.3	41.8	41.8
	2 NO	521	34.7	53.2	95.0
	8 DK	49	3.3	5.0	100.0
	Total	979	65.3	100.0	
Missing	0 NAP	519	34.6		
	9 NA	2	.1		
	Total	521	34.7		
Total		1500	100.0		

ABSINGLE NOT MARRIED

		Frequency	Percent	Valid Percent	Cumulativ e Percent
Valid	1 YES	388	25.9	39.7	39.7
	2 NO	540	36.0	55.3	95.0
	8 DK	49	3.3	5.0	100.0
	Total	977	65.1	100.0	
Missing	0 NAP	519	34.6		
	9 NA	4	.3		
	Total	523	34.9		
Total		1500	100.0		

The assumption that these reasons would garner less support proves accurate. It is also interesting that virtually the same proportions of respondents— 39 percent to 42 percent—support this second set of reasons.

Unconditional Support for Abortion

Finally, let's see what proportion of the population would support a woman having unrestricted freedom to choose an abortion for any reason.

ABANY ABORTION IF WOMAN WANTS FOR ANY REASON

		Frequency	Percent	Valid Percent	Cumulativ e Percent
Valid	1 YES	365	24.3	37.4	37.4
	2 NO	563	37.5	57.6	95.0
	8 DK	49	3.3	5.0	100.0
	Total	977	65.1	100.0	
Missing	0 NAP	519	34.6		
	9 NA	4	.3		
	Total	523	34.9		
Total		1500	100.0		

Notice that about the same proportion (37 percent) supports a woman's unrestricted freedom to choose abortion as supported by the specific situations described in ABNOMORE, ABPOOR, and ABSINGLE.

Support for Abortion—An Overview

Let's construct a table that summarizes those tables we've just examined. It is often useful to bring related tables such as these together in an abbreviated format.

Percentage Who Support a Woman's Right to Choose Abortion Because:

the woman's health would be seriously endangered	85
the pregnancy resulted from rape	76
there is a strong chance of a serious defect	76
a family is too poor to afford more children	42
the woman is unmarried	40
a family wants no more children	39
the woman wants it, for any reason	37

The tables we've just examined suggest that attitudes toward abortion fall into three basic groups. There is a small minority of no more than 15 percent who are opposed to abortion under any circumstances. We conclude this because 85 percent would support abortion if the woman's life were seriously endangered.

Another group, just under 40 percent of the population, would support a woman's free choice of abortion for any reason. The remainder of the population would support abortion in only a few circumstances involving medical danger and/or rape.

Demonstration 8.3 Producing Crosstabs[1]

Now that we have had a chance to produce and analyze frequency tables for the seven abortion items in your subsample, we want to add a little more sophistication to the process. In this section we are going to continue our focus on abortion attitudes by showing you how to use the *crosstabs procedure* to examine the structure of attitudes toward this issue in more depth.

The crosstabs procedure is used to create a *crosstabulation*, a matrix that shows the distribution of one variable for each category of a second variable. While we begin in this chapter by focusing on how you can use this procedure to learn more about the structure of abortion attitudes, in Part IV we will broaden this discussion to focus on how you can use this procedure to answer questions empirically and to test hypotheses. For example, we can use crosstab tables to begin to address questions such as whether liberals are more likely to support abortion than conservatives; whether those who attend church regularly are less likely to support abortion than those who do not attend church regularly; or whether women are more likely to support abortion under any circumstances than men. For now, however, we will concentrate on using this procedure to examine the structure of abortion attitudes in-depth.

---

1. The discussion concerning how to set missing values in Define Variable comes in the beginning of the next chapter (Chapter 9, Demonstration 9.1 "Defining Missing Values"). We make note of that here only because some instructors may find it useful to introduce that discussion at this point.

To begin, let's try a simple example. The command pathway to this technique is

Analyze → Descriptive Statistics → Crosstabs...

Work your way through these menu selections and you should reach a window that looks like the following:

Because the logic of a crosstab will be clearer when we have an example to look at, just follow these steps on faith and we'll justify your faith in a moment.

Let's analyze the relationship between the answers people gave to the question about whether a woman should be able to have an abortion if her health was seriously endangered (ABHLTH) and if she was too poor to have more children (ABPOOR).

In the Crosstabs window, click **ABHLTH** and then click the **arrow** pointing toward the Row(s): field. Next, click on **ABPOOR** and transfer it to the Column(s): field, producing the result shown below.

You will notice that there are several other options available in the Crosstabs dialog box. We are going to explore these more later on. For now, once your window looks like the one above, you can click **OK**. After a few seconds, you'll be rewarded with the following data in your Output window.

ABHLTH WOMANS HEALTH SERIOUSLY ENDANGERED * ABPOOR LOW INCOME--CANT AFFORD MORE CHILDREN Crosstabulation

Count

		ABPOOR LOW INCOME--CANT AFFORD MORE CHILDREN			
		1 YES	2 NO	8 DK	Total
ABHLTH WOMANS HEALTH SERIOUSLY ENDANGERED	1 YES	408	389	35	832
	2 NO		107	1	108
	8 DK	1	24	13	38
Total		409	520	49	978

SPSS COMMAND 8.3   Producing Crosstabs[2]

> Click **Analyze** → **Descriptive Statistics** → **Crosstabs...** →
>
> Highlight the **name of the variable** → Click on **arrow** pointing to the **Row(s):** box →
>
> Highlight the **name of the variable** → Click on **arrow** pointing to the **Column(s):** box →
>
> Click **OK**

Notice that the crosstabs table demonstrates the logic of the command we asked you to make. By specifying ABPOOR as the Column variable, we have caused it to appear across the top of the table with its attributes of "Yes" and "No" representing the two columns of figures.

ABHLTH, the Row variable, appears to the left of the table, and its attributes constitute the rows of the table.

More important, this table illustrates a logic that operates within the system of attitudes that people hold about abortion. First, we notice that 408 people say they would support a woman's right to choose abortion if her health were seriously endangered or if she were poor and felt she couldn't afford more children. At the opposite corner of the table, we find 107 people who would oppose abortion in both cases.

Another 389 respondents said they would support the right to choose if the woman's health were seriously endangered, but not on the basis of poverty. Notice that no respondents said they would support abortion on the basis of poverty but deny it on the basis of health. There are probably two elements involved in this pattern. On the one hand, threats to the woman's life are probably seen as more serious than the suffering presented by another mouth to feed in a poor family. At the same time, few, if any, would hold a woman responsible for having a pregnancy that seriously threatened her health. Some people, however, do blame the poor for their poverty and would probably say that the woman in question should have avoided getting pregnant if she knew that it would be hard for her to feed another child. As a consequence, then, 389 of the respondents oppose abortion under some circumstances but are willing to make an exception in the case of a woman's health being threatened.

There is additional information in the SPSS table that will become more useful to us in later analyses. The rightmost column in the table, for example, tells us that a total of 797 (832 – 35) of those with an opinion said that they would approve an abortion for a woman whose health was seriously endangered, and 107 (108 – 1) said they would not. The bottom row of numbers in the table gives us the breakdown regarding the other variable.

---

2. While the dependent variable normally goes in the Row(s): box and the independent variable goes in the Column(s): box, we have not introduced this or other useful options available in the Crosstabs dialog box yet because we will not be focusing on hypotheses testing until Part IV.

Let's try another example of the same phenomenon. The threat of a birth defect was considered a more compelling reason for abortion by the respondent than was the fact that the woman was not married. Why don't you run that table now? Use **Analyze → Descriptive Statistics → Crosstabs...** to get to the Crosstabs window. If ABHLTH and ABPOOR are still specified as the Row(s): and Column(s): variables, simply click **Reset** or **highlight** them and transfer them to the list of variables on the left-hand side of the dialog box using the **left-pointing arrows**. Now specify **ABDEFECT** as the **row** variable and **ABSINLGE** as the **column** variable.

Click **OK** and here's what the output should look like.

ABDEFECT STRONG CHANCE OF SERIOUS DEFECT * ABSINGLE NOT MARRIED Crosstabulation

Count

		ABSINGLE NOT MARRIED			Total
		1 YES	2 NO	8 DK	
ABDEFECT STRONG CHANCE OF SERIOUS DEFECT	1 YES	382	320	35	737
	2 NO	3	186	1	190
	8 DK	3	34	13	50
Total		388	540	49	977

This table presents a strikingly similar picture. We see that 382 support the woman's right to choose in both situations, and 186 oppose abortion in both instances. Of those who would approve abortion in only one of the two situations, almost all of them (320) make the exception for the threat of birth defects. Only 3 respondents would allow abortion for a single woman but deny it in the case of birth defects. What are we to make of the 3 people who responded in this way? One possibility is that these respondents misunderstood one or both of the questions, or perhaps they have some complex point of view that demands such answers. Either way, they are few enough in number that they will not seriously affect the analysis of this topic.

We could continue examining tables like these, but the forthcoming conclusion remains the same: There are three major positions regarding abortion. One position approves it unconditionally on the basis of the woman's choice; another position opposes it under all circumstances; and the third position approves abortion only in certain circumstances—those involving medical complications or rape.

While we have used the crosstabs procedure to examine the structure of abortion attitudes in more depth, keep in mind that we could also (and will) use this procedure beginning in Part IV to test hypotheses. For instance, we will move beyond crosstabulating two attitudes and begin exploring questions such as whether women are more supportive of abortion than men by crosstabulating one of our measures of attitudes toward abortion with SEX. Before we do that, however, we want to conclude our discussion in this section by learning how to combine two or more indicators of a concept to create a composite index (Chapter 9). Then in Chapter 10 we will offer suggestions for further univariate analyses before we refocus our attention on how the crosstabs procedure can be used to examine the relationship between two variables and test hypotheses.

Conclusion

In this initial analysis of abortion attitudes, we have had an opportunity to explore the structure of attitudes on this controversial topic. Although abortion is generally discussed as an all-or-nothing proposition, we've seen that relatively few Americans reject abortion completely. A sizable minority appear to have reservations about abortion but are willing to make exceptions in certain circumstances.

We are going to explore this structuring of attitudes further in Chapter 9, where you will learn how to create a new variable in the data set—one that captures the variations of attitudes about abortion.

Main Points

- In this chapter we moved from univariate to bivariate analysis to introduce you to an important procedure, crosstabs.
- The file DEMO.SAV contains seven abortion items.
- In this chapter we reviewed two ways you can use SPSS to identify the abbreviated variable names of each of these items.
- You can produce frequency tables for all these items at once by following the commands listed in SPSS Command 8.1.
- The frequency tables for the abortion variables show that attitudes toward abortion fall into three main categories.
- A minority of respondents (15 percent) would not support abortion under any circumstances.
- Just under 40 percent of respondents would support a woman's right to choose under any circumstances, whereas the remainder of the population would support abortion only in the case of a medical emergency or rape.
- The crosstabs procedure is used to create crosstabulations.
- Crosstabulations allow you to cross-classify respondents in terms of their answers to more than one question.
- While we used this procedure primarily to examine the structure of abortion attitudes in more depth, beginning in Part IV we are going to begin to use this procedure to test hypotheses when we focus on bivariate analyses in more depth.

Key Terms

Univariate analysis
Bivariate analysis
Crosstabulations
Crosstabs

Bivariate distributions
Contingency tables
Two-way frequency distributions

SPSS Commands Introduced in This Chapter

8.1:   Identifying Variables

> **Option 1:**
>
> Click **Utilities** → **Variables...**
>
> **Option 2:**
>
> Click **Utilities** → **File Info...**

8.2:   Running Frequencies for Several Variables at Once

> **Option 1:**
>
> If the variables are clustered together
> Click **Analyze** → **Descriptive Statistics** → **Frequencies...** →
> **Scroll** down list of variable names until all appropriate items are **highlighted** →
> Click on the **arrow** pointing toward the "Variable(s):" field → **OK**
>
> **Option 2**
>
> If the variables are not clustered together
> Click **Analyze** → **Descriptive Statistics** → **Frequencies...** →
> Hold down the **Shift key** on your keyboard as you **click on the names of the variables** →
> Click on the **arrow** pointing toward the "Variable(s):" field → **OK**

8.3:   Producing Crosstabs

> Click **Analyze** → **Descriptive Statistics** → **Crosstabs...** →
> Highlight the **name of the variable** → Click on **arrow** pointing to the **Row(s):** box →
> Highlight the **name of the variable** → Click on **arrow** pointing to the **Column(s):** box →
> Click **OK**

Review Questions

1. If you wanted to identify the names of the abortion items in your DEMO.SAV file, would you use the Utilities → File... command or the Analyze → Descriptive Statistics... command?

2. List the abbreviated variable names for three of the abortion items in your DEMO.SAV file.

3. Which of the seven abortion variables is most likely to garner support from respondents?

4. Which of the seven abortion variables is least likely to garner support from respondents?

5. What is a crosstabulation?

6. A researcher produced a crosstabulation analyzing the relationship between the answers people gave to the question about whether a woman should be able to have an abortion if her pregnancy was the result of rape (ABRAPE) and if she was married but did not want any more children (ABNOMORE). Based on what you know about the structure of abortion attitudes, estimate generally what you think the table would display in terms of levels of support for abortion in both cases? How about levels of support for abortion in the case of rape but not in the case of a married woman who does not want more children?

7. Thinking back to the crosstabulation discussed in Question 6, approximately how many respondents would you estimate are likely to support abortion in the case of a married woman who wants no more children but not in the case of a pregnancy that resulted from rape? Do you think the number would be closer to 5, 50, or 500?

8. If respondents answered that they support abortion in the case of a married woman who wants no more children, but not in the case of a pregnancy that resulted from rape, how might you explain these answers?

9. Thinking back again to the crosstabulation discussed in Question 6, what would the column of numbers on the far right of the table indicate?

10. What would the row of numbers on the bottom of the table indicate?

11. Now go ahead and generate a crosstab between ABRAPE and ABNOMORE to check your answers to the previous series of Questions (6–10).

12. Construct a hypothesis regarding abortion attitudes that a crosstabulation might be used to test. Be sure it includes both an independent and a dependent variable (as discussed in Chapter 2).

NAME _____

CLASS _____

INSTRUCTOR _____

DATE _____

To complete the following exercises, you need to load the data file EXER.SAV. You will find answers to Questions 1–14 in Appendix A.

1. List the abbreviated variable names and a short description of the five items in your EXER.SAV data set that measure whether or not respondents would approve of a police officer striking a citizen and, if so, under what circumstances.

   Abbreviated Variable Name   Description

   A. _____   _____

   B. _____   _____

   C. _____   _____

   D. _____   _____

   E. _____   _____

   Run Frequencies *for all five variables listed above at once and then use the results to answer the following questions.*

2. (POLHITOK) _____% [Valid %] of those who answered said they can imagine a situation in which they would approve of a police officer striking a citizen.

3. (POLHITOK) _____% [Valid %] of those who answered reported they would not approve of a police officer striking a citizen under any circumstances.

4. Excluding POLHITOK, which two items enjoy the most support (i.e., under what circumstances would the majority of respondents approve of a police officer striking a citizen)? List the variable name and the percentage of those who responded "Yes" for both variables.

   Variable Name   % Answered "Yes" [Valid %]

   A. _____   _____

   B. _____   _____

5. Excluding POLHITOK, which two items enjoy the least support?

       Variable Name   % Answered "Yes" [Valid %]

    A. _____   _____

    B. _____   _____

6. In the space provided below, construct a table that summarizes four of the frequency tables we just examined (POLABUSE, POLATTAK, POLESCAP, POLMURDR). Your new table should be titled:

"Percentage Who Support a Police Officer Striking a Citizen when..."

[conditions under which support   [% of respondents
police officer striking citizen]   who support]

    A.

    B.

    C.

    D.

7. Describe the table you just created in a few sentences.

Run Crosstabs *to analyze the relationship between the answers people gave to the question about whether they would support a police officer striking a citizen if the citizen attacked the officer with his fists (POLATTAK—row variable) and if the citizen said vulgar and obscene things (POLABUSE—column variable). Then use your table to answer the questions below (Questions 8–13).*

8. _____ respondents said they would support a police officer striking a citizen in both cases.

9. _____ respondents said they would support a police officer striking a citizen if the citizen attacked the officer with his fists, but not if the citizen said vulgar and obscene things.

10. _____ respondents said they would not support a police officer striking a citizen in either situation.

NAME _____

CLASS _____

INSTRUCTOR _____

DATE _____

11. Only _____ respondent(s) said he/she/they would support an officer striking a citizen if the citizen said vulgar and obscene things, but not if the citizen attacked the officer with his fists.

12. _____ of those with an opinion said they would approve of a police officer striking a citizen if the citizen attacked the officer with his fists, whereas _____ said they would not.

13. _____ of those with an opinion said they would approve of a police officer striking a citizen if the citizen said vulgar and obscene things, whereas _____ said they would not.

14. There was more support for a police officer striking a citizen if the citizen was trying to escape custody than if the citizen was being questioned as a murder suspect. Run Crosstabs for POLESCAP (row variable) and POLMURDR (column variable) and then summarize your findings in a few paragraphs in the space provided below.

15. Construct a hypothesis involving either the variables RACE or CLASS and the variable POLHITOK. Make sure your hypothesis includes one independent variable (RACE or CLASS) and one dependent variable (POLHITOK) as discussed in Chapter 2. Write your hypotheses in the space on the back of this sheet.

Chapter 9   Creating Composite Measures: Exploring Attitudes Toward Abortion in More Depth

Now that you've had a chance to become familiar with univariate analysis, we're going to add a little more sophistication to the process.

You will recall that in the last chapter we used seven separate items to examine the complexity of attitudes toward abortion. By running Crosstabs we were able to distinguish between three major positions on this issue: unconditional approval, conditional approval, and unconditional disapproval. We were also able to see that many respondents make fine distinctions between those situations in which they would and would not support abortion.

While the separate abortion items were helpful in this regard, they also made it difficult for us to get a clear picture of how Americans feel about abortion overall. Consequently, to explore attitudes toward abortion further, it may be useful for us to have a single variable, a *composite measure*, which captures the complexities of attitudes towards abortion overall—in other words, a single variable that takes into account the complexity of attitudes by capturing the three major positions on this issue.

Now that we have raised the issue, you will probably not be surprised to learn that SPSS allows us to create such a variable or composite measure made up of multiple indicators of a single concept. By employing the *Compute* command we can use the scores on two or more existing items to compute a new variable that summarizes attitudes toward a complicated issue or ambiguous concept such as abortion, sexual permissiveness, religiosity, prejudice, and so on.

The Compute command allows us to create composite measures of varying degrees of complexity. This chapter focuses on how you can use this command to compute two indices. We will begin with a fairly simple index based on two abortion items. Then we will construct a somewhat more complicated measure employing *Count*.

Demonstration 9.1: Defining Missing Values

Before we begin, we should make one small change to our data file which will be useful when we validate our new indices. Load **SPSS** and open **DEMO.SAV**. Once you are in the Data Editor, click on **ABANY** to highlight the column. Now choose **Data** from the menubar and **Define Variable...** from the drop-down menu. Once you are looking at the Define Variable box, choose **Missing Values...** to open the Define Missing Values box.

You will see that SPSS gives us several options for defining missing values: No missing values, Discrete missing values, Range of missing values, and Range plus one discrete missing value. For now, we want to select **Discrete missing values**. You can go ahead and click on the **circle next to this option** if it is not selected already. In the rectangles below you may already see the numeric values (codes) "0" (NAP) and "9" (NA). This tells us that those codes have already been defined as Missing values.[1]

We want to designate "8" (DK) as a missing value as well. To do that, we simply type **8** in the space provided under Discrete Missing Values. Once you have done that you can click **Continue** and **OK** and SPSS will make the necessary changes.

By doing this we have simply told SPSS that for the variable ABANY, "8" should be treated as a missing value. This small change will be useful when we validate our indices later in this chapter by running Crosstabs with column percentages.

If you are analyzing ABANY in the future and decide that you want to include DK (or any other value designated as missing) in your analysis, all you have to do is open the **Define Variable...** dialog box, select **Missing Values...**, and make the appropriate changes.

Now that you are comfortable with the procedure for defining missing values, why don't you go ahead and designate "8" (DK) as a missing value for the

---

1. If you did not recall the labels pertaining to each code, don't worry. You can find this information easily by selecting **Labels...** in the Define Variables box. You will then see the numeric values and labels for ABANY displayed.

six other abortion variables: ABDEFECT, ABHLTH, ABNOMORE, ABPOOR, ABRAPE, and ABSINGLE.

SPSS COMMAND 9.1:   Defining Missing Values

> Click on **Variable name** in Data Editor to highlight the column →
> Click **Data** → **Define Variable...** → **Missing Values...** →
> Select one of the four available options...
> Click **Continue** → **OK**

Keep in mind that as you continue to work through the demonstrations and exercises in the rest of the text, you will want to remember to define "Don't knows" as missing for all your variables before computing percentages.

Demonstration 9.2: Index 1—ABORT

Index—A Form of Composite Measure

An *index* is a form of composite measure, composed of more than one indicator of the variable under study. The score on a multiple-choice quiz is an example of a very simple index. Each question is an "item" that indicates some of the student's knowledge of the subject matter. Together, all the items form an index of the student's knowledge. Just as we would not think a single-question quiz would give us a very accurate assessment of a student's knowledge, so it is also when we measure attitudes. We do a better job measuring respondent's attitudes with multiple items.

In addition, there are two other advantages to using an index. First, they include multiple dimensions of the subject under study. In this case, an index composed of ABDEFECT and ABSINGLE will combine two aspects of the debate over abortion rather than being limited to only one (e.g., the impact of birth defects).

Second, composite measures tap into a greater range of variation between the extremes of a variable. If we were to simply use one of the abortion items, we would distinguish two groups of respondents: the pros and the antis. Combining two items will allow us to distinguish three groups. A later example will extend this range of variation even further.

ABORT Index

As we noted, the Compute command allows us to create a new summary variable based on information from existing items. The new variable can then be saved in your data set and used like any other variable.[2]

---

2. If you follow the demonstrations and exercises in this chapter, you will be asked to compute a number of new variables. Consequently, anyone using the Student Version of SPSS should be sensitive to the fact that it is limited to 50 variables. You may also want to review the discussion in Chapter 6 regarding saving changes to your data set.

There are many ways to use the Compute command to create new measures of varying degrees of complexity and sophistication. In this section we are going to compute a fairly simple index that we'll call ABORT (for anti-ABORTion index).[3]

Our index will be based on the two variables mentioned above: ABDEFECT and ABSINGLE. As you probably recall, ABDEFECT measures respondents' support for abortion if there is a chance of serious defect in the baby, whereas ABSINGLE measures respondents' support for abortion if the woman is not married and does not want to marry the man. You may want to look back at the list of variables in Chapter 4 to find the exact wording of each question. If you do that, you will notice that both items are coded as follows:

Value/ Code		Value Label
0	—	NAP [Missing Value]
1	—	Yes
2	—	No
8	—	DK [Missing Value]
9	—	NA [Missing Value]

We are going to treat ABDEFECT and ABSINGLE as if they were items on a quiz designed to find out how much our respondents disapproved of abortion. On this quiz, for each "right" answer, "No," respondents will be given 1 point. Consequently, a respondent who answered "No" to both questions would get 2 points. Someone answering "No" to only one question and "Yes" to the other would get 1 point, and a respondent answering "Yes" to both would get a score of 0. On this quiz then, the higher the score, the more respondents disapprove of abortion.

We will use the Compute command to instruct SPSS to create a new variable (ABORT) based on respondents' scores on ABDEFECT and ABSINGLE. Our index (ABORT) will be made up of three possible scores as discussed above:

ABORT Index Scores

0—Respondent approves of abortion in both cases (if there is a chance of a serious birth defect and if the woman is single).

1—Respondent approves of abortion in one circumstance (primarily birth defects) but not the other.

2—Respondent disapproves of abortion in both cases (if there is a chance of a serious birth defect and if the woman is single).

---

3. You can choose any name you like for your new variable, provided it is no longer than 8 characters and begins with a letter.

We'll use the Compute command to accomplish three tasks:

Task 1: Use Compute to create the new variable ABORT with the score for each respondent set to 0. Just like a quiz, an index starts with no points!

Task 2: Use the logical IF capability of Compute to see if respondents gave us the "right" answer for ABDEFECT or ABSINGLE. If they did, we will add a point to their index score, ABORT.

Task 3: Use the logical IF in Compute to check for missing values due to nonresponses or "Don't knows." When scoring a quiz, a nonresponse is counted the same as getting it wrong. When creating an index, missing information means we don't know the respondent's opinion. For our ABORT index, missing information means we know nothing about a respondent's disapproval or approval of abortion. Rather than making the mistake of assuming that people who did not respond (or for whom information was missing) approved of abortion, we eliminate them from our analysis by setting their score on ABORT to "Missing."

When we are done, if a respondent had a 1 ("Yes") on both ABDEFECT and ABSINGLE, her score will be a 0 on our new index. If a respondent had a 1 ("Yes") on ABDEFECT and a 2 ("No") on ABSINGLE (or vice versa), his score will be a 1 on our new index. And if a respondent had a 2 ("No") for both component variables, her score will be 2 on our index.

Four steps are involved in the process of computing our new variable, ABORT. We are going to walk you through them one at a time.

Step 1: Creating Our New Variable ABORT

To do this, simply click **Transform** in the menubar and then select **Compute...** in the drop-down menu to open the Compute Variable dialog box as shown below.

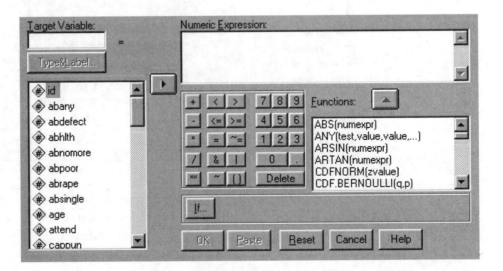

In the upper-left hand corner of the box you will see a rectangle followed by an equal sign that is labeled Target Variable:. Click in that rectangle and type the name of the new variable we want to create, **ABORT**.

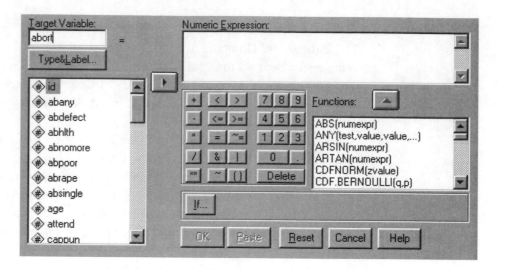

Once you do that you will see that we have already begun a numeric expression that says "ABORT =". Our task from now on is to specify what ABORT equals by filling in the field titled Numeric Expression:.

We will begin by entering 0 in the Numeric Expression: field. You can do this in one of two ways. You can simply type it in or you can use the calculator pad in the center of the window (under the Numeric Expression: field) to "paste" it in. To use the latter, simply click **0** in the calculator pad. Once you do that, the 0 will magically appear in the Numeric Expression: field.

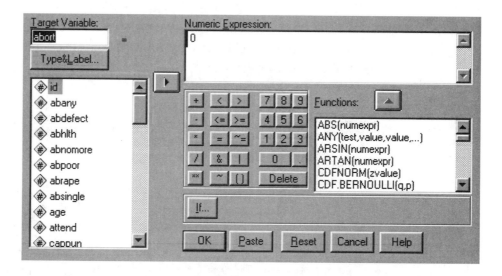

In either case, we've now instructed SPSS to create a new variable named ABORT and to give everyone a score of 0 on it. Click the **OK** button at the bottom of the window to have SPSS execute the command.

You will now be back in the Data Editor window. If you **scroll to the far right** of the window using the **horizontal scroll bar** that runs along the bottom of the matrix, you will see your new variable ABORT, and if you look down the column you will see that everyone has been given a score of 0 as we requested.

Step 2: Adding Points for Not Approving Abortion

Now, let's start adding points to the index scores based on the answers people gave to the component items (ABDEFECT and ABSINGLE). We do this by creating a *counter* in the compute procedure. Counters are small computer *algorithms* that accumulate some number each time it is executed. To add points to our index, we will use the following counter:

Abort = Abort + 1

Each time SPSS is told to do this algorithm, it will find the current ABORT score for each respondent and add 1 to it.

Select **Transform** and **Compute...** once again. Keep our new variable name ABORT in the Target Variable: field. In the Numeric Expression: field replace 0 with **Abort + 1**. This tells SPSS that we want to add 1 to respondents' index scores.

Now we need to tell SPSS which respondents should have a "1" added to their score. To do this, select **If...** at the bottom of your window to open the Compute Variable: If Cases box as shown below.

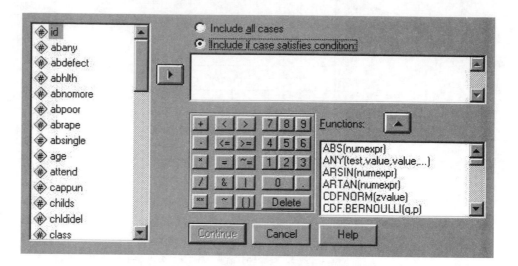

We can now tell SPSS that we want to give respondents a "1" on the ABORT index if they had a score of 1 on both ABDEFECT and ABSINGLE.

Begin by clicking the button **Include if case satisfies condition:**, and you will notice that we can now begin using our keypad. Either type or paste the following expression in the rectangle under Include if case satisfies condition box:

ABDEFECT = 2

Once again, all we have told SPSS to do is to give 1 point to any respondent who said they did not approve of abortion in the case of a strong chance of a birth defect.

To execute this command simply click **Continue** and then choose **OK** and **OK** once again when SPSS asks you if you want to "Change the existing Variable." If you look at ABORT on the Data Editor screen, you will find that for a few of the respondents, ABORT has been changed to a 1. These are the people who said "No" to ABDEFECT.

Now that points have been added for all those who said "No" to ABDE-FECT, repeat the process for ABSINGLE. Its really quite easy. All you have to do is get back to the screen where you said "ABDEFECT = 2" and change it to "ABSINGLE = 2." After SPSS has completed this task, you should be able to see 0s, 1s, and 2s under the ABORT variable in the Data Editor.[4]

Step 3: Assign a $SYSMIS to ABORT If Either ABDEFECT or ABSINGLE Is Missing

Now we want to follow the same basic procedure to tell SPSS to set respondents' index scores to the system missing value, *$SYSMIS*, if data were not present for

---

4. Using the logical capabilities of Compute also allows the building of indexes from variables that are not all coded the same.

either ABDEFECT or ABSINGLE. When a $SYSMIS code is encountered by SPSS, the case is removed from any statistical computations. $SYSMIS codes are displayed as a "." in the Data Editor window.

To do this simply follow these commands:

Click **Transform** → **Compute…**

In the "Numeric Expression:" field type **$SYSMIS**

Click **If…**

Make sure **"Include if case satisfies condition:"** is selected.

Change the expression to read **MISSING(ABDEFECT) I MISSING(ABSINGLE)**

It should look like this.

You can either type **MISSING** into the window, or, if you wish, you can enter it with the mouse by scrolling down the list of Functions until you come to MISSING(), clicking on **MISSING()**, and then clicking the **up arrow** button. Once in the window, you will see a "?" between the parentheses. It can be replaced by clicking on the **name of the appropriate variable** and the **right arrow** button.

When your window looks like the one above, click **Continue** → **OK** → **OK** to carry out the operation.

Step 4: Defining ABORT

You should now be back in the Data Editor window. To complete our index we need to do one more thing. Highlight **ABORT** and then select **Define Variable…** under the **Data** menu.

Go to the Define Variable box, select **Type...**, and change the decimal places to **0**.

Click **Continue** once again.

Now select **Labels...** and go through and fill in the *variable label* any way you choose (for example "Simple Abortion Index"). Then add the *values* and *labels* for ABORT as follows:

0 = Yes/Approve (in both cases)

1 = Conditional Support (Yes in only one case)

2 = No/Disapprove (in both cases)

Then click **Continue** and **OK**.

Running Frequencies on ABORT

To see if we really accomplished what we set out to do, run **Frequencies** for the variable ABORT and you should see the following table (refer to the SPSS commands listed at the end of Chapter 6 or on-line in E-Appendix F if you need to review the commands for running Frequencies).

ABORT Simple Abortion Index

		Frequency	Percent	Valid Percent	Cumulative Percent
Valid	0 yes/approve	382	25.5	42.9	42.9
	1 conditional support	323	21.5	36.3	79.1
	2 no/disapprove	186	12.4	20.9	100.0
	Total	891	59.4	100.0	
Missing	System	609	40.6		
Total		1500	100.0		

If you compare the index score in this table with the crosstabs of the two component variables we ran in the last chapter, you'll see a logical correspondence. In the earlier table, 186 people disapproved of abortion under both of the specified conditions; here we find that 186 people scored 2 on the index. We also found that 320 people would approve abortion for birth defects but not for a single woman, and 3 had the reverse view; the index shows 323 people (320 + 3) with a score of 1. Finally, the 382 people who approved of abortion in both cases previously have a score of 0 on the index. Notice also that 609 people were excluded on the basis of missing data.

Congratulations! You've just created a composite index. We realize you may still be wondering why that's such good news. After all, it wasn't your idea to create the thing in the first place.

SPSS COMMAND 9.2:   Computing a Simple Index

Step 1: Create New Variable

Click **Transform** → **Compute...** → **Target Variable:** →

Type name of new variable → Type/Paste **0** in "Numeric Expression:" field →

Click **OK** →

Step 2+: Add Points to Index Score

Click **Transform** → **Compute...** → Type/Paste counter you are using in the Numeric Expression: field [ex. Abort + 1] → ...

Click **If...** → Select **"Include if case..."** → Type/Paste expression in field →

Click **Continue** → **OK** → **OK...**

Repeat Step 2 as many times as necessary until complete index...

Step 3: $SYSMIS

Click **Transform** → **Compute...** → Type **$SYSMIS** in "Numeric Expression:" field →

Click **If...** → Select **"Include if case..."** → Type/Paste expression in field (put all variables used in index joined by | (logical OR signs)) →

Click **Continue** → **OK** → **OK...**

Step 4: Define Variable

Highlight name of new variable in Data Editor →

Click **Data** → **Define Variable...** →

Type...

Labels...

Demonstration 9.3: Validating ABORT

To get a clearer idea of the value of such a composite measure, let's move on to the next step in the process we've launched. Let's validate the index; that is, let's make sure it really measures what we are attempting to measure. If you recall the earlier discussion of validity and reliability in Chapter 3, you'll see the link to this discussion of index validation.

In creating this simple index, we've tried to put respondents in one of three groups: those very supportive of abortion, those very opposed, and those in the middle. If we've succeeded in that effort, the scores we've assigned people on the new index, ABORT, should help us to predict how people answered other abortion items in the questionnaire. Let's begin with their answers to ABHLTH: approving abortion for a woman whose health is in danger.

To undertake this test of the index's validity, we'll return to the Crosstabs command, introduced in Chapter 8. As you'll see, it has some additional features that can be used to good effect. In this instance, we want to cross-classify people in terms of their scores on the index and on the variable ABHLTH.

Run the **Crosstabs** command with **ABHLTH** as the **row** variable and **ABORT** as the **column** variable (if you need to review the Crosstabs command, refer to the discussion in Chapter 8, the SPSS Commands listed at the end of Chapter 8, or on-line in E-Appendix F). Here's the result you should get:

ABHLTH WOMANS HEALTH SERIOUSLY ENDANGERED * ABORT Simple Abortion Index Crosstabulation

Count

		ABORT Simple Abortion Index			
		0 yes/approve	1 conditional support	2 no/disapprove	Total
ABHLTH WOMANS HEALTH SERIOUSLY ENDANGERED	1 YES	380	309	80	769
	2 NO	2	7	94	103
Total		382	316	174	872

You may be able to look at this table and see the relationship between the index and ABHLTH, but the analysis will be much simpler if we convert the data in the table to percentages. Let's express the assumption of validity that we are testing in terms of percentages. If those with a score of 0 on the index are the most supportive of abortion, then we should expect to find a higher percentage of them approving abortion in the case of the woman's health being endangered than we would find among the other groups. Those who scored 2 on the index, by contrast, should be the least likely—the smallest percentage—to approve abortion based on the woman's health.

Looking first at those who scored 0, in the leftmost column of the table, we would calculate the percentage as follows. Of the 382 people who scored 0, we see that 380 approved of abortion in the case of ABHLTH. Dividing 380 by 382 indicates that those 380 people are 99.47 percent of the total 382. Looking at those with a score of 2, in the rightmost column, we find that the 80 who approve represent 45.97 percent of the 174 with that score. These two percentages support the assumption we are making about the index.

Happily, SPSS can be instructed to calculate these percentages for us. In fact, we are going to be looking at percentage tables for the most part in the rest of this book.

Before we instruct SPSS to make these calculations, it is important to note that our first task in this chapter, designating "Don't knows" as "Missing," was done in anticipation of this procedure. In other words, in running Crosstabs with percentages we do not want SPSS to include responses such as "Don't know" in its calculation.

Go back to the **Crosstabs** window. Your previous request should still be in the appropriate fields. Notice a button at the bottom of this window called **Cells...**. Click it. This will take you to a new window, as shown below:

Notice that you can choose to have SPSS calculate percentages for you in one of three ways: using row totals, column totals, or the total number of cases. Click **Column** and then select **Continue** and **OK** in the Crosstabs window to have SPSS run the table for you. Your reward should look like the following:

ABHLTH WOMANS HEALTH SERIOUSLY ENDANGERED * ABORT Simple Abortion Index Crosstabulation

| | | | ABORT Simple Abortion Index | | | |
			0 yes/appro ve	1 conditional support	2 no/disapp rove	Total
ABHLTH WOMANS HEALTH SERIOUSLY ENDANGERED	1 YES	Count	380	309	80	769
		% within ABORT Simple Abortion Index	99.5%	97.8%	46.0%	88.2%
	2 NO	Count	2	7	94	103
		% within ABORT Simple Abortion Index	.5%	2.2%	54.0%	11.8%
Total		Count	382	316	174	872
		% within ABORT Simple Abortion Index	100.0%	100.0%	100.0%	100.0%

Take a moment to examine the logic of this table. For each score on the index, we have calculated the percentage saying they support (yes) or oppose (no) a woman's right to an abortion if her health is seriously endangered. It is as though we limited our attention to one of the index-score groups (those who scored 0, for example) and described them in terms of their attitudes on the abortion item; then we repeated the process for each of the index-score groups. Once we've described each of the subgroups, we can compare them.

When you have created a table with the percentages totaling 100 down each column, the proper way to read the table is across the rows. Rounding off the percentages to simplify matters, we would note, in this case (reading across the first two of the table), that

100 percent of those with a score of 0 on the index,

98 percent of those with a score of 1 on the index, and

46 percent of those with a score of 2 on the index

said they would approve of abortion if the woman's health were seriously endangered. This table supports our assumption that the index measures levels of support for a woman's freedom to choose abortion.

Now let's validate the index using the other abortion items not included in the index itself. Repeat the **Crosstabs** command, substituting the four abortion items—**ABNOMORE, ABRAPE, ABPOOR**, and **ABANY**—for ABHLTH.

Run the Crosstabs command now and see what results you get. Look at each of the four tables and see what they say about the ability of the index to measure attitudes toward abortion. Here is an abbreviated table format that you might want to construct from the results of that command. SPSS doesn't create a table like this, but it's a useful format for presenting data in a research report.

ABORT Index

Percentage Who Approve of Abortion When	0	1	2
the woman was raped	98	83	28
the couple can't afford more children	93	14	2
the couple doesn't want more children	90	11	—
the woman wants an abortion	89	8	1

Whereas the earlier table showed the percentages who approved and those who disapproved of abortion in a specific situation, this table presents only those who approved. The first entry in the table, for example, indicates that 98 percent of those with a score of 0 on the index approve of abortion in the case of rape. Of those with a score of 1 on the index, 83 percent approved of abortion for this reason, and 28 percent of those with a score of 2 approved.

As you can see, the index accurately predicts differences in responses to each of the other abortion items. In each case, those with lower scores on the index are more likely to support abortion under the specified conditions than are those with higher scores on the index.

By building this composite index, we've created a more sophisticated measure of attitudes toward abortion. Whereas each of the individual items allows only for approval or disapproval of abortion under various circumstances, this index reflects three positions on the issue: unconditional disapproval (2), conditional approval (1), and unconditional approval (0).

SPSS COMMAND 9.3:   Producing Crosstabs with Column Percentages

> Click **Analyze** → **Descriptive Statistics** → **Crosstabs...** →
> Highlight **variable name** → Click **arrow** pointing to the **Row(s): box** →
> Highlight **variable name** → Click **arrow** pointing to the **Column(s): box** →
> Click **Cells...** → choose **Column** in Percentages box → **Continue** → **OK**

Demonstration 9.4: Index 2—ABINDEX Employing Count

Whereas the first index was created from only two of the abortion items, we can easily create a more elaborate index using more items. This larger index will tap into more dimensions of the abortion debate and provide a wider range of variation between the extremes.

To illustrate, let's use all the abortion items except for ABANY, supporting a woman's unrestricted choice. While we could create this new index following the same procedures as before, there is also a shortcut that we can use when we want to score several items the same way in creating the index. Suppose, for example, that we want to create a larger index by giving people one point for agreeing to an abortion in each of the six special circumstances.

Step 1: Missing values

Select **Transform** in the menubar and this time choose **Count...** (as opposed to Compute...) from the drop-down menu. This will present you with the following window:

The Count Occurrences of Values within Cases box creates a new variable that literally counts the occurrences of the same value(s) for each case in a list of variables. This will become clearer as we move through this process.

In creating our new index, we will, once more, need to deal with the problem of missing values. In using Count, we are going to handle that matter somewhat differently from the way we did before. Specifically, we are going to begin by creating a variable that tells us whether people had missing values on any of the six items we are examining.

To do this, we'll create a variable called MISS. Once you are in the Count Occurrences of... box, type **MISS** in the Target Variable: field. Next, we want to specify the items to be considered in creating MISS. Transfer the following variable names to the Variables: field: ABDEFECT, ABHLTH, ABNOMORE, ABPOOR, ABRAPE, and ABSINGLE. You can do this by selecting a variable in the list on the left side of the window and clicking the **arrow** pointing to the Variables: field, or you can simply double-click a variable name. (Where several variables are together in the list, you can drag your cursor across the several names, selecting them all, and then click the arrow.)

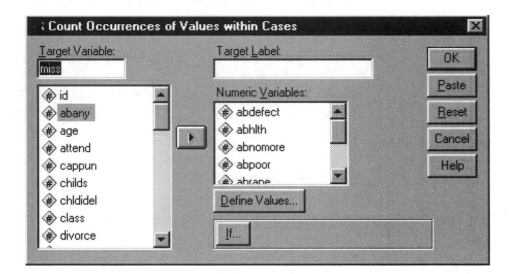

Having selected the variables to be counted, click **Define Values...**.

The left side of the window offers several options for counting, but we want to use the simplest: a single value. Click the **button** beside System- or user-missing. Click the **Add** button to transfer the value to the Values to Count: field.

Click **Continue** to return to the Count Occurrences... window.

Click **OK** to launch the procedure. When SPSS has completed the procedure, you will find that the Data window now has a new variable called MISS, with scores ranging from 0 to 6, indicating the number of missing values people had on the six items. (If you are looking at the Output window, you can use the Window menu to shift to the Data window.)

Step 2: Creating Our New Variable ABINDEX

Now we are ready to create our new abortion index. Choose **Count...** under the **Transform** menu again. Replace MISS with **ABINDEX** in the Target Variable: field. Leave the six abortion items where they are in the Variables: field.

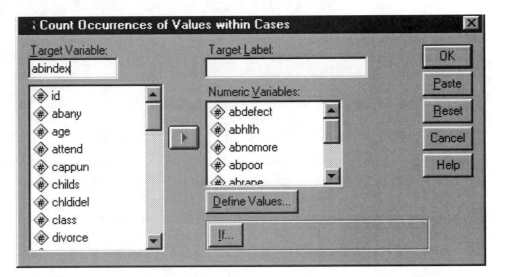

Now click **Define Values...**.

In the Count Values within... window, you'll notice that MISSING is still showing in the specification field. Click **MISSING** to select it. Then click **Remove**. Now the field is empty.

Click the first option on the left, **Value:**, and type "**1**" in the field beside it. Click **Add** to transfer the value to the appropriate field. Then click **Continue** and **OK**.

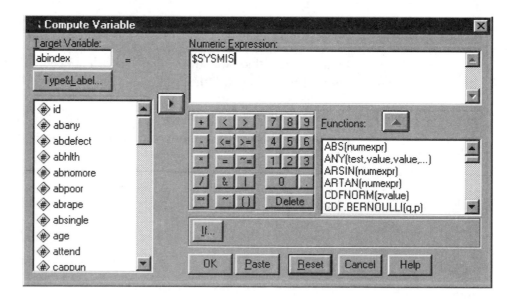

Since we left the six variable names in Numeric Variables:, we have now told SPSS to count the number of times a person had a score of "1" on any of those six items.

Step 3: Discarding Cases with $SYSMIS

Before we can use our new ABINDEX variable, we have to inform SPSS which respondents did not answer all six abortion questions. We can do that easily using the variable MISS we created a moment ago.

From the Data screen, select **Transform** and **Compute...**. Identify **ABINDEX** as the target variable. In the Numeric Expression: window, type **$SYSMIS** (again, an SPSS keyword that causes cases to be eliminated from analysis).

Don't click OK yet! If you did, all of our respondents would be eliminated from further analysis. Instead, click **If...**. Click the **button** that lightens Include if case satisfies condition:. In the Condition window, type in or click **MISS ~= 0**. (The "~=" means "not equal to.") Now you can click **Continue** and then **OK** in the Compute Variable box. If you get another message, click **OK** again.

We have now told SPSS that we want it to count pro-choice answers only for those who had no missing values on any of the six items.

Step 4: Defining ABINDEX

Now we need to tidy up our new variable. Select **ABINDEX** in the Data window and then select **Define Variable...** under **Data**.

Click **Type...** and change the number of decimal places to **0**.

You can label your new variable, as well as add values and labels by selecting **Labels...**.

Click **Continue** and **OK** to put SPSS to work.

Running Frequencies

Once you've entered and executed these commands, let's see what these instructions produced. Get the **Frequency** distribution of **ABINDEX**. Here's what you should find.

ABINDEX

		Frequency	Percent	Valid Percent	Cumulative Percent
Valid	0	84	5.6	10.2	10.2
	1	49	3.3	5.9	16.1
	2	86	5.7	10.4	26.5
	3	192	12.8	23.2	49.8
	4	54	3.6	6.5	56.3
	5	46	3.1	5.6	61.9
	6	315	21.0	38.1	100.0
	Total	826	55.1	100.0	
Missing	System	674	44.9		
Total		1500	100.0		

This table shows the distribution of scores on the new index, ABINDEX. As you can see, there are 315 people—38 percent of those with opinions—who support abortion in all the specified circumstances (score 6 on the index). A total of 84 disapprove of abortion in any of those circumstances. The rest are spread out according to the number of conditions they feel would warrant abortion.

Validating ABINDEX

For validation purposes, this time we have only one item not included in the index itself: ABANY. Let's see how well the index predicts respondents' approval of a woman's unrestricted choice of abortion.

Run the **Crosstabs** procedure specifying:

- **ABANY** as the **row** variable

- **ABINDEX** as the **column** index

- **Cells** to be percentaged by **column**

ABANY ABORTION IF WOMAN WANTS FOR ANY REASON * ABINDEX Crosstabulation

| | | | ABINDEX | | | | | | | |
			0	1	2	3	4	5	6	Total
ABANY ABORTION IF WOMAN WANTS FOR ANY REASON	1 YES	Count			2	8	11	25	298	344
		% within ABINDEX			2.4%	4.2%	20.8%	54.3%	95.8%	42.3%
	2 NO	Count	84	49	80	181	42	21	13	470
		% within ABINDEX	100.0%	100.0%	97.6%	95.8%	79.2%	45.7%	4.2%	57.7%
Total		Count	84	49	82	189	53	46	311	814
		% within ABINDEX	100.0%	100.0%	100.0%	100.0%	100.0%	100.0%	100.0%	100.0%

As we can see, answers to ABANY are closely related to scores on ABINDEX. None of the persons who scored either a 0 or 1 on ABINDEX favored a woman's right to an abortion for any reason. For scores 2 through 6, the percentage continues increasing across the index until we find that 95.8 percent of those who scored 6 on the index say a woman has the unconditional right to an abortion.

Once again, we find the index validated. This means that if we wish to analyze peoples' attitudes toward abortion further (and we will), we have the choice of using a single item to represent those attitudes or using a composite measure. We've seen, moreover, that we can create such an index in different ways.

SPSS COMMAND 9.4:   Creating a More Complex Index with Count

Step 1: Missing Values

Click **Transform** → **Count...** → **Target Variable:** → Type **MISS** →

Transfer variable names to "Variables:" field → Click **Define Values...** →

Select **"System-or user-missing"** → Click **Add** → **Continue** → **OK** →

Step 2: Creating the New Index

Click **Transform** → **Count...** →

In **Target Variable:** field **replace MISS with new variable name** [ABINDEX] →

Leave items where they are in the "Variables:" field → Click **Define Values...** →

Click on **MISSING** in the specification field → Click **Remove** → **Value** →

Type "**1**" in the field next to Value → Click **Add** → **Continue** → **OK** →

Step 3: Discarding Cases with $SYSMIS

Click **Transform** → **Compute...** → **Target Variable:** → Type **ABINDEX** →

Type **$SYSMIS** in the "Numeric Expression:" field →

Click **If** → Select **button** next to **"Include if case satisfies condition:"** →

In the condition window type or click "**MISS ~=0**" →

Click **Continue** → **OK** → **OK** →

Step 4: Define Variable

Highlight the name of the new variable in the Data Editor →

Click **Data** → **Define Variable...** →

Type...

Labels...

That is enough for now. However, before ending this session, make sure you **Save** both of your new variables (**ABORT** and **ABINDEX**) so we can use them later (see Chapter 6, Demonstration 6.7 and SPSS Command 6.11). It is important to reiterate that anyone using the Student Version of SPSS has to be sensitive to the fact that it is limited to 50 variables. Consequently, you may need to follow the instructions in Chapter 6 regarding saving your data. For those of you using the Professional Version of SPSS, this is obviously not an issue.

Conclusion

In this chapter, we've seen that it is often possible to measure social scientific concepts in a number of ways. Sometimes, the data set contains a single item that does the job nicely. Measuring gender by asking people for their gender is a good example.

In other cases, the mental images that constitute our concepts (e.g., religiosity, political orientations, prejudice) are varied and ambiguous. Typically, no single item in a data set provides a complete representation of what we have in mind. Often, we can resolve this problem by combining two or more indicators of the concept into a composite index. As we've seen, SPSS offers the tools necessary for such data transformations.

If you continue your studies in social research, you will discover that there are many more sophisticated techniques for creating composite measures. However, the simple indexing techniques you have learned in this chapter will serve you well in the analyses that lie ahead.

Main Points

- Concepts can be measured in a number of different ways.
- In some cases a single item is enough to measure a concept.
- In the case of a controversial and emotionally charged issue such as abortion, where opinion is varied and intricate, no one item is capable of capturing the complexity of opinion.
- In such cases, composite measures made up of multiple indicators of a single concept can be very useful.
- There are a variety of advantages to using composite measures.
- An index is a form of composite measure.
- The Compute command allows us to create a new summary variable or index based on the scores of existing variables.
- The Compute command is very flexible and can be used to create items/indexes of varying degrees of complexity.
- We created one fairly simple index (ABORT) and one more complicated index with Count (ABINDEX) to measure overall feelings about abortion.

Key Terms

Composite measure	Counter
Compute	Algorithms
Count	$SYSMIS
Index	

SPSS Commands Introduced in This Chapter

9.1:   Defining Missing Values

> Click on **Variable name** in Data Editor to highlight the column →
> Click **Data** → **Define Variable…** → **Missing Values…** →
> Select one of the four available options…
> Click **Continue** → **OK**

9.2:   Computing a Simple Index

> Step 1: Create New Variable
> Click **Transform** → **Compute…** → **Target Variable:** →
> **Type name of new variable** → Type/Paste **0** in "Numeric Expression:"
>   field →
> Click **OK** →
>
> Step 2+: Add Points to Index Score
> Click **Transform** → **Compute…** → Type/Paste counter you are using
>   in the Numeric Expression: field [ex. Abort + 1] → …
> Click **If…** → Select **"Include if Case…"** → Type/Paste expression in
>   field →
> Click **Continue** → **OK** → **OK**…
> Repeat Step 2 as many times as necessary until complete index…
>
> Step 3: $SYSMIS
> Click **Transform** → **Compute…** → Type **$SYSMIS** in "Numeric
>   Expression:" field →
> Click If… → Select "Include if Case…" → Type/paste expression in
>   field (put all variables used in index joined by | (logical OR signs)) →
> Click **Continue** → **OK** → **OK**…
>
> Step 4: Define Variable
> **Highlight name of new variable** in Data Editor →
> Click **Data** → **Define Variable…** →
> **Type…**
> **Labels…**

9.3:   Producing Crosstabs with Column Percentages

Click **Analyze** → **Descriptive Statistics** → **Crosstabs...** →
Highlight **variable name** → Click **arrow** pointing to the **Row(s): box** →
Highlight **variable name** → Click **arrow** pointing to the **Column(s): box** →
Click **Cells...** → choose **Column** in Percentages box → **Continue** → **OK** →

9.4:   Creating a More Complex Index with COUNT

Step 1: Missing Values

Click **Transform** → **Count...** → **Target Variable:** → Type **MISS** →
Transfer variable names to "Variables:" field → Click **Define Values...** →
Select "**System-or user-missing**" → Click **Add** → **Continue** → **OK** →

Step 2: Creating the New Index

Click **Transform** → **Count...** →
In **Target Variable:** field **replace MISS with new variable name** [ABINDEX] →
Leave items where they are in the "Variables:" field → Click **Define Values...** →
Click on **MISSING** in the specification field → Click **Remove** → **Value** →
Type "**1**" in the field next to Value → Click **Add** → **Continue** → **OK** →

Step 3: Discarding Cases with $SYSMIS

Click **Transform** → **Compute...** → **Target Variable:** → Type **ABINDEX** →
Type **$SYSMIS** in the "Numeric Expression:" field →
Click **If** → Select **button** next to "**Include if case satisfies condition:**" →
In the condition window type or click "**MISS ~=0**" →
Click **Continue** → **OK** → **OK** →

Step 4: Define Variable

Highlight the name of the new variable in the Data Editor →
Click **Data** → **Define Variable...** →
Type...
Labels...

Review Questions

1. What is a composite measure?

2. If you wanted to designate a missing value, would you be better off choosing the command path Analyze → Descriptives or Data → Define Variable?

3. The Discrete missing values option allows you to specify up to how many individual missing values?

4. What is an index?

5. What are two of the advantages of using an index?

6. What information is used to compute a new summary variable?

7. How do we test an index's validity?

8. What are the commands to run Crosstabs with column percentages?

9. Can indexes be based on the scores of more than two items?

10. What is the Count procedure used for?

NAME _____

CLASS _____

INSTRUCTOR _____

DATE _____

In this exercise you will be given a chance to compute two indices. The first will be based on two variables contained in your EXER.SAV data file, POLABUSE and POLATTAK. Simply follow the steps below and supply the information requested as you go along. You will find answers to the Questions 1–18 in Appendix A.

1. What does the variable POLABUSE measure?

2. What does the variable POLATTAK measure?

3. List the values and labels for POLABUSE and POLATTAK.

Value   Label

_____   _____

_____   _____

_____   _____

_____   _____

_____   _____

4. Designate DKs as "Missing" for the following variables: POLABUSE and POLATTAK. For use later, do the same for POLESCAP, POLHITOK, POLMURDR. In addition, be sure that NAP and NA are defined as missing values as well.

5. The value for DK for the variables listed in Question 4 is _____.

6. List the commands used to define DK as missing, beginning with DATA →

Our new variable/index will be named POLIN (for POLice INdex).

> *POLIN scores are:*
> 0 — Approve/Yes in both cases.
> 1 — Conditional Approval/Yes in one case, but not the other.
> 2 — Disapprove/No in both cases.

7. The _____[higher/lower] the index score, the more the respondent agrees that there are situations in which they would approve of a police officer striking an adult male citizen.

8. The _____[higher/lower] the index score, the less the respondent agrees that there are situations in which they would approve of a police officer striking an adult male citizen.

9. Compute new variable/index – POLIN

   [Hint: Click **Transform → Compute → Target Variable...**]

10. Define POLIN (set decimal places and indicate variable label, values, and labels).

    [Hint: Click **Data → Define Variable → Type...**]

11. Run and print Frequencies for POLIN.

12. Of those who answered,

    _____ % received a score of 0 on the index.

    _____ % received a score of 1 on the index.

    _____ % received a score of 2 on the index.

13. Now validate your index by cross-classifying people in terms of their response to POLIN and the following variables: POLESCAP, POLHITOK, and POLMURDR.

    • Run Crosstabs with column percentages

    • Specify POLIN as the Column variable

    [Hint: **Analyze → Descriptive Statistics → Crosstabs...**]

NAME _____

CLASS _____

INSTRUCTOR _____

DATE _____

14. POLESCAP by POLIN

_____ % of those with a score of 0 on the index

_____ % of those with a score of 1 on the index

_____ % of those with a score of 2 on the index

agree that it is okay for a police officer to hit someone if he is trying to escape from custody.

15. POLMURDR by POLIN

_____% of those with a score of 0 on the index

_____% of those with a score of 1 on the index

_____% of those with a score of 2 on the index

agree that it is okay for a police officer to hit someone if he is being questioned as a murder suspect.

16. POLHITOK by POLIN

_____ % of those with a score of 0 on the index

_____ % of those with a score of 1 on the index

_____ % of those with a score of 2 on the index

17. Was the index POLIN validated? Explain.

18. Now it is time to compute an index on your own. Create a more complex index (POLFORCE) employing Count based on the four following variables: POLABUSE, POLATTAK, POLESCAP, and POLMURDR. If you need to review the commands, refer back to SPSS Command 9.4. Make sure you run Frequencies, validate your index using POLHITOK, print your output, and summarize your findings below.

Chapter 10 Suggestions for Further Univariate Analysis

In the preceding chapters, we've given you a number of research possibilities to begin exploring based on the variables contained in your DEMO.SAV file. The topics we have focused on so far include religion, politics, and abortion. In the event that you've exhausted those possibilities and want to look beyond them, here are some additional topics for you to consider.

Desired Family Size

One of the major social problems facing the world today is that of overpopulation. A brief summary of population growth on the planet should illustrate what we mean.

Year	Population	Doubling Time
0	.25 billion	—
1650	.50 billion	1,650 years
1850	1.00 billion	200 years
1930	2.00 billion	80 years
1975	4.00 billion	45 years
1994	5.64 billion	39 years
1998	5.93 billion	49 years

These data show several things. For example, the world's population has increased more than 20-fold since the beginning of the Christian era. More important, however, the rate of increase has been steadily increasing. This is most easily seen in the rightmost column above, showing what demographers call the **doubling time**. It took 1,650 years for the world's population to increase from a quarter of a billion people to half a billion. The time required to double dramatically shortened until 1994. As of 1998, the doubling time increased to about 49 years. However, even with the slight increase in doubling time, today's children can expect to live out their older years in a world with nearly 12 billion people.

This astounding increase in the pace of population growth has been caused by the fact that during most of human existence, extremely high death rates have been matched by equally high birth rates. During the past few generations, however, death rates have plummeted around the world because of improved public health measures, medical discoveries, and improved food production.

The current pace of population growth simply cannot go on forever. Although scientists may disagree on the number of people the planet can support, there is simply no question that there is some limit. At some point, population growth must be slowed even more and stopped—perhaps even reversed.

There are two ways to end population growth: Either death rates can be returned to their former high levels or birth rates can be reduced. Because most of us would choose the latter solution, demographers have been very interested in variables that measure desired family size.

Your data set contains a variable, CHLDIDEL, that presents responses to the question, "What do you think is the ideal number of children for a family to have?" If every family had only two children, then births and deaths would eventually roughly balance each other out, producing a condition of population stabilization, or zero population growth (excluding the effect of migration). What percentage of the population do you suppose chose that as the ideal? Some favored larger families, and others said they thought only one child was the ideal. Why don't you find out what the most common response was?

Later in this book, you may want to explore the causes of people's attitudes about ideal family size. For instance, it may be interesting to consider whether the number of siblings that respondents have (SIBS) impacts their conception of ideal family size (CHLDIDEL).

Child Training

What do you think are the most important qualities for children to develop as they grow up? Respondents to the General Social Survey were asked that question also. To frame the question more specifically, they were presented with several of the answers people commonly give and were asked how important each was. If you had to choose, which thing on this list would you pick as the most important for a child to learn to prepare him or her for life?

The interviewer read the following list (which we've annotated with the GSS variable names):

OBEY	to obey
POPULAR	to be well-liked or popular
THNKSELF	to think for himself or herself
WORKHARD	to work hard
HELPOTH	to help others when they need help

Once the respondents indicated which of these they felt were most important, they were asked:

Which comes next in importance?

Which comes third?

Which comes fourth?

This set of responses allowed the researchers to code the final responses as "Least important."

As with earlier topics, take a moment to notice how you feel about such matters. Then see if you can anticipate what public opinion is on these qualities of children. It will be useful, by the way, to observe your reasoning process as you attempt to anticipate public opinion. What observations, clues, or cues prompt you to think OBEY is the most important, or POPULAR, or whichever one you picked as the one most people would choose?

Then you can see how people actually responded to the questions. Once you've done that, you should review your earlier reasoning, either to confirm your predictions or to figure out where you went wrong. What can you infer from the differences among your opinions, your predictions, and the actual results?

Attitudes About Sexual Behavior

As with most other things, Americans differ in their feelings about sexual behavior. We thought you might be interested in this area of public opinion, so we've included three GSS variables dealing with different kinds of sexual behavior.

HOMOSEX asks about homosexual sex relations, PREMARSX focuses on premarital sex, and XMOVIE asks whether the respondent has attended an X-rated movie during the past year. Notice that the first two variables measure respondents' attitudes toward the behavior of others, while the last variable measures the respondent's own behavior. Either might be taken as an indication of overall orientation, but it is important always to remember exactly what variables represent. One question this raises, however, is whether self-reports of behavior can be considered generally reliable? A second question you may want to think about is whether this method of data collection (surveys) should be used primarily to measure opinions and attitudes rather than behavior, or doesn't it matter?

We realize that you may very well have strong opinions about each of these issues. Your job as a social science researcher, however, is to find out what Americans as a whole think and do. What percentage do you suppose have gone to an X-rated movie? Which do you think people tolerate more: premarital sex or homosexuality? Give it some thought and then check it out.

It's not too early to begin asking yourself what would cause people to be more tolerant or less so in these regards. When we turn to bivariate analysis later on, you'll have a chance to test some of your expectations.

Here's an idea that could take you deeper into this general topic. See if you can use the **Transform → Count...** command to create a composite measure of sexual permissiveness, combining the three items. If you do this, be sure you take into account the differences in coding for the first two variables (HOMOSEX and PREMARSX) and XMOVIE.

Prejudice

Prejudice is a topic that has concerned social scientists for a long time, and the persistence of the problem keeps it a topic of interest and research. Your disk includes three items from the GSS that deal with aspects of anti-Black prejudice: RACMAR, RACPUSH, and RACDIF4.

All three items deal with different components of prejudice and racial attitudes. RACMAR measures respondents' attitudes toward the legality of interracial marriage, RACPUSH measures attitudes toward Black-White relations, whereas RACDIF4 deals with the causes of differences in socioeconomic status. You may want to look back at Chapter 4 for the exact wording of these questions. Remember, it's always important to know exactly how survey questions were asked in order to understand what the responses really mean.

These items present you with an interesting picture of racial attitudes and prejudice in the United States. Where, for instance, do you think the majority of adult Americans stand on the issue of interracial marriage? Do you think most respondents feel that interracial marriage should be outlawed or not?

You may be able to guess that general opposition to interracial marriage has decreased over the years. Before you look at this variable, however, take a moment to try to guess what the level of public support for making interracial marriage illegal might be. Then see how well you've been able to anticipate opinion on this issue.

Next, try to estimate overall opinion on the other two variables: RACPUSH and RACDIF4. It may be somewhat more difficult for you to estimate opinion on these issues, but after you have come up with an estimate, check to see whether you were correct.

If these items really interest you, you may want to consider creating a composite measure of prejudice from two or three of the variables.

Conclusion

There are several other variables in the data set. As you no doubt recall, you can get an overview of the whole thing by the command **Utilities → Variables...**. Once you see the list of variables on the left side of the window, you can click on any of the **variable names** to get short descriptions and the codes used for categorical responses.

By the time you finish this chapter, you should be feeling fairly comfortable with SPSS and the GSS data set. Now you can add more strength to the facility you are developing. In Part IV, you are going to try your hand at bivariate analysis, which lets you start to search for the reasons people are the way they are.

Main Points

- DEMO.SAV contains a variety of variables that open up a number of different research possibilities.

- In addition to religion, politics, and abortion, the data set also contains variables that deal with issues such as desired family size, child training, attitudes toward sexual behavior, and prejudice.

- Overpopulation is an issue of grave concern that can be dealt with in two primary ways.

■ Because most people prefer a solution that deals with decreasing birth rates as opposed to increasing death rates, public opinion regarding ideal family size is an issue of great interest to many researchers.

■ If you are interested in child development and child rearing, public attitudes regarding child training may be of particular interest to you.

■ Attitudes toward sexual behavior can be combined to create an interesting measure of sexual permissiveness.

■ It is important to note that while two of the variables dealing with sexual behavior measure public attitudes toward the behavior of others, the third variable focuses on the respondents' own behavior.

■ Three variables deal with different aspects of prejudice, specifically anti-Black prejudice.

■ It may be interesting to create a composite measure of prejudice based on two or three of these items in order to get a more complete view of American attitudes toward this controversial and often volatile issue.

Key Term

Doubling time

SPSS Commands Introduced in This Chapter

No new commands were introduced in this chapter.

Review Questions

1. What topics besides religion, politics, and abortion are represented by the variables contained in your DEMO.SAV file?

2. List the variables on your DEMO.SAV file that pertain to ideal family size.

3. Try to estimate public opinion on each of these variables.

4. List the variables on your DEMO.SAV file that pertain to child training.

5. Try to estimate public opinion on each of these variables.

6. List the variables on your DEMO.SAV file that pertain to attitudes about sexual behavior.

7. Try to estimate public opinion on each of these variables.

8. List the variables on your DEMO.SAV file that pertain to prejudice.

9. Try to estimate public opinion on each of these variables.

10. Of the four new topics introduced in this chapter, which interests you the most? Why?

NAME _____

CLASS _____

INSTRUCTOR _____

DATE _____

Your EXER.SAV data file contains a number of additional topics and research possibilities for you to consider, including sex roles, police, health and health insurance, mass media use, national government spending priorities, teen sex, and affirmative action. Choose one of these topics/issues and then answer the following questions.

1. State the issue/topic you have chosen from the list above.

2. Use the **Utilities → Variables...** command to identify the variables in your EXER.SAV file which pertain to this issue/topic. Then list below the abbreviated variable names and a short description of each variable.

    Abbreviated Variable Name   Description

3. Using the World Wide Web, the library, or another research tool, investigate the issue/topic you have chosen. Then write a few short paragraphs (similar to those in Chapter 10) that give a general introduction to this issue/topic. You should state why this issue/topic interests you and highlight some of the central questions and controversies that make this issue/topic ripe for social research.

4. Write a short paragraph or two explaining how you might use some of the procedures and/or commands we have discussed so far to explore this issue further. Be as specific as possible.

Part IV   Bivariate Analysis

This set of chapters adds another dimension to your analyses. By moving from the analysis of one variable, univariate analysis, to the analysis of two variables at a time, bivariate analysis, we open the possibility of exploring matters of cause and effect. Thus, in Chapter 11, we'll begin to examine what factors cause some people to be more religious than others. In this analysis, we'll be guided by an earlier analysis, which put forward a "deprivation theory" of church involvement.

In Chapter 12, we'll begin to discover why some people are liberal and others conservative, as well as why some are Democrats, others Republicans, and still others Independents. In addition, we'll begin to explore some of the consequences of political orientations. What differences do they make in terms of other attitudes and orientations?

Chapter 13 is going to take us deep inside the hotly controversial issue of abortion. You probably already have a few ideas about why some people are supportive of a woman's right to choose an abortion and others are opposed. Now you are going to have an opportunity to test your expectations and learn something about the roots of different points of view in this national debate.

In Chapters 11 through 13, we are going to limit our analyses to percentage tables, a basic format for investigations in social research. However, there are many other methods for measuring the extent to which variables are related to one another. We'll examine some of these in Chapter 14 where we focus on some common measures of association such as lambda, gamma, Pearson's r, and simple regression. You'll learn the logic that lies behind these measures, how they help us assess the strength (and in some cases, the direction) of association between variables, and you'll see how to use them through SPSS.

Chapter 15 adds another set of techniques for your use in assessing the associations that you discover among variables. Whenever samples have been chosen from a larger population, as is the case with the GSS data, there is always some danger that the associations we discover among variables in our sample are merely results of sampling error and do not represent a genuine pattern in the larger population. Chapter 15 will demonstrate several techniques used by social researchers to guard against being misled in that fashion.

Finally, as we did in Part III, we'll conclude our examination of bivariate analysis in Chapter 16 with suggestions for other lines of inquiry.

Chapter 11   Examining the Sources of Religiosity

You may recall that in Chapter 8 we gave you a sense of bivariate analysis by showing you how to run Crosstabs, an important bivariate technique. You may also recall that while we utilized this technique to examine attitudes toward abortion in more depth, we noted that it is primarily used to examine the relationships between variables and to test hypotheses. Consequently, in this chapter we are going to turn our attention to Crosstabs once again, paying particular attention to how this technique can be use to help us understand why some people are more religious than others.

Except for our brief foray into Crosstabs, up to this point we have largely limited our discussion to *unviariate analysis*, the analysis of one variable. Now, however, we are going to turn our attention to *bivariate analysis*, the analysis of two variables at a time. This will allow us to shift our focus from *description* (mainly the province of univariate analysis) to the more exciting world of *explanation*.

It may be useful for you to think about the differences between univariate and bivariate analyses in terms of the number of variables, major questions, and primary goals.

	Univariate Analysis	Bivariate Analysis
Number of Variables	1	2
Major Question	What?	Why?
Primary Goal	Description	Explanation

Consequently, whereas in the previous section we looked at the extent of people's religiosity, we now turn our attention to trying to explain "why": *Why* are some people more religious than others? What *causes* some people to be more religious than others? How can we *explain* the fact that some people are more religious than others?

The Deprivation Theory of Religiosity

The reading titled "A Theory of Involvement," by Charles Y. Glock, Benjamin B. Ringer, and Earl R. Babbie, on-line in E-Appendix G of this book, presents one explanation for differing degrees of religiosity. In it, the authors explain their social deprivation theory of religiosity. Simply put, they say that people who are denied gratification within the secular society will be more likely to turn to the church as an alternative source of gratification.

In their analysis, they looked for variables that distinguished those who were getting more gratification in the secular society from those who were getting less. For example, they reasoned that the United States is still a male-dominated society, meaning that women are denied the level of gratification enjoyed by men. Women often earn less for the same work, are denied equal access to prestigious occupations, are underrepresented in politics, and so on. According to the deprivation theory, therefore, women should be more religious than men.

The data analyses done by Glock et al., based on a sample of Episcopalian church members in 1952, confirmed their hypothesis. The question we might now ask is whether the same is true of the general U.S. population in 1998. Our data allow us to test that hypothesis.

Demonstration 11.1: Testing Our Hypothesis— Correlating Religiosity and Gender

As we noted earlier, this analysis requires us to advance our analytic procedures to bivariate analysis, involving two variables: a cause and an effect. If you think back to our discussion of theory and hypotheses in Chapter 2, you may recall that in this case religiosity would be the effect or *dependent variable* and gender the cause or *independent variable*. This means that your gender causes—to some extent—your degree of religiosity. Based on this notion we might construct a *hypothesis* which states:

> You are more likely to be religious [dependent variable]
> if you are a woman [category of independent variable—gender]
> than if you are a man [category of independent variable—gender].

It is often easy to confuse the *categories of the variable* with the variable itself. Keep in mind that in this case, "woman" and "man" are categories of the independent variable, "gender."

To test this hypothesis, we need measures of both the independent and dependent variables. The independent variable (gender) is easy: The variable SEX handles that nicely. But what about our dependent variable (religiosity)? As you'll recall from our earlier discussion, there are several measures available to us. For the time being, let's use church attendance as our measure, even though we've noted that it is not a perfect indicator of religiosity in its most general meaning.

You will remember that when we looked at ATTEND in Chapter 6, it had nine categories. If we were to crosstabulate ATTEND and SEX without recoding ATTEND, we would expect a table with 18 (9 × 2) cells. To make our table more manageable, we are going to use the recoded CHATT as our measure of church attendance.[1]

---

1. If you did not save the recoded variable CHATT, simply go back to Chapter 6 and follow the recode commands to create CHATT before moving ahead with the discussion and demonstrations in this chapter.

When running **Crosstabs** it is customary to specify the *dependent variable* as the *row variable* and the *independent variable* as the *column variable*. We will follow this convention by specifying:

- **CHATT** (dependent variable) as the **row** variable
- **SEX** (independent variable) as the **column** variable
- **Cells** to be percentaged by **column**

If you execute this command, you should get the following result.

CHATT * SEX RESPONDENTS SEX Crosstabulation

			SEX RESPONDENTS SEX		Total
			1 MALE	2 FEMALE	
CHATT	1 About weekly	Count	166	314	480
		% within SEX RESPONDENTS SEX	25.6%	38.0%	32.5%
	2 About monthly	Count	98	132	230
		% within SEX RESPONDENTS SEX	15.1%	16.0%	15.6%
	3 Seldom	Count	234	250	484
		% within SEX RESPONDENTS SEX	36.1%	30.2%	32.8%
	4 Never	Count	151	131	282
		% within SEX RESPONDENTS SEX	23.3%	15.8%	19.1%
Total		Count	649	827	1476
		% within SEX RESPONDENTS SEX	100.0%	100.0%	100.0%

The first row of percentages in the table tells us that 25.6 percent of the men reported attending church about weekly, contrasted to 38 percent of the women. If we want, we can also note that 40.7 percent of the men attend church about monthly (25.6 + 15.1, "About weekly" + "About monthly"). Note also that 54 percent of the women attend about monthly (38 + 16, "About weekly" + "About monthly").

SPSS COMMAND 11.1: Running Crosstabs—Specifying the Dependent and Independent Variables

> Click **Analyze** → **Descriptive Statistics** → **Crosstabs...** →
>
> Highlight the name of the **dependent variable(s)** → Click **arrow** pointing to the **Row(s): box** →
>
> Highlight the name of the **independent variable(s)** → Click **arrow** pointing to the **Column(s): box** →
>
> Click **Cells...** → Select **Column** in the Percentages box →
>
> Click **Continue** → **OK**

Epsilon

Epsilon is a simple statistic often used to summarize percentage differences such as those in the table above. Epsilon is calculated by identifying the largest and smallest percentages in either row and then subtracting the smallest from the largest. For example, in comparing men and women in terms of "About weekly" church attendance, the percentage difference (epsilon) is 12.4 points (38 – 25.6). This simple statistic is useful because it gives us a tool for comparing sex differences on other measures of religiosity.

When discussing epsilon it is important to note that technically, tables that have more than two columns have several epsilons—one for each pair of cells being compared. In these cases, researchers will often use epsilon to refer to the largest difference in any row of cell percentages.

These data then make it clear that women are more likely than men to attend church frequently. This would seem to support the deprivation theory of religiosity. Let's see if other indicators of religiosity produce the same result.

Demonstration 11.2: Further Hypothesis Testing— Correlating Other Measures of Religiosity and Gender

We can request more than one table in the Crosstabs window. You will notice that the commands for this procedure are the same as those listed above (SPSS Command 11.1), except in this case we are going to click on two dependent variables and place them both in the Row(s): field.

Before we do this, however, we want to remind you that it is important to check that the "Don't knows" (DK) for all your variables are designated as "missing values" before you instruct SPSS to run Crosstabs with column percentages.[2] In this case, you should designate "DK" as missing for both **PRAY** and **POSTLIFE**. As we noted in Chapter 9, you can do this by **highlighting the name of the variable** in your Data Editor and then clicking **Data → Define Variable... → Missing Values...**. If you need to check the numeric value of "DK," simply select **Labels...** in the Define Variable window (the value of "DK" is **8** for both PRAY and POSTLIFE). If you need to review the commands for designating variables as missing, see the discussion in Chapter 9 or the SPSS commands listed in the end of that chapter or on-line in E-Appendix F.

Throughout the rest of the book it will be your responsibility to keep in mind which values have been designated as missing and which have not. If you discover that your screens do not match the screens reproduced in the text, it may be because you have forgotten to designate "DK" as a "missing value" for one or more variables.

2. This was not an issue in the first correlation we ran in this chapter (SEX by CHATT) because we know that in coding gender, DK is not an option. Moreover, in the case of CHATT, keep in mind it is based on our recoding of ATTEND, and DK is already designated as a missing value for that variable. Nevertheless, just to be safe, you may have wanted to verify this information by **highlighting the variable name** in your Data Editor and then selecting **Data → Define Variable... → Missing Values...** before running Crosstabs with percentages.

Once you have designated "DK" as a missing value for both variables, you should open the **Crosstabs** window. Now highlight **CHATT** in the **Row(s):** field, and then click on the **left-pointing arrow** to move it back to the list of variables. Now highlight **PRAY** in the list of variables and click on the **arrow** pointing toward the **Row(s):** field. Do the same with **POSTLIFE**, placing it in the **Row(s):** field directly below PRAY.

Leave SEX (our independent variable) in the **Column(s):** field and then execute the command. After you do that, we'll review both of the tables in turn.

PRAY HOW OFTEN DOES R PRAY * SEX RESPONDENTS SEX Crosstabulation

| | | | SEX RESPONDENTS SEX | | Total |
			1 MALE	2 FEMALE	
PRAY HOW OFTEN DOES R PRAY	1 SEVERAL TIMES A DAY	Count	62	121	183
		% within SEX RESPONDENTS SEX	17.8%	30.8%	24.7%
	2 ONCE A DAY	Count	97	135	232
		% within SEX RESPONDENTS SEX	27.8%	34.4%	31.3%
	3 SEVERAL TIMES A WEEK	Count	49	54	103
		% within SEX RESPONDENTS SEX	14.0%	13.7%	13.9%
	4 ONCE A WEEK	Count	31	21	52
		% within SEX RESPONDENTS SEX	8.9%	5.3%	7.0%
	5 LT ONCE A WEEK	Count	99	56	155
		% within SEX RESPONDENTS SEX	28.4%	14.2%	20.9%
	6 NEVER	Count	11	6	17
		% within SEX RESPONDENTS SEX	3.2%	1.5%	2.3%
Total		Count	349	393	742
		% within SEX RESPONDENTS SEX	100.0%	100.0%	100.0%

A quick review of this table indicates that women are more likely than men to report that they pray at least once a day. Combining the first two categories, we calculate 45.6 (17.8 + 27.8) percent for men and 65.2 (30.8 + 34.4) percent for women. Or, we could look at the other end of the table and note that men are more likely to report infrequency of prayer. This table would also seem to confirm the deprivation thesis.

In terms of praying at least daily, the epsilon is 19.6 (65.2 – 45.6) percentage points, pointing to a greater sex difference than we observed in the case of church attendance. Because the epsilon is greater for this table than it was for the previous table (CHATT by SEX), you may conclude that the dependent variable PRAY has a stronger relationship with SEX than does the dependent variable CHATT.

Finally, let's consider beliefs in life after death: the variable POSTLIFE.

POSTLIFE BELIEF IN LIFE AFTER DEATH * SEX RESPONDENTS SEX Crosstabulation

			SEX RESPONDENTS SEX		
			1 MALE	2 FEMALE	Total
POSTLIFE BELIEF IN LIFE AFTER DEATH	1 YES	Count	385	520	905
		% within SEX RESPONDENTS SEX	79.5%	83.2%	81.6%
	2 NO	Count	99	105	204
		% within SEX RESPONDENTS SEX	20.5%	16.8%	18.4%
Total		Count	484	625	1109
		% within SEX RESPONDENTS SEX	100.0%	100.0%	100.0%

The epsilon is smallest in this case (3.7), meaning that both CHATT and PRAY have a stronger relationship with SEX than does POSTLIFE. Nonetheless, women are slightly more likely to say that they believe in life after death than are men.

Each of these bivariate analyses, therefore, has supported the thesis put forth by Glock and his coauthors, suggesting that people who were deprived of gratification in the secular society would be more likely to turn to religion as an alternative source of gratification. More specifically, we have found evidence that supports the thesis with regard to gender differences—that women are still deprived of gratification in American society in comparison with men.

That said, it is important to note that while we have found relationships between the three religiosity variables and gender, we have not necessarily *proven* our theory. For instance, while there seems to be a strong association between PRAY and SEX, this is probably best looked at as *evidence of*, *not proof of*, a causal relationship. Because two variables can be associated without it necessarily being a causal relationship, we need to proceed with care when interpreting our findings.

Demonstration 11.3: Correlating Religiosity and Age

Glock et al. also argue that the United States is a youth-oriented society, with gratification being denied to old people. Whereas some traditional societies tend to revere the elders, this is not the case in the United States. The deprivation thesis, then, would predict that older respondents would be more religious than younger ones. The researchers confirmed this expectation in their 1952 data from Episcopalian church members.

Let's check out the relationship between age and religiosity in 1998. To make the table manageable, we'll use the recoded AGECAT variable created earlier in Chapter 6.[3]

3. Once again, if you did not save the recoded variable AGECAT, simply go back to Chapter 6 and follow the recode commands to create AGECAT before continuing with this chapter. Also, be sure that DK is designated as a missing value for all your variables before running Crosstabs.

So, request a **Crosstab** using:

- **CHATT**, **POSTLIFE**, and **PRAY** (our dependent variables) as **row** variables
- **AGECAT** (our independent variable) as a **column** variable
- **Cells** to be percentaged by **column**

The resulting tables look like this:

CHATT * AGECAT Recoded Age Categories Crosstabulation

			AGECAT Recoded Age Categories				Total
			1 Under 21	2 21-39	3 40-64	4 65 and older	
CHATT	1 About weekly	Count	5	132	215	128	480
		% within AGECAT Recoded Age Categories	11.4%	23.0%	35.5%	51.0%	32.5%
	2 About monthly	Count	12	99	85	34	230
		% within AGECAT Recoded Age Categories	27.3%	17.2%	14.0%	13.5%	15.6%
	3 Seldom	Count	16	221	197	50	484
		% within AGECAT Recoded Age Categories	36.4%	38.4%	32.5%	19.9%	32.8%
	4 Never	Count	11	123	109	39	282
		% within AGECAT Recoded Age Categories	25.0%	21.4%	18.0%	15.5%	19.1%
Total		Count	44	575	606	251	1476
		% within AGECAT Recoded Age Categories	100.0%	100.0%	100.0%	100.0%	100.0%

POSTLIFE BELIEF IN LIFE AFTER DEATH * AGECAT Recoded Age Categories Crosstabulation

			AGECAT Recoded Age Categories				Total
			1 Under 21	2 21-39	3 40-64	4 65 and older	
POSTLIFE BELIEF IN LIFE AFTER DEATH	1 YES	Count	27	354	372	152	905
		% within AGECAT Recoded Age Categories	87.1%	80.6%	81.9%	82.2%	81.6%
	2 NO	Count	4	85	82	33	204
		% within AGECAT Recoded Age Categories	12.9%	19.4%	18.1%	17.8%	18.4%
Total		Count	31	439	454	185	1109
		% within AGECAT Recoded Age Categories	100.0%	100.0%	100.0%	100.0%	100.0%

PRAY HOW OFTEN DOES R PRAY * AGECAT Recoded Age Categories Crosstabulation

			AGECAT Recoded Age Categories				Total
			1 Under 21	2 21-39	3 40-64	4 65 and older	
PRAY HOW OFTEN DOES R PRAY	1 SEVERAL TIMES A DAY	Count	5	55	80	43	183
		% within AGECAT Recoded Age Categories	22.7%	19.2%	26.1%	34.1%	24.7%
	2 ONCE A DAY	Count	5	82	103	42	232
		% within AGECAT Recoded Age Categories	22.7%	28.6%	33.6%	33.3%	31.3%
	3 SEVERAL TIMES A WEEK	Count	4	45	42	12	103
		% within AGECAT Recoded Age Categories	18.2%	15.7%	13.7%	9.5%	13.9%
	4 ONCE A WEEK	Count	2	30	15	5	52
		% within AGECAT Recoded Age Categories	9.1%	10.5%	4.9%	4.0%	7.0%
	5 LT ONCE A WEEK	Count	5	67	63	20	155
		% within AGECAT Recoded Age Categories	22.7%	23.3%	20.5%	15.9%	20.9%
	6 NEVER	Count	1	8	4	4	17
		% within AGECAT Recoded Age Categories	4.5%	2.8%	1.3%	3.2%	2.3%
Total		Count	22	287	307	126	742
		% within AGECAT Recoded Age Categories	100.0%	100.0%	100.0%	100.0%	100.0%

With some slight variations, we can see that older respondents are more likely to report that they attend church and pray regularly than younger respondents. This would tend to support the deprivation thesis in terms of age, at least to some extent. Interestingly, the oldest group—those 65 and older—are just about as likely to believe in life after death as those who are 21 to 64 but less likely to believe in life after death as those under 21, although more than 80 percent do believe in it. You should be aware that some variations like this become more common as the number of groups being compared increases. Looking at the several tables as a whole, however, we find that the general pattern of religiosity increasing with age is supported.

This completes our initial foray into the world of bivariate analysis. We hope you've gotten a good sense of the potential for detective work in social research.

Conclusion

In this chapter, we made a critical logical advance in the analysis of social scientific data. Up to now, we have focused our attention on description. With this examination of religiosity, we've crossed over into explanation. We've moved from asking *what* to asking *why*.

Much of the excitement in social research revolves around discovering why people think and act as they do. You've now had an initial exposure to the logic and computer techniques that make such inquiries possible.

Let's apply your new capabilities to other subject matter. In the next two chapters, we're going to examine, respectively, the sources of different political orientations and why people feel as they do about abortion.

Main Points

- In this chapter we shifted our focus from univariate analysis to bivariate analysis.
- Univariate analysis is the analysis of one variable at a time.
- Bivariate analysis is the analysis of two variables.
- You can think of the differences between univariate and bivariate analysis in terms of the number of variables, major questions, and primary goals.
- We began our bivariate analysis by considering why some people are more religious than others.
- In this analysis we were guided by the social depravation theory of religiosity, first discussed in Chapter 2.
- We used this theory to develop a hypothesis stating that women are more likely to be religious than men.
- This hypothesis contains two variables: gender (independent/cause) and religiosity (dependent variable/effect).
- It is important not to confuse the categories of a variable with the variable itself.
- We tested this hypothesis by running Crosstabs with column percentages.
- When running Crosstabs, it is customary to specify the dependent variable as the row variable and the independent variable as the column variable.

- Throughout the chapter we ran several crosstabs correlating religiosity (as measured by CHATT, PRAY, and POSTLIFE) with gender (as measured by SEX) and then age (as measured by AGECAT).

- Epsilon is a simple statistic used to summarize percentage differences.

- Finding an association between variables is best looked at as evidence of, not proof of, a causal relationship.

Key Terms

Univariate analysis

Bivariate analysis

Dependent variable

Independent variable

Hypothesis

Categories of the variable

Epsilon

SPSS Commands Introduced in This Chapter

11.1:   Running Crosstabs – Specifying the Dependent and Independent Variables

> Click **Analyze** → **Descriptive Statistics** → **Crosstabs...** →
>
> Highlight the name of the **dependent variable(s)** → Click **arrow** pointing to the **Row(s): box** →
>
> Highlight the name of the **independent variable(s)** → Click **arrow** pointing to the **Column(s): box** →
>
> Click **Cells...** → Select **Column** in the Percentages box →
>
> Click **Continue** → **OK**

Review Questions

1. What is univariate analysis?

2. What is bivariate analysis?

3. What are the major differences between univariate and bivariate analysis in terms of the number of variables, major questions, and primary goals?

4. In a hypothesis, the variable is said to "cause" (to some extent) variation in another variable is referred to as what type of variable?

   Identify the independent and dependent variables in the following hypotheses (Questions 5 and 6):

5. Those employed by companies with more than twenty employees are more likely to have some form of managed-choice health care than those employed by companies with fewer employees.

6. In the United States, women are more likely to vote for Democrats than men are.

7. What are the categories of the independent variable in the hypothesis in Question 6?

8. When running Crosstabs, is it customary to specify the dependent variable as the row or column variable?

9. If you were running Crosstabs to test the relationship between the variables in the hypothesis in Question 5, which variable would you specify as the row variable and which would you specify as the column variable?

10. What is epsilon?

11. How is epsilon calculated?

12. Can there be more than one epsilon in a table that has more than two columns?

13. If you run Crosstabs and find a strong relationship between the independent and dependent variable in your hypothesis, are you better off looking at this association as evidence of or proof of a causal relationship?

NAME _____

CLASS _____

INSTRUCTOR _____

DATE _____

To complete the following exercises, you need to load the data file EXER.SAV. You can find answers to Questions 1–8 in Appendix A.

A number of studies have addressed the relationship between race and attitudes toward sex roles. For instance, in a 1992 study Jill Grisby argued that Whites are more likely than Blacks to believe that if a woman works it has a detrimental impact on her children. We are going to test this hypothesis using the variables RACE (as a measure of race) and FECHLD (as a measure of opinions regarding the impact of working women on their children). Simply follow the steps listed below and supply the information requested in the spaces provided (Questions 1–8).

1. Restate the hypothesis linking RACE and FECHLD.

2. Identify the independent and dependent variables in the hypothesis.

3. When running Crosstabs, which variable should you specify as the row variable?

4. Which variable should you specify as the column variable?

5. Now run Crosstabs with column percentages to test the hypothesis (do not forget to specify DK as a missing value for each variable before you begin). When you have produced your table, present your results by filling in the following information:

   A. List the categories of the independent variable in the spaces provided on Line A.

B. List the percentage of respondents who "Strongly agree" and "Agree" with the statement that the fact that a woman works does not hurt children in the spaces provided on Line B (i.e., sum of those who "Strongly agree" + "Agree" on FECHLD).

FECHLD by RACE

LINE A _____ _____ _____
LINE B _____ _____ _____

6. Are the results consistent with your hypothesis as stated in response to Question 1?

7. Compare Blacks and Whites in terms of agreement ("Strongly agree" + "Agree") with the statement that the fact that a woman works does not hurt children and give the percentage difference (epsilon) below.

8. Do your findings show that there is evidence of a causal relationship between RACE and FECHLD? Explain.

Continue to research the causes of differing attitudes toward sex roles by selecting one independent variable and one dependent variable from the following lists:[4]

Independent variables: SEX, EDCAT, AGE [select one][5]
Dependent variables: FEFAM, FEHELP, FEPRESCH [select one]

As before, run Crosstabs *with column percentages to test your hypothesis and then fill in the information requested in the spaces provided (Questions 9–13).*

9. State and explain your hypothesis involving the [one] independent variable and [one] dependent variable you chose from the list above.

---

4. You can access a list of references to papers, articles, and books dealing with attitudes toward sex roles by visiting the General Social Survey Data and Information Retrieval System (GSSDIRS) at http://www.icpsr.umich.edu/GSS99/. Once you access the web site, one option is to search for the codebook variable FEHELP (or another "sex role" variable) and then consult the section subtitled "Bibliography."

5. We recoded EDUC to create the new variable EDCAT in the exercises at the end of Chapter 6 (SPSS Lab Exercise 6.1). If you did not save the variable EDCAT, you will need to recode EDUC in order to make the table more manageable.

NAME _____

CLASS _____

INSTRUCTOR _____

DATE _____

10. Run Crosstabs with column percentages to test your hypothesis. Remember to designate DK as a missing value for both your variables. In addition, if you chose AGE as your independent variable, you may need to recode it and create a new variable to make your table more manageable.

   Once you have produced your table, present your results by filling in the following information:

   A. List the abbreviated variable names of your independent and dependent variables on Line A.

   B. List the categories of the independent variable in the spaces provided on Line B (use only as many blank spaces as necessary).

   C. List the percentage of respondents who "Strongly agree" and "Agree" for either FEFAM, FEHELP, or FEPRESCH on Line C (i.e., sum of those who "Strongly agree" + "Agree" for the variable you have chosen); use only as many blank spaces as necessary.

   LINE A _____ by _____
                       [Dependent Variable]   [Independent Variable]

   LINE B _____ _____ _____ _____ _____ _____

   LINE C _____ _____ _____ _____ _____ _____

11. Are these results consistent with your hypothesis as stated in response to Question 9?

12. Compute epsilon.

13. Do your findings show that there is evidence of a causal relationship between your independent and dependent variables? Explain.

Chapter 12   **Political Orientations as Cause and as Effect**

In looking for the sources of religiosity, we worked with a coherent theory. As we noted in Chapter 2, this process is called ***deduction***, and it is usually the preferred approach to data analysis. Sometimes, however, it's appropriate to take a less structured route beginning with data and then proceeding to theory. As you may recall, this process is known as ***induction***. As we turn our attention to politics in this chapter, we're going to be more inductive than deductive so that you can become familiar with this approach as well.

In Chapter 7, we examined two GSS variables: POLVIEWS and PARTYID. In the analyses to follow, we'll begin by looking at the relationship between these two variables. You can do that now that you understand the **Crosstabs** command. Next, we'll explore some of the variables that cause differences in political philosophies and party identification, such as age, religion, gender, race, education, class, and marital status. Finally, we'll look at POLVIEWS and PARTYID as independent variables to determine what impact they have on other variables.

Demonstration 12.1: The Relationship Between POLVIEWS and PARTYID

Let's begin with the recoded forms of our two key political variables, POLVIEWS and PARTYID. You may recall that when we recoded these items in Chapter 7, we named them POLREC and PARTY, respectively.[1]

As we indicated earlier, there is a consensus that Democrats are more liberal than Republicans and that Republicans are more conservative than Democrats, although everyone recognizes the existence of liberal Republicans and conservative Democrats.

The GSS data allow us to see what the relationship between these two variables actually is. Because neither is logically prior to the other, we could treat either as the independent variable. For our present purposes, it is probably use-

---

1. If you did not save these recoded variables (PARTY and POLREC), simply go back to Chapter 7 and follow the recode instructions before moving ahead with the demonstrations in this chapter.

ful to explore both possibilities: (a) political philosophy causes party identification (political philosophy as the independent variable), and (b) party identification causes political philosophy (party identification as the independent variable).

POLREC by PARTY

To begin, then, let's see if Democrats are more liberal or more conservative than Republicans.[2] To check this out, you will want to run the **Crosstab** procedure specifying:

- **POLREC** as the **row** variable
- **PARTY** as the **column** variable
- **Cells** to be percentaged by **Column**

POLREC Recoded polviews * PARTY Recoded party ID Crosstabulation

			PARTY Recoded party ID				
			1 Democrat	2 Independent	3 Republican	4 Other	Total
POLREC Recoded polviews	1 Liberal	Count	191	145	41	10	387
		% within PARTY Recoded party ID	41.5%	26.5%	10.6%	32.3%	27.2%
	2 Moderate	Count	184	239	103	10	536
		% within PARTY Recoded party ID	40.0%	43.6%	26.8%	32.3%	37.6%
	3 Conservative	Count	85	164	241	11	501
		% within PARTY Recoded party ID	18.5%	29.9%	62.6%	35.5%	35.2%
Total		Count	460	548	385	31	1424
		% within PARTY Recoded party ID	100.0%	100.0%	100.0%	100.0%	100.0%

The data in this table confirm the general expectation. Of the Democrats in the GSS sample, 42 percent describe themselves as liberals in contrast to 11 percent of the Republicans. The Independents fall halfway between the two parties, with 27 percent saying they are liberals. The relationship can also be seen by reading across the bottom row of percentages: 19 percent of the Democrats, versus 63 percent of the Republicans, call themselves conservatives.

PARTY by POLREC

We can also turn the table around logically and ask whether liberals or conservatives are more likely to identify with the Democratic party (or which are more likely to say they are Republicans). You can get this table by simply reversing the location of the two variable names in the earlier command. Run the **Crosstab** procedure again, only this time make **PARTY** the **row** variable and **POLREC** the **column** variable. Here's what you'll get:

2. Keep in mind that "Don't knows" should be defined as missing values for all the variables used in this chapter.

PARTY Recoded party ID * POLREC Recoded polviews Crosstabulation

			POLREC Recoded polviews			
			1 Liberal	2 Moderate	3 Conserva tive	Total
PARTY Recoded party ID	1 Democrat	Count	191	184	85	460
		% within POLREC Recoded polviews	49.4%	34.3%	17.0%	32.3%
	2 Independent	Count	145	239	164	548
		% within POLREC Recoded polviews	37.5%	44.6%	32.7%	38.5%
	3 Republican	Count	41	103	241	385
		% within POLREC Recoded polviews	10.6%	19.2%	48.1%	27.0%
	4 Other	Count	10	10	11	31
		% within POLREC Recoded polviews	2.6%	1.9%	2.2%	2.2%
Total		Count	387	536	501	1424
		% within POLREC Recoded polviews	100.0%	100.0%	100.0%	100.0%

Again, the relationship between the two variables is evident. Liberals are more likely (49 percent) to say they are Democrats than are moderates (34 percent are Democrats) or conservatives (only 17 percent are Democrats).

Now, why don't you state the relationship between these two variables in terms of the likelihood that they will support the Republican party? Either way of stating the relationship is appropriate.

In summary, then, there is an affinity between liberalism and the Democrats and between conservatism and the Republicans. At the same time, it is not a perfect relationship, and you can find plenty of liberal Republicans and conservative Democrats in the tables.

Now, let's switch gears and see if we can begin to explain *why* people are liberals or conservatives, Democrats or Republicans. Whereas in the last chapter when we began our discussion of bivariate analyses we examined why some people are more religious than others, in this chapter we are going to ask similar questions regarding political orientation and party identification: *Why* are some people more liberal (or conservative) than others? *Why* do some people identify themselves as Democrats, while others identify themselves as Republicans, Independents, or "Other"? What *causes* people to be liberals or conservatives, Democrats or Republicans?

Demonstration 12.2: Age and Politics

Often the search for causal variables involves the examination of *demographic* (or background) *variables*, such as: age, religion, sex, race, education, class, and marital status. Such variables often have a powerful impact on attitudes and behaviors. Let's begin with age.

There is a common belief that young people are more liberal than old people—that people get more conservative as they get older. As you can imagine, liberals tend to see this as a trend toward stodginess, whereas conservatives tend to explain it as a matter of increased wisdom. Regardless of the explanation you might prefer, let's see if it's even true that old people are more conservative than young people.

POLREC by AGECAT

To find out, run a **Crosstab**. In this case, age (as measured by AGECAT) would be the independent variable and political views (as measured by POLREC) would be the dependent variable.[3] Consequently, you should specify **POLREC** as the **row** variable and **AGECAT** as the **column** variable. Here's what you should get:

POLREC Recoded polviews * AGECAT Recoded Age Categories Crosstabulation

			AGECAT Recoded Age Categories				
			1 Under 21	2 21-39	3 40-64	4 65 and older	Total
POLREC Recoded polviews	1 Liberal	Count	14	174	152	49	389
		% within AGECAT Recoded Age Categories	34.1%	31.1%	25.9%	20.5%	27.3%
	2 Moderate	Count	12	211	221	93	537
		% within AGECAT Recoded Age Categories	29.3%	37.7%	37.6%	38.9%	37.6%
	3 Conservative	Count	15	175	214	97	501
		% within AGECAT Recoded Age Categories	36.6%	31.3%	36.5%	40.6%	35.1%
Total		Count	41	560	587	239	1427
		% within AGECAT Recoded Age Categories	100.0%	100.0%	100.0%	100.0%	100.0%

Which of the following statements is a more accurate interpretation of the table above?

Older age groups appear to be more conservative than younger age groups.

Older age groups appear to be more liberal than younger age groups.

If you chose the first answer, you have just won the right to continue with the analysis. (Oh, never mind—you can continue even if you got it wrong.) Notice, however, that the strength of the relationship is not terribly strong.

PARTY by AGECAT

What would you expect to find in terms of political party identification (as measured by PARTY)? If that relationship corresponds to the one we've just examined, we'd expect to find growing strength for Republicans as people grow older. Young people should be more likely to identify themselves as Democrats. Here's an opportunity to test common sense. Why don't you try it yourself and see what you get? And then compare your table to the following one.

---

3. We recoded AGE to create a new variable AGECAT in Chapter 6. We then used this variable again in Chapter 11. If you did not save this recode, go back to Chapter 6 and follow the recode instructions before moving ahead.

PARTY Recoded party ID * AGECAT Recoded Age Categories Crosstabulation

			AGECAT Recoded Age Categories				
			1 Under 21	2 21-39	3 40-64	4 65 and older	Total
PARTY Recoded party ID	1 Democrat	Count	5	173	199	103	480
		% within AGECAT Recoded Age Categories	11.4%	29.6%	32.5%	40.6%	32.1%
	2 Independent	Count	28	254	240	69	591
		% within AGECAT Recoded Age Categories	63.6%	43.4%	39.2%	27.2%	39.5%
	3 Republican	Count	10	140	163	80	393
		% within AGECAT Recoded Age Categories	22.7%	23.9%	26.6%	31.5%	26.3%
	4 Other	Count	1	18	10	2	31
		% within AGECAT Recoded Age Categories	2.3%	3.1%	1.6%	.8%	2.1%
Total		Count	44	585	612	254	1495
		% within AGECAT Recoded Age Categories	100.0%	100.0%	100.0%	100.0%	100.0%

Interpreting Your Table: The Relationship Between Age and Party Identification

How would you interpret this table? What's the relationship between age and party identification? See if you can interpret this table yourself before moving on.

As you can see, the relationship between AGECAT and PARTY is not as clear as the relationship between AGECAT and POLREC.

In fact, as you probably noticed, the first row of percentages goes directly contrary to our expectations: Older people are substantially more likely to call themselves Democrats than are young people. When we examine the Republicans, however, we discover virtually the same thing, although it is not as clear. How can this be?

One explanation may be found among those identifying themselves as Independents. This identification is much more common among the young than it is among the old. The clearest relationship in this table is that the likelihood of identifying with *some* political party increases dramatically with age in the table, but there is no clear tendency for that identification to favor one party over another.

Realize that the observed pattern is amenable to more than one explanation. It could be that people become more likely to identify with the major parties as they grow older. On the other hand, the relationship might reflect a *trend* phenomenon: a disenchantment with the major parties in recent years, primarily among young people. To test these competing explanations, you would need to analyze ***longitudinal data***, those representing the state of affairs at different points in time. Because the GSS has been conducting surveys since 1972, we have such data extending back more than a quarter century.

Demonstration 12.3: Religion and Politics

In the United States, the relationship between religion and politics is somewhat complex, especially with regard to Roman Catholics. Let's begin with political philosophies. We will ask SPSS to run Crosstabs connecting RELIG with POLREC.

Defining Missing Values: Range Plus One...

Before we run Crosstabs, however, we need to recode our measure of religious preference (RELIG) to make it more manageable. You may recall from our discussion in Chapter 6 that RELIG contains 16 categories. Because we are primarily interested in the 4 largest categories (Protestant, Catholic, Jewish, Agnostics/Atheists) as opposed to the smaller categories labeled "Other" (Mormon, Buddhist, Moslem), we want to instruct SPSS to define the latter as "Missing."

You can review the labels and values for this item by highlighting **RELIG** in the Data Editor, opening the **Define Variable...** box, and clicking **Labels...** (or by looking in the list of variables at the end of Chapter 4). Do that now and you will see that we want to define the values 0, 5–13, 98, and 99 as missing.

To do this, highlight **RELIG** in the Data Editor, go back to the **Define Variable...** box, and select **Missing Values....** This time, however, instead of selecting Discrete missing values, click the **button** next to **Range plus one discrete missing value**. This option allows us to designate a range of numeric values, plus one additional value, as missing. In this case we want to list the range of values as **5** through **99** and the discrete value as **0**. Now click **Continue** and **OK** to return to the Data Editor.

Keep in mind that while we are designating these categories as missing for our present purposes, we can easily go back and change this if we want to include them in future analyses.

SPSS COMMAND 12.1: Defining Missing Values Using "Range plus one..."

> Click **Data** → **Define Variable...** → **Missing Values...** →
> Select **"Range plus one discrete missing value"** →
> Type in the appropriate range of values and one discrete missing
>   value →
> Click **Continue** → **OK**

POLREC by RELIG

Once you have returned to the Data Editor you will be ready to run your **Crosstabs** connecting **RELIG** (independent/**column** variable) and **POLREC** (dependent/**row** variable).

As we see in the table, Jews are the most likely to identify themselves with the Democratic party. While Protestants are slightly more likely to identify themselves as Democrats than are Catholics, there is not a meaningful difference between the two groups in this regard.

If you are interested in these two variables, you might want to explore the relationship between politics and the other religious variables we've examined: POSTLIFE and PRAY.

On the other hand, you could look for other consequences of RELIG. What else do you suppose might be affected by differences of religious affiliation?

Demonstration 12.4: Gender and Politics

Gender is a demographic variable associated with a great many attitudes and behaviors. Take a minute to think about the reasons women might be more liberal or more conservative than men. Once you've formed an expectation in this regard, why don't you use SPSS to look for the actual relationship?

PARTY Recoded party ID * RELIG RS RELIGIOUS PREFERENCE Crosstabulation

| | | | RELIG RS RELIGIOUS PREFERENCE | | | | |
			1 Protestant	2 Catholic	3 Jewish	4 None	Total
PARTY Recoded party ID	1 Democrat	Count	257	122	13	62	454
		% within RELIG RS RELIGIOUS PREFERENCE	33.0%	30.8%	48.1%	30.2%	32.3%
	2 Independent	Count	263	178	10	98	549
		% within RELIG RS RELIGIOUS PREFERENCE	33.8%	44.9%	37.0%	47.8%	39.0%
	3 Republican	Count	247	91	4	37	379
		% within RELIG RS RELIGIOUS PREFERENCE	31.7%	23.0%	14.8%	18.0%	26.9%
	4 Other	Count	12	5		8	25
		% within RELIG RS RELIGIOUS PREFERENCE	1.5%	1.3%		3.9%	1.8%
Total		Count	779	396	27	205	1407
		% within RELIG RS RELIGIOUS PREFERENCE	100.0%	100.0%	100.0%	100.0%	100.0%

As you can see, there is no apparent relationship between gender and political philosophy, although slightly more women are more likely to identify with the Democratic party (36 percent) than are men (28 percent). This latter relationship may reflect the fact that the Democratic party has been more explicit in its support for women's issues in recent years than has the Republican party. Still, the relationship is not a particularly strong one.

Demonstration 12.5: Race and Politics

Given our brief discussion above about politics and ethnic minority groups such as Jews and Roman Catholics, what relationship do you expect to find between politics and race? The variable available to you for analysis (RACE) codes only "White," "Black," and "Other," so it's not possible to examine this relationship in great depth, but you should be able to make some educated guesses about how Caucasians and African-Americans might differ politically.

POLREC by RACE

After you've thought about the likely relationship between race and politics, why don't you run the tables and test your ability to predict such matters?

Recoded polviews * RACE OF RESPONDENT Crosstabulation

			RACE OF RESPONDENT			Total
			WHITE	BLACK	OTHER	
Recoded polviews	Liberal	Count	303	48	38	389
		% within RACE OF RESPONDENT	27.0%	24.4%	35.8%	27.3%
	Moderate	Count	405	94	38	537
		% within RACE OF RESPONDENT	36.0%	47.7%	35.8%	37.6%
	Conservative	Count	416	55	30	501
		% within RACE OF RESPONDENT	37.0%	27.9%	28.3%	35.1%
Total		Count	1124	197	106	1427
		% within RACE OF RESPONDENT	100.0%	100.0%	100.0%	100.0%

The first table shows that Whites are somewhat more conservative (37 percent) than African-Americans (28 percent). Interestingly, both groups are about equally liberal (although Whites are just slightly more liberal than African-Americans). This can be explained by the fact that African-Americans identify themselves as somewhat more moderate (48 percent) than Whites (36 percent).

PARTY by RACE

Recoded party ID * RACE OF RESPONDENT Crosstabulation

			RACE OF RESPONDENT			Total
			WHITE	BLACK	OTHER	
Recoded party ID	Democrat	Count	317	130	33	480
		% within RACE OF RESPONDENT	27.0%	61.9%	29.5%	32.1%
	Independent	Count	465	63	63	591
		% within RACE OF RESPONDENT	39.6%	30.0%	56.3%	39.5%
	Republican	Count	368	15	10	393
		% within RACE OF RESPONDENT	31.4%	7.1%	8.9%	26.3%
	Other	Count	23	2	6	31
		% within RACE OF RESPONDENT	2.0%	1.0%	5.4%	2.1%
Total		Count	1173	210	112	1495
		% within RACE OF RESPONDENT	100.0%	100.0%	100.0%	100.0%

While the correlation between political views and race may not have been as pronounced as you might have expected, the relationship between race and political party identification is very strong, reflecting the Democratic party's orientation toward minority groups.

Demonstration 12.6: Education and Politics

Education, a common component of social class, is likely to be of interest to you, especially if you are currently a college student. From your own experience, what would you expect to be the relationship between education and political philosophy?

Before we test the relationship between these variables, we need to **Recode** our measure of education (**EDUC**) to make it more manageable. We will create a new variable called **EDCAT**. You may recall that we already recoded EDUC on our EXER.SAV file in the exercises at the end of Chapter 6. We need to recode it once again in a similar manner and this time save it on our DEMO.SAV file:

Old Values	New Values	Labels
Lowest through 11 →	1	Less than high school
12 →	2	High school graduate
13 through 15 →	3	Some college
16 →	4	College graduate
17 through 20 →	5	Graduate studies (beyond college)

If you need to review the instructions for recoding, see the SPSS Commands listed at the end of Chapter 6 or on-line in E-Appendix F.

Once you have successfully recoded and **labeled** EDCAT, check your results by running **Frequencies** on the new variable. Your table should look like the one below:

EDCAT

		Frequency	Percent	Valid Percent	Cumulativ e Percent
Valid	Less than high school	255	17.0	17.1	17.1
	High school graduate	468	31.2	31.4	48.5
	Some college	385	25.7	25.8	74.3
	College graduate	213	14.2	14.3	88.5
	Graduate studies	171	11.4	11.5	100.0
	Total	1492	99.5	100.0	
Missing	System	8	.5		
Total		1500	100.0		

POLREC by EDCAT

Now we are ready to run the **Crosstabs** for **EDCAT** (independent/**column** variable) and **POLREC** (dependent/**row** variable), so you can find out whether your expectations regarding the relationship between these variables are accurate.

POLREC Recoded polviews * EDCAT Crosstabulation

| | | | EDCAT | | | | | |
			1 Less than high school	2 High school graduate	3 Some college	4 College graduate	5 Graduate studies	Total
POLREC Recoded polviews	1 Liberal	Count	55	91	123	58	61	388
		% within EDCAT	23.6%	20.8%	32.5%	28.4%	36.1%	27.3%
	2 Moderate	Count	95	197	128	67	48	535
		% within EDCAT	40.8%	45.1%	33.9%	32.8%	28.4%	37.6%
	3 Conservative	Count	83	149	127	79	60	498
		% within EDCAT	35.6%	34.1%	33.6%	38.7%	35.5%	35.0%
Total		Count	233	437	378	204	169	1421
		% within EDCAT	100.0%	100.0%	100.0%	100.0%	100.0%	100.0%

As you can see, while liberalism seems to increase slightly with education, this does not mean that conservatism declines with increasing education. Instead, the rise in liberalism is accounted for by a decline in the number of moderates as education increases.

PARTY by EDCAT

But how about political party? You decide how to structure your Crosstab instruction to obtain the following table.

Recoded party ID * EDCAT Crosstabulation

| | | | EDCAT | | | | | |
			Less than high school	High school graduate	Some college	College graduate	Graduate studies	Total
Recoded party ID	Democrat	Count	94	149	126	60	48	477
		% within EDCAT	37.0%	32.0%	32.8%	28.2%	28.2%	32.1%
	Independent	Count	110	196	140	83	58	587
		% within EDCAT	43.3%	42.1%	36.5%	39.0%	34.1%	39.5%
	Republican	Count	44	115	108	65	60	392
		% within EDCAT	17.3%	24.7%	28.1%	30.5%	35.3%	26.4%
	Other	Count	6	6	10	5	4	31
		% within EDCAT	2.4%	1.3%	2.6%	2.3%	2.4%	2.1%
Total		Count	254	466	384	213	170	1487
		% within EDCAT	100.0%	100.0%	100.0%	100.0%	100.0%	100.0%

The relationship here is fairly consistent, but it is possibly in the opposite direction from what you expected. We've seen throughout these analyses that the association of liberalism with the Democratic party is hardly a perfect one, and these latest two tables point that out very clearly.

Whereas liberalism increases somewhat with rising educational levels, Democratic party identification decreases for all educational categories. Why do you suppose that would be the case? Think about this, and we'll return to this issue in Chapter 18, when you have the ability to analyze multivariate tables.

Some Surprises—Class, Marital Status, and Politics

Sometimes the inductive method of analysis produces some surprises. As an example, you might take a look at the relationship between our political variables and the demographic variables CLASS and MARITAL.

Social Class

You might expect that social class is related to political philosophy and party identification because the Democratic party has traditionally been strong among the working class, whereas the well-to-do have seemed more comfortable as Republicans. If you are so inclined, why don't you check to see if this relationship still holds true in the late 1990s? You can use the variable CLASS, which is a measure of subjective social class, asking respondents how they view themselves in this regard.

After you have done that, try to interpret your tables in much the same way we did with the tables above. What do your tables show? Is there a relationship between subjective social class and political philosophy or party identification? Are the results consistent with your expectations or are they surprising in some way?

Marital Status

In addition, you may also want to take a look at the relationship between marital status and political orientations. If even the suggestion that there is a relationship between marital status and political orientations sounds far-fetched to you, the results of this analysis may be surprising.

Once you've run the tables, try to interpret them and think of any good reasons for the observed differences. Here's a clue: Try to think of other variables that might account for the patterns you've observed. Then, in Chapter 18, when we engage in multivariate analysis, you'll have a chance to check out some of your explanations.

The Impact of Party and Political Philosophy

Let's shift gears now and consider politics as an independent variable. What impact do you suppose political philosophy and/or political party might have in determining people's attitudes on some of the political issues we looked at earlier?

Ask yourself where liberals and conservatives would stand on the following issues. Then run the tables to find out if your hunches are correct.

GUNLAW   registration of firearms
CAPPUN   capital punishment

Remember, when POLREC is the independent variable, you need to alter its location in the Crosstabs command, making it the column variable.

Once you've examined the relationship between political philosophies and these more specific political issues, consider the impact of political party. In forming your expectations in this latter regard, you might want to review recent political platforms of the two major parties or the speeches of political candidates from the two parties. Then see if the political party identification of the American public falls along those same lines.

Conclusion

We hope this chapter has given you a good look at the excitement possible in the detective work called social science research. We're willing to bet that some of the results you've uncovered in this chapter pretty much squared with your understanding of American politics, whereas other findings came as a surprise.

The skills you are learning in this book, along with your access to SPSS and the GSS data, make it possible for you to conduct your own investigations into the nature of American politics and other issues that may interest you. In the chapter that follows, we're going to return to our examination of attitudes toward abortion. This time, we want to learn what causes differences in attitudes on this hotly controversial topic.

Main Points

- While in the last chapter we began with a theory of religiosity, in this chapter we took a more inductive approach.

- We examined the causes (and effects) of political orientations by focusing primarily on the recoded forms of our two main political variables: POLVIEWS and PARTYID.

- After looking at the relationship between these two variables in their recoded form (POLREC and PARTY), we concluded that there is an affinity between liberalism and Democrats and conservatism and Republicans, although it is by no means a perfect relationship.

- We then resumed our focus on bivariate analyses by examining what causes some people to be liberals or conservatives, Democrats or Republicans.

- In searching for causal variables, we focused primarily on demographic items such as age, religion, gender, race, education, class, and marital status.

- In some cases our results did not match our expectations.

- The bulk of the chapter was devoted to explaining what causes people to hold various political views or to identify with one political party or another. In these analyses we identified POLREC and PARTY as dependent variables.

- It is also possible to look at political views and party identification as independent variables to see what role they might have in determining people's attitudes on political issues such as gun control and capital punishment.

Key Terms

Deduction   Demographic variables
Induction   Longitudinal data

SPSS Commands Introduced in this Chapter

12.1:   Defining Missing Values Using "Range plus one…"

> Click **Data** → **Define Variable…** → **Missing Values…** →
> Select **"Range plus one discrete missing value"** →
> Type in the appropriate range of values and one discrete missing
>   value →
> Click **Continue** → **OK**

Review Questions

1. What is the difference between deductive and inductive data analysis?

2. Which approach did we use in Chapter 11 to examine religiosity?

3. Which approach did we use to examine political orientations in this chapter (Chapter 12)?

4. What did we find when we crosstabulated POLREC and PARTY?

5. Do our findings suggest that all conservatives are Republican and all liberals are Democrats?

6. Name three demographic variables in either your DEMO.SAV or EXER.SAV files.

7. Is the variable CAPPUN a demographic variable? How about INCOME98?

8. Our findings show that older age groups appear to be slightly more conservative than younger age groups. Does this mean that older age groups are more likely than younger age groups to identify themselves as Republicans?

9. Of the three religious categories we examined, which is the most liberal? Which is the most conservative?

10. Summarize the relationship between gender and our political variables.

11. There is a very strong relationship between race and party identification, with 62 percent of African-Americans identifying themselves as Democrats, compared to 27 percent of Whites. Can we conclude from this that there is an equally strong relationship between race and political views?

12. Why do you suppose Democratic party identification decreases with rising educational levels?

13. Summarize the relationship between marital status and our political orientations. How can we explain these results?

14. Does either political philosophy or party identification determine attitudes about issues such as gun control or capital punishment?

NAME _____

CLASS _____

INSTRUCTOR _____

DATE _____

To complete the following exercises you need to load the data file EXER.SAV. You can find answers to Questions 1–2 in Appendix A.

In Questions 1–7 we are going to examine what causes some people to feel that the national government is spending too little on improving and protecting Americans' health. As you move through the exercises, remember to designate DK as missing for all relevant variables.

1. Run Crosstabs with NATHEAL as your dependent variable, HEALTH as your independent variable, and cells to be percentaged by column. After you run Crosstabs, print your output.

   Then on Line A below write the names of the categories of HEALTH using as many spaces as necessary. On Line B, fill in the spaces noting the percentage who answered "Too little" on NATHEAL for each category of HEALTH.

   NATHEAL by HEALTH

   Line A _____ _____ _____ _____ _____

   Line B _____ _____ _____ _____ _____

2. Do the column percentages in the summary table above change, suggesting that there is a relationship between the variables?

3. Choose one demographic variable from your data file EXER.SAV and state your expectations regarding the relationship between that variable (as the independent variable) and NATHEAL (as the dependent variable). (Depending on which variable you chose, you may need to recode it to make it more manageable).

4. Was it necessary for you to recode the demographic variable you chose as your independent variable? If so, explain how you recoded the variable by listing the name of the variable you recoded, the name of the new (recoded) variable, the old value labels, and the new value labels.

5. Run Crosstabs with NATHEAL as your dependent variable and the variable you chose as the independent variable and print your table. Then on Line A below write the name of your independent variable. On Line B write the names of the categories of your independent variable using as many spaces as necessary. On Line C, fill in the spaces noting the percentage who answered "Too little" on NATHEAL for each category of the independent variable.

   Line A NATHEAL by _____

   Line B _____ _____ _____ _____ _____

   Line C _____ _____ _____ _____ _____

6. Do the column percentages in the summary table you created above change, suggesting that there is a relationship between the variables?

7. Summarize and explain your findings below. You may want to note, for instance, whether the findings match your expectations and whether you were surprised by the findings.

8. Choose one of the following variables as your dependent variable: NATE-DUC, NATRACE, or NATFARE and note the name of the variable you chose and what it measures below.

9. Now choose a second variable from your data set as your independent variable. Note the name of the variable and what it measures below. If it is necessary to recode your variable, note how you did that below.

10. What are your expectations regarding the relationship between your independent and dependent variables?

11. Run Crosstabs and print your table. Then summarize and explain your findings below. You may want to note, for instance, whether there is a relationship between your independent and dependent variables? Do the findings match your expectations? Were you at all surprised by the results? If so, why? If not, why not?

Chapter 13   What Causes Different Attitudes Toward Abortion?

One of the most controversial issues of recent years has concerned whether a woman has the right to have an abortion. Partisans on both sides of this issue are often extremely vocal and demonstrative.

As we saw in Chapter 8, there appear to be three main positions on this issue among the GSS respondents in 1998. Just under 40 percent support a woman's right to have an abortion for any reason, whereas 15 percent oppose abortion under all circumstances, and the rest are opposed to unrestricted abortions but are willing to make exceptions when pregnancy results from rape or when it risks the mother's health or is likely to result in serious birth defects.

In this chapter, we're going to use your new analytic skills to begin exploring the causes of these different points of view on abortion. Why are some people permissive and others not? As we pursue this question, we can profit from an excellent review of the research on abortion attitudes: Cook, Jelen, and Wilcox's *Between Two Absolutes: Public Opinion and the Politics of Abortion* (1992). Chapter 2 from that book is reprinted on-line in E-Appendix G to serve as background for the analyses we'll undertake in this chapter and to suggest additional directions of analysis if you would like to pursue this topic beyond these first steps.

Demonstration 13.1: Gender and Abortion

As you think about possible causes of different attitudes about abortion, the first one that probably comes to mind is gender, given that abortion affects women more directly than it does men. In a quote that has become a popular pro-choice bumper sticker, Florynce Kennedy put it this way several years ago: "If men could get pregnant, abortion would be a sacrament." There is reason to believe, therefore, that women would be more supportive of abortion than men. Let's see.

Here is a table that summarizes attitudes toward abortion by gender. It is *not* SPSS output, but we've *created it* from several SPSS tables. Your task is to figure out how to get the SPSS tables that would allow you to create this table.[1]

---

1. If you are having trouble figuring out how to access the information used to create the table on page 212, don't worry, the commands are as follows: Run **Crosstabs** for the **seven abortion variables** (**row** variables) and **SEX** (**column** variable), **cells** to be percentaged by **column**. You should get seven crosstabs that can be used to create the table (i.e., the percent of men and women who responded "Yes" to each item). Make sure you are clear as to how we created this table because we will be asking you to create and interpret similar tables involving different items later in the chapter.

Percentage Approving of Abortion under the Following Conditions

		Men	Women
ABHLTH	woman's health endangered	90	88
ABDEFECT	serious defect likely	81	79
ABRAPE	resulted from rape	82	77
ABPOOR	too poor for more children	44	44
ABSINGLE	woman is unmarried	43	41
ABNOMORE	family wants no more	42	41
ABANY	for any reason	41	39

Contrary to what we expected, women are not more supportive of abortion than men. Actually, men are consistently a little more supportive, representing a difference of from one to two percentage points on several items and even more in the case of ABRAPE.

We used the individual items concerning abortion for this analysis because it was possible that men and women would differ on some items but not on others. For example, we might have expected women to be more supportive on the item concerning the woman's health, but this was not the case.

As an alternative strategy for examining the sources of attitudes toward abortion, let's make use of the index, **ABORT**, that we created in Chapter 9, combining responses to ABDEFECT and ABSINGLE.

Based on the summary table above, we would certainly expect little difference between women and men in their index scores. And our modified expectations are more accurate, as you'll discover when you create the following table.

Simple Abortion Index * RESPONDENTS SEX Crosstabulation

			RESPONDENTS SEX		Total
			1 MALE	2 FEMALE	
Simple Abortion Index	0 yes/approve	Count	169	213	382
		% within RESPONDENTS SEX	44.1%	41.9%	42.9%
	1 conditional support	Count	137	186	323
		% within RESPONDENTS SEX	35.8%	36.6%	36.3%
	2 no/disapprove	Count	77	109	186
		% within RESPONDENTS SEX	20.1%	21.5%	20.9%
Total		Count	383	508	891
		% within RESPONDENTS SEX	100.0%	100.0%	100.0%

Recall that a score of 0 on the index represents those who supported a woman's right to have an abortion in both circumstances: if there was a chance of a birth defect and if she was single. Overall, 43 percent of the sample took that position. This table indicates little difference between men and women, with men slightly *more likely* (44 percent) to score 0 on the index than women (42 percent).

So far, then, we have learned that gender is not the explanation for differences in attitudes toward abortion. Let's see if age has an impact.

Demonstration 13.2: Age and Abortion

As Cook and her colleagues (1992) point out, abortion is somewhat more relevant to young people because they are more likely to experience unwanted pregnancies than are older people. What would that lead you to expect in the way of a relationship between age and support for abortion? Think about that, and then use SPSS to run the tables that answer the question for you.

Recall that we recoded AGE into AGECAT in Chapter 6. We'll want to use **AGECAT** for our examination of the relationship between age and abortion attitudes.

Now you can request the SPSS tables that relate age to abortion attitudes. Here's a summary of the tables you should have created.

Percentage Approving of Abortion
under the Following Conditions

		Under 21	21–39	40–64	Over 64
ABHLTH	woman's health endangered	96	90	88	84
ABDEFECT	serious defect likely	80	80	78	82
ABRAPE	resulted from rape	80	82	76	81
ABPOOR	too poor for more children	60	48	42	37
ABSINGLE	woman is unmarried	32	44	41	40
ABNOMORE	family wants no more	42	45	40	36
ABANY	for any reason	33	43	39	34

Take a minute to look over the data presented in this summary table. How do the analytic results square with your expectations?

These data suggest that younger people are more likely than older people to support abortion if a woman's health is at risk, although there is a great deal of support for abortion in this situation across all age groups. Interestingly, those under 21 are almost twice as likely as those 65 and older to support abortion if the woman is too poor to have any more children. However, there is little or no relationship between age and the other abortion items.

Now let's run **Crosstabs** using our **ABORT** index and **AGECAT** to see what we find.

Simple Abortion Index * Recoded Age Categories Crosstabulation

| | | | \multicolumn{4}{c|}{Recoded Age Categories} | |
			1 Under 21	2 21-39	3 40-64	4 65 and older	Total
Simple Abortion Index	0 yes/approve	Count	8	157	158	59	382
		% within Recoded Age Categories	32.0%	46.0%	41.6%	40.7%	42.9%
	1 conditional support	Count	12	115	138	58	323
		% within Recoded Age Categories	48.0%	33.7%	36.3%	40.0%	36.3%
	2 no/disapprove	Count	5	69	84	28	186
		% within Recoded Age Categories	20.0%	20.2%	22.1%	19.3%	20.9%
Total		Count	25	341	380	145	891
		% within Recoded Age Categories	100.0%	100.0%	100.0%	100.0%	100.0%

This table indicates that there is no relationship between age and abortion as measured by our ABORT index. Based on the analyses above then, we could say that there is not convincing evidence of a strong relationship between age and abortion attitudes. Or, perhaps it is just more complex than we have been allowing for in these analyses. We'll find out once we are able to undertake multivariate analysis in Part V.

Demonstration 13.3: Religion and Abortion

If we began this analysis by asking you what variable you thought might account for attitudes toward abortion, there is a good chance that you would have guessed religion, given the unconditional and public opposition of the Roman Catholic church. Your growing facility with SPSS and the GSS data make it possible for you to test that expectation.

Let's start with the possible impact of religious affiliation. Here's a summary of what you should discover if you run the **several abortion items** by **RELIG**.[2]

Percentage Approving of Abortion
under the Following Conditions

		Prot.	Cath.	Jew	None
ABHLTH	woman's health endangered	88	84	100	97
ABDEFECT	serious defect likely	77	75	100	95
ABRAPE	resulted from rape	76	74	100	96
ABPOOR	too poor for more children	39	35	75	75
ABSINGLE	woman is unmarried	37	33	87	70
ABNOMORE	family wants no more	35	32	100	74
ABANY	for any reason	34	30	77	70

There are several observations you might make about these data. To begin with, the expectation that Catholics would be the most opposed to abortion is

---

2. Those values of the variable RELIG designated as "missing" in the last chapter (0, 5–99) will not be included in this analysis either.

confirmed. They are the least likely to approve of abortion under any of the conditions asked about.

At the same time, the level of support for abortion among American Catholics is greatly at variance with the church's official position. Under the traumatic conditions summarized at the top of the table, 74 to 84 percent of the Catholics say they would approve abortion. Even under the less traumatic conditions, 30 to 35 percent of the Catholics would support a woman's right to an abortion: 30 percent support it "for any reason."

In contrast, Jews and those with no religion are consistently more supportive of a woman's right to an abortion. It is interesting to note that all the Jewish respondents said they would support abortion in four of the seven cases: ABHLTH, ABDEFECT, ABRAPE, and ABNOMORE.

To examine this relationship further, you could also use the index **ABORT** to see if this pattern is reflected in scores on a composite measure. Your table should look like the one below.

Simple Abortion Index * RS RELIGIOUS PREFERENCE Crosstabulation

| | | | RS RELIGIOUS PREFERENCE | | | | |
			1 Protestant	2 Catholic	3 Jewish	4 None	Total
Simple Abortion Index	0 yes/approve	Count	176	79	13	91	359
		% within RS RELIGIOUS PREFERENCE	37.3%	34.3%	86.7%	70.5%	42.4%
	1 conditional support	Count	187	90	2	32	311
		% within RS RELIGIOUS PREFERENCE	39.6%	39.1%	13.3%	24.8%	36.8%
	2 no/disapprove	Count	109	61		6	176
		% within RS RELIGIOUS PREFERENCE	23.1%	26.5%		4.7%	20.8%
Total		Count	472	230	15	129	846
		% within RS RELIGIOUS PREFERENCE	100.0%	100.0%	100.0%	100.0%	100.0%

In our earlier examinations of religion, we've sometimes gone beyond affiliation to examine the measure of religiosity, or religiousness. How do you suppose church attendance would relate to abortion attitudes? To find out, let's use **CHATT**, the recoded variable created in Chapter 6.

Run the appropriate tables. Here's a summary of what you should have learned.

Percentage Approving of Abortion under the Following Conditions

		Weekly	Monthly	Seldom	Never
ABHLTH	woman's health endangered	78	91	93	96
ABDEFECT	serious defect likely	63	86	87	91
ABRAPE	resulted from rape	65	85	83	92
ABPOOR	too poor for more children	24	52	49	64
ABSINGLE	woman is unmarried	25	49	45	61
ABNOMORE	family wants no more	23	46	45	63
ABANY	for any reason	21	49	43	57

What does this table tell you about religion and abortion attitudes? The over-all relationship is pretty clear: Increased church attendance is related to decreased support for abortion. There is a substantial difference, however, between those who attend church about weekly and those who attend less often. Those who attend one to three times per month are more than twice as likely to support unconditional abortion as those who attend church weekly. Even in the case of the traumatic conditions at the top of the table, only those who attend church weekly stand out in their relatively low level of support.

The fact that the other three groups do not differ much from one another, by the way, is a result of what we call a *ceiling effect*. Whenever the overall percentage of people agreeing with something approaches 100 percent, it's not possible for there to be much variation among subgroups. In the extreme case, if everyone agreed on something, there would be no way for men and women to differ because 100 percent of both would have to agree. Similarly, there could be no differences among age groups, religions, and so on. When the overall percentage approaches zero, a similar situation occurs that we call a *floor effect*.

Now check the relationship between **CHATT** and the abortion index, **ABORT**, and then compare your results with ours below.

Simple Abortion Index * CHATT Crosstabulation

			CHATT				
			1 About weekly	2 About monthly	3 Seldom	4 Never	Total
Simple Abortion Index	0 yes/approve	Count	75	64	137	96	372
		% within CHATT	25.7%	48.5%	46.3%	61.9%	42.5%
	1 conditional support	Count	105	49	120	46	320
		% within CHATT	36.0%	37.1%	40.5%	29.7%	36.6%
	2 no/disapprove	Count	112	19	39	13	183
		% within CHATT	38.4%	14.4%	13.2%	8.4%	20.9%
Total		Count	292	132	296	155	875
		% within CHATT	100.0%	100.0%	100.0%	100.0%	100.0%

Are these results consistent with those in the summary table we created? Do you find evidence of a ceiling effect in this table as well?

The GSS data we've provided for your use permit you to explore this general topic even further, if you wish. Why don't you check out the effect of **POSTLIFE** and **PRAY** on abortion attitudes? Before running the tables, however, take some time to reflect on what might logically be expected. How should beliefs about an afterlife affect support for or opposition to abortion? You may be surprised by what you learn. Then again, maybe you won't be surprised.

Demonstration 13.4: Politics and Abortion

There is a strong and consistent relationship between political philosophy and abortion attitudes. What do you suppose that relationship is? Who would you expect to be the more supportive of abortion: liberals or conservatives? To carry out this investigation, you'll probably want to use the recoded variable, **POLREC**.

Now you can examine the relationship between political philosophy and abortion attitudes to see if your hunch is correct. Here's a summary of what you should discover.

Percentage Approving of Abortion
under the Following Conditions

		Liberal	Moderate	Conservative
ABHLTH	woman's health endangered	95	89	84
ABDEFECT	serious defect likely	90	82	69
ABRAPE	resulted from rape	90	80	71
ABPOOR	too poor for more children	64	42	29
ABSINGLE	woman is unmarried	61	41	25
ABNOMORE	family wants no more	62	40	26
ABANY	for any reason	62	36	24

How would you describe these results? Try your hand at writing a sentence or two to report on the impact of political philosophy on abortion attitudes before reading ahead.

One way to summarize the relationship between political philosophy and abortion attitudes is to say the following: Liberals are strongly and consistently more supportive of a woman's right to an abortion than are conservatives, with moderates falling in between.

To pursue this relationship further, you may want to use the **ABORT** index.

Simple Abortion Index * Recoded polviews Crosstabulation

			Recoded polviews			
			1 Liberal	2 Moderate	3 Conservative	Total
Simple Abortion Index	0 yes/approve	Count	160	128	74	362
		% within Recoded polviews	61.5%	42.8%	25.9%	42.8%
	1 conditional support	Count	75	116	122	313
		% within Recoded polviews	28.8%	38.8%	42.7%	37.0%
	2 no/disapprove	Count	25	55	90	170
		% within Recoded polviews	9.6%	18.4%	31.5%	20.1%
Total		Count	260	299	286	845
		% within Recoded polviews	100.0%	100.0%	100.0%	100.0%

Are these results consistent with those in the summary table above? Does the interpretation of the relationship between political philosophy and abortion attitudes as strong and consistent hold up?

Another direction you might want to follow in investigating the relationship between politics and abortion attitudes concerns political party identification. As you no doubt realize, the Democratic party has been generally more supportive of a woman's right to have an abortion than has the Republican party. This difference was dramatically portrayed by the presidential and vice presidential candidates during the 1996 election.

How do you suppose the official differences separating the parties show up in the attitudes of the rank and file? Among the general public, who do you suppose are the most supportive of abortion: Democrats or Republicans? See if you can find out for yourself by creating a summary table similar to those above and then running **Crosstabs** with **PARTY** (as our measure of party identification) and **ABORT** (our index of abortion attitudes). Once you have done that, see if the findings are consistent with your expectations.

Demonstration 13.5: Sexual Attitudes and Abortion

Recalling that abortion attitudes are related to differences in political philosophy, it might occur to you that other philosophical differences might be relevant as well. As you may recall from Chapter 10, the GSS data set contains three items dealing with sexual permissiveness/restrictiveness:

PREMARSX   attitudes toward premarital sex

HOMOSEX   attitudes toward homosexual sex relations

XMOVIE   attendance at an X-rated movie during the year

Here's the relationship between attitudes toward premarital sex and toward abortion. Notice how permissiveness on one is related to permissiveness on the other.[3]

Simple Abortion Index * SEX BEFORE MARRIAGE Crosstabulation

			SEX BEFORE MARRIAGE				
			1 ALWAYS WRONG	2 ALMST ALWAYS WRG	3 SOMETIME S WRONG	4 NOT WRONG AT ALL	Total
Simple Abortion Index	0 yes/approve	Count	22	14	37	116	189
		% within SEX BEFORE MARRIAGE	18.3%	31.1%	47.4%	60.7%	43.5%
	1 conditional support	Count	35	23	34	56	148
		% within SEX BEFORE MARRIAGE	29.2%	51.1%	43.6%	29.3%	34.1%
	2 no/disapprove	Count	63	8	7	19	97
		% within SEX BEFORE MARRIAGE	52.5%	17.8%	9.0%	9.9%	22.4%
Total		Count	120	45	78	191	434
		% within SEX BEFORE MARRIAGE	100.0%	100.0%	100.0%	100.0%	100.0%

Now, why don't you check to see if the same pattern holds for the other sexual permissiveness items?

Simple Abortion Index * HOMOSEXUAL SEX RELATIONS Crosstabulation

			HOMOSEXUAL SEX RELATIONS				
			1 ALWAYS WRONG	2 ALMST ALWAYS WRG	3 SOMETIME S WRONG	4 NOT WRONG AT ALL	Total
Simple Abortion Index	0 yes/approve	Count	125	27	34	167	353
		% within HOMOSEXUAL SEX RELATIONS	26.3%	45.0%	59.6%	69.9%	42.4%
	1 conditional support	Count	204	21	20	57	302
		% within HOMOSEXUAL SEX RELATIONS	42.9%	35.0%	35.1%	23.8%	36.3%
	2 no/disapprove	Count	147	12	3	15	177
		% within HOMOSEXUAL SEX RELATIONS	30.9%	20.0%	5.3%	6.3%	21.3%
Total		Count	476	60	57	239	832
		% within HOMOSEXUAL SEX RELATIONS	100.0%	100.0%	100.0%	100.0%	100.0%

---

3 Since a "Don't know" response indicates the absence of an opinion, these responses were eliminated from the table by declaring them missing values.

Simple Abortion Index * SEEN X-RATED MOVIE IN LAST YEAR Crosstabulation

			SEEN X-RATED MOVIE IN LAST YEAR		Total
			1 YES	2 NO	
Simple Abortion Index	0 yes/approve	Count	55	129	184
		% within SEEN X-RATED MOVIE IN LAST YEAR	48.2%	39.7%	41.9%
	1 conditional support	Count	40	131	171
		% within SEEN X-RATED MOVIE IN LAST YEAR	35.1%	40.3%	39.0%
	2 no/disapprove	Count	19	65	84
		% within SEEN X-RATED MOVIE IN LAST YEAR	16.7%	20.0%	19.1%
Total		Count	114	325	439
		% within SEEN X-RATED MOVIE IN LAST YEAR	100.0%	100.0%	100.0%

As you probably expected, abortion attitudes are related to attitudes toward homosexuality and to attendance at an X-rated movie. In other words, those who are sexually permissive tend to be permissive in the area of abortion as well.

Other Factors You Can Explore on Your Own

There are a number of other factors that can affect attitudes toward abortion. We'll suggest a few more demographic variables for you to check out. You may want to review the excerpt from Cook et al. in E-Appendix G for further ideas.

You might suspect that education is related to abortion attitudes. If so, which direction do you suppose that relationship goes? Why do you suppose that is?

Race is another standard demographic variable that might be related to abortion attitudes. You should examine the relationship between attitudes toward abortion in particular circumstances and race carefully, because race may have slightly different effects on different items.

Finally, you might like to explore the relationship between abortion attitudes and some family variables. How do you suppose abortion attitudes relate to respondents' views of the ideal number of children to have?

The family variable that may surprise you in its relationship to abortion attitudes is MARITAL. You may recall that we also uncovered a surprising effect of marital status on political philosophy. Check this one out, and we'll take a more in-depth look once we begin our multivariate analyses.

Conclusion

In this chapter, you've had an opportunity to search for explanations for the vast differences in people's feelings about abortion. We've found that religion and politics, for example, are powerful influences. We've also just seen that permissiveness and restrictiveness regarding abortion are strongly related to permissiveness and restrictiveness on issues of sexual behavior.

Thus far, we've opened up the search only for explanations, limiting ourselves to bivariate analyses. In the analyses to come, we'll dig ever deeper into the reasons for differences in the opinions people have. Ultimately, you should gain a well-rounded understanding of the logic of social scientific research as well as master some of the fundamental techniques for acting on that logic through SPSS.

Main Points

- This chapter focused on the causes of differing attitudes toward abortion.
- Cook, Jelen, and Wilcox's book *Between Two Absolutes* was used as a starting point for our analysis.
- Throughout the chapter we examined the relationship between attitudes toward abortion and several potential independent or causal variables.
- In addition to examining SPSS output (primarily crosstabs), we also created our own summary tables based on several SPSS tables. These summary tables made it easy to examine the relationship between attitudes toward abortion and several independent variables.
- Gender and age are not related to attitudes toward abortion, whereas religion, politics, and sexual attitudes are.
- In the case of religion, for example, we found that those who attend church weekly are much less likely to support abortion than those who attend less often.
- We also found that those attending less often (monthly, seldom, or never) do not differ much from one another. Here we see evidence of what we call a ceiling effect.
- You may also want to try looking for relationships between attitudes toward abortion and other demographic variables such as race, education, and family.

Key Terms

Ceiling effect
Floor effect

SPSS Commands Introduced in This Chapter

No new commands were introduced in this chapter.

Review Questions

1. One way we explored the relationship between attitudes toward abortion and several potential independent variables was by constructing a summary table based on SPSS output. How were these tables constructed?

2. What are the commands used to instruct SPSS to construct a table looking at the relationship between our abortion index ABORT and gender?

3. Do our findings support the contention that women are more likely to be supportive of abortion than men?

4. Why did we use the recoded variable AGECAT as opposed to the variable AGE to examine the relationship between age and attitudes toward abortion?

5. Summarize the relationship between abortion attitudes and religious affiliation.

6. Do the majority of American Catholics differ from the Catholic church on abortion in particular circumstances? If so, what circumstances?

7. What is the ceiling effect?

8. What is the floor effect?

9. We found that liberals are more likely than conservatives to support abortion. Does this mean that Democrats are more likely to support abortion than Republicans?

10. Are those favoring small families more or less likely to support abortion?

11. Is there any difference between those who are separated and those who are divorced in terms of their unconditional support for abortion?

12. Is there a relationship between attitudes toward sexual behavior and attitudes toward abortion?

NAME _____

CLASS _____

INSTRUCTOR _____

DATE _____

To complete the following exercises, you need to load the data file EXER.SAV. Answers to Questions 1–9 can be found in Appendix A.

We are going to begin by looking at what causes people to be permissive (or restrictive) in the area of teen sex. We will focus primarily on the three variables from your EXER.SAV file that deal with this issue: PILLOK, SEXEDUC, and TEEN-SEX.

1. What do each of the following variables measure?

   A. PILLOK

   B. SEXEDUC

   C. TEENSEX

2. List the values and labels of each of the following variables in the spaces provided below.

   A. PILLOK
   Value   Label

   _____   _____
   _____   _____
   _____   _____
   _____   _____
   _____   _____
   _____   _____
   _____   _____

   B. SEXEDUC
   Value   Label

   _____   _____
   _____   _____
   _____   _____
   _____   _____
   _____   _____
   _____   _____

   C. TEENSEX
   Value   Label

   _____   _____
   _____   _____
   _____   _____
   _____   _____
   _____   _____
   _____   _____
   _____   _____

3. Recode/Relabel the following variables. Once you have done that, open the Define Variable box and set Type, Value Labels, and Missing Values for each new, recoded variable.

   A. PILLOK recode to create PILLREC
      [The three values listed as "missing values" (0, 8, 9) will automatically be defined as missing when you recode the PILLOK as shown below.]

    1–2 →   1   Permissive
    3–4 →   2   Restrictive
    [0,8,9 Missing Values]

   B. TEENSEX recode to create TEENREC
      [Once again, the four items listed as "missing values" will automatically be defined as "missing" when you recode TEENSEX as shown below.]

    3–4 →   1   Permissive
    1–2 →   2   Restrictive
    [0,5,8,9 Missing Values]

   C. SEXEDUC label in the following manner
      [Designate the "missing values" by opening the Define Variables box: **Data → Define Variable... → Missing Values...→ Range plus one discrete missing value.** Low: = 3, High: = 9. Discrete value: = 0 → **Continue → OK**]

    1   Permissive
    2   Restrictive
    0,3–9 Missing Values

4. Use SEX and our three measures of permissiveness on teen sex (PILLREC, TEENREC, and SEXEDUC) to instruct SPSS to run tables that can be used to fill in the summary table below.

Percentage Permissive on Teen Sex Given the Following Situations	Men	Women
PILLREC	_____	_____
SEXEDUC	_____	_____
TEENREC	_____	_____

5. What does this table tell you about the strength of the relationship between gender and permissiveness on teen sex? Do the column percentages change? If so, specify how the dependent variable changes with changes in the independent variable.

NAME _____

CLASS _____

INSTRUCTOR _____

DATE _____

6. Now we will move away from demographic variables. Try using FEFAM (which as you may recall is one of our measures of attitudes toward family and sex roles) and our three measures of permissiveness on teen sex (PILL-REC, TEENREC, and SEXEDUC) to instruct SPSS to run tables that can be used to fill in the summary table below. (Don't forget to designate DK "8" as missing for FEFAM.)

Percentage Permissive on Teen Sex Given the Following Situations	Strongly Agree	Agree	Disagree	Strongly Disagree
PILLREC	_____	_____	_____	_____
SEXEDUC	_____	_____	_____	_____
TEENREC	_____	_____	_____	_____

7. What does this table tell you about the strength of the relationship between attitudes toward family/sex roles and permissiveness on teen sex? Do the column percentages change? If so, specify how the dependent variable changes with changes in the independent variable.

8. Use FEPRESCH and our three measures of permissiveness on teen sex (PILLREC, TEENREC, and SEXEDUC) to instruct SPSS to run tables that can be used to fill in the following summary table. (Don't forget to designate DK "8" as missing for FEPRESCH.)

Percentage Permissive on Teen Sex Given the Following Situations	Strongly Agree	Agree	Disagree	Strongly Disagree
PILLREC	_____	_____	_____	_____
SEXEDUC	_____	_____	_____	_____
TEENREC	_____	_____	_____	_____

9. What does this table tell you about the strength of the relationship between attitudes toward family/sex roles and permissiveness on teen sex? Do the column percentages change? If so, specify how the dependent variable changes with changes in the independent variable.

10. Now choose another variable that you think may be related to permissiveness on teen sex. Write the name of the variable and explain why you chose it (i.e., how it might be related to permissiveness on teen sex).

11. List the values and labels of the item you chose and indicate whether it is necessary to recode/relabel. If so, explain how you did that below.

12. Examine the relationship between the variable you chose and our three measures of permissiveness on teen sex (PILLREC, SEXEDUC, and TEENREC). Then fill in the following summary table below with the results of your analysis. If you need more space, use a separate sheet of paper. (Don't forget, depending on which variable you choose, you may have to designate DK as missing.)

Percentage Permissive
on Teen Sex
LABELS OF
VARIABLE CHOSEN _____

PILLREC

SEXEDUC

TEENREC

13. What does this table tell you about the strength of the relationship between _____ [name of variable you chose] and permissiveness on teen sex? Do the column percentages change? If so, specify how the dependent variable changes with changes in the independent variable.

Chapter 14   Measures of Association

In the preceding analyses, we depended on percentage tables as our format for examining the relationships among variables. In this chapter, we are going to explore some other formats for that examination. By and large, these techniques, called *measures of association*, summarize relationships in contrast to the way percentage tables lay out the details.

Another way you might think of measures of association is in contrast to the statistics (measures of central tendency and dispersion) we introduced in Chapter 6. Both are considered *descriptive statistics*, but measures of central tendency and dispersion summarize the distribution of categories of a single variable, whereas measures of association summarize the strength of association between two variables. Additionally, when two variables are at either the ordinal or interval/ratio level of measure, measures of association also indicate the direction of association. These capabilities enable us to use measures of association to answer two important questions:

1. How *strong* is the association or relationship between two variables?
2. And, for ordinal and interval/ratio variables, what is the *direction* of association between two variables?

We begin our discussion with a thought experiment designed to introduce you to the logic of statistical association. We will then focus on four of the most commonly used measures of association, each of which is appropriate for variables at different levels of measurement: lambda, gamma, Pearson's *r,* and regression. In each case we will begin by introducing the logic of the measure and then show you how it can be calculated using SPSS. Finally, we will briefly discuss measures appropriate for mixed types of variables.

Before we begin, it is important to note that while our focus will be limited primarily to the four statistics mentioned above, there are a variety of other measures of association that social researchers find useful. Depending on your statistical background, you may already be familiar with some of them. While it is beyond the scope of this text to review them all, this chapter serves as an introduction to the logic of some of the basic measures.

The Logic of Statistical Association: Proportionate Reduction of Error (PRE)

To introduce the logic of statistical association, we would like you to take a minute for a "thought experiment." Imagine that there is a group of 100 people in a lecture hall, and you are standing in the hallway outside the room. The people will come out of the room one at a time, and your task will be to guess the gender of each before he or she comes into view. Take a moment to consider your best strategy for making these guesses.

If you know nothing about the people in the room, there really is no useful strategy for guessing—no way to make educated guesses. But now suppose you know that 60 of the people in the room are women. This would make educated guesses possible: You should guess "woman" every time. By doing this, you would be right 60 times and wrong 40 times.

Now suppose that every time a person prepares to emerge from the room, his or her first name is announced. This would probably improve your guessing substantially. You'd guess "woman" for every Nancy or Joanne and "man" for every Joseph and Wendell. Even so, you probably wouldn't be totally accurate, given the ambiguity of names like Pat, Chris, and Leslie.

It is useful to notice that we could actually calculate how much knowing first names improved your guessing. Let's say you would have made 40 errors out of 100 guesses without knowing names and only 10 errors when you knew the names. You would have made 30 fewer mistakes. Out of an original 40 mistakes, that's a 75 percent improvement. Statisticians refer to this as a ***proportionate reduction of error***, which they abbreviate as ***PRE***. The measures of association we are going to focus on are largely based on this logic.

Lambda: A Measure Appropriate for Nominal Variables

Lambda is a measure of association appropriate for use with two nominal variables, and it operates on the PRE logic. Essentially, this means that the two variables are related to one another to the extent that knowing a person's attribute on one will help you guess his or her attribute on the other (i.e., the extent to which one variable is "associated" with affects, or has an impact on, another variable).

An Indication of Strength of Association

The value of lambda, which can vary between 0.00 and 1.00, indicates the *strength* of association or relationship between two nominal variables. The closer the value of lambda is to 1.00, the stronger the relationship between the variables. Conversely, the closer the value of lambda is to 0.00, the weaker the relationship between the variables.

You'll remember that nominal variables are just sets of categories with no greater-than or less-than relationships between them. Based on that, you have probably already correctly surmised that lambda provides *no* indication of the direction of association. In the absence of an order between categories, there can be no direction of relationship. Even if there were a strong relationship between eye color and hair color, it would make no sense to say it was positive or negative!

Example 1: The Logic of Lambda [1]

Here's a very simple example of lambda. Suppose that we have data on the employment status of 1,000 people. Half are employed; half are unemployed. If

---

1. Throughout this chapter we review how measures of association are computed in an effort to provide the rationale for matching the measure to the level of the data. Instructors and students who would rather focus on interpretation are encouraged to skip these sections.

we were to begin presenting you with person after person, asking you to guess whether each was employed or not, you'd get about half wrong and half right by guessing blindly. So, the logic of lambda begins with the assumption that you'd make 500 errors in this case. Let's call these your "uneducated errors."

Now, take a look at the table below, which gives you additional information: the ages of the subjects.

	Young	Old	Total
Employed	0	500	500
Unemployed	500	0	500
Total	500	500	1,000

Suppose now that we were to repeat the guessing exercise. This time, however, you would know whether each person is young or old. What would be your strategy for guessing employment status?

Clearly, you should make an educated guess of "unemployed" for every young person and "employed" for every old person. Do that and you'll make no errors. You will have reduced your errors by 500, in comparison with the first attempt. Given that you will have eliminated all your former errors, we could also say that you have reduced your errors by 100 percent.

Here's the simple equation for lambda that allows you to calculate the reduction of errors:

$$\frac{\text{(uneducated errors)} - \text{(educated errors)}}{\text{(uneducated errors)}} = \frac{500 - 500}{500} = 1.00$$

Notice that the calculation results in 1.00, which we treat as 100 percent in the context of lambda.

Example 2: The Logic of Lambda

To be sure the logic of lambda is clear to you, let's consider another hypothetical example, similar to the previous example:

	Young	Old	Total
Employed	250	250	500
Unemployed	250	250	500
Total	500	500	1,000

In this new example, we still have half young and half old, and we also have half employed and half unemployed. Notice the difference in the relationship between the two variables, however. Just by inspection, you should be able to see that they are independent of one another. In this case, age has no impact on employment status.

The lack of a relationship between age and employment status here is reflected in the "educated" guesses you would make about employment status if you knew a person's age. It wouldn't help you at all, and you would get half the young people wrong and half the old people wrong. You would have made 500 errors in uneducated guesses, and you wouldn't have improved by knowing their ages.

Lambda reflects this new situation:

$$\frac{\text{(uneducated errors)} - \text{(educated errors)}}{\text{(uneducated errors)}} = \frac{500 - 500}{500} = 0.00$$

Knowing age would have reduced your errors by zero percent.

Demonstration 14.1: Instructing SPSS to Calculate Lambda

The real relationships between variables are seldom this simple, of course, so let's look at a real example using SPSS and the General Social Survey data. You'll be pleased to discover that you won't have to calculate the errors or the proportion of reduction because SPSS does it for you.

Set up a **Crosstabs** request using **ABANY** as the **row** variable and **RELIG** as the **column** variable. For the time being, it will be useful to request no percentaging of the cells in the table.[2] Click on **Cells...**, and **turn off "Column"** if that's still selected. Then return to the Crosstabs window by clicking **Continue**. Before executing the Crosstabs command, however, click the **Statistics...** button. Here's what you should see:

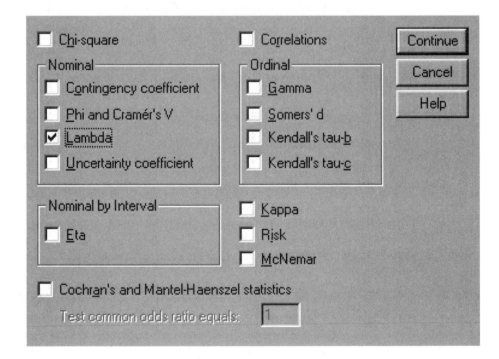

---

2. Usually percentages are requested in order to see how the column percentages change or move. We omitted them here only to make the table somewhat easier to read.

You will notice that SPSS gives you a variety of options, including some of the measures of association we are going to introduce in this chapter (as well as some we will not introduce, but which you may want to explore on your own). You can see that lambda is listed in the box on the left-hand side under Nominal because, as we know, lambda is a measure of association used for two nominal variables. Click **Lambda** and a check mark will appear in the small box to the left. Once you have done that, you can leave the Statistics window by clicking **Continue** and then execute the Crosstabs command by selecting **OK**. Here's the result that should show up in your Output window:

ABANY ABORTION IF WOMAN WANTS FOR ANY REASON * RELIG RS RELIGIOUS PREFERENCE Crosstabulation

Count

		RELIG RS RELIGIOUS PREFERENCE				Total
		1 Protestant	2 Catholic	3 Jewish	4 None	
ABANY ABORTION IF WOMAN WANTS FOR ANY REASON	1 YES	168	72	13	89	342
	2 NO	325	168	4	39	536
Total		493	240	17	128	878

We've omitted the request for percentages in this table because it will be useful to see the actual number of cases in each cell of the table. However, keep in mind that in most cases you want to request percentages to see how the column percentages change or move. At the far right of the table, notice that 342 people supported the idea of a woman being able to get an abortion just because she wanted one; 536 were opposed. If we were to make uneducated guesses about people's opinions on this issue, we'd do best always to guess "opposed." But by doing that, we would make 342 errors.

If we knew each person's religion, however, we would improve our record somewhat. Here's what would happen.

Religion	Guess	Errors
Protestant	No	168
Catholic	No	72
Jewish	Yes	4
None	Yes	39
Total		283

Compare this table to your output to insure that you understand how we created it.

To calculate lambda, then,

$$\frac{\text{(uneducated errors)} - \text{(educated errors)}}{\text{(uneducated errors)}} = \frac{342 - 283}{342} = .172514$$

This indicates, therefore, that we have improved our guessing of abortion attitudes by 17 percent as a result of knowing religious affiliation. Here's how SPSS reports this result:

Directional Measures

			Value	Asymp. Std. Error[a]	Approx. T[b]	Approx. Sig.
Nominal by Nominal	Lambda	Symmetric	.081	.015	4.968	.000
		ABANY ABORTION IF WOMAN WANTS FOR ANY REASON Dependent	.173	.032	4.968	.000
		RELIG RS RELIGIOUS PREFERENCE Dependent	.000	.000	c	c
	Goodman and Kruskal tau	ABANY ABORTION IF WOMAN WANTS FOR ANY REASON Dependent	.084	.018		.000[d]
		RELIG RS RELIGIOUS PREFERENCE Dependent	.024	.006		.000[d]

SPSS reports more information than we need right now, so let's focus our attention on the second row of numbers. Because we have been testing whether we could predict abortion attitudes (ABANY) by knowing religion, that makes ABANY the dependent variable. As you can see, the value of lambda in that instance is 0.173, the value we got by calculating it for ourselves.

Knowing a person's religious affiliation, then, allows us to predict his or her attitude on abortion 17 percent more accurately. The implicit assumption in this analysis is that religious affiliation *causes*, to some degree, attitudes toward abortion. We use the value of lambda as an indication of how strong the causal link is.

However, it is important that you bear in mind that *association alone does not prove causation*. When we observe a statistical relationship between two variables, that relationship strengthens the probability that one causes the other, but it is not sufficient proof. To be satisfied that a causal relationship exists, social scientists also want the link to make sense logically (in this case, the role of churches and clergy in the abortion debate offer that reasoning). And finally, we want to be sure that the observed relationship is not an artifact produced by the effects of a third variable. This latter possibility will be examined in Part V on multivariate analysis.

For curiosity's sake, notice the third row, which treats RELIG as the dependent variable. This deals with the possibility that we might be able to guess people's religions by knowing where they stand on abortion. Take a moment to look at the crosstabulation above.

If we were to make uneducated guesses about people's religions, we'd always guess Protestant, because Protestants are by far the largest group. Knowing attitudes toward abortion wouldn't help matters, however. In either case, we'd still guess Protestant, even among those who were in favor of abortion rights.

If RELIG were the dependent variable, then, knowing ABANY would improve our guessing by zero percent, which is the calculation presented by SPSS.

Interpreting Lambda and Other Measures

After all this discussion about lambda, you may still be wondering what a value of .173, for instance, actually means in terms of the strength of the relationship between these two variables. Does it signify a strong, relatively strong, moderate, or weak association? Is it something worth noting or does it indicate such a weak relationship that it is not even worth paying attention to? Unfortunately, there are no easy answers to these questions. While we are going to say more about statistical significance in the next chapter, we do want to give you some (albeit general) basis for interpreting these values.

We can say for certain that not only for lambda, but also for all the PRE measures of association we are considering in this chapter, a value of 1.00 (positive or negative in the case of gamma and Pearson's *r)* indicates a perfect association or the strongest possible relationship between two variables. Conversely, a value of 0.00 indicates no relationship between the variables. We can also say that the closer the value is to 1.00 (positive or negative in the case of gamma and Pearson's *r),* the stronger the relationship. And the closer the value is to 0.00, the weaker the relationship.

Determining whether or not a relationship is noteworthy depends on what other researchers have found. If other researchers had not discovered any variables that related to abortion attitudes, then our lambda of .173 would be important. As you will see later, there are variables that have much stronger relationships to abortion than religion, so strong that they make our .173 quite unremarkable. In short, all relationships must be interpreted in the context of other findings in the same general area of inquiry.

That said, in order to give you a sense of one way you can approach these statistics, we include some general guidelines for interpreting the strength of association between variables in Table 14.1. As the title of the table clearly indicates, these are merely loose guidelines with arbitrary cut-off points that must be understood within the context of our discussion above regarding the absence of any absolute "rules" of interpretation.

You will note that Table 14.1 lists the possible values as positive or negative. While the value of lambda is, as we noted, always a positive value between 0.00 and 1.00, *the values of the other measures that we will discuss later in this chapter* (see discussions of gamma and Pearson's *r* below) *run from –1.00 to +1.00, and thus include both positive and negative values.*

Table 14.1:   Some General Guidelines for Interpreting Strength of Association (Lambda, Gamma, Pearson's *r*...)[3]

Strength of Association	Value of Measures of Association Lambda, Gamma, Pearson's *r*...)
None	0.00
Weak/Uninteresting association	±.01 to .09
Moderate/Worth noting	±.10 to .29
Evidence of strong association/ Extremely interesting	±.30 to .99
Perfect/Strongest possible association	±1.00

3. This table is adapted from a more in-depth discussion in Healey et al. 1999, 84. In the text the authors note that whereas "[t]his scale may strike you as too low . . . [r]emember that, in the social sciences, we deal with probabilistic causal relationships . . . expecting measures of association to approach 1 is unreasonable. Given the complexity of the social world, the (admittedly arbitrary) the guideline presented is serviceable in most instances."

Based on these general guidelines, what might you say about the strength of the relationship between ABANY and RELIG?

Now, why don't you choose some nominal variables and then experiment with instructing SPSS to calculate lambda?

SPSS COMMAND 14.1: Running Crosstabs and Lambda

Click **Analyze** → **Descriptive Statistics** → **Crosstabs...** →
Specify **dependent variable** as the **Row(s)**: variable →
Specify **independent variable** as the **Column(s)**: variable →
Click **Cells...** →
[Make sure "Column" under "Percentages" is *not* selected (there should *not* be a check mark next to "Column")][4] →
Click **Continue** →
Click **Statistics...** → **Lambda** → **Continue** → **OK**

Gamma: A Measure Appropriate for Ordinal Variables

Whereas lambda is used to examine the association between two nominal variables, *gamma* is a measure of association based on the logic of proportionate reduction of error appropriate for two ordinal variables.

An Indication of Strength and Direction (with a Caveat) of Association

Unlike lambda, gamma not only indicates the *strength of association* but it also indicates the *direction of association* between two ordinal variables. With each variable having a greater than/less than between its categories, we can observe whether or not high values of one variable are associated with high values on the other (a *positive association*) or if high values of one variable are associated with low values of the other (a *negative association*). The values of gamma range from −1.00 to 1.00.

In terms of the *strength of association*, the closer to −1.00 or 1.00, the stronger the relationship between the two variables, whereas the closer to 0.00, the weaker the association between the variables.

In terms of the *direction of association*, a negative sign indicates a *negative association*; as one variable increases, the other decreases (the items change in opposite directions). Conversely, a *positive* sign indicates a *positive association*; both items change in the same direction (they both either increase or decrease).

For instance, a negative association between social class and prejudice indicates that the variables change in opposite directions: As one increases, the other decreases. Conversely, a positive association between social class and prejudice indicates that the variables change in the same direction: They both either increase or decrease.

---

4. Usually percentages are requested in order to see how the column percentages change or move. In this table, we purposely omitted percentages to make the table easier to read.

We want to underscore the fact that you can *only* determine the direction of association between two variables if they are *both measured on scales that express greater than/less than relationships between their points*. Furthermore, if an ordinal variable's codes have been arbitrarily assigned in such a way that high number codes indicate an absence of what is being measured and low number codes indicate a presence of the phenomenon, the sign (– or +) of the relationship will be reversed.

For an example of what we mean by *arbitrary values*, think back to when we reduced the number of ordinal categories on the variable ATTEND to create CHATT. In that case, we chose the value of 1 to represent "About weekly," 2 to represent "About monthly," and so on. These are arbitrary values in the sense that we could just as easily have arranged the categories in the opposite direction so that 1 represented "Never," 2 represented "Seldom," 3 represented "About monthly," and 4 represented "About weekly." With reversed codes, you need to keep in mind that a negative value for gamma in this case would not correctly indicate a direction of association, it would merely be a result of the way we arbitrarily arranged the categories of an item.

Example 1: The Logic of Gamma

We judge two variables to be related to each other to the extent that knowing what a person is like in terms of one variable helps us to guess what he or she is like on the other. Whereas the application of this logic in the case of lambda lets us make predictions for individuals (e.g., if a person is Protestant, we guess he or she is also Republican), the logic is applied to pairs of people in the case of gamma.

To see the logic of gamma, let's consider the following nine people, placed in a matrix that indicates their social class standing and their level of prejudice: two ordinal variables.

Prejudice	Lower Class	Middle Class	Upper Class
Low	Jim	Tim	Kim
Medium	Mary	Harry	Carrie
High	Nan	Jan	Fran

Our purpose in this analysis is to determine which of the following best describes the relationship between social class and prejudice:

1. The higher your social class, the more prejudiced you are.
2. The higher your social class, the less prejudiced you are.
3. Your social class has no effect on your level of prejudice.

To begin our analysis, we should note that the only pairs who are appropriate to our question are those who differ in both social class and prejudice. Jim and Harry are an example; they differ in both social class and level of prejudice.

Here are the 18 pairs that qualify for analysis:

Jim-Harry	Kim-Mary	Harry-Nan
Jim-Carrie	Kim-Harry	Harry-Fran
Jim-Jan	Kim-Nan	
Jim-Fran	Kim-Jan	

Tim-Mary	Mary-Jan	Carrie-Nan
Tim-Nan	Mary-Fran	Carrie-Jan
Tim-Carrie		
Tim-Fran		

Take a minute to assure yourself that no other pair of people satisfies the criterion that they differ in both social class and prejudice.

If you study the table, you should be able to identify pairs of people who would support conclusions 1 and 2—we'll come back to conclusion 3 a little later.

Suppose now that you have been given the list of pairs, but you've never seen the original table. Your task is to guess which member of each pair is the more prejudiced. Given that you will simply be guessing blind, chances are that you'll get about half right and half wrong: nine correct answers and nine errors. Gamma helps us determine whether knowing how two people differ on social class would reduce the number of errors we'd make in guessing how they differ on prejudice.

Let's consider Jim-Harry for a moment. If they were the only two people you could study, and if you had to reach a conclusion about the relationship between social class and prejudice, what would you conclude? Notice that Harry is higher in social class than Jim (middle class versus lower class), and Harry is also higher in prejudice (medium versus low). If you were to generalize from this single pair of observations, there is only one conclusion you could reach: "The higher your social class, the more prejudiced you are."

As we noted earlier, this is referred to as a positive association: The higher on one variable, the higher on the other. In the more specific language of gamma, we'll refer to this as a *same pair*: The direction of the difference between Jim and Harry on one variable is the same as the direction of difference on the other. Harry is higher than Jim on both.

Suppose you had to base your conclusion on the Jim-Jan pair. What would you conclude? Look at the table and you'll see that Jan, like Harry, is higher than Jim on both social class and prejudice. This pair would also lead you to conclude that the higher your social class, the more prejudiced you are. Jim-Jan, then, is another same pair in the language of gamma.

Suppose, on the other hand, we observed only Tim and Mary. They would lead us to a very different conclusion. Mary is lower than Tim on social class, but she is higher on prejudice. If this were the only pair you could observe, you'd have to conclude that the higher your social class, the lower your prejudice. In the language of gamma, Tim-Mary is an *opposite pair*: The direction of their difference on one variable is the opposite of their difference on the other.

Now, we hope you've been feeling uncomfortable about the idea of generalizing from only one pair of observations, although that's what many people often do in everyday life. In social research, however, we would never do that.

Moving a little bit in the direction of normal social research, let's assume that you have observed all nine of the individuals in the table. What conclusion would you draw about the association between social class and prejudice? Gamma helps you answer this question.

Let's see how well each of the alternative conclusions might assist you in guessing people's prejudice based on knowing about their social class. If you operated on the basis of the conclusion that prejudice increases with social class, for example, and I told you Fran is of a higher social class than Harry, you would correctly guess that Fran is more prejudiced. If, on the other hand, I told you that Harry is higher in social class than Nan, you would incorrectly guess that he is more prejudiced.

Take a minute to go through the list of pairs above and make notations of which ones are same pairs and which ones are opposite. Once you've done that, count the numbers of same and opposite pairs.

You should get nine of each type of pair. This means that if you assume that prejudice increases with social class, you will get the nine opposite pairs wrong; if you assume prejudice decreases with social class, you will get the nine same pairs wrong. In other words, neither strategy for guessing levels of prejudice based on knowing social class will do you any good in this case. In either case, we make as many errors as we would have made if we didn't know the social class differences in the pairs. Gamma gives us a method for calculating that result.

The formula for gamma is as follows:

$$\frac{\text{same} - \text{opposite}}{\text{same} + \text{opposite}}$$

To calculate gamma, you must first count the number of same pairs and the number of opposite pairs. Once you've done that, the mathematics is pretty simple.

Now, you can complete the formula as follows:

$$\frac{9-9}{9+9} = \frac{0}{18} = 0$$

In gamma, this result is interpreted as 0 percent, meaning that knowing how two people differ on social class would improve your guesses as to how they differ on prejudice by 0—or not at all.

Consider the following modified table, however. Suppose for the moment that there are only three people to be studied:

Prejudice	Lower Class	Middle Class	Upper Class
Low	Jim		
Medium		Harry	
High			Fran

Just by inspection, you can see how perfectly these three people fit the pattern of a positive association between social class and prejudice. Each of the three pairs—Jim-Harry, Harry-Fran, Jim-Fran—is a same pair. There are no opposite pairs. If we were to give you each of these pairs, telling you who was higher in social class, the assumption of a positive association between the two variables would let you guess who was higher in social class with perfect accuracy.

Let's see how this situation would look in terms of gamma.

$$\frac{\text{same} - \text{opposite}}{\text{same} + \text{opposite}} = \frac{3 - 0}{3 + 0} = 1.00 \text{ or } 100 \text{ percent}$$

In this case, we would say gamma equals 1.00, with the meaning that you have reduced the number of errors by 100 percent. To understand this meaning of gamma, we need to go back to the idea of guessing prejudice differences without knowing social class.

Recall that if you were guessing blind, you'd be right about half the time and wrong about half the time. In this hypothetical case, you'd be wrong 1.5 times (that would be your average if you repeated the exercise hundreds of times). As we've seen, however, knowing social class in this instance lets us reduce the number of errors by 1.5—down to zero. It is in this sense that we say we have reduced our errors by 100 percent.

Now, let's consider a slightly different table.

Prejudice	Lower Class	Middle Class	Upper Class
Low			Nan
Medium		Harry	
High	Kim		

Notice that in this case we could also have a perfect record if we use the assumption of a negative association between social class and prejudice: The higher your social class, the lower your prejudice. The negative association shows up in gamma as follows:

$$\frac{(\text{same} - \text{opposite})}{(\text{same} + \text{opposite})} = \frac{0 - 3}{0 + 3} - 1.00 \text{ or } -100 \text{ percent}$$

Once again, the gamma indicates that we have reduced our errors by 100 percent. The minus sign in this result simply signals that the relationship is negative.

Example 2: The Logic of Gamma

We are finally ready for a more realistic example. Just as you would not want to base a generalization on as few cases as we've been considering so far, neither would it make sense to calculate gamma in such situations. Notice how gamma helps you assess the relationship between two variables when the results are not as obvious to the nonstatistical eye.

Prejudice	Lower Class	Middle Class	Upper Class
Low	200	400	700
Medium	500	900	400
High	800	300	100

In this table, the names of individuals have been replaced with the numbers of people having a particular social class and level of prejudice. There are 200 lower-class people in the table, for example, who are low on prejudice. On the other hand, there are 100 upper-class people who are high on prejudice.

Perhaps you can get a sense of the relationship in this table by simple observation. The largest cells are those lying along the diagonal running from lower left to upper right. This would suggest a negative association between the two variables (*direction of association*). Gamma lets us determine with more confidence whether that's the case and gives us a yardstick for measuring how strong the relationship is (*strength of association*).

In the simpler examples, every pair of cells represented one pair because there was only one person in each cell. Now it's a little more complex. Imagine for a moment just one of the people in the upper left cell (lower class, low prejudice). If we match that person up with the 900 people in the center cell (middle class, medium prejudice), we'd have 900 pairs. The same would result from matching each of the people in the first cell with all those in the second. We can calculate the total number of pairs produced by the two cells by simple multiplication: 200 times 900 gives us 180,000 pairs. Notice, by the way, that these are same pairs.

As a further simplification, notice that there are 900 + 400 + 300 + 100 people who will match with the upper left cell to form same pairs. That makes a total of 1,700 × 200 = 340,000. Here's an overview of all the "same" pairs in the table:

200 × (900 + 300 + 400 + 100) = 340,000
500 × (300 + 100) = 200,000
400 × (400 + 100) = 200,000
900 × 100 = 90,000
Total same pairs = 830,000

Following the same procedure, here are all the opposite pairs:

700 × (500 + 800 + 900 + 300) = 1,750,000
400 × (800 + 300) = 440,000
400 × (500 + 800) = 520,000
900 × 800 = 720,000
Total opposite pairs = 3,430,000

Even though this procedure produces quite a few more pairs than we've been dealing with, the formula for gamma still works the same way:

$$\frac{(\text{same} - \text{opposite})}{(\text{same} + \text{opposite})} = \frac{830,000 - 3,430,000}{830,000 + 3,430,000} = \frac{-2,6000,000}{4,260,000} = -.61$$

The minus sign in this result confirms that the relationship between the two variables is a negative one (direction). The numerical result indicates that knowing the social class ranking in each pair reduces our errors in predicting their ranking in terms of prejudice by 61 percent (strength).

Suppose, for the moment, that you had tried to blindly predict differences in prejudice for each of the 4,260,000 pairs. You would have been wrong about 2,130,000 times. By assuming that the person with higher social class is less prejudiced, you would have made only 830,000 errors, or 2,130,000 – 830,000 = 1,300,000 fewer errors. Dividing the 1,300,000 improvement by the 2,130,000 baseline gives .61, indicating you have reduced your errors by 61 percent.

Demonstration 14.2: Instructing SPSS to Calculate Gamma

Now, here's the good news. Although it's important for you to understand the logic of gamma, it is no longer necessary for you to do the calculations by hand. Whenever you run Crosstabs in SPSS, you can request that gamma be calculated by making that request when you set up the table.

Go to **Crosstabs**. Make **CHATT** the **row** variable and **AGECAT** the **column** variable.[5] Then click on **Statistics....**

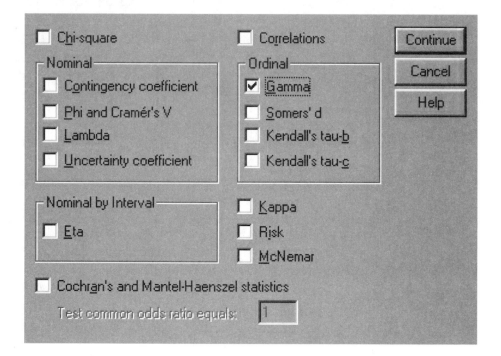

Notice that **Gamma** is appropriately a choice for ordinal data. Click it. If Lambda still has a check mark next to it, turn it off before selecting **Continue** to return to the main window. Once you have returned to the Crosstabs window, you can instruct SPSS to run the procedure by selecting **OK**. You should get the following table and report on gamma.

---

5. Note to Instructors: In an effort to build on the previous discussion of gamma and direction of association, we use CHATT as an example here because it makes the reverse scoring/interpretation point. However, you may also want to demonstrate gamma using another variable that is scored differently or ask students to choose such a variable when completing SPSS Lab Exercises 14.1, Questions 22–28.

CHATT * AGECAT Recoded Age Categories Crosstabulation

Count

		AGECAT Recoded Age Categories				
		1 Under 21	2 21-39	3 40-64	4 65 and older	Total
CHATT	1 About weekly	5	132	215	128	480
	2 About monthly	12	99	85	34	230
	3 Seldom	16	221	197	50	484
	4 Never	11	123	109	39	282
Total		44	575	606	251	1476

Symmetric Measures

		Value	Asymp. Std. Error[a]	Approx. T[b]	Approx. Sig.
Ordinal by Ordinal	Gamma	-.230	.032	-7.172	.000
N of Valid Cases		1476			

Notice that gamma is reported as −.230. This means that knowing a person's age would improve our estimate of his or her church attendance by 23 percent.

Although you might think the negative sign means there is a negative relationship between age and church attendance, we know now that this is not the case. In this example the minus sign results from our choosing to arbitrarily arrange attendance categories from the most frequent at the top to the least frequent at the bottom. If we had arranged the categories in the opposite direction, the gamma would have been positive.

Whenever you ask SPSS to calculate gamma, it is important that you note how the variable categories are arranged. If coding is not consistent—that is, if low codes indicate low amounts of what is being measured and vice versa—gamma's signs will be reversed. You can also determine the direction of the association by inspecting the table. Looking at the first row in the table above, it is fairly clear that church attendance tends to increase as age increases; hence the relationship between the two variables is a positive one.

To gain some more experience with gamma, why don't you select some ordinal variables that interest you and examine their relationships with one another by using gamma?

As you do that, you may want to keep in mind that the general guidelines for interpreting the strength of the relationship indicated by the value of gamma are the same as those discussed previously in regard to lambda and summarized in Table 14.1.

SPSS COMMAND 14.2: Running Crosstabs and Gamma

> Click **Analyze** → **Descriptive Statistics** → **Crosstabs...** →
> Specify **dependent variable** as the **Row(s)**: variable →
> Specify **independent variable** as the **Column(s)**: variable →
> Click **Cells...** →
> [Make sure "Column" under "Percentages" is not selected (there should not be a check mark next to "Column")][6] →
> Click **Continue** →
> Click **Statistics...** → **Gamma** → **Continue** → **OK**

Pearson's *r*: A Measure Appropriate for I/R Variables

Finally, we are going to work with ***Pearson's r,*** also known as a *product-moment correlation coefficient.* Pearson's *r* is a measure of association that reflects the PRE logic and is appropriate to continuous, interval-ratio (I/R) variables such as age, education, and income.

An Indication of Strength and Direction of Association

Like gamma, the value of Pearson's *r* ranges from −1.00 to +1.00, indicating both the strength and direction of the relationship between two I/R variables. Once again, a −1.00 indicates a perfect negative association, a +1.00 indicates a perfect positive association, and a 0.00 indicates no association.

Example 1: The Logic of Pearson's *r*

Although this measure also reflects the PRE logic, its meaning in that regard is not quite so straightforward as it is for the discrete variables analyzed by lambda and gamma. Although it made sense to talk about "guessing" someone's gender or employment status and being either right or wrong, there is little chance that we would ever guess someone's annual income in exact dollars or his or her exact age in days. Our best strategy would be to guess the mean income, and we'd be wrong almost every time. Pearson's *r* lets us determine whether knowing one variable would help us come closer in our guesses of the other variable and calculates how much closer we would come.

To understand *r,* let's take a simple example of eight young people and see whether there is a correlation between their heights (in inches) and their weights (in pounds). To begin, then, let's meet the eight subjects.

---

6. See footnote 3.

	Height	Weight
Eddy	68	144
Mary	58	111
Marge	67	137
Terry	66	153
Albert	61	165
Larry	74	166
Heather	67	92
Ruth	61	128

Take a minute to study the heights and weights. Begin with Eddy and Mary, at the top of the list. Eddy is both taller and heavier than Mary. If we were forced to reach a conclusion about the association between height and weight based only on these two observations, we would conclude there is a positive correlation: The taller you are, the heavier you are. We might even go a step further and note that every additional inch of height corresponds to about 3 pounds of weight.

On the other hand, if you needed to base a conclusion on observations of Eddy and Terry, see what that conclusion would be. Terry is 2 inches shorter but 9 pounds heavier. Our observations of Eddy and Terry would lead us to just the opposite conclusion: The taller you are, the lighter you are.

Sometimes, it's useful to look at a ***scattergram***, which graphs the cases at hand in terms of the two variables.[7] The diagram on the next page presents the eight cases in this fashion. Notice that there seems to be a general pattern of increasing height being associated with increasing weight, although there are a couple of cases that don't fit that pattern.

---

7. We are going to review how you can instruct SPSS to produce a scattergram (also called a scatterplot) toward the end of the chapter.

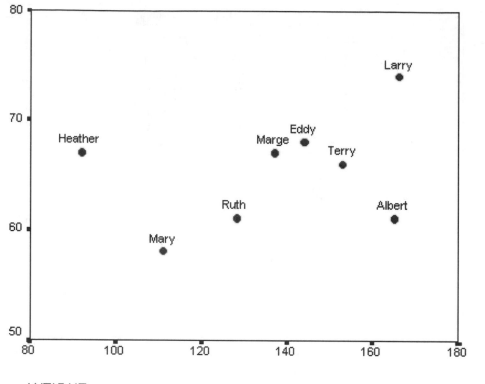

WEIGHT

Pearson's *r* allows for the fact that the relationship between height and weight may not be completely consistent, but nevertheless it lets us discover any prevailing tendency in that regard. In the gamma logic presented above, we might consider a strategy of guessing who is heavier or lighter on the basis of who is taller or shorter, assuming either a positive (taller means heavier) or negative (taller means lighter) relationship between the two variables. With *r*, however, we'll take account of *how much* taller or heavier.

To calculate *r*, we need to know the mean value of each variable. As you recall, this is calculated by adding all the values on a variable and dividing by the number of cases. If you do these calculations in the case of height, you'll discover that the eight people, laid end to end, would stretch 522 inches, for a mean height of 65.25 inches. Do the same calculation for their weights, and you'll discover that the eight people weigh a total of 1,096 pounds, for a mean of 137 pounds.

From now on, we are going to focus less on the actual heights and weights of our eight people and deal more with the extent to which they differ from the means. The table below shows how much each person differs from the means for height and weight. Notice that plus and minus signs have been used to indicate whether a person is above or below the mean. (If you want to check your calculations in this situation, you should add all the deviations from height and notice they total 0; the same is true for deviations from mean weight.)

	Height	Weight	H-dev	W-dev
Eddy	68	144	+2.75	+7
Mary	58	111	−7.25	−26
Marge	67	137	+1.75	0
Terry	66	153	+0.75	+16
Albert	61	165	−4.25	+28
Larry	74	166	+8.75	+29
Heather	67	92	+1.75	−45
Ruth	61	128	−4.25	−9
Means	65.25	137		

As our next step, we want to determine the extent to which heights and weights vary from their means overall. Although we have shown the plus and minus signs above, it is important to note that both +2.00 and −2.00 represent deviations of 2 inches from the mean height. For reasons that will become apparent shortly, we are going to capture both positive and negative variations by squaring each of the deviations from the means. The squares of both +2.00 and −2.00 are the same: 4.00. The table below shows the squared deviations for each person on each variable. We've also totaled the squared deviations and calculated their means.

	Height	Weight	H-dev	W-dev	Sq H-dev	Sq W-dev
Eddy	68	144	+2.75	+7	7.5625	49
Mary	58	111	−7.25	−26	52.5625	676
Marge	67	137	+1.75	0	3.0625	0
Terry	66	153	+0.75	+16	0.5625	256
Albert	61	165	−4.25	+28	18.0625	784
Larry	74	166	+8.75	+29	76.5625	841
Heather	67	92	+1.75	−45	3.0625	2,025
Ruth	61	128	−4.25	−9	18.0625	81
Means =	65.25	137			Totals = 179.5000	4,712

Now we're going to present a couple of steps that would require more complicated explanations than we want to subject you to in this book, so if you can simply hear what we say without asking why, that's sufficient at this point. (If you are interested in learning the logic of the intervening steps, that's great. You should check discussions of variance and standard deviations in statistics textbooks.)

Dividing the sum of the squared deviations by 1 less than the number of cases ($N - 1$) yields a quantity statisticians call the **variance**. With a large number of cases, this quantity is close to the mean of the sum of squared deviations.

The variances in this case are 25.643 for height and 673.143 for weight. The square root of the variance is called the **standard deviation**. (Perhaps you are already familiar with these concepts, or perhaps you have heard the terms but haven't known what they mean.) Thus, the standard deviation for height is 5.063891; for weight, 25.94499.

Now, we are ready to put all these calculations to work for us. We are going to express all the individual deviations from mean height and mean weight in units equal to the standard deviations. For example, Eddy was +2.75 inches taller than the average. Eddy's new deviation from the mean height becomes +0.54 (+2.75 ÷ 5.064). His deviation from the mean weight becomes +0.27 (+7 ÷ 25.945).

Our purpose in these somewhat complex calculations is to standardize deviations from the means of the two variables because the values on those variables are of very different scales. Whereas Eddy was 1.75 inches taller than the mean and 7 pounds heavier than the mean, we didn't have a way of knowing whether his height deviation was greater or lesser than his weight deviation. By dividing each deviation by the standard deviation for that variable, we can now see that Eddy's deviation on height is actually greater than his deviation in terms of weight. These new measures of deviation are called *z scores*. The table below presents each person's z score for both height and weight.

	Height	Weight	zheight	zweight	zcross
Eddy	68	144	.54	.27	.15
Mary	58	111	−1.43	−1.00	1.43
Marge	67	137	.35	.00	.00
Terry	66	153	.15	.62	.09
Albert	61	165	−.84	1.08	−.91
Larry	74	166	1.73	1.12	1.93
Heather	67	92	.35	−1.73	−.60
Ruth	61	128	−.84	−.35	.29
				Total	2.38

You'll notice that there is a final column of the table called "zcross." This is the result of multiplying each person's z score on height by the z score on weight. You'll notice we've begun rounding off the numbers to two decimal places. That level of precision is sufficient for our present purposes.

Thanks to your perseverance, we are finally ready to calculate Pearson's r product-moment correlation. By now, it's pretty simple.

r = sum of (z scores for height × z scores for weight) divided by $N − 1$

In our example, this amounts to

$r = 2.38 ÷ 8 - 1 = .34.$

There is no easy, commonsense way to represent the meaning of r. Technically, it has to do with the extent to which variations in one variable can explain variations in the other. In fact, if you square r, .12 in this case, it can be interpreted as follows: 12 percent of the variance in one variable can be accounted for by the variance in the other. Recall that the variance of a variable reflects the extent to which individual cases deviate from the mean value. Reverting to the logic of PRE, this means that knowing a person's height reduces by 12 percent the extent of our errors in guessing how far he or she is from the mean weight.

In large part, r's value comes with use. When you calculate correlations among several pairs of variables, the resulting r's will tell which pairs are more highly associated with one another than is true of other pairs.

Demonstration 14.3: Instructing SPSS to Calculate Pearson's *r*

Here's the really good news. Your reward for pressing through all the calculations above, in order to gain some understanding of what r represents, is that you'll never have to do it again. SPSS will do it for you.

Let's consider the possible relationship between two of the continuous variables in the data set: AGE and RINCOM98. If you think about it, you should expect that people tend to earn more money as they grow older, so let's check the correlation between age and respondents' incomes. (Note: RINCOM98 is the respondent's personal income; INCOME98 is family income.)

You might be reluctant to calculate the deviations, squared deviations, and so on for the 1,372 respondents in your data set (if not, you need a hobby), but computers thrive on such tasks.

Recoding RINCOM98 → RINC98A

Before we tell SPSS to take on the task of computing correlations for us, we need to do a little housekeeping. If you run a **Frequency** distribution on **RINCOM98**, you will see this:

RINCOM98 RESPONDENTS INCOME

		Frequency	Percent	Valid Percent	Cumulativ e Percent
Valid	1 UNDER $1 000	25	1.7	2.3	2.3
	2 $1 000 to 2 999	21	1.4	2.0	4.3
	3 $3 000 to 3 999	23	1.5	2.2	6.5
	4 $4 000 to 4 999	13	.9	1.2	7.7
	5 $5 000 to 5 999	11	.7	1.0	8.7
	6 $6 000 to 6 999	25	1.7	2.3	11.1
	7 $7 000 to 7 999	20	1.3	1.9	13.0
	8 $8 000 to 9 999	32	2.1	3.0	16.0
	9 $10000 to 12499	56	3.7	5.3	21.2
	10 $12500 to 14999	48	3.2	4.5	25.8
	11 $15000 to 17499	46	3.1	4.3	30.1
	12 $17500 to 19999	57	3.8	5.4	35.4
	13 $20000 to 22499	73	4.9	6.9	42.3
	14 $22500 to 24999	67	4.5	6.3	48.6
	15 $25000 to 29999	85	5.7	8.0	56.6
	16 $30000 to 34999	91	6.1	8.6	65.1
	17 $35000 to 39999	52	3.5	4.9	70.0
	18 $40000 to 49999	94	6.3	8.8	78.9
	19 $50000 to 59999	59	3.9	5.5	84.4
	20 $60000 to 74999	41	2.7	3.9	88.3
	21 $75000 - $89999	15	1.0	1.4	89.7
	22 $90000- $109999	9	.6	.8	90.5
	23 $110 000 over	22	1.5	2.1	92.6
	24 REFUSED	65	4.3	6.1	98.7
	98 DK	14	.9	1.3	100.0
	Total	1064	70.9	100.0	
Missing	0 NAP	414	27.6		
	99 NA	22	1.5		
	Total	436	29.1		
Total		1500	100.0		

There is a problem in using the codes for RINCOM98. The code categories are not equal in width. Code category 8 includes respondents whose incomes were between $8,000 and $9,999, whereas code category 9 includes incomes between $10,000 and $12,499. The categories form an ordinal scale that is not appropriate for use with Pearson's *r*.

We can use **Recode** to improve on the coding scheme used for recording incomes.[8] If we assume incomes are spread evenly across categories, then we can simply substitute the midpoints of the interval widths for the codes used in RINCOM98. That way, we can approximate an I/R scale and rid ourselves of the problems created by the interval widths not being equal. Code 23, $110,000 or more, has no upper limit. We just took a guess that the midpoint would be about $130,000. Even though we don't have each respondent's actual income, this approach will enable us to use Pearson's *r* to search for relationships between income and other variables. As SPSS commands, the recoding looks like this:

8. The authors greatly appreciate the suggestion of this analysis by Professor Gilbert Klajman, Montclair State College.

Transform → Recode → Into Different Variables...

Old Variable → New Variable
RINCOM98 → RINC98A
Old and New Values
1 → 500

2 → 2000

3 → 3000

4 → 4000

5 → 5000

6 → 6000

7 → 7000

8 → 8000

9 → 11,250

10 → 13,750

11 → 16,250

12 → 18,750

13 → 21,250

14 → 23,750

15 → 27,500

16 → 32,500

17 → 37,500

18 → 45,000

19 → 55,000

20 → 67,500

21 → 82,500

22 → 100,000

23 → 130,000

Notice that we did not specify new values for codes 0 (Not applicable), 24 (Refused), 98 (Don't know), or 99 (No answer). SPSS assigns SYSMIS, the system missing value, to any of the cases not specifically identified with an old value in the Old and New Values list. By ignoring RINCOM98's codes 0, 24, 98, 99, the corresponding cases in RINC98A are set to SYSMIS.

Once you have completed the recode, highlight **RINC98A** in the Data Editor, go to the Define Variables window, select **Type...**, and change the number of decimal places to **0**. Then run **Frequencies** for RINC98A. Here's what the recoded variable looks like.

RINC98A

		Frequency	Percent	Valid Percent	Cumulativ e Percent
Valid	500	25	1.7	2.5	2.5
	2000	21	1.4	2.1	4.7
	3000	23	1.5	2.3	7.0
	4000	13	.9	1.3	8.3
	5000	11	.7	1.1	9.4
	6000	25	1.7	2.5	12.0
	7000	20	1.3	2.0	14.0
	8000	32	2.1	3.2	17.3
	11250	56	3.7	5.7	22.9
	13750	48	3.2	4.9	27.8
	16250	46	3.1	4.7	32.5
	18750	57	3.8	5.8	38.3
	21250	73	4.9	7.4	45.7
	23750	67	4.5	6.8	52.5
	27500	85	5.7	8.6	61.1
	32500	91	6.1	9.2	70.4
	37500	52	3.5	5.3	75.6
	45000	94	6.3	9.5	85.2
	55000	59	3.9	6.0	91.2
	67500	41	2.7	4.2	95.3
	82500	15	1.0	1.5	96.9
	100000	9	.6	.9	97.8
	130000	22	1.5	2.2	100.0
	Total	985	65.7	100.0	
Missing	System	515	34.3		
Total		1500	100.0		

Computing *r*

With the housekeeping out of the way, you need only move through this menu path to launch SPSS on the job of computing *r*. Unlike the previous measures we have discussed, Pearson's *r* is not available in the **Crosstabs** window. Instead it is appropriately available in the **Bivariate Correlations** window. To access this window simply follow the steps below:

Analyze → Correlate → Bivariate...

This will bring you to the following window:

Transfer **AGE** and **RINC98A** to the Variables: list. (Be sure to use AGE and not AGECAT, because we want the uncoded variable.)

Below the Variables: list, you'll see that we can choose from among three forms of correlation coefficients. Our discussion above has described Pearson's *r,* so click **Pearson** if it is not selected already.

Did you ever think about what we would do if we had an AGE for someone, but we did not know his or her RINC98A? Because we would have only one score, we would have to throw that person out of our analysis. But suppose we had three variables and we were missing a score on a case? Would we throw out just the pair that had a missing value, or would we throw out the whole case?

SPSS lets us do it either way. Click on **Options...**, and you will see that we can choose to exclude cases either *pairwise* or *listwise*. If we exclude pairwise, we discard a pair only when either score is missing, but with listwise exclusion, we discard the entire case if only one pair is missing.

We will use listwise exclusion. With a sample as large as ours, it does not hurt to lose a few cases. However, if our sample were small, we would probably want to use pairwise deletion.

Once you have selected **Exclude cases listwise**, click on **Continue** and then **OK**. Your reward will be a *correlation matrix,* a table that shows the correlations among all variables (including, as we will see, the correlation of each item with itself).

Correlations[a]

		AGE AGE OF RESPONDENT	RINC98A
AGE AGE OF RESPONDENT	Pearson Correlation	1.000	.233**
	Sig. (2-tailed)	.	.000
RINC98A	Pearson Correlation	.233**	1.000
	Sig. (2-tailed)	.000	.

**. Correlation is significant at the 0.01 level (2-tailed).

a. Listwise N=985

The Pearson's *r* product-moment correlation between AGE and RINC98A is .233.[9] Notice that the correlation between AGE and itself is perfect (1.000), which makes sense if you think about it.

You now know that the .233 is a measure of the extent to which deviations from the mean income can be accounted for by deviations from the mean of age. By squaring *r*, we learn that about 5.4 percent of the variance in income can be accounted for by how old people are.

We are going to ignore the references to "Significance" until the next chapter. This indicates the *statistical significance* of the association.

SPSS COMMAND 14.3: Producing a Correlation Matrix and Pearson's *r*

Click **Analyze** → **Correlate** → **Bivariate...** →

Highlight **variable name** → Click right-pointing **arrow** to transfer it to the "Variables:" field →

Repeat previous step until all variables have been transferred →

Click **Pearson** → **Options...** → **Exclude cases** either list or pairwise → **Continue** → **OK**

Demonstration 14.4: Requesting Several Correlation Coefficients

What else do you suppose might account for differences in income? If you think about it, you might decide that education is a possibility. Presumably, the more education you get, the more money you'll make. Your understanding of *r* through SPSS will let you check it out.

The Correlations command allows you to request several correlation coefficients at once. Go back to the **Bivariate Correlations** window and add **EDUC**

9. The discussion and general guidelines for interpreting Pearson's *r* can be found in Demonstration 14.1 and Table 14.1.

to the list of variables being analyzed. Once again, exclude cases listwise before executing the command.

Here's what you should get in your Output window. (Hint: If you didn't get this, check what happened to the "Don't knows.")

Correlations^a

		AGE AGE OF RESPON DENT	RINC98A	EDUC HIGHEST YEAR OF SCHOOL COMPLET ED
AGE AGE OF RESPONDENT	Pearson Correlation	1.000	.232**	.043
	Sig. (2-tailed)	.	.000	.176
RINC98A	Pearson Correlation	.232**	1.000	.410**
	Sig. (2-tailed)	.000	.	.000
EDUC HIGHEST YEAR OF SCHOOL	Pearson Correlation	.043	.410**	1.000
	Sig. (2-tailed)	.176	.000	.

**. Correlation is significant at the 0.01 level (2-tailed).

a. Listwise N=982

This new correlation matrix is a little more complex than the previous one. The fact that each variable correlates perfectly with itself should offer assurance that we are doing something right. The new matrix also tells us that there is a stronger correlation between EDUC and RINCOME: .410. Squaring the r tells us that 16.8 percent of the variance in income can be accounted for by how much education people have.

A Note of Caution

We'll be using the Correlations command and related statistics as the book continues. In closing this discussion, we'd like you to recall that Pearson's r is appropriate only for I/R variables. It would not be appropriate in the analysis of nominal variables such as **RELIG** and **MARITAL**, for example. But what do you suppose would happen if we asked SPSS to correlate r for those two variables? This time, exclude cases pairwise before you execute the command.

Correlations

		RELIG RS RELIGIOUS PREFERENCE	MARITAL MARITAL STATUS
RELIG RS RELIGIOUS PREFERENCE	Pearson Correlation	1.000	.171**
	Sig. (2-tailed)	.	.000
	N	1411	1410
MARITAL MARITAL STATUS	Pearson Correlation	.171**	1.000
	Sig. (2-tailed)	.000	.
	N	1410	1499

**. Correlation is significant at the 0.01 level (2-tailed).

As you can see, SPSS does not recognize that we've asked it to do a stupid thing. It stupidly complies. It tells us there is a significant (see next chapter) relationship between a person's marital status and the religion he or she belongs to, whereas the correlation calculated here has no real meaning.

SPSS has been able to do the requested calculation because it stores "Married" as 1 and "Widowed" as 2 and stores "Protestant" as 1, "Catholic" as 2, and so on, but these numbers have no numerical meaning in this instance. Catholics are not "twice" Protestants, and widowed people are not "twice" married people.

Here's a thought experiment we hope will guard against this mistake: (a) Write down the telephone numbers of your five best friends; (b) add them up and calculate the "mean" telephone number; (c) call that number and see if an "average" friend answers. Or go to a Chinese restaurant with a group of friends and have everyone in your party select one dish by its number in the menu. Add all those numbers and calculate the mean. When the waiter comes, get several orders of the "average" dish and see if you have any friends left.

Pearson's r is designed for the analysis of relationships among continuous, interval/ratio variables. We have just entrusted you with a powerful weapon for understanding. Use it wisely. Remember: Statistics don't mislead—those who calculate statistics stupidly mislead.

Regression

The discussion of Pearson's r correlation coefficient opens the door for discussion of a related statistical technique that is also appropriate for I/R level variables: *regression*. When we looked at the scattergram of weight and height in the hypothetical example that introduced the discussion of correlation, you will recall that we tried to "see" a general pattern in the distribution of cases. Regression makes that attempt more concrete.

Example 1: The Logic of Regression

To begin, let's imagine an extremely simple example that relates the number of hours spent studying for an examination and the grades students got on the exam. Here are the data in a table:

Student	Hours	Grade
Fred	0	0
Mary	2	25
Sam	4	50
Edith	6	75
Earl	8	100

First question: Can you guess which of us prepared this example? Second question: Can you see a pattern in the data presented?

The pattern, pretty clearly, is this: The more you study, the better the grade you get. Let's look at these data in the form of a graph. (This is something you can do by hand, using graph paper.)

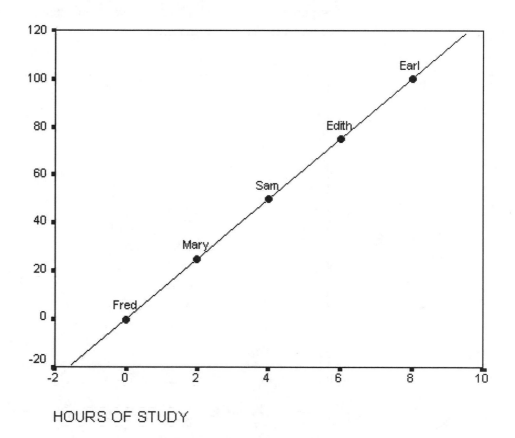

HOURS OF STUDY

As you can see, the five people in this example fall along a straight line across the graph. This line is called the *regression line*. As you may recall from plane geometry, it is possible to represent a straight line on a graph in the form of an equation. In this case the equation would be as follows:

Grade = 12.5 × Hours

To determine a person's grade using this equation, you need only multiply the number of hours he or she studied by 12.5. Multiply Earl's 8 hours of study by 12.5 and you get his grade of 100. Multiply Edith's 6 hours by 12.5 and you get 75. Multiply Fred's 0 hours by 12.5 and, well, you know Fred.

Whereas correlation considers the symmetrical association between two variables, regression adds the notion of causal direction. One of the variables is the *dependent variable*—grades, in this example—and the other is the *independent variable* or cause—hours of study. Thus, the equation we just created is designed to predict a person's grade based on how many hours he or she studied. If we were to tell you that someone not included in these data studied 5 hours for the exam, you could predict that that person got a 62.5 on the exam (5 × 12.5).

If all social science analyses produced results as clear as these, you probably wouldn't need SPSS or a book like this one. In practice, however, the facts are usually a bit more complex, and SPSS is up to the challenge.

Given a set of data with an imperfect relationship between two variables, SPSS can discover the line that *comes closest* to passing through all the points on the graph. To understand the meaning of the notion of coming close, we need to recall the squared deviations found in our calculation of Pearson's *r*.

Suppose Sam had gotten 70 on the exam, for example. Here's what he would look like on the graph we just drew.

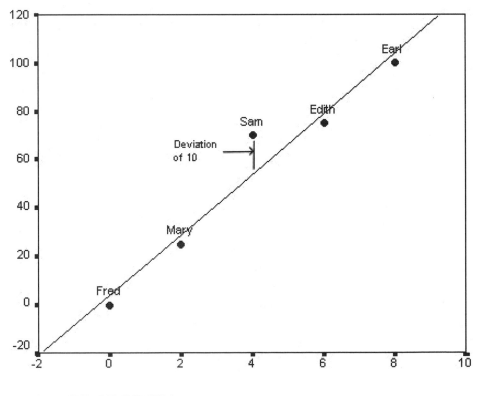

HOURS OF STUDY

Notice that the improved Sam does not fall on the original regression line: His grade represents a deviation of 10 points. With a real set of data, most people fall to one side or the other of any line we might draw through the data. SPSS, however, is able to determine the line that would produce the smallest deviations overall—measured by squaring all the individual deviations and adding them. This calculated regression line is sometimes called the ***least-squares regression line***.

Requesting such an analysis from SPSS is fairly simple. To use this technique to real advantage, you need more instruction than is appropriate for this book. However, we wanted to introduce you to regression because it is a popular technique among many social scientists.

Demonstration 14.5: Regression

To experiment with the regression technique, let's make use of a new variable: SEI. This variable rates the socioeconomic prestige of respondents' occupations on a scale from a low of 0 to a high of 100, based on other studies that have asked a sample from the general population to rate different occupations.

Here's how we would ask SPSS to find the equation that best represents the influence of EDUC on SEI. You should realize that there are a number of ways to request this information, but we'd suggest you do it as follows. (Just do it this way and nobody gets hurt, okay?)

Under **Analyze**, select **Regression** → **Linear....** Here's what you get.

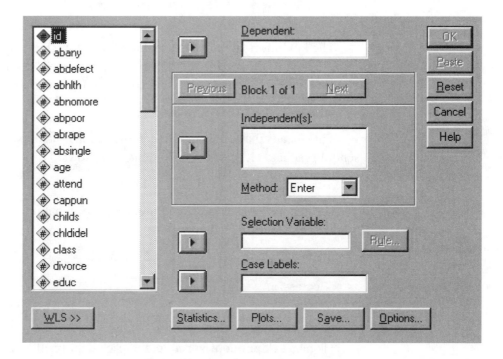

Select **SEI** as the Dependent: variable and **EDUC** as the Independent(s): variable. Click **OK**, and SPSS is off and running. Here's the output you should get in response to this instruction.

Model Summary

Model	R	R Square	Adjusted R Square	Std. Error of the Estimate
1	.576ª	.332	.331	15.780

a. Predictors: (Constant), EDUC HIGHEST YEAR OF SCHOOL COMPLETED

ANOVAᵇ

Model		Sum of Squares	df	Mean Square	F	Sig.
1	Regression	175458.9	1	175458.9	704.592	.000ª
	Residual	353113.1	1418	249.022		
	Total	528572.0	1419			

a. Predictors: (Constant), EDUC HIGHEST YEAR OF SCHOOL COMPLETED

b. Dependent Variable: SEI RESPONDENT SOCIOECONOMIC INDEX

Coefficientsª

Model		Unstandardized Coefficients		Standardized Coefficients	t	Sig.
		B	Std. Error	Beta		
1	(Constant)	-2.015	1.978		-1.019	.309
	EDUC HIGHEST YEAR OF SCHOOL COMPLETED	3.833	.144	.576	26.544	.000

a. Dependent Variable: SEI RESPONDENT SOCIOECONOMIC INDEX

The key information we are looking for is contained in the final table titled "Coefficients": the *intercept* (–2.015) and the *slope* (3.833). These are the data we need to complete our regression equation. Use them as follows:

SEI = –2.015 + (EDUC × 3.833).

This means that we would predict the occupation prestige ranking of a high school graduate (12 years of schooling) as follows:

SEI = –2.015 + (12 × 3.833) = 43.981.

On the other hand, we would predict the occupational prestige of a college graduate (16 years of schooling) as

SEI = –2.015 + (16 × 3.833) = 59.313.

SPSS COMMAND   14.4: Regression

> Click **Analyze → Regression → Linear... →**
>
> Highlight **dependent variable** and click right-pointing **arrow** to transfer it to Dependent: field →
>
> Highlight **independent variable** and click right-pointing **arrow** to transfer it to Independent(s): field →
>
> Click **OK**

Demonstration 14.6: Presenting Data Graphically: Producing a Scatterplot with Regression Line

Another way to explore the relationship between SEI and EDUC is to instruct SPSS to produce a *scatterplot* with a *regression line*. Scatterplot is a term SPSS uses to identify what we referred to earlier in our discussion of Pearson's *r* as a scattergram. A scatterplot/scattergram is simply a graph with a *horizontal (x) axis* and a *vertical (y) axis*. As you saw earlier, each dot on the graph represents the point of intersection for each individual case. It is the "scatter" of dots taken as a whole which, along with the regression line, indicate the strength and direction of association between the variables.

Instructing SPSS to produce a scatterplot with a regression line allows us to see the distribution and array of cases, while saving us the time-consuming task of creating the graph on our own (which as you can imagine with approximately 1,500 cases would be quite a daunting task).

To produce a scatterplot, all you have to do is open the Scatterplot window by clicking **Graphs** and then choosing **Scatter...** in the drop-down menu.

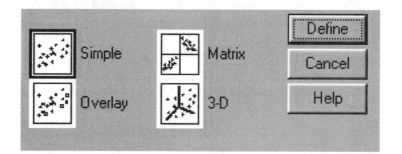

When you have opened the Scatterplot window as shown above, select **Simple** if it is not already highlighted and then click **Define**. You should now be looking at the Simple Scatterplot dialog box as shown below:

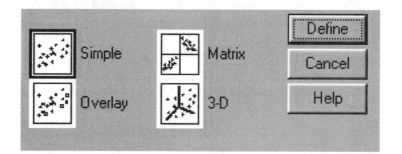

Following the example we used above, place **EDUC** (the independent variable) along the **X Axis:**. And then place **SEI** (the dependent variable) along the **Y Axis:**. When you are finished with this process you can hit **OK** and very shortly the following graph should appear on your screen.

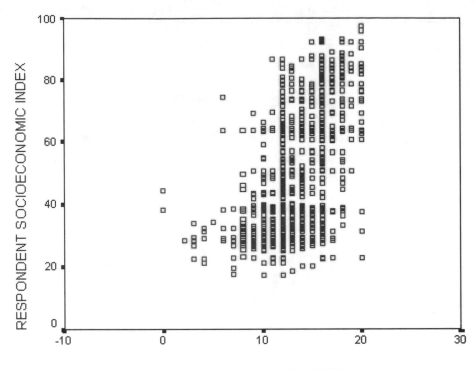

HIGHEST YEAR OF SCHOOL COMPLETED

As requested, our independent variable EDUC is arrayed along the *x* (horizontal) axis and our dependent variable SEI is arrayed along the *y* (vertical axis). You can also see the splatter of dots on the graph, each representing a particular case.

Now **double-click on the graph** and the SPSS Chart Editor will appear.

We are going to use the Chart Editor to add our regression line which, as we saw earlier, is simply a single straight line that will run through our scatterplot and come as close as possible to touching all the "dots" or data points.

Now select the **Chart Options** button, which is the second button from the right on the lower button bar. Once you have done that the Scatterplot Options dialog window will open as shown below.

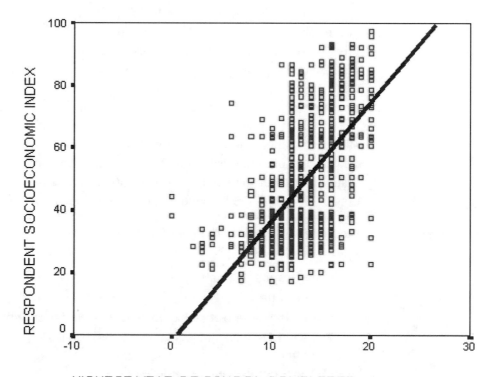

Click on the **box** next to **Total** in the upper right-hand side of the window below Fit Line. Once you see a check mark appear in the box, you can click **OK**. You will soon see that the regression line we requested has been added to your scatterplot as shown below. To close the Chart Editor, simply click **File → Close**.

An Indication of Direction and Strength of Association

The scatterplot and regression line shown above serve as a visual indication of the direction and strength of association between EDUC and SEI.

The direction of association can be determined based on the way the regression line sits on the scatterplot. Generally, when the line moves from the bottom left-hand side of the graph to the upper right-hand side of the graph (uphill), this indicates a positive association between the variables (they both either increase or decrease in the same direction), whereas a regression line that runs from the upper left to the lower right side of the scatterplot (downhill) indicates a negative association between the items (as one increases, the other decreases).

The strength of association can be estimated based on the extent to which the dots (cases) are scattered around the regression line. The closer the dots are to the regression line, the stronger the association between the variables (in the case of a "perfect relationship," the dots will sit exactly on the regression line, indicating the strongest possible association between the variables). Conversely, the further spread out or scattered the dots are, the weaker the relationship between the items.

We want to emphasize that although this type of visual representation allows us to estimate the strength of association between variables, there is no agreement regarding what constitutes a "strong" versus a "moderate" or "weak" association. Consequently, your best option may be to use the scatterplot with a regression line in conjunction with a measure such as Pearson's r, which allows you to obtain a value that summarizes the association between variables more precisely than just the scatterplot and regression line do. Keep in mind that because both options are appropriate for continuously distributed I/R variables, they can be used to examine the same types of items.

Now try to see if you can describe the strength and direction of association between EDUC and SEI as shown in the scatterplot with a regression line above. What is the direction of association? Are the variables positively or negatively related (i.e., does the regression line run uphill or downhill)? What can you estimate in terms of the strength of association between EDUC and SEI? Are the dots or cases clustered around the regression line or spread out?

SPSS COMMAND 14.5:   Producing a Scatterplot with Regression Line

> Click **Graphs** → **Scatter...** → In Scatterplot dialog box click **Simple** → **Define** →
>
> In Simple Scatterplot dialog box **highlight independent variable** →
>
> Transfer independent variable to **X Axis:** by clicking right-pointing **arrow** →
>
> Highlight **dependent variable** →
>
> Transfer to **Y Axis:** by clicking right-pointing **arrow** →
>
> Click **OK** →
>
> **Double-click on the Scatterplot** in your Data Editor →
>
> Click **Chart Options** button (second button from right on lower button bar) →
>
> In Scatterplot Options dialog box click **Total** → **OK**

That's enough fun for now. We'll return to regression later, when we discuss multivariate analysis in Chapter 17.

Analyzing the Association Between Variables at Different Levels of Measurement

The measures of association we have focused on are each appropriate for variables at a particular level of measurement. For instance, lambda is used to examine the association between two nominal variables, whereas gamma is used to explore the relationship between two ordinal variables and Pearson's r and regression are appropriate for two I/R items. Table 14.2 lists the measures we have reviewed along with their appropriate level of measurement.

Table 14.2:   Measures of Association Reviewed in Chapter

Level of Measurement	Measure of Association (Range of Values)of Each Variable
Nominal × Nominal	Lambda [0 to +1]
Ordinal × Ordinal	Gamma [−1 to +1]
I/R × I/R	Pearson's r [−1 to +1]
	Regression

In some cases, however, you may discover that you want to analyze the association between two variables at different levels of measurement: for instance, nominal by ordinal, nominal by I/R, and so on. While there are specialized bivariate measures of association for use when two variables are on different levels of measure, the safest course of action for the novice is to use a measure of association that meets the assumptions for the variable with the lowest level of measurement. This usually means that one variable will have to be recoded to reduce its level of measurement. For instance, when we examined the relationship between church attendance (ordinal) and age (I/R), we recoded peoples' ages into ordinal categories. While it would not be appropriate to use Pearson's r to correlate our CHATT and AGE, it is perfectly legitimate to use gamma to correlate CHATT with AGECAT.

While it is beyond the scope of this chapter to review all the statistical measures appropriate for each particular situation, those of you who are interested in pursuing the relationship between mixed variables may want to consult a basic statistics[10] or research methods text for a discussion of appropriate measures.[11] Keep in mind that a variety of these texts can now be accessed quite easily on

---

10. Two of the many basic statistics texts that you may want to consult are: Freeman's *Elementary Applied Statistics* (1968) and Siegel and Castellan's *Nonparametric Statistics for the Behavioral Sciences* (1988).

11. In *The Survey Research Handbook*, for instance, Alreck and Settle (1985) provide a table titled "Statistical Measures of Association" which, depending on the type of independent and dependent variables you are working with (i.e., categorical or continuous), specifies which measures of association are appropriate. The table is accompanied by a discussion of statistical analysis and interpretation (287–362; Figure 10-5, 303).

the world wide web.[12] In addition, you may want to access some of the many web sites that have been established in recent years to help students identify appropriate statistical tests. The following are just two examples of the numerous sites available:

"Selecting Statistics"
http://trochim.human.cornell.edu/selstat/ssstart.htm

"Descriptive Statistics for Data Analysis"
http://www.becker.edu/~jstone/soc/courses3/soc401/dstatistics.htm

Conclusion

In this chapter, we've seen a number of statistical techniques that can be used to summarize the degree of relationship or association between two variables. We've seen that the appropriate technique depends on the level of measurement represented by the variables involved. Lambda is appropriate for nominal variables, gamma for ordinal variables, and Pearson's *r* product-moment correlation and regression for ratio variables.

We realize that you may have had trouble knowing how to respond to the results of these calculations. How do you decide, for example, if a gamma of .25 is high or low? Should you get excited about it or yawn and continue looking? The following chapter on statistical significance offers one basis for making such decisions.

Main Points

- In this chapter we looked at new ways to examine the relationships among variables.
- Measures of association summarize the strength (and in the case of numeric items, the direction) of association between two variables in contrast to the way percentage tables lay out the details.
- This chapter focuses on only some of the many measures available: lambda, gamma, Pearson's *r,* and regression.
- The measures are largely based on the logic of PRE.
- Lambda is appropriate for two nominal variables; its values range from 0 to 1.
- Gamma is appropriate for two ordinal variables; its values range from –1 to +1.
- Pearson's *r* is appropriate for two I/R items; its values range from –1 to +1.
- The closer the value is to positive or negative 1, the stronger the relationship between the items (with +1 or –1 indicating a perfect association). The closer the

12. A few examples include: William M. Trochim's Research Methods Knowledge Base at http://trochim.human.cornell.edu/kb/index.htm; David M. Lane's Hyperstat Online at http://www.ruf.rice.edu/~lane/hyperstat/index.html; and David Stockburger's Introductory Statistics: Concepts, Models, and Applications at http://www.psychstat.smsu.edu/introbook/sbkoo.htm. These are just three of the many research methods and statistics texts now available on the world wide web.

value is to 0, the weaker the relationship between the items (with 0 indicating no association between the items).

■ There are no set rules for interpreting strength of association.

■ Like Pearson's *r*, regression is also appropriate for two I/R items.

■ Another way to explore the strength and direction of association between two I/R items is to produce a scatterplot with a regression line.

■ There are a variety of appropriate statistics for examining the relationship between mixed types of variables.

Key Terms

Measures of association
PRE (proportionate reduction of error)
Lambda
Gamma
Positive association
Negative association
Strength of association
Direction of association
Same pair
Opposite pair
Pearson's *r*
Scattergram (scatterplot)

Variance
Standard deviation
z scores
Correlation matrix
Statistical significance
Regression
Least-squares regression line
Intercept
Slope
Regression line
x (horizontal) axis
y (vertical) axis

SPSS Commands Introduced in This Chapter

14.1:   Running Crosstabs and Lambda

> Click **Analyze** → **Descriptive Statistics** → **Crosstabs...** →
> Specify **dependent variable** as the **Row(s)**: variable →
> Specify **independent variable** as the **Column(s)**: variable →
> Click **Cells...** →
> [Make sure "Column" under "Percentages" is *not* selected (there should *not* be a check mark next to "Column")] →
> Click **Continue** →
> Click **Statistics...** → **Lambda** → **Continue** → **OK**

14.2:   Running Crosstabs and Gamma

> Click **Analyze** → **Descriptive Statistics** → **Crosstabs**... →
>
> Specify **dependent variable** as the **Row(s)**: variable
>
> Specify **independent variable** as the **Column(s)**: variable →
>
> Click **Cells**... →
>
> [Make sure "Column" under "Percentages" is *not* selected (there should *not* be a check mark next to "Column")] →
>
> Click **Continue** →
>
> Click **Statistics...** → **Gamma** → **Continue** → **OK**

14.3:   Producing a Correlation Matrix and Pearson's *r*

> Click **Analyze** → **Correlate** → **Bivariate...** →
>
> Highlight **variable name** → Click right-pointing **arrow** to transfer it to the "Variables:" field →
>
> Repeat previous step until all variables have been transferred →
>
> Click **Pearson** → **Options...** → **Exclude cases** either list or pairwise →
>
> **Continue** → **OK**

14.4:   Regression

> Click **Analyze** → **Regression** → **Linear...** →
>
> Highlight **dependent variable** and click right-pointing **arrow** to transfer it to Dependent: field →
>
> Highlight **independent variable** and click right-pointing **arrow** to transfer it to Independent(s): field →
>
> Click **OK**

14.5:   Producing a Scatterplot with Regression Line

> Click **Graphs** → **Scatter...** → In Scatterplot dialog box click **Simple** → **Define** →
>
> In Simple Scatterplot dialog box **highlight independent variable** →
>
> Transfer independent variable to **X Axis**: by clicking right-pointing **arrow** →
>
> Highlight **dependent variable** →
>
> Transfer to **Y Axis**: by clicking right-pointing **arrow** →
>
> Click **OK** →
>
> **Double-click on the Scatterplot** in your Data Editor →
>
> Click **Chart Options** button (second button from right on lower button bar) →
>
> In Scatterplot Options dialog box click **Total** → **OK**

Review Questions

1. If two variables are strongly associated, does that mean that they are necessarily causally related?
2. What is PRE?
3. List three measures of association.
4. Measures of association give us an indication of the _____ of association and in the case of numeric items the _____ of association between two variables.
5. Lambda is appropriate for variables at which level of measurement?
6. Gamma is appropriate for variables at which level of measurement?
7. Pearson's *r* is appropriate for variables at which level of measurement?
8. List the range of values for each of the following measures:
   • lambda
   • gamma
   • Pearson's *r*
9. The closer to _____ or _____ (value) the stronger the relationship between the variables.
10. The closer to _____ (value) the weaker the relationship between the variables.
11. A value of _____ or _____ indicates a perfect (or the strongest) relationship between the variables.
12. What does a positive association between two variables indicate? What does a negative association between two variables indicate?
13. Does a negative value for gamma necessarily indicate that the variables are negatively associated? Explain.
14. Regression is appropriate for two variables at which level of measurement?
15. What type of graph did we review in this chapter which allows us to examine the strength and direction of association between two I/R variables?

NAME _____

CLASS _____

INSTRUCTOR _____

DATE _____

To complete these exercises, load your data file EXER.SAV. You will find answers to selected Questions (1–7, 13–21, and 29–38) in Appendix A.

Run Crosstabs *with column percentages for the variables RACE (independent) and POLHITOK (dependent). Then request the appropriate measure of association and answer Questions 1–7. Reminder: Be sure to define DKs as missing values.*

1. What is the level of measurement for the variable RACE?

2. What is the level of measurement for the variable POLHITOK?

3. What measure of association is appropriate to examine the relationship between these variables?

4. Record the percentage of respondents who said "Yes" to POLHITOK for each category of the variable RACE.

   Race

	White	Black	Other
Yes	_____	_____	_____

5. Do the column percentages change or move, signifying a relationship between RACE and POLHITOK? Explain.

6. The strength/value of _____ (measure of association) is _____ (value/strength of measure of association).

7. Would you characterize the relationship between these two variables as weak, moderate, or strong? Explain.

Choose two nominal variables from your data set. Run Crosstabs *with column percentages for the variables. Then request the appropriate measure of association and answer Questions 8–12. Reminder: Be sure to label DKs as missing values.*

8. List the two variables you chose, designating one as the independent and one as the dependent variable. Then state briefly why you chose them and what you expect to find in terms of the relationship between these items.

9. What measure of association is appropriate to examine the relationship between these variables?

10. Do the column percentages change or move, signifying a relationship between these variables? Explain.

11. The strength/value of _____ (measure of association) is _____ (value/strength of measure of association).

12. Would you characterize the relationship between these two variables as weak, moderate, or strong? Explain.

Run Crosstabs *with column percentages for the variables RACWORK (independent) and DISCAFF (dependent). Then request the appropriate measure of association and answer Questions 13–21. Reminder: Be sure to label DKs as missing values for your variables. For the variable RACWORK, you should designate the following numeric values as missing: 0, 6, 8, 9.*

13. What is the level of measurement for the variable RACWORK?

14. What is the level of measurement for the variable DISCAFF?

15. What measure of association is appropriate to examine the relationship between these variables?

NAME _____

CLASS _____

INSTRUCTOR _____

DATE _____

16. Record the percentage of respondents who said "Very likely" and "Somewhat likely" to DISCAFF for each category of the variable RACWORK.

	All White	Mstly. Wt.	Half-Half	Mstly. Blk.	All Black
Very Likely	_____	_____	_____	_____	_____
Somewhat Likely	_____	_____	_____	_____	_____

17. Do the column percentages change or move, signifying a relationship between RACWORK and DISCAFF? Explain.

18. The strength/value of _____ (measure of association) is _____ (value/strength of measure of association).

19. Are either of the variables numeric? If so, which?

20. Would you characterize the relationship between these two variables as weak, moderate, or strong? Explain

21. What is the direction of association between these variables?

Choose two ordinal variables from your data set. Run Crosstabs with column percentages for the variables. Then request the appropriate measure of association and answer Questions 22–28. Reminder: Be sure to label DKs as missing values for your variables whenever requesting percentages.

22. List the two variables you chose, designating one as the independent and one as the dependent variable. Then state briefly why you chose them and what you expect to find in terms of the relationship between these items.

23. What measure of association is appropriate to examine the relationship between these variables?

24. Do the column percentages change or move, signifying a relationship between these variables? Explain.

25. The strength/value of _____ (measure of association) is _____ (value/strength of measure of association).

26. Are either of the variables numeric? If so, which?

27. Would you characterize the relationship between these two variables as weak, moderate, or strong? Explain.

28. What is the direction of association between these variables?

Produce a correlation matrix, exclude cases pairwise, and request Pearson's r for the variables AGE (independent) and SEI (dependent). Then answer Questions 29–32. Define DK, NA, and NAP as missing values for the variable AGE.

29. What is the level of measurement for the variable AGE?

NAME _____

CLASS _____

INSTRUCTOR _____

DATE _____

30. What is the level of measurement for the variable SEI?

31. Pearson's *r* for AGE and SEI is _____.

32. Would you characterize the relationship between these two variables as weak, moderate, or strong? Explain.

Produce a scatterplot with a regression line for the variables EDUC (independent) and TVHOURS (dependent). Then answer Questions 33–37. Designate the labels NA, NAP, and DK as missing for each of the variables.

33. What is the level of measurement for the variable EDUC?

34. What is the level of measurement for the variable TVHOURS?

35. What is the direction of the relationship between the variables?

36. As years of education increases, does the number of hours of television watched increase or decrease?

37. The relationship of the "dots" or cases to the regression line suggests what about the strength of the relationship between these two variables?

38. Produce a correlation matrix with Pearson's *r*, exclude cases pairwise, and then further describe the strength of the relationship between EDUC and TVHOURS by noting what the value of Pearson's *r* is and whether the relationship is weak, moderate, or strong.

39. Choose two nominal, ordinal, or I/R variables from the data set; instruct SPSS to calculate the appropriate measure of association; and then describe the relationship between the variables below. (If you choose two I/R variables, also produce a scatterplot with a regression line and use that to aid in your analysis of the relationship between the variables.) In particular, you may want to consider noting the following type of information: what variables you chose, the levels of measurement of each, whether they are numeric, whether you had to recode either item or designate any values as missing, what measure of association you instructed SPSS to calculate, the value of that measure, what it indicates about the relationship between these variables (strength and direction), etc....

Chapter 15 **Tests of Significance**

Thus far, in Chapters 11 through 14, we've been looking at the relationships between pairs of variables. In all that, you may have been frustrated over the ambiguity as to what constitutes a "strong" or a "weak" relationship. As we noted in the last chapter, ultimately there is no absolute answer to this question. The strength and significance of a relationship between two variables depend on many things.

If you are trying to account for differences among people on some variable, such as prejudice, the explanatory power of one variable, such as education, needs to be contrasted with the explanatory power of other variables. Thus you might be interested in knowing whether education, political affiliation, or region of upbringing has the greatest impact on a person's prejudice.

Sometimes the importance of a relationship is based on practical policy implications. Thus the impact of some variable in explaining (and potentially reducing) auto theft rates, for example, might be converted to a matter of dollars. Other relationships might be expressed in terms of lives saved, students graduating from college, and so forth.

Statistical Significance

In this chapter, we're going to introduce you to another standard for judging the relationships among variables—one that is commonly used by social scientists. Whereas in Chapter 14 we discussed measures of association that allow us to examine the *strength* (and in the case of ordinal and I/R variables, the *direction*) of association, in this chapter we explore tests that will allow you to estimate *statistical significance*. Tests of statistical significance allow us to estimate the likelihood that a relationship between variables in a sample actually exists in the population as opposed to being an illusion due to chance or sampling error.

For instance, whenever analyses are based on random samples selected from a population rather than on data collected from everyone in that population, there is always the possibility that what we learn from the samples may not truly reflect the whole population. Thus we might discover in a sample that women are more religious than men, but that could be simply an artifact of our sample: We happened to pick too many religious women and/or too few religious men. Tests of significance allow us to estimate the likelihood that our finding, a relationship between gender and religiosity in this case, could have happened by chance. If the chances of our finding are very unlikely, say only about five in a hundred, then we have the confidence needed to generalize our finding from the sample to the population from which it was drawn.

Significance Tests: Part of the Larger Body of Inferential Statistics[1]

Significance tests are part of a larger body of statistics known as *inferential statistics*. Inferential statistics can probably best be understood in contrast to *descriptive statistics*, which you are already familiar with. Together, descriptive and inferential statistics constitute two of the main types of statistics that social researchers use. Up to this point (Chapters 6 through 14) our focus has been largely on descriptive statistics that allow us to describe or summarize the main features of our data or the relationships between variables in our data set. In contrast, inferential statistics allows us to go a step further by making it possible to draw conclusions or make inferences that extend beyond the items in our particular data set to the larger population. In short, we can use inferential statistics to help us learn what our sample tells us about the population from which it was drawn. In the case of tests of significance, for instance, we can estimate whether an observed association between variables in our sample is generalizable to the larger population.

Statistical Significance Versus Measures of Association

Social scientists often test the statistical significance of relationships discovered among variables. Although these tests do not constitute a direct measure of the *strength* of a relationship, they tell us the likelihood that the observed relationship could have resulted from the vagaries of probability sampling, which we call *sampling error*. These tests relate to the strength of relationships in that the stronger an observed relationship, the less likely it is that it could be the result of sampling error. Correspondingly, it is more likely that the observed relationship represents something that exists in the population as a whole.

You will find that social scientists use measures of association and tests of significance in conjunction with one another because together they allow us to address three important questions about the relationships between variables:

1. *How strong is the relationship?* (Measures of Association/Descriptive Statistics such as lambda, gamma, etc. . . . Chapter 14)

2. In the case of ordinal and I/R variables, *what is the direction of association?* (Measures of Association/Descriptive Statistics such as gamma, Pearson's *r*, etc. . . . Chapter 14)

3. *Is the relationship statistically significant?* (Tests of Significance/Inferential Statistics such as chi-square, *t* test, etc. . . .)

---

1. Because we cannot hope to provide you with an in-depth discussion of the complexities of inferential statistics, we encourage you to refer to basic statistics and social research texts for a more complete discussion. To that end, throughout this chapter we will try to point you to various resources that you may find useful. A web site that provides a very brief and accessible overview of inferential statistics (among many other things) is the "Inferential Statistics" part of "Sociology—UTSA Style Index to the Sociological World" at http://csbs.utsa.edu/social&policy/soc/masters/inferential.htm. The home page also contains links to many other sites that you may find useful, including introductory research and statistics texts that you can access on-line.

In this chapter we turn our attention to Question 3 and some of the measures that can be used to estimate statistical significance, primarily chi-square, *t* tests, and ANOVA.

Chi-Square

To learn the logic of statistical significance, let's begin with a measure, ***chi-square***, that is based on the kinds of crosstabulations we've been examining in previous chapters. Chi-square is a test of significance that is most appropriate for nominal items, although it can be used with ordinal variables or a combination of nominal and ordinal variables. Chi-square, one of the most widely used tests of significance, estimates the probability that the association between variables is a result of random chance or sampling error by comparing the actual or observed distribution of responses with the distribution of responses we would expect if there were absolutely no association between two variables.

To help make this more clear, let's take some time now to look at the logic of statistical significance in general and chi-square in particular.

The Logic of Statistical Significance: Chi-Square

For a concrete example, let's return to one of the tables that examines the relationship between religion and abortion attitudes.

Let's reexamine the relationship between religious affiliation and unconditional support for abortion.

Do a **Crosstab** of **ABANY** (**row** variable) and **RELIG** (**column** variable) and request Cells percentaged by **column**.

ABANY ABORTION IF WOMAN WANTS FOR ANY REASON * RELIG RS RELIGIOUS PREFERENCE Crosstabulation

| | | | RELIG RS RELIGIOUS PREFERENCE | | | | |
			1 Protestant	2 Catholic	3 Jewish	4 None	Total
ABANY ABORTION IF WOMAN WANTS FOR ANY REASON	1 YES	Count	168	72	13	89	342
		% within RELIG RS RELIGIOUS PREFERENCE	34.1%	30.0%	76.5%	69.5%	39.0%
	2 NO	Count	325	168	4	39	536
		% within RELIG RS RELIGIOUS PREFERENCE	65.9%	70.0%	23.5%	30.5%	61.0%
Total		Count	493	240	17	128	878
		% within RELIG RS RELIGIOUS PREFERENCE	100.0%	100.0%	100.0%	100.0%	100.0%

The question this table (which contains the actual or *observed* frequencies) is designed to answer is whether a person's religious affiliation affects his or her attitude toward abortion. You'll recall that we concluded it does: Catholics and Protestants are the most opposed to abortion, and Jews and those with no religion are the most supportive. The question we now confront is whether the observed differences point to some genuine pattern in the U.S. population at large or whether they result from a quirk of sampling.

To assess the *observed relationship* as shown in the table above, we are going to begin by asking what we should have *expected* to find if there were no relationship between religious affiliation and abortion attitudes. An important part of the answer lies in the rightmost column in the preceding table. It indicates that 39 percent of the whole sample supported a woman's unconditional right to an abortion (Yes), and 61 percent did not (No).

If there were no relationship between religious affiliation and abortion attitudes, we should expect to find 39 percent of the Protestants approving (Yes), 39 percent of the Catholics approving, 39 percent of the Jews approving, and so forth. But we recall that the earlier results did not match this perfect model of no relationship, so the question is whether the disparity between the model and our observations would fall within the normal degree of sampling error.

To measure the extent of the disparity between the model and what's been observed, we need to calculate the number of cases we'd expect in each cell of the table if there were no relationship. The table below shows how to calculate the expected cell frequencies.

ABANY	Protestant	Catholic	Jewish	None
Yes	493	240	17	128
	×.39	×.39	×.39	×.39
No	493	240	17	128
	×.61	×.61	×.61	×.61

Make sure you know how we constructed this table before moving ahead.

Consequently, if there were no relationship between religious affiliation and abortion attitudes, we would expect 39 percent of the 493 Protestants ($493 \times .39 = 192$) to approve and 61 percent of the 493 Protestants ($493 \times .61 = 301$) to disapprove. If you continue this series of calculations, you should arrive at the following set of *expected cell frequencies*.

ABANY	Protestant	Catholic	Jewish	None
Yes	192	94	7	50
No	301	146	10	78

The next step in calculating chi-square is to calculate the *difference between expected and observed values* in each cell of the table. For example, if religion had no affect on abortion, we would have expected to find 192 Protestants approving; in fact, we observed only 168. Thus the discrepancy in that cell is −24. The discrepancy for Catholics approving is −22 (observed − expected = 72 − 94). The table below shows the discrepancies for each cell.

ABANY	Protestant	Catholic	Jewish	None
Yes	−24	−22	6	39
No	24	22	−6	−39

Finally, for each cell we square the discrepancy and divide it by the expected cell frequency. For the Protestants approving of abortion, then, the squared discrepancy is 576 (-24×-24). Dividing it by the expected frequency of 192 yields 3. When we repeat this for each cell, we get the following results.

ABANY	Protestant	Catholic	Jewish	None
Approve	3	5.15	5.14	30.42
Disapprove	1.91	3.32	3.6	19.5

Chi-square is the sum of all these latest cell figures: 72.04. We have calculated a summary measure of the discrepancy between what we would have expected to observe if religion did not affect abortion and what we actually observed. Now the only remaining question is whether that resulting number should be regarded as large or small. Statisticians often speak of the **goodness of fit** in this context: How well do the observed data fit a model of two variables being unrelated to each other?

The answer to this latest question takes the form of a probability: the probability that a chi-square this large could occur as a result of sampling error. A probability of .05 in this context would mean that it should happen five times in 100 samples. A probability of .001 would mean it should happen only one time in 1,000 samples.

To evaluate our chi-square of 72.04, we need to look it up in a table of chi-square values, which you'll find in the back of any statistics textbook. Such tables have several columns marked by different probabilities (e.g., .30, .20, .10, .05, .01, .001). The tables also have several rows representing different **degrees of freedom** (df).

If you think about it, you'll probably see that the larger and more complex a table is, the greater the likelihood that there will be discrepancies from the perfect model of expected frequencies. We take account of this by one final calculation.

Degrees of freedom are calculated from the data table as (rows − 1) × (columns − 1). In our table, there are four columns and two rows, giving us (3 × 1) degrees of freedom. Thus, we would look across the third row in the table of chi-square values, which would look, in part, like this:

df	.05	.01	.001
3	7.815	11.341	16.268

These numbers tell us that a chi-square as high as 7.815 from a table like ours would occur only 5 times in 100 samples if there were no relationship between religious affiliation and abortion attitudes among the whole U.S. population. A chi-square as high as 11.341 would happen only once in 100 samples, and a chi-square as high as 16.268 would only happen once in 1,000.

Thus we conclude that our chi-square of 72.04 could result from sampling error less than once in 1,000 samples. This is often abbreviated as $p < .001$: The probability is less than 1 in 1,000.

They have no magical meaning, but the .05 and .001 levels of significance are often used by social scientists as a convention for concluding that an observed relationship reflects a similar relationship in the population rather than arising from sampling error. Most social scientists agree that relationships with significance values of .05 or less are so unlikely to have occurred by chance that they can be called *significant*. The lower the probability, the more statistically significant the relationship. Accordingly, if a relationship is significant at the .001 level, we can be more confident of our conclusion than if it is significant only at the .05 level.

Going back to our example then, if the value of chi-square is *greater* than the value printed in the reference table for the appropriate degree of freedom and at the probability level of .05 or less, then the relationship between the variables can be considered statistically significant.

As we noted, in our example the value of chi-square is 72.04, which is greater than the value printed in the reference table for the appropriate df at the probability of .05, .01 and .001. This then tells us that the relationship between our variables (ABANY and RELIG) can be considered statistically significant.

There you have it: far more than you ever thought you'd want to know about chi-square.[2] By sticking it out and coming to grasp the logical meaning of this statistical calculation, you've earned a reward.

Demonstration 15.1: Instructing SPSS to Calculate Chi-Square

Rather than going through all the preceding calculations, we could have simply modified our **Crosstabs** request slightly (and after seeing how easy it is to instruct SPSS to run chi-square, you will probably wish we had just done this much earlier). In the Crosstabs window, click **Statistics...** and select **Chi-Square** in the upper left corner of the Statistics window. Then click **Continue** and **OK** to run the Crosstab request.

Chi-Square Tests

	Value	df	Asymp. Sig. (2-sided)
Pearson Chi-Square	73.412[a]	3	.000
Likelihood Ratio	72.232	3	.000
Linear-by-Linear Association	51.328	1	.000
N of Valid Cases	878		

---

2. "Sociology—UTSA Style Index to the Sociological World" contains a "Chi Square Tutorial" that provides a brief and very accessible introduction to the logic of chi-square; see http://csbs.utsa.edu/social&policy/soc/masters/chisquare.htm.

Reading Your Output

We are interested primarily in the first row of figures in this report. Notice that the 73.41 value of chi-square is slightly different from our hand calculation. This is because of our rounding off in our cell calculations, and it shouldn't worry you. Notice that we're told that there are three degrees of freedom. Finally, SPSS has calculated the probability of getting a chi-square this high with three degrees of freedom and has run out of space after three zeros to the right of the decimal point. Thus the probability is far less than .001, as we determined by checking a table of chi-square values.

The reference to a *minimum expected frequency* of 6.62 is worth noting. Because the calculation of chi-square involves divisions by expected cell frequencies, it can be greatly inflated if any of them are very small. By convention, adjustments to chi-square should be made if more than 20 percent of the expected cell frequencies are below 5. You should check a statistics text if you want to know more about this.

SPSS COMMAND 15.1:   Producing Crosstabs with Chi-Square

> Click **Analyze** → **Descriptive Statistics** → **Crosstabs...** →
>
> Highlight name of **dependent variable** → Transfer to **Row(s):** box by selecting right-pointing **arrow** →
>
> Highlight name of **independent variable** → Transfer to **Column(s):** box by selecting right-pointing **arrow** →
>
> Click **Cells...** → Select **Column** in Percentages box → Click **Continue** →
>
> Click **Statistics...** → Select **Chi-Square** → Click **Continue** → **OK**

Practice Running Chi-Square

While it is fresh in your mind, why don't you have SPSS calculate some more chi-squares for you? You may recall that sex had little impact on abortion attitudes. Why don't you see what the chi-square is?

To experiment more with chi-square, you might rerun some of the other tables relating various demographic variables to abortion attitudes. Notice how chi-square offers a basis for comparing the relative importance of different variables in determining attitudes on this controversial topic.

Significance and Association

It bears repeating here that tests of significance are different from measures of association, although they are related to one another. The stronger an association between two variables, the more likely it is that the association will be judged statistically significant—that is, not a simple product of sampling error. Other factors also affect statistical significance, however. As we've already mentioned, the number of degrees of freedom in a table is relevant. So is the size of the sample: The larger the sample, the more likely it is that an association will be judged significant.

Researchers often distinguish between *statistical significance* (examined in this section) and ***substantive significance***. The latter refers to the importance of an association, and it can't be determined by empirical analysis alone. As we suggested at the outset of this chapter, substantive significance depends on practical and theoretical factors. All this notwithstanding, social researchers often find statistical significance a useful device in gauging associations.

That said, you may still be wondering how you should interpret findings which show, for instance, that there is a strong but not statistically significant relationship between two variables. Or, conversely, what you should say if you find that there is a fairly weak but nonetheless statistically significant relationship between two items. Table 15.1 is intended to help as you approach the sometimes daunting task of interpreting tests of significance and association. While there are no "rules" of interpretation, this table can be looked at as a general guide of sorts to help you as you begin to bring together the concepts of association and significance. However, we do want to add one note of caution. This table is meant to serve only as a general guide to interpreting tests of association and significance. Consequently, you may (and probably should) find that you do not agree with the interpretation offered in every instance.

For instance, if your findings show that the association between two variables is strong and statistically significant, you can look across the first row of the table to get some guidance in interpreting these results.

Table 15.1: A Guide to Interpreting Tests of Association and Significance

Strength of Association	Statistical Significance	Interpretation	Comment
Strong	Significant	Knowledge of the independent variable improves prediction of dependent variable and relationship can be generalized from the sample to the population.	Look what I've discovered!
Strong	Not Significant	Although knowledge of the independent variable improves prediction of dependent variable in the sample, the relationship cannot be generalized to the population.	Close, but no banana.
Weak	Significant	Knowledge of the independent variable is of little help in predicting the dependent variable but may be generalized to the population.	That's no big thing.
Weak	Not Significant	Knowing about the independent variable provides little help in the prediction of the dependent variable in the sample and cannot be generalized to the population.	Back to the drawing board.

Whereas chi-square operates on the logic of the contingency table, which you've grown accustomed to through the crosstabs procedure, we're going to turn next to a test of significance based on means.

t Tests

Who do you suppose lives longer, men or women? Whichever group lives longer should, as a result, have a higher average age at any given time. Regardless of whether you know the answer to this question for the U.S. population as a whole, let's see if our GSS data can shed some light on the issue.

We could find the average ages of men and women in our GSS sample with the simple command path:

Analyze → Compare Means → Means...

Because age is the characteristic on which we want to compare men and women, **AGE** is the **dependent** variable; **SEX** the **independent**. Transfer those variables to the appropriate fields in the window. Then click **OK**.

Report

AGE AGE OF RESPONDENT

SEX RESPONDENTS SEX	Mean	N	Std. Deviation
1 MALE	44.84	661	16.77
2 FEMALE	46.51	839	17.53
Total	45.78	1500	17.21

As you can see, our sample reflects the general population in that women have a mean age of 46.51, compared with the mean age of 44.84 for men. The task facing us now parallels the one pursued in the discussion of chi-square. Does the observed difference reflect a pattern that exists in the whole population, or is it simply a result of a sampling procedure that happened to get too many old women and/or too many young men this time? Would another sample indicate that men are older than women or that there is no difference?

In the last section we ran Crosstabs with chi-square to estimate the statistical significance of the observed association between gender and religiosity, two nominal variables. We will not rely on crosstabs and chi-square here because our dependent variable, AGE, is an I/R item that contains many categories. Consequently, the crosstabs procedure would produce a table that is too large and unwieldy to analyze easily. Instead we will rely on one of the most commonly used inferential statistics—t tests. While there are three types of t tests available on SPSS, we are going to utilize the ***Independent-samples t test (two sample t test)***.

Given that we've moved very deliberately through the logic and calculations of chi-square, we are going to avoid such details in the present discussion.[3] The ***t test***, which is best suited for dependent variables at the I/R level of measurement, examines the distribution of values on one variable (AGE) among different groups (men and women—two categories of one variable SEX) and calculates the probability that the observed difference in means results from sampling error alone. As with chi-square, it is customary to use the value of .05 or less to identify a statistically significant association.

Demonstration 15.2: Instructing SPSS to Run Independent-Samples *t* Test

To request a *t* test from SPSS to examine the relationship between AGE and SEX, you enter the following command path:

Analyze → Compare Means → Independent-Samples T Test...

You will notice that the drop-down menu lists the three types of *t* tests available on SPSS: One-Sample T Test..., Independent-Samples T Test..., and Paired-Samples T Test.... As noted above, we are interested in the Independent-Samples T Test... option. After following the command path above, you should see the following screen:

---

3. For a brief description and overview of how to calculate the *t* test see "The T-Test for Differences Between Two Groups" at http://csbs.utsa.edu/social&policy/soc/masters/t-test.htm.

In this window, we want to enter **AGE** as the **Test Variable(s):** and **SEX** as the **Grouping Variable:**. This means that SPSS will group respondents by sex and then examine and compare the mean ages of the two gender groups.

Notice than when you enter the Grouping Variable, SPSS puts "SEX[??]" in that field. Although the comparison groups are obvious in the case of SEX, it might not be so obvious with other variables so SPSS wants some guidance. Click **Define Groups...**.

Type **1** (male) into Group 1: and **2** (female) into Group 2:. Click **Continue**, then **OK**.

Group Statistics

	SEX RESPONDENTS SEX	N	Mean	Std. Deviation	Std. Error Mean
AGE AGE OF RESPONDENT	1 MALE	661	44.84	16.77	.65
	2 FEMALE	839	46.51	17.53	.61

Independent Samples Test

		Levene's Test for Equality of Variances		t-test for Equality of Means						
		F	Sig.	t	df	Sig. (2-tailed)	Mean Difference	Std. Error Difference	95% Confidence Interval of the Difference Lower	Upper
AGE AGE OF RESPONDENT	Equal variances assumed	2.987	.084	-1.864	1498	.062	-1.67	.89	-3.42	8.69E-02
	Equal variances not assumed			-1.874	1443.193	.061	-1.67	.89	-3.41	7.77E-02

Reading Your Output

The program gives you much more information than you need for the present purposes, so let's identify the key elements. Some of the information is a repeat of what we got earlier from the Means command: means, standard deviations, and standard errors for men and women.

In the Group Statistics box under Mean, for example, we see once again that the average age is 44.84 for men and 46.51 for women.

The results regarding significance that we are most interested in now are given in the box below labeled Independent Samples Test, under the heading t-test for Equality of Means. If you look there under the subheading "Sig. (2-tailed)," in the top row labeled Equal variances assumed, you will see the probability we are looking for: .062.

As you will anticipate, .062 in this context indicates a probability of 62 in 1,000. The "2-tailed" notation requires just a little more explanation.

In our sample, the average age for women is 1.67 years higher than for men (46.51 – 44.84). SPSS has calculated that about 62 times in 1,000 samples, sampling error might produce a difference this great in either direction. That is, if the average age of men and the average age of women in the population were exactly the same, and we were to select 1,000 samples like this one, we could expect 62 of those samples to show women at least 1.67 years older than men or men as much as 1.67 years older than women.

When you don't have theoretical reasons to anticipate a particular relationship, it is appropriate for you to use the "2-tailed" probability in evaluating differences in means like these. In some cases—when you have deduced specific expectations from a theory, for example—you might come to the data analysis with a hypothesis that "women are older than men." In such a case, it might be more appropriate to note that there is a probability of 31 in 1,000 ($p = .031$) that sampling error would have resulted in women being as much as 1.67 years older than men. For our purposes in this book, however, we'll stick with the 2-tailed test.

SPSS COMMAND 15.2: Running T Test (Independent Samples T Test)

> Click **Analyze → Compare Means → Independent-Samples T Test...→**
>
> Highlight **name of test variable** in variable list → Click **arrow** pointing to the **Test Variable(s): box →**
>
> Highlight **name of grouping variable** in variable list → Click **arrow** pointing to the **Grouping Variable: box →**
>
> Click **Define Groups... → Define Group 1: and Group 2: →** Click
>
> **Continue → OK**

Demonstration 15.3: *t* Test—EDUC by SEX

Some of the variables in your GSS data set allow you to explore this issue further. For example, it would be reasonable for better-educated workers to earn more than poorly educated workers, so if the men in our sample have more education than the women, that might explain the difference in pay. Let's see.

Return to the T Test window and substitute **EDUC** for AGE as the Test Variable(s):.[4] Leave "SEX[1 2]" as the Grouping Variable:. Run the new *t* test.

Group Statistics

	SEX RESPONDENTS SEX	N	Mean	Std. Deviation	Std. Error Mean
EDUC HIGHEST YEAR OF SCHOOL COMPLETED	1 MALE	655	13.39	3.00	.12
	2 FEMALE	837	13.23	2.83	9.78E-02

Independent Samples Test

		Levene's Test for Equality of Variances		t-test for Equality of Means						
									95% Confidence Interval of the Difference	
		F	Sig.	t	df	Sig. (2-tailed)	Mean Difference	Std. Error Difference	Lower	Upper
EDUC HIGHEST YEAR OF SCHOOL COMPLETED	Equal variances assumed	3.320	.069	1.073	1490	.283	.16	.15	-.13	.46
	Equal variances not assumed			1.066	1365.396	.287	.16	.15	-.14	.46

What conclusion do you draw from these latest results? Notice first that the men and women in our sample have very similar mean number of years of education (men = 13.39, women = 13.23). The difference is very small, and it is one we could expect to find in 283 of 1,000 samples. With the significance level far greater than the usual .05, this small difference could have occurred far too easily by chance for us to generalize it to the whole population.

With such a small difference between men's and women's educational backgrounds, it is unlikely that education can be used as a "legitimate reason" for women earning less than men. That's not to say that there aren't other legitimate reasons that may account for the difference in pay. For instance, it is often argued that women tend to concentrate in less prestigious jobs than men: nurses rather than doctors, secretaries rather than executives, teachers rather than principals. Leaving aside the reasons for such occupational differences, that might account for the differences in pay. As you may recall, your GSS data contain a measure of socioeconomic status (SEI). We used that variable in our experimentation with Correlations. Let's see if the women in our sample have lower-status jobs, on average, than the men.

Demonstration 15.4: *t* Test—SEI by SEX

Go back to the T Test window and replace EDUC with **SEI**. Run the procedure, and you should get the following result.

---

4. Before proceeding, make sure DK for the variable EDUC is defined as missing.

Group Statistics

	SEX RESPONDENTS SEX	N	Mean	Std. Deviation	Std. Error Mean
SEI RESPONDENT SOCIOECONOMIC INDEX	1 MALE	648	50.645	19.839	.779
	2 FEMALE	778	48.210	18.773	.673

Independent Samples Test

		Levene's Test for Equality of Variances		t-test for Equality of Means						
		F	Sig.	t	df	Sig. (2-tailed)	Mean Difference	Std. Error Difference	95% Confidence Interval of the Difference	
									Lower	Upper
SEI RESPONDENT SOCIOECONOMIC INDEX	Equal variances assumed	1.691	.194	2.377	1424	.018	2.435	1.025	.425	4.445
	Equal variances not assumed			2.365	1347.736	.018	2.435	1.030	.415	4.455

The mean difference in occupational prestige ratings of men and women is 2.4 on a scale from 0 to 100. SPSS tells us that such a difference could be expected just as a consequence of sampling error in only about 18 samples in 1,000 ($p = .018$). How would you interpret this finding? Do you think this difference is statistically significant enough to have any social significance?

To pursue this line of inquiry further, you will need additional analytic skills that will be covered shortly in the discussion of multivariate analysis.

Analysis of Variance

The *t* test is limited to the comparison of two groups at a time (for example, male and female). If we wanted to compare the levels of education of different religious groups, we'd have to compare Protestants and Catholics, Protestants and Jews, Catholics and Jews, and so forth. And if some of the comparisons found significant differences and other comparisons did not, we'd be hard pressed to reach an overall conclusion about the nature of the relationship between the two variables.

The *analysis of variance* (*ANOVA*) is a technique that resolves the shortcoming of the *t* test. It examines the means of subgroups in the sample and analyzes the variances as well. That is, it examines more than whether the actual values are clustered around the mean or spread out from it.

If we were to ask ANOVA to examine the relationship between RELIG and EDUC, it would determine the mean years of education for each of the different religious groups, noting how they differed from one another. Those "between-group" differences would be compared with the "within-group" differences (variance): how much Protestants differed among themselves, for example. Both sets of comparisons are reconciled by ANOVA to calculate the likelihood that the observed differences are merely the result of sampling error.

Demonstration 15.5: Instructing SPSS to Run ANOVA

To get a clearer picture of ANOVA, ask SPSS to perform the analysis we've been discussing. You can probably figure out how to do that, but here's a hint.

Analyze → General Linear Model → Univariate...[5]

---

5. If you have used earlier versions of SPSS, you will notice a difference here. The simple factorial ANOVA procedure has been replaced with the GLM univariate procedure (General Factorial). This allows for ANOVA tables but does not require a defined range of factor variables. See SPSS's extensive Help option for further details.

Put **EDUC** into the **Dependent Variable**: field and **RELIG** in the **Fixed Factor(s):** field. It is that simple (at least for our purposes). Once you have done that, click **OK** to launch the procedure.

Tests of Between-Subjects Effects

Dependent Variable: EDUC HIGHEST YEAR OF SCHOOL COMPLETED

Source	Type III Sum of Squares	df	Mean Square	F	Sig.
Corrected Model	232.355[a]	3	77.452	9.218	.000
Intercept	68140.509	1	68140.509	8110.246	.000
RELIG	232.355	3	77.452	9.218	.000
Error	11754.091	1399	8.402		
Total	259156.0	1403			
Corrected Total	11986.446	1402			

a. R Squared = .019 (Adjusted R Squared = .017)

Reading Your Output

Here's the SPSS report on the analysis. Again, we've gotten more information than we want for our present purposes.

For our immediate purposes, let's look simply at the row titled Corrected Model. This refers to the amount of variance in EDUC that can be explained by variations in RELIG. Because our present purpose is to learn about tests of statistical significance, let's move across the row to the statistical significance of the explained variance. You can see that the value listed here is .000. This means that if religion and education were unrelated to each other in the population, we might expect samples that would generate this amount of explained variance less than once in 1,000 samples.

Perhaps you will find it useful to think of ANOVA as something like a statistical broom. We began by noting a lot of variance in educational levels of our respondents; imagine people's educations spread all over the place. In an attempt to find explanatory patterns in that variance, we use ANOVA to sweep the respondents into subgroups based on religious affiliation (stay with us on this). The questions are whether variations in education are substantially less within each of the piles than we originally observed in the whole sample, and whether the mean years of education in each of the subgroups are quite different from one another. Imagine a set of tidy piles that are quite distant from one another. ANOVA provides a statistical test of this imagery.

SPSS COMMAND 15.3:   ANOVA (GLM Univariate)

Click **Analyze** → **General Linear Model** → **Univariate...** →

Highlight name of **dependent variable** → Click **arrow** pointing **to Dependent Variable:** field →

Highlight name of **factor variable** → Click **arrow** pointing to **Fixed Factor(s):** field → **OK**

It is also possible for ANOVA to consider two independent variables, but that goes beyond the scope of this book. We have introduced you to ANOVA because we feel it is useful, and we wanted to open up for you the possibility of your using this popular technique; however, you will need more specialized training in the performance of analysis of variance to use it effectively.

A Statistical Toolbox: A Summary

As we near the end of our discussion of bivariate analysis, we think it may be useful as a review and summary of sorts, to provide you with a table listing descriptive and inferential statistics by their appropriate level of measurement.

You will note that those statistics we reviewed in depth are listed in bold. In addition, we included a few references to some basic statistics we did not cover, but which you may find useful as you pursue your own research.

Please keep in mind that this table is not exhaustive. It references only a few of the many statistics social researchers find useful when working with items at various levels of measurement.

Table 15.2:   A Statistical Toolbox

Statistics for Measuring:	Level of Measurement		
	Nominal	Ordinal	I/R
DESCRIPTIVE STATISICS			
Central Tendency	**MODE**	**MEDIAN**	**MEAN**
Dispersion		**RANGE**	**VARIANCE**
		Interquartile Range	**STANDARD DEVIATION**
Association	**LAMBDA**	**GAMMA**	*r*^{2}
(PRE and non-PRE)	Cramer's *V*	Somer's *D*	Pearson's *r*
	Phi	Tau *B*	beta
	Contingency Coefficient		
INFERENTIAL STATISTICS			
Tests of Significance	**CHI-SQUARE**	**CHI-SQUARE**	**INDEPENDENT SAMPLES T TEST ANOVA**

Conclusion

This chapter has taken on the difficult question of whether the observed relationship between two variables is important or not. It is natural that you would want to know whether and when you have discovered something worth writing home about. No one wants to shout, "Look what I've discovered!" and have others say, "That's no big thing."

Ultimately, there is no simple test of the substantive significance of a relationship between variables. If we found that women earn less than men, who can say if that amounts to a lot less or just a little bit less? In a more precise study, we could calculate exactly how much less in dollars, but we would still not be in a position to say absolutely whether that amount was a lot or a little. If women made a dollar a year less than men on the average, we'd all probably agree that was not an important difference. If men earned a hundred times as much as women, on the other hand, we'd probably all agree that was a big difference. However, few of the differences we discover in social science research are that dramatic.

In this chapter, we've examined a very specific approach that social scientists often take in addressing the issue of significance. As distinct from notions of *substantive* significance, we have examined *statistical* significance. In each of the measures we've examined—chi-square, *t* test, and analysis of variance— we've asked how likely it would be that sampling error could produce the observed relationship if there were actually no relationship in the population from which the sample was drawn.

This assumption of "no relationship" is sometimes referred to as the **null hypothesis**. The tests of significance we've examined all deal with the probability that the null hypothesis is correct. If the probability is relatively high, we conclude that there is no relationship between the two variables under study in the whole population. If the probability is small that the null hypothesis could be true, then we conclude that the observed relationship reflects a genuine pattern in the population.

Main Points

- In this chapter we introduced tests of statistical significance.

- As opposed to measures of association that focus on the strength and direction of the relationship, tests of significance allow us to estimate whether the relationship can be considered statistically significant.

- Statistical significance generally refers to the likelihood that an observed relationship between variables in a sample could have occurred as a result of chance or sampling error.

- Tests of significance also allow you to determine whether or not an observed association between items in a sample is likely to exist in the population.

- In this chapter we moved from focusing primarily on descriptive statistics to inferential statistics.

- The three tests of significance we reviewed are part of the larger body of inferential statistics: chi-square, t tests, and ANOVA.

- Chi-square is most appropriate for nominal variables, although it can be used with ordinal variables.

- Traditionally, a chi-square with a probability of .05 or less is considered significant.

- The t test is most appropriate if the dependent variable is at the I/R level of measurement.

- ANOVA builds on the shortcomings of the t test.

- There is an important difference between substantive and statistical significance.

Key Terms

Statistical significance
Inferential statistics
Descriptive statistics
Sampling error
Chi-square
Goodness of fit
Degrees of freedom (df)

Substantive significance
Independent Samples T Test
(two sample t test)
t test
Analysis of variance (ANOVA)
Null hypothesis

SPSS Commands Introduced in This Chapter

15.1:   Producing Crosstabs with Chi-Square

> Click **Analyze** → **Descriptive Statistics** → **Crosstabs...** →
>
> Highlight name of **dependent variable** → Transfer to **Row(s):** box by selecting right-pointing **arrow** →
>
> Highlight name of **independent variable** → Transfer to **Column(s):** box by selecting right-pointing **arrow** →
>
> Click **Cells...** → Select **Column** in Percentages box → Click **Continue** →
>
> Click **Statistics...** → Select **Chi-Square** → Click **Continue** → **OK**

15.2:   Running T Test (Independent Samples T Test)

> Click **Analyze** → **Compare Means** → **Independent-Samples T Test...**→
>
> Highlight **name of test variable** in variable list → Click **arrow** pointing to the **Test Variable(s):** box →
>
> Highlight **name of grouping variable** in variable list → Click **arrow** pointing to the **Grouping Variable:** box →
>
> Click **Define Groups...** → **Define Group 1: and Group 2:** → Click **Continue** → **OK**

15.3:   ANOVA (GLM Univariate)

> Click **Analyze** → **General Linear Model** → **Univariate...** →
>
> Highlight name of **dependent variable** → Click **arrow** pointing **to Dependent Variable:** field →
>
> Highlight name of **factor variable** → Click **arrow** pointing to **Fixed Factor(s):** field → **OK**

Review Questions

1. What does the term *statistical significance* mean?
2. If you are interested in estimating the strength of association between variables, would you rely on tests of significance or measures of association?
3. If you are interested in determining whether or not an observed relationship between variables in your sample is likely to exist in the population, would you rely on tests of significance or measures of association?
4. What are inferential statistics?
5. How do they differ from descriptive statistics?
6. Chi-square is considered appropriate for variables at what level of measurement?
7. Chi-square is based on a comparison of _____ frequencies and _____ frequencies.

8. If a chi-square has a probability level greater than .05, is it generally considered significant by traditional social science standards?

9. Would a chi-square with a probability of .01 be considered significant by traditional social science standards?

10. Would we have more confidence if an association was significant at the .05 or .001 level?

11. The t test is considered appropriate if your dependent variable is at what level of measurement?

12. Does the t test allow us to determine whether the means, the variances, or both the means and variances of two groups are statistically different from each other?

13. How does ANOVA resolve the shortcomings of the t test? Explain.

14. Does ANOVA examine the means, variances, or both the means and variances of subgroups in a sample?

15. In this chapter we have focused primarily on statistical significance. How does this differ from substantive significance?

NAME _____

CLASS _____

INSTRUCTOR _____

DATE _____

To complete the following exercises you need to load the data file EXER.SAV. You will find answers to selected questions in Appendix A.

1. Recode the variable AFFRMACT as follows to create a new variable AFFREC (if you recode the values as follows, values 0, 8, and 9 for the variable AFFRMACT will be listed as system missing for your new variable AFFREC). When you have done that, be sure to set the decimal places for AFFREC to "0" and add value labels.

Old Values	New Values	New Value Labels
1 – 2	→ 1	Support
3 – 4	→ 2	Oppose

   Run Crosstabs *listing RACE and SEX as the independent variables and AFFREC as the dependent variable. Request column percentages and chi-square. Then answer Questions 2–8. Make sure all "Don't knows" are labeled as missing values.*

2. Record the percentage who said "Support" to AFFREC for each independent variable (RACE and SEX).

	Percentage "Support"	Significance Chi-Square
RACE		_____
White	_____	
Black	_____	
Other	_____	
SEX		_____
Male	_____	
Female	_____	

3. (RACE) Do the percentages change or move, signifying a relationship between RACE and AFFREC? Explain how you know.

4. (RACE) What is the significance of chi-square? Is it less than, equal to, or more than .05?

5. (RACE) Is the relationship between RACE and AFFREC statistically significant?

6. (SEX) Do the percentages change or move, signifying a relationship between SEX and AFFREC? Explain how you know.

7. (SEX) What is the significance of chi-square? Is it less than, equal to, or more than .05?

8. (SEX) Is the relationship between SEX and AFFREC statistically significant?

Run the t test, specifying AGE, SEI, and EDUC as the **Test Variables** *and RACE as the* Grouping Variable. *Keep in mind that you will have to ask SPSS to limit the comparison to Whites and Blacks, omitting the "Other" category. Once you have run the procedure, complete Questions 9–16.*

9. Fill in the blanks with the appropriate information.

	RACE	
	White	Black
AGE		
Mean	_____	_____
Sig.		
(2-Tailed)	_____	
EDUC		
Mean	_____	_____
Sig.		
(2-Tailed)	_____	
SEI		
Mean	_____	_____
Sig.		
(2-Tailed)	_____	

10. (AGE) Is the mean age of Whites higher than, lower than, or the same as Blacks?

11. (AGE) Is the difference significant? Why or why not? Explain.

NAME _____

CLASS _____

INSTRUCTOR _____

DATE _____

12. (EDUC) Is the mean education of Whites higher than, lower than, or the same as Blacks?

13. (EDUC) Is the difference significant? Why or why not? Explain.

14. (SEI) Is the mean SEI of Whites higher than, lower than, or the same as Blacks?

15. (SEI) Is the difference significant? Why or why not? Explain.

16. On the basis of these results, what conclusions if any can you draw about racial inequality in the United States in 1998? How much inequality is there? Is there inequality in education, the work force, or both? Do your data indicate that Whites have a higher average age, suggesting that they live longer? What if anything does this say about racial inequality today?

Run ANOVA, *putting EDUC in the* Dependent Variable: *field and CLASS in the* Fixed Factor(s) *field*.

17. What is the statistical significance of the explained variance?

18. Is this finding significant? Explain

19. Run ANOVA, putting AGE in the Dependent Variable: field and CLASS in the Fixed Factor(s) field. Summarize your findings below.

Chapter 16 Suggestions for Further Bivariate Analyses

By now, you've amassed a powerful set of analytic tools. In a world where people make casual assertions about sociological topics, you're now in a position to determine the facts. You can determine *how* the U.S. population feels about a variety of topics, and with your new bivariate skills, you can begin to explain *why* they feel as they do.

In this chapter, we are going to suggest some additional analyses you might undertake. They will allow you to perfect your skills, and these suggestions open the possibility of your thinking more for yourself. What are you interested in? What would you like to learn more about? Here are some possibilities.

In Chapter 10, we suggested some topics, drawn from the items on your DEMO.SAV file, which you might pursue with the techniques of univariate analysis. Let's start by returning to those topics.

Desired Family Size

CHLDIDEL asked respondents what they considered the ideal number of children for a family. A little more than half of the respondents said that two or fewer was best. Because that is also the number of children that would represent population stabilization, you might want to begin by recoding this variable to create two response categories. If you are having difficulty with this, here is a "hint" to point you in the right direction:

Select **Transform → Recode → Into Different Variables...**

Then recode CHLDIDEL to create a new variable CHLDNUM with the following values and labels:

CHLDIDEL		New Variable CHLDNUM	
Old Values		New Values	Value Labels
0 through 2	→	1	0–2
3 through highest	→	2	3 or more

Once you've recoded **CHLDIDEL** into the more manageable variable **CHLDNUM**, you can start looking for the causes of differences. As a start, you might want to see if the variables we examined in relation to abortion attitudes are related to opinions about ideal family size.

We found that gender was basically unrelated to abortion attitudes. How about ideal family size? Do you think men and women differ in their images of the perfect family? If you think so, in which direction do you think that difference goes?

How about age? Support for small families is a fairly recent development in the United States, against a historical backdrop of large farm families. Does this mean that young people would be more supportive of small families than older people? You find out.

The better-educated members of the population are generally more concerned about environmental issues. Are they also more committed to small families?

Religion and race are good candidates for shaping opinions about ideal family size because the nature of family life is often central to subcultural patterns. We saw that Catholics and Protestants were resistant to abortion. How do they feel about limiting family size in general? You can know the answer in a matter of minutes.

Several family variables may very well relate to attitudes toward ideal family size. Marital status and whether respondents have ever been divorced might be relevant. Can you see why that would be worth exploring? What would you hypothesize?

Of possibly direct relevance, the data set contains SIBS (the number of brothers and sisters the respondent has). You might want to see if the experience of having brothers and sisters has any impact on opinions about what's best in family size.

If you would like to explore the issue of ideal family size further, you might want to look into Judith Blake's *Family Size and Achievement* (1989).[1]

Child Training

In Chapter 10, we took an initial look at different opinions about what was important in the development of children. The key variables were as follows:

OBEY	to obey
POPULAR	to be well-liked or popular
THNKSELF	to think for himself or herself
WORKHARD	to work hard
HELPOTH	to help others when they need help

If you examined these variables, you discovered some real differences in how people want their children to turn out. Now let's see what causes those differences, because opinions on this topic can reflect some more general attitudes and worldviews.

---

1. Throughout this chapter we are going to recommend sources you may want to consult if you are interested in pursuing a particular issue or topic further. In addition, we want to remind you that the NORC maintains an Internet site called GSSDIRS (the General Social Survey Data and Information Retrieval System). Among other things, this site contains a list of articles, books, papers, studies, and so on, which pertain to each topic and variable in the GSS. You can access the site at http://www.icpsr.umich.edu/GSS99/ and then select "GSS Search Engine" under "Main Applications." Once you have done that, you can search for a particular variable by typing "Codebook Variable:" and the variable name (i.e., CHLDIDEL, SIBS, etc...). Once you access the Codebook, Page Down until you see "Bibliography." You can also access the Codebook directly at http://www.icpsr.umich.edu/GSS99/codebook.htm and then search by subject or variable name.

Once again, such demographic variables as sex, age, race, and religion might make a difference. OBEY, for example, reflects a certain authoritarian leaning. Perhaps it is related to political variables, such as PARTYID and POLVIEWS; perhaps not. There's only one way to find out.

HELPOTH measures an altruistic dimension. That's something religions often encourage. Maybe there's a relation between this variable and some of the religion variables.

Also consider the variable THNKSELF, which values children's learning to think for themselves. What would you expect to influence this? Education, perhaps? How about age and sex? Do you think older respondents would be relatively cool to children thinking for themselves? Would men or women be more supportive? Don't rule out religious and political variables. Some of these results are likely to confirm your expectations; some do not.

When it comes to the value of children thinking for themselves, you may find some of the other attitudinal variables in the GSS data set worth looking at. Consider those who have told us they are permissive on premarital sex and homosexuality. Do you think they would be more or less likely to value children's learning to think for themselves?

There are any number of directions you might want to pursue in looking for the causes of different attitudes toward the qualities most valued for children. For more ideas in this arena, you might want to look at Duane Alwin's *Changes in Qualities Valued in Children* (1989).

Attitudes about Sexual Behavior

You may want to focus on the three sexual variables per se. What do you suppose would cause differences of opinion regarding premarital sexual relations and homosexuality? What do you suppose determines who goes to X-rated movies? You have the ability and the tools to find out for yourself.

Near the end of the movie *Casablanca*, the police chief instructs his officers to "round up the usual suspects." You might do well to round up the usual demographic variables as a way of beginning your examination of sexual attitudes: age, gender, race, religion, education, social class, and marital status, for example.

Before examining each of these relationships, take some time to think about any links you might logically expect. Should men or women be more permissive about homosexuality? Should married, single, or divorced people be more supportive of premarital sex? How do you expect young and old people to differ?

As you investigate these attitudes, be careful about assuming that the three items are just different dimensions of the same orientation. The kinds of people who are permissive about premarital sex are not necessarily the same ones who are permissive about homosexuality.

If you are interested in exploring this topic further, you may want to consult Tom Smith's *The Polls: A Report: The Sexual Revolution?* (1990) or Kaye Wellings et al.'s *Sexual Attitudes* (1994).

Prejudice

At least two items in your DEMO.SAV file address different aspects of racial prejudice about African-Americans. RACMAR measures respondents attitudes toward the legality of interracial marriage, whereas RACPUSH measures attitudes toward Black–White relations.

Certainly, RACE is the most obvious variable to examine, and you probably won't be surprised at what you find. Don't stop there, however. There are other variables that provide even more dramatic relationships.

Education, politics, and social class offer fruitful avenues for understanding the roots of attitudes on these variables. You may be surprised by the impact of religious variables.

As a different approach, you might look at the opinion that homosexuality is morally wrong as is prejudice against gays and lesbians. It's worth checking whether responses to that item are related to prejudice against African-Americans.

To get a sense of how other researchers have explored racial prejudice, you may want to see Edward Carmines et al.'s *The Changing Content of American Racial Attitudes: A Fifty Year Portrait* (1990) or Howard Schuman et al.'s *Racial Attitudes in America: Trends and Interpretations* (1985).

Conclusion

The preceding suggestions should be enough to keep you busy, but you shouldn't feel limited by them. The most fruitful guides to your analyses should be your own personal interests. Consequently, while we have focused our suggestions on the DEMO.SAV file, we encourage you to explore the EXER.SAV file as well. Keep in mind the EXER.SAV file contains a number of additional variables, covering issues such as health care, mass media use, national government spending priorities, sex roles, law enforcement, teen sex, and equalization. Think about which of the topics from either the DEMO.SAV file or the EXER.SAV file most interest or concern you. Now you have a chance to learn something about them on your own. You don't have to settle for polemical statements about "the way things are." You now have the tools you need to find out for yourself.

In examining these bivariate relationships, you may want to begin with Crosstabs, because that technique gives you the most detailed view of the data. At the same time, you should use this exercise as an opportunity to experiment with the other bivariate techniques we've examined. Try chi-squares where appropriate, for example. As you find interesting relationships between variables, you may want to test their statistical significance to get another window on what they mean.

What you've learned so far may be sufficient for most of your day-to-day curiosities. Now you can learn what public opinion really is on a given topic, and you can determine what kinds of people hold differing views on that topic. In the remaining chapters of this book, however, we are going to show you an approach to understanding that goes much deeper. As we introduce you to multivariate analysis, you're going to have an opportunity to sample a more complex mode of understanding than most people are even aware of.

Main Points

- Now that you are capable of describing both what Americans think about a variety of issues and why, we suggest some additional bivariate analysis for you to pursue on your own.

- We focus specifically on four topics drawn from the items in your DEMO.SAV file as examples of the types of investigations you may want to pursue: desired family size, child training, attitudes about sexual behavior, and prejudice.

- Don't be limited by these suggestions, however. Pursue topics and issues that interest or concern you. After all, this is your adventure.

- Keep in mind that your DEMO.SAV and EXER.SAV files each contain more than forty GSS items covering a number of important and controversial issues in American life.

- When pursuing relations between two variables, you should begin with Crosstabs, then experiment with the other techniques we reviewed in this section, including measures of association and tests of statistical significance.

Key Terms

No new terms were introduced in this chapter.

SPSS Commands Introduced in This Chapter

No new commands were introduced in this chapter.

Review Questions

Discuss how you might apply the techniques and procedures we covered in Part IV (Chapters 11–16) on bivariate analysis to examine the following topics. In particular, be sure to explain how you might apply some or all of the bivariate techniques we discussed (i.e., crosstabs, measures of association, and tests of statistical significance).

1. Desired family size
2. Child training
3. Attitudes toward sexual behavior
4. Prejudice

NAME _____

CLASS _____

INSTRUCTOR _____

DATE _____

The following topics/issues are based on items in your EXER.SAV file: sex roles, law enforcement, health insurance, mass media (use and confidence), national government spending priorities, teen sex, affirmative action, and equalization.

1. Choose a topic or issue from the list above that interests you and identify it in the space below.

2. List the names of the variables in your EXER.SAV file that pertain to this topic/issue.

3. Think about how you want to begin exploring these items, and then list the uni-variate techniques we learned in Part III (Chapters 6–10), which you are going to use to examine each of the variables above (for instance, frequencies, measures of central tendency and dispersion, recoding, graphic displays of data—bar chart, line chart...). Be as specific as possible regarding your data analysis plans.

4. Run the univariate analysis you suggested in response to Question 3 and then detail your findings below. Attach any relevant output (tables, charts, graphs, etc...) to this page.

5. Choose one of the variables that you have been focusing on in Questions 2–4. Make sure it is an item that you are interested in examining further and list it in the space below.
   Dependent variable _____

6. List the names of two other items (independent variables) from the EXER.SAV file which you think may be causally related to or associated with your dependent variable.

Independent variable 1 _____

Independent variable 2 _____

7. Write two hypotheses linking your dependent (Question 5) and independent variables (Question 6).

Hypothesis 1:

Dependent variable _____

Independent variable 1 _____

Hypothesis 2:

Dependent variable _____

Independent variable 2 _____

8. List the bivariate techniques you are going to use to test hypothesis 1. Begin with Crosstabs and then move to specific measures of association and tests of significance. Be as specific as possible.

9. List the bivariate techniques you are going to use to test hypothesis 2. Begin with Crosstabs and then move to specific measures of association and tests of significance. Be as specific as possible.

10. Run the bivariate analysis you suggested to test hypothesis 1 (Question 8) and then detail your findings below. Be as specific as possible regarding the findings of each test/procedure. Make sure you explain whether or not your findings confirm your hypothesis. When you are done, attach any relevant output (tables, charts, graphs, etc...) to this sheet.

11. Run the bivariate analysis you suggested to test hypothesis 2 (Question 9) and then detail your findings below. Be as specific as possible regarding the findings of each test/procedure. Make sure you explain whether or not your findings confirm your hypothesis. When you are done, attach any relevant output (tables, charts, graphs, etc...) to this sheet.

Part V Multivariate Analysis

Now that you've mastered the logic and techniques of bivariate analysis, we are going to take you one step further: to the examination of three or more variables at a time, known as multivariate analysis.

In Chapter 17, we'll delve more deeply into religious orientations to gain a more comprehensive understanding of this variable. Chapter 18 will pick up some loose threads of our bivariate analysis and pursue them further with our new analytic capability.

In Chapter 19, we will set as our purpose the prediction of attitudes toward abortion. We'll progress, step-by-step, through a number of variables previously found to have an impact on abortion attitudes, and we'll accumulate them in a composite measure that will offer a powerful predictor of opinions.

Finally, Chapter 20 launches you into uncharted areas of social research, which you should now be empowered to chart for yourself.

Chapter 17 Multiple Causation: Examining Religiosity in Greater Depth

In the last section we focused primarily on the relationship between two variables: a single independent and a single dependent variable. If we continued to limit ourselves solely to the examination of two variables at a time, our understanding of the social world would remain incomplete, not to mention dissatisfying. Bivariate analysis alone cannot help us understand the social world, because in the "real world" two or more factors often have an impact on, influence, or cause variation in a single dependent variable. Consequently, to understand the complexities of the social world, we need to introduce a more sophisticated form of statistical analysis that allows us to examine the impact of more than one independent variable on a single dependent variable.

Social scientists refer to this type of analysis as *multivariate analysis*, the *simultaneous* analysis of three or more variables. Multivariate analysis is the next step beyond bivariate analysis. By helping us move beyond the limitations of unviariate and bivariate analysis, it allows us to develop a more complete understanding of the complexities of the social world.

We are going to begin our introduction to multivariate analysis by looking at the simplest of outcomes, multiple causation.

Demonstration 17.1: Multiple Causation— The Impact of Age and Sex on Religiosity

In Chapter 11, we discussed several variables that might affect the levels of respondents' religiosity. Women, we found, were more religious than men. Old people were more religious than young people.

It is often the case with social phenomena that people's attitudes and behaviors are affected by more than one factor. It is the task of the social scientist, then, to discover all those factors that influence the dependent variable under question and discover how those factors work together to produce a result. If both age and gender affect religiosity independently, perhaps a combination of the two would predict it even better.

To begin our multivariate analysis, let's see how well we can predict religiosity if we consider AGE and SEX simultaneously. Does religiosity increase with age among both men and women separately? Moreover, do the two variables have a cumulative effect on religiosity? That is, are old women the most religious and young men the least religious?

To begin our exploration of this topic, let's open our DEMO.SAV file and use CHATT as the dependent variable; that is, let's see how well we can predict or explain attendance at worship services. To examine the simultaneous impact of AGECAT and SEX on CHATT, simply make an additional modification to the now-familiar **Crosstabs** command.

■ Enter **CHATT** as the **row** variable
■ Enter **AGECAT** as the **column** variable

Now select **SEX** in the list of variables. Notice that the arrows activated would let you transfer SEX to the row or column fields—but don't do that! Instead, transfer it to the **third field**, near the bottom of the window.[1]

Check that the cells are set to be percentaged by columns by selecting **Cells...** and **Column**. Then click **Continue** and **OK** to execute the command.

This command produces more than one table. We have asked SPSS to examine the impact of AGECAT on CHATT separately for men and women. Thus, we are rewarded with the following three-variable crosstabulation.

---

1. In doing this we are also introducing a technique called *elaboration* or *controlling for a third variable*. Elaboration is a technique that helps us to examine the relationship between two variables (independent and dependent) while controlling for a third variable. In this example, for instance, we have specified CHATT as our dependent variable, AGECAT as our independent variable, and SEX as our *control variable*. Essentially this will allow us to look at the relationship between church attendance (religiosity) and age, while controlling for gender. Our output will be two tables: one showing the relationship between CHATT and AGECAT for men only and the other showing the relationship between CHATT and AGECAT for women only.

CHATT * AGECAT Recoded Age Categories * SEX RESPONDENTS SEX Crosstabulation

SEX RESPONDENTS SEX				AGECAT Recoded Age Categories				
				1 Under 21	2 21-39	3 40-64	4 65 and older	Total
1 MALE	CHATT	1 About weekly	Count	1	45	75	45	166
			% within AGECAT Recoded Age Categories	5.9%	17.2%	28.0%	44.1%	25.6%
		2 About monthly	Count	3	45	36	14	98
			% within AGECAT Recoded Age Categories	17.6%	17.2%	13.4%	13.7%	15.1%
		3 Seldom	Count	7	109	95	23	234
			% within AGECAT Recoded Age Categories	41.2%	41.6%	35.4%	22.5%	36.1%
		4 Never	Count	6	63	62	20	151
			% within AGECAT Recoded Age Categories	35.3%	24.0%	23.1%	19.6%	23.3%
	Total		Count	17	262	268	102	649
			% within AGECAT Recoded Age Categories	100.0%	100.0%	100.0%	100.0%	100.0%
2 FEMALE	CHATT	1 About weekly	Count	4	87	140	83	314
			% within AGECAT Recoded Age Categories	14.8%	27.8%	41.4%	55.7%	38.0%
		2 About monthly	Count	9	54	49	20	132
			% within AGECAT Recoded Age Categories	33.3%	17.3%	14.5%	13.4%	16.0%
		3 Seldom	Count	9	112	102	27	250
			% within AGECAT Recoded Age Categories	33.3%	35.8%	30.2%	18.1%	30.2%
		4 Never	Count	5	60	47	19	131
			% within AGECAT Recoded Age Categories	18.5%	19.2%	13.9%	12.8%	15.8%
	Total		Count	27	313	338	149	827
			% within AGECAT Recoded Age Categories	100.0%	100.0%	100.0%	100.0%	100.0%

Notice that the table is divided into two parts, male and female. For our purposes, we can create a summary table as follows that is easier to read:

Percentage Who Attend Worship Services about Weekly

	Under 21	21–39	40–64	65 and Older
Men	6	17	28	44
Women	15	28	41	56

There are three primary observations to be made regarding this table. First, women are more likely to attend worship services than are men within each age group. Second, with a minor exception, the previously observed relationship between AGE and ATTEND is true for both men and women. Finally, the question we asked earlier about the cumulative effect of the two causal variables is answered with a clear "Yes." A mere 6 percent of the youngest men attend worship services weekly, contrasted to 56 percent of the oldest women.

SPSS COMMAND 17.1: Running Crosstabs to Examine the Impact of Two (or More) Independent Variables on One Dependent Variable

---

Click **Analyze** → **Descriptive Statistics** → **Crosstabs...** →

Highlight **dependent variable** → Click arrow pointing toward the **Row(s):** field →

Highlight one **independent variable** → Click arrow pointing toward the **Column(s):** field →

Highlight second **independent variable** [control variable] → Click arrow pointing toward **bottom field** →

Click **Cells...** → **Column** in Percentages box → **Continue** → **OK**

Demonstration 17.2: The Impact of Family Status on Religiosity

If you read the excerpt by Glock et al. on-line in E-Appendix G, you will recall that, according to social deprivation theory, "family status" is also related to religiosity. Those who had complete families (spouse and children) were the least religious among the 1,952 Episcopal church members, suggesting that those lacking families were turning to the church for gratification.

Using **Crosstabs**, set **CHATT** as the **row** variable and **MARITAL** as the **column** variable. Here's what you should get:

CHATT * MARITAL MARITAL STATUS Crosstabulation

| | | | MARITAL MARITAL STATUS | | | | | |
			1 MARRIED	2 WIDOWED	3 DIVORCED	4 SEPARATED	5 NEVER MARRIED	Total
CHATT	1 About weekly	Count	291	65	53	10	61	480
		% within MARITAL MARITAL STATUS	40.6%	50.0%	23.6%	20.4%	17.2%	32.5%
	2 About monthly	Count	94	17	42	17	60	230
		% within MARITAL MARITAL STATUS	13.1%	13.1%	18.7%	34.7%	16.9%	15.6%
	3 Seldom	Count	218	26	83	15	141	483
		% within MARITAL MARITAL STATUS	30.4%	20.0%	36.9%	30.6%	39.8%	32.7%
	4 Never	Count	114	22	47	7	92	282
		% within MARITAL MARITAL STATUS	15.9%	16.9%	20.9%	14.3%	26.0%	19.1%
Total		Count	717	130	225	49	354	1475
		% within MARITAL MARITAL STATUS	100.0%	100.0%	100.0%	100.0%	100.0%	100.0%

These data certainly do not confirm the earlier finding. Although the widowed are the most religious, those currently married are next. It would not appear that those deprived of conventional family status are turning to the church for an alternative source of gratification. Perhaps the explanation for this lies in historical changes.

In the 46 years separating these two studies, there have been many changes with regard to family life in the United States. Divorce, single-parent families, unmarried couples living together—these and other variations on the traditional family have become more acceptable and certainly more common. It would make sense, therefore, that people who lacked regular family status in 1998 would not feel as deprived as such people may have in the early 1950s.

Before setting this issue aside, however, we should take a minute to consider whether the table we've just seen is concealing anything. In particular, can you think of any other variable that is related to both attendance at worship services and marital status? If so, that variable might be clouding the relations between marital status and religiosity.

The variable we are thinking of is age. We've already seen that age is strongly related to church attendance. It is also probably related to marital status in that young people (low in church attendance) are the most likely to be "never married." And old people (high in church attendance) are the most likely to be widowed. It is possible, therefore, that the widowed are high in church attendance only because they're mostly old, and those never married are low in church attendance only because they're young. This kind of reasoning lies near the heart of multivariate analysis, and the techniques you've mastered allow you to test this possibility.

Return to the **Crosstabs** window and add **AGECAT** as the **third variable**.

Once you've reviewed the resulting tables, see if you can construct the following summary table.

Percentage Who Attend Church about Weekly

	Married	Widowed	Divorced	Separated	Never Married
Under 21	—	—	—	—	12
21–39	34	—	22	—	15
40–64	42	48	19	—	28
65 & older	51	52	48	—	—

Dashes in this table indicate that there are too few cases for meaningful percentages. We required at least 10 cases, a common standard.

Once again, these findings do not seem to confirm the theory that those lacking families turn to the church for gratification, whereas those with families are the least religious. Indeed, the widowed and married appear to be among the most religious in each category. This is followed by those who are divorced. Those never married indicate comparatively low levels of church attendance in almost every age group, except for the 40–64 age category.

You can also observe in this table that the effect of age on church attendance is maintained regardless of marital status. Older respondents are more likely to attend religious services than the younger ones in each category. Social scientists often use the term *replication* for the analytic outcome we've just observed. Having discovered that church attendance increases with age overall, we've now found that this relationship holds true regardless of marital status. That's an important discovery in terms of the generalizability of what we have learned about the causes of religiosity.

Demonstration 17.3: Social Class and Religiosity

In the earlier study, Glock and his colleagues found that religiosity increased as social class decreased; that is, those in the lower class were more religious than those in the upper class. This fit nicely into the deprivation thesis, that those deprived of status in the secular society would turn to the church as an alternative source of gratification. The researchers indicated, however, that this finding might be limited to the Episcopalian church members under study. They suggested that the relationship might not be replicated in the general public. You have the opportunity to check it out.

Let's begin with our measure of subjective social class. Run **Crosstabs** with **column** percentages, requesting **CHATT** as the **row** variable and **CLASS** as the **column** variable.[2] Here's what you should get:

2. Do not forget to designate the following numeric values for the variable CLASS as missing: 0, 5, 8, 9.

CHATT * CLASS SUBJECTIVE CLASS IDENTIFICATION Crosstabulation

			CLASS SUBJECTIVE CLASS IDENTIFICATION				
			1 LOWER CLASS	2 WORKING CLASS	3 MIDDLE CLASS	4 UPPER CLASS	Total
CHATT	1 About weekly	Count	30	207	221	20	478
		% within CLASS SUBJECTIVE CLASS IDENTIFICATION	34.1%	30.9%	33.7%	35.1%	32.5%
	2 About monthly	Count	12	106	98	13	229
		% within CLASS SUBJECTIVE CLASS IDENTIFICATION	13.6%	15.8%	14.9%	22.8%	15.6%
	3 Seldom	Count	21	228	214	20	483
		% within CLASS SUBJECTIVE CLASS IDENTIFICATION	23.9%	34.1%	32.6%	35.1%	32.9%
	4 Never	Count	25	128	123	4	280
		% within CLASS SUBJECTIVE CLASS IDENTIFICATION	28.4%	19.1%	18.8%	7.0%	19.0%
Total		Count	88	669	656	57	1470
		% within CLASS SUBJECTIVE CLASS IDENTIFICATION	100.0%	100.0%	100.0%	100.0%	100.0%

This table suggests that there is little relationship between social class and church attendance. In fact, the findings seem to run almost contrary to our expectations in some regards. To be sure of this conclusion, you might want to rerun the table, controlling for sex and for age. At the same time, you can test the generalizability of the previously observed effects of sex and age on church attendance. Do they hold up among members of different social classes?

Other Variables to Explore

Notice that our analyses so far in this chapter have used CHATT as the dependent variable: the measure of religiosity. Recall, however, our earlier comments on the shortcomings of single-item measures of variables. Perhaps our analyses have been misleading by seeking to explain church attendance. Perhaps different conclusions might be drawn if we had studied beliefs in an afterlife, or frequency of prayer. Why don't you test some of the earlier conclusions by using other measures of religiosity? If you are really ambitious, you can create a composite index of religiosity and look for causes.

Similarly, we have limited our preceding investigations in this chapter to the variables examined by Glock and his colleagues. Now that you have gotten the idea about how to create and interpret multivariate tables, you should broaden your exploration of variables that might be related to religiosity. What are some other demographic variables that might affect religiosity? Or you might want to explore the multivariate relationships between religiosity and some of the attitudinal variables we've been exploring: political philosophies, sexual attitudes, and so forth. In each instance, you should examine the bivariate relationships first, and then move on to the multivariate analyses.

Chi-Square and Measures of Association

Thus far, we've introduced the logic of multivariate analysis through the use of Crosstabs. You've already learned some other techniques that can be used in your examination of several variables simultaneously.

Chi-Square

First, we should remind you that you may want to use a chi-square test of statistical significance when you use Crosstabs. It's not required, but you may find it useful as an independent assessment of the relationships you discover.

Measures of Association

Second, you may also want to experiment using an appropriate measure of association such as lambda or gamma to test the strength and, in certain cases, the direction of association.

Multiple Regression

You may recall our fairly brief discussion of regression at the end of Chapter 14. At that point, we discussed a form of regression known as *simple linear regression* or just *linear regression*, which involves one independent and one dependent variable.

Regression can also be a powerful technique for exploring multivariate relationships. When you are conducting multivariate analysis involving one dependent and more than one independent variable, the technique is referred to as *multiple regression*. In both cases, regression is appropriate for two or more I/R or continuous variables.

To use either linear or multiple regression effectively, you need much more instruction than we propose to offer in this book. Still, we want to give you a brief overview of multiple regression, much in the same way we did when we introduced linear regression earlier.

Demonstration 17.4: Multiple Regression

In our previous use of regression (linear regression, Chapter 14), we examined the impact of EDUC on SEI, respondents' socioeconomic status scores. Now we'll open the possibility that other variables in the data set might also affect occupational prestige.

Dummy Variables

In addition to EDUC, we are also going to consider two additional independent variables: SEX and RACE. These variables were chosen because many argue that in today's workforce, men are still treated differently than women, and Whites are still treated differently than African-Americans.

You will notice, however, that both SEX and RACE are nominal variables, not I/R variables. Since we told you that regression is appropriate for I/R continuous variables, you may begin to wonder how we can propose to use two nominal variables in a regression equation. That's a very good question.

The answer lies in the fact that researchers sometimes treat such items as *dummy variables* appropriate to a regression analysis.[3] In regard to the variable SEX, for example, the logic used here transforms gender into a measure of "maleness," with men respondents being 100 percent male and the women 0 percent male.

Recoding SEX to Create a Dummy Variable—MALE

Let's recode **SEX** as described above into the new variable **MALE**. So take the following steps:

Transform → **Recode** → **Into Different Variables...**

Select **SEX** as the **Numeric Variable**. Let's call the new variable **MALE**. Using the **Old and New Values...** window, make these assignments.

Execute the Recode command by clicking **Continue** and then **OK**.

Before moving on to the variable RACE, make sure you set the *decimal places* for MALE to **0**. You may also want to give a brief *description* of MALE and define your *values* and *labels*.

---

3. For a brief overview of dummy variables, see: "Dummy Variables" at http://www.csbs.utsa.edu/social&policy/soc/masters/dummyvars.htm.

SPSS COMMAND 17.2:   Recoding to Create a Dummy Variable

> Click **Transform → Recode → Into Different Variables... →**
>
> **Highlight name of variable recoding** → Click **arrow** pointing toward "**Numeric Variable...**" field →
>
> Type **name of new variable** in rectangle under "Output Variable" labeled "**Name:**" →
>
> Click **Change → Old and New Values... →**
>
> Recode Old/Add New Values... →
>
> Click **Continue → OK**

Recoding RACE to Create a Dummy Variable—WHITE

We will use the same basic procedure to recode RACE as we used to recode SEX. Open the Recode dialog box by selecting **Transform → Recode → Into Different Variables...**

Designate **RACE** as the Numeric Variable and name the new variable **WHITE**. Then use the **Old and New Values** window to accomplish your recode.

You will notice that unlike the variable SEX, RACE contains three numeric values: 1 (White), 2 (Black), and 3 (Other). Consequently, in this case we are going to recode RACE as follows:

RACE		WHITE
Old Values		New Values
1	→	1
2–3	→	0

With this coding scheme, the dummy code "1" designates 100 percent majority group status, "0" designates 0 percent majority (or minority) group status. Once you have set the new values, click **Continue** and **OK** to execute the command.

Before we ask SPSS to run our regression analysis, make sure you set the *decimal places* for your new variable (WHITE) to **0**. In addition, you may want to provide a brief *description of the variable* and *define the values and labels*.

Multiple Regression[4]

Now that we have created our dummy variables, we are ready to request the multiple regression analysis.

Analyze → Regression → Linear... takes us to the window we want. Select **SEI** and make it the Dependent: Variable. Then place **EDUC, MALE,** and **WHITE** in the Independent(s): field. In the window labeled Method:, click the **down arrow** and highlight **Stepwise**.

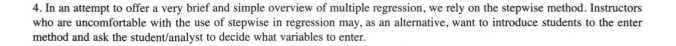

4. In an attempt to offer a very brief and simple overview of multiple regression, we rely on the stepwise method. Instructors who are uncomfortable with the use of stepwise in regression may, as an alternative, want to introduce students to the enter method and ask the student/analyst to decide what variables to enter.

Run this command by clicking **OK**, and you will receive a mass of output. Without going into all the details, we are simply going to show you how it establishes the equation we asked for. We'll take the output a piece at a time. For our purposes, we'd like you to skip through the output on your screen until you find the following two tables (probably the second and fourth tables displayed):

Model Summary

Model	R	R Square	Adjusted R Square	Std. Error of the Estimate
1	.576ª	.332	.331	15.780
2	.579ᵇ	.335	.335	15.745
3	.581ᶜ	.338	.336	15.723

a. Predictors: (Constant), EDUC HIGHEST YEAR OF SCHOOL COMPLETED

b. Predictors: (Constant), EDUC HIGHEST YEAR OF SCHOOL COMPLETED, MALE

c. Predictors: (Constant), EDUC HIGHEST YEAR OF SCHOOL COMPLETED, MALE, WHITE

Coefficientsᵃ

Model		Unstandardized Coefficients B	Unstandardized Coefficients Std. Error	Standardized Coefficients Beta	t	Sig.
1	(Constant)	-2.015	1.978		-1.019	.309
	EDUC HIGHEST YEAR OF SCHOOL COMPLETED	3.833	.144	.576	26.544	.000
2	(Constant)	-3.013	2.007		-1.501	.134
	EDUC HIGHEST YEAR OF SCHOOL COMPLETED	3.830	.144	.576	26.583	.000
	MALE	2.292	.839	.059	2.731	.006
3	(Constant)	-4.375	2.096		-2.088	.037
	EDUC HIGHEST YEAR OF SCHOOL COMPLETED	3.799	.145	.571	26.278	.000
	MALE	2.246	.838	.058	2.679	.007
	WHITE	2.286	1.026	.048	2.228	.026

We have given SPSS three variables that it might use to predict occupational prestige. In a stepwise regression, it begins by creating the most effective equation possible with only one independent variable. As you can see, it chose EDUC for that role. In other words, if you had to measure prestige on the basis of only one of the three independent variables, SPSS is telling us we'd do best with EDUC. It also reminds us of the variables not used in this first equation.

To create our equation for Model 1, we take two numbers from the Unstandardized Coefficients column: the constant (–2.015) and the *B* value (called the *slope*) for EDUC (3.833). Locate those in your output. We use these numbers to create the following equation:

$$SEI = -2.015 + (EDUC \times 3.833)$$

If someone had 10 years of education, then we would estimate his or her occupational prestige as follows:

$$SEI = -2.015 + (10 \times 3.833) = 36.315$$

Model 2 adds MALE as a predictor of occupational prestige. The meaning of this is that if we could use two variables to predict PRESTIGE, we should use

EDUC and MALE. Notice that the slope for EDUC changes only slightly when we add another independent variable.

$$SEI = -3.013 + (EDUC \times 3.830) + (MALE \times 2.292)$$

Based on this, what equation would you use to predict the occupational prestige of a male with 10 years of education? Here is a hint to get you started:

$$SEI = -3.013 + (10 \times 3.830) + (\underline{} \times \underline{}) = \underline{}$$

Model 3, the last row in the chart, uses all three variables. It's your turn to convert these data into a regression equation and experiment with it. Determine whether being White is worth any additional points of prestige when education and sex are held constant.

The column headed Standardized Coefficients gives you a guide to the relative impact of the different variables. Take a minute to consider some independent variable that has no impact on the dependent variable. What slope would it be given?

If you think about it, the only proper weight would be zero. That would mean that a person's value on that variable would never make any difference in predicting the dependent variable. By the same token, the larger the slope for any given variable, the larger its part in determining the resulting prediction.

It is possible (although it is not the case in this example) that a variable that is supposed to be a better predictor, such as EDUC, could have a smaller scope than an item such as MALE, which is not supposed to be as good a predictor of SEI. How can this happen?

The solution to this puzzle lies in the different scales used in the different variables. MALE only goes as high as 1 (Male), whereas EDUC obviously goes much higher to accommodate the different levels of educational attainment of respondents. Slopes must be standardized before they can be compared. Standardized slopes are what the slopes would be if each of the variables used the same scale. SPSS prints standardized slopes under the column Standardized Coefficients. The data presented above indicate that EDUC (.571) has the greatest impact on SEI, followed distantly by MALE (.058) and WHITE (.048). Interpreted, this means that education has the greatest impact on socioeconomic status, followed by "maleness" and "majorityness."

SPSS COMMAND 17.3:   Multiple Regression

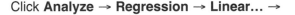

> Click **Analyze** → **Regression** → **Linear...** →
>
> **Highlight name** of **dependent variable** → Click **arrow** pointing to **Dependent**: field →
>
> **Highlight name** of 1st **independent variable** → Click **arrow** pointing to **Independent(s)**: field →
>
> Repeat last steps as many times as necessary until all Independent variables are listed in Independent(s): field →
>
> Click **arrow pointing down** next to box labeled "Method" → Select **Stepwise** → Click **OK**

Conclusion

In this chapter, we have given you an initial peek into the logic and techniques of multivariate analysis. As you've seen, the difference between bivariate and multivariate analysis is much more than a matter of degree. Multivariate analysis does more than bring in additional variables: It represents a new logic for understanding social scientific relationships.

For this contact, we've looked at how multivariate analysis lets us explore the nature of multiple causation, seeing how two or more independent variables affect a dependent variable. In addition, we've used multivariate techniques for the purpose of testing the generalizability of relationships.

In the latter regard, we have begun using multivariate techniques for the purpose of considering hidden relationships among variables, as when we asked whether the widowed attended church frequently just because they were mostly older people. We'll pursue this kind of detective work further in the chapters to come.

Main Points

- This chapter introduced a new, more sophisticated form of statistical analysis: multivariate analysis.

- Multivariate analysis is the simultaneous analysis of three or more variables.

- The Crosstabs procedure can be used to analyze the relationship between two independent variables and one dependent variable while controlling for a third variable.

- We examined multiple causes of religiosity in more depth by focusing on items such as: AGECAT, SEX, MARITAL, and SEI.

- Other analytic techniques may aid in the examination of several items at once, including chi-square, measures of association, and regression.

- We introduced simple linear regression in Chapter 14.

- In this chapter we introduced another regression procedure: multiple regression.

- Nominal and ordinal items can be recoded to create dummy variables that are suitable for regression analysis.

Key Terms

Multivariate analysis	Simple linear regression
Elaboration	Linear regression
Controlling for a third variable	Multiple regression
Control variable	Dummy variables
Replication	

SPSS Commands Introduced in This Chapter

17.1: Running Crosstabs to Examine the Impact of Two (or More) Independent Variables on One Dependent Variable

> Click **Analyze** → **Descriptive Statistics** → **Crosstabs...** →
>
> Highlight **dependent variable** → Click arrow pointing toward the **Row(s)**: field →
>
> Highlight one **independent variable** → Click arrow pointing toward the **Column(s)**: field →
>
> Highlight second **independent variable** [control variable] → Click arrow pointing toward **bottom field** →
>
> Click **Cells...** → **Column** in Percentages box → **Continue** → **OK**

17.2: Recoding to Create a Dummy Variable

> Click **Transform** → **Recode** → **Into Different Variables** →
>
> **Highlight name of variable recoding** → Click **arrow** pointing toward **"Numeric Variable..."** field →
>
> Type **name of new variable** in rectangle under "Output Variable" labeled **"Name:"** →
>
> Click **Change** → **Old and New Values...** →
>
> Recode Old/Add New Values... →
>
> Click **Continue** → **OK**

7.3: Multiple Regression

> Click **Analyze** → **Regression** → **Linear...** →
>
> **Highlight name** of **dependent variable** → Click **arrow** pointing to **Dependent:** field →
>
> **Highlight name** of 1st **independent variable** → Click **arrow** pointing to **Independent(s):** field →
>
> Repeat last steps as many times as necessary until all Independent variables are listed in Independent(s): field →
>
> Click **arrow pointing down** next to box labeled "Method" → Select **Stepwise** → Click **OK**

Review Questions

1. What is multivariate analysis?
2. If you are doing multivariate analysis and you ask SPSS to run **Crosstabs** with more than one independent variable, does the second independent variable belong below the first independent item in the box marked **Column(s):**?
3. Describe the relationship between social class and church attendance. Do the findings support the "social deprivation" theory? Why or why not?
4. What does "replication" refer to?
5. Name at least two other techniques you learned (before reading Chapter 17) that you could use in your multivariate examinations.
6. Simple linear regression involves the analysis of _____ [number] independent and _____ [number] dependent variables.
7. Multiple regression involves the analysis of _____ [number] independent and _____ [number] dependent variables.
8. Regression is appropriate for variables at what level(s) of measurement?
9. What is a dummy variable?
10. Why did we recode SEX to create MALE for our multiple regression example? Why didn't we just use SEX as our measure of gender?
11. What is a better predictor of SEI, EDUC or MALE?
12. When reading your multiple regression output, which of the following rows gives a sense of the relative impact of the independent variable: Unstandardized Coefficients, Standardized Coefficients, *t,* or sig.?

NAME —————————————————————————

CLASS —————————————————————————

INSTRUCTOR —————————————————————————

DATE —————————————————————————

To complete the following exercises, you need to load the data file EXER.SAV. Answers to selected questions can be found in Appendix A. For all these exercises, remember to define DKs as missing when necessary.

1. Examine the simultaneous impact of class and race on support for national spending on crime. Run Crosstabs and then complete the following summary table. Before running Crosstabs, be sure to designate the values indicated below as missing for each item.

   Dependent variable—NATCRIME [define 0, 8, 9 as missing]
   Independent variable 1—CLASS [define 5–9 & 0 as missing]
   Independent variable 2—RACE [define 3 "Other" as missing]

   NATCRIME: Percentage who feel the national government is spending too little fighting crime

	LOWER	WORKING	MIDDLE	UPPER
WHITE	_____	_____	_____	_____
BLACK	_____	_____	_____	_____

2. For WHITES: The percentage who feel the national government is spending too little fighting crime _____ [increases, decreases, stays about the same] as class increases.

3. For BLACKS: The percentage who feel the national government is spending too little fighting crime _____ [increases, decreases, stays about the same] as class increases.

4. Summarize the major findings from the table below. Explain the primary observations that can be made regarding the table. You may want to note, for instance, the relationship between race and support for government spending on crime, as well as the relationship between class and support for government spending on crime. Also note whether the two variables have a cumulative effect on support for national spending on crime. That is, are lower-class Blacks more likely to feel the government is spending too little fighting crime as opposed to upper-class Whites?

5. Examine the simultaneous impact of class and gender on support for national spending on welfare. Run Crosstabs and request chi-square. Then complete the following summary table. Before running Crosstabs, be sure to define DK for NATFARE as missing.

   Dependent variable—NATFARE [define 0, 8, 9 as missing]
   Independent variable 1—CLASS
   Independent variable 2—SEX

   NATFARE: Percentage who feel the national government is spending too little on welfare.

	LOWER	WORKING	MID	UPPER	Chi-square
MALE	_____	_____	_____	_____	_____
FEMALE	_____	_____	_____	_____	_____

6. For MALES: The percentage who feel the government is spending too little on welfare _____ [increases, decreases, stays about the same] as class increases. The value of chi-square indicates that there _____ [is/is not] a statistically significant relationship.

7. For FEMALES: The percentage who feel the government is spending too little on welfare _____ [increases, decreases, stays about the same] as class increases. The value of chi-square indicates that there _____ [is/is not] a statistically significant relationship.

8. Summarize the major findings from the table below. Explain the primary observations that can be made regarding the table. You may want to note, for instance, the relationship between gender and support for government spending on welfare, as well as the relationship between class and support for government spending on welfare. Also note whether the two variables have a cumulative effect on support for national spending on welfare. That is, are lower-class women more likely to feel the government is spending too little on welfare as opposed to upper-class men? In addition, be sure to discuss whether the findings are statistically significant.

NAME   _____

CLASS   _____

INSTRUCTOR _____

DATE   _____

Examine the simultaneous impact of two independent variables of your choice on support for the national governments spending on education [NATEDUC]. Run Crosstabs, *request chi-square, and then answer the following questions and complete the summary table (use as many spaces as necessary). Don't forget to define DK as missing for NATEDUC and the other variables you choose. In addition, if you need to recode one or both of your independent variables, indicate how you did that in response to Question 9.*

9. List the two independent variables you chose.

10. Justify your choice of the two independent variables and explain how you expect them to be related to NATEDUC.

11. NATEDUC: Percentage who feel that the government is spending too little on education

              _____   _____   _____   _____   Chi-square

      _____
      _____
      _____
      _____
      _____

12. Summarize your findings in detail below. Be sure to explain the primary observations that can be made regarding the table and discuss whether the findings are statistically significant.

13. Choose one dependent and two independent variables and write the names of the variables you chose below.

Dependent variable _____

Independent variable 1 _____

Independent variable 2 _____

14. Write two hypotheses explaining the relationship between each independent variable and the dependent variable.

Hypothesis 1:

Hypothesis 2:

Examine the simultaneous impact of the two independent variables on the dependent variable. Run Crosstabs *with chi-square and an appropriate measure of association. Then create a summary table detailing the relationship below [Question 16]. Remember to define DKs as missing and, if necessary, recode your variables and indicate how you did that in the space below Question 15.*

15. Measure of association _____

16. Summary Table:

NAME _____

CLASS _____

INSTRUCTOR _____

DATE _____

17. Summarize your findings in detail below. Be sure to explain the primary observations that can be made regarding the table. Discuss the strength and, if possible, the direction of association. Also indicate whether the findings are statistically significant and whether they support your hypotheses.

18. Recode the variable RACE to create a new dummy variable WHITE.

RACE Old Values		WHITE New Value
1	→	1
2–3	→	0

When you are done set the decimal places to 0.

Examine the impact of education [EDUC], race [RACE], and age [AGE] on the hours of television viewed each day. Designate the following values as missing (if they are not already defined as missing) before beginning your regression analysis.

EDUC—designate 97–99 as missing

AGE—designate 0, 98–99 as missing

TVHOURS—designate –1, 98–99 as missing

Open the Linear regression *window and designate TVHOURS as the dependent variable and EDUC, WHITE, and AGE as the independent variables. Then answer the following questions.*

19. What is the constant for EDUC?

20. What is *B* value (slope) for EDUC?

21. Fill in the blanks to create the following equation.

TVHOURS = _____ + (EDUC × _____)

22. If someone had 10 years of education, we would estimate his or her hours of watching television per day as follows: [fill in the blanks]

TVHOURS = _____ + (10 × _____) = _____

23. Fill in the blanks to create the following equation.

TVHOURS = _____ + (EDUC × _____) + (WHITE × _____)

24. If a White person had 10 years of education, how many hours of television would you estimate he/she watches every day?

25. Which of the three independent variables is most strongly related to TVHOURS? Explain the logic of your choice.

Chapter 18   Dissecting the Political Factor

In Chapter 12, we began exploring some of the causes of political philosophies and party identification. Now you are equipped to dig more deeply. Let's start with the relationship between political philosophy and party identification. As you'll recall, our earlier analysis showed a definite relationship, although it was not altogether consistent. Perhaps we can clarify it.

Political Philosophy and Party Identification

On the whole, Democrats in our sample were more liberal than Independents or Republicans. Also, Republicans were the most conservative, although there wasn't as large a distinction between Democrats and Independents as you might have expected. Here's the basic table from Chapter 12 examining the relationship between political philosophy (POLREC) and party identification (PARTY).[1]

POLREC Recoded polviews * PARTY Recoded party ID Crosstabulation

			PARTY Recoded party ID				
			1 Democrat	2 Independent	3 Republican	4 Other	Total
POLREC Recoded polviews	1 Liberal	Count	191	145	41	10	387
		% within PARTY Recoded party ID	41.5%	26.5%	10.6%	32.3%	27.2%
	2 Moderate	Count	184	239	103	10	536
		% within PARTY Recoded party ID	40.0%	43.6%	26.8%	32.3%	37.6%
	3 Conservative	Count	85	164	241	11	501
		% within PARTY Recoded party ID	18.5%	29.9%	62.6%	35.5%	35.2%
Total		Count	460	548	385	31	1424
		% within PARTY Recoded party ID	100.0%	100.0%	100.0%	100.0%	100.0%

For purposes of this analysis, let's focus on the percentages who identify themselves as "Conservative." In the table above, the percentage difference separating the Democrats and Republicans in calling themselves conservative amounts to 44 points. You'll recall, perhaps, that percentage differences are sometimes designated by the Greek letter *epsilon* or abbreviated with the letter ε.

---

1. You may recall that in Chapter 7 we recoded the variables POLVIEWS and PARTYID to create POLREC and PARTY, respectively.

Demonstration 18.1: Controlling for Education

If you were to undertake a study of the political party platforms and/or the speeches of political leaders from the two major parties, you would conclude that Democrats are, in fact, somewhat more liberal than Republicans, and that Republicans are, in fact, somewhat more conservative than Democrats. If the relationship between political philosophy and party identification is not as clear as we might like, then perhaps some of the respondents simply don't know how the two parties are generally regarded.

Who do you suppose would be the least likely to know the philosophical leanings of the two parties? Perhaps those with the least education would be unaware of them. If that were the case, then we should expect a clearer relationship between political philosophy and party identification among the more educated respondents than among the less educated.

Why don't you open your DEMO.SAV file and run the SPSS command that lets you create the following three-variable summary table?[2]

Percentage Saying They Are Conservative	Less Than HS	HS Grad	Some College	College Grad	Grad Studies
Democrat	21	23	18	12	8
Independent	39	29	28	29	25
Republican	52	58	61	75	67
ε	31	35	43	63	59

Our suspicion seems to be confirmed. The clearest relationship between party and political philosophy appears among college graduates, followed by those with post-college education and then those with some college. Notice that Democrats and Republicans are separated by an epsilon of 31 percentage points among the least educated group. As we would expect, the epsilon is slightly larger (35 percentage points) among high school graduates. Independents of every education level say they are more conservative than Democrats but much less so than Republicans.

This table reveals something else that relates to our earlier analysis. You may recall that we found only a weak and inconsistent relationship between education and political philosophy in our Chapter 12 analysis. There was a tendency for liberalism to increase with education, although only 12 percentage points separated the least from the most educated groups in that respect. There was no relationship between conservatism and education, with the moderate point of view decreasing with education.

This new table clarifies the situation somewhat. The relationship between political philosophy and education occurs primarily among Democrats. Although the more highly educated Republicans are the most conservative, there are few differences among the other educational groups.

---

2. To construct this summary table, instruct SPSS to run **Crosstabs** with **column** percentages, specifying **EDCAT** as the **column** variable, **POLREC** as the **row** variable, and **PARTY** as the **control** variable. In the controlled table, the number of cases in the "Other" category of POLREC is very small. With numbers so small, it is easy to compute percentages that exaggerate differences. We'll avoid the problem by not including the "Other" category of POLREC in our summary table.

This table represents what social scientists call a ***specification***. We have specified the relationship between education and political philosophy: It occurs primarily among Democrats. On the other hand, we could say that we have specified the relationship between political philosophy and party identification: It occurs primarily among the better educated.

Specification stands as an alternative to ***replication***. You'll recall from our discussion in the last chapter that replication indicates that a relationship between two variables can be generalized to all kinds of people. Specification indicates that it cannot.

When we look at the relationship between two variables, such as political philosophy and party identification, among subgroups determined by some other variable, such as education, we often say that we are ***controlling for a third variable***. Social scientists use the expression "controlling for" in the sense of creating controlled conditions: only college graduates, only those with some college, and so on. We also speak of "holding education ***constant***" in the sense that education is no longer a variable (it is a constant) when we look at only one educational group at a time.

Why don't you experiment with this logic, testing the generalizability of the relationship between political philosophy and party identification among other subgroups, formed by holding other variables constant?

Demonstration 18.2: The Mystery of Politics and Marital Status

In Chapter 12, we encouraged you to explore the relationship between marital status and politics. If you took us up on the invitation, you should have found an interesting relationship between marital status and political philosophy.

Recoding MARITAL

Because relatively few respondents were "Separated," we should combine them with some other group. It would seem to make sense to combine the separated with the divorced, reasoning that separation is often experienced as an interim step toward divorce.

Let's recode MARITAL into a new variable, MARITAL2, with

Transform → Recode → Into Different Variables...

Once in the Recode window, you should enter **MARITAL** as the Input Variable and **MARITAL2** as the Output Variable. Click on **Change** to move MARITAL2 to the recode list. Then, in the **Old and New Values** window, recode as follows:

MARITAL Old Values		MARITAL2 New Values	Labels
1	→	1	Married
2	→	2	Widowed
3–4	→	3	Divorced/separated
5	→	4	Never married

Don't forget to use **Add** to record the instructions. Then, you can **Continue** and **OK** your way to the recoded variable.

Before we move on, make sure you *set the decimal places* for your new variable to **0**, as well as *define the values and labels* for MARITAL2.

POLREC by MARITAL2

Now create a **Crosstab** with **MARITAL2** as the **column** variable and **POLREC** as the **row** variable. Ask SPSS for **column** percentages. Here's what you should get:

POLREC Recoded polviews * MARITAL2 Crosstabulation

			MARITAL2				
			1 married	2 widowed	3 divorced/s eparated	4 never married	Total
POLREC Recoded polviews	1 Liberal	Count	155	20	101	113	389
		% within MARITAL2	22.2%	16.5%	37.8%	33.1%	27.3%
	2 Moderate	Count	255	58	92	132	537
		% within MARITAL2	36.5%	47.9%	34.5%	38.7%	37.6%
	3 Conservative	Count	288	43	74	96	501
		% within MARITAL2	41.3%	35.5%	27.7%	28.2%	35.1%
Total		Count	698	121	267	341	1427
		% within MARITAL2	100.0%	100.0%	100.0%	100.0%	100.0%

If you had run the chi-square test of statistical significance, you would have found this relationship to exceed the .001 level of significance. So, why is it that married and widowed respondents are more conservative than the divorced, separated, or never married? Your multivariate skills will allow you to explore this matter in more depth than was possible before.

POLREC by MARITAL2 by AGECAT

Perhaps age is the key. The widowed are likely to be older than others, and the never married are likely to be younger. As we've seen, people tend to become more conservative with age. Here is a summary table created from the results of the Crosstab of POLREC by MARITAL2 by AGECAT. See if you can duplicate this yourself.

Percentage Who Say They Are Conservative	Married	Widowed	Divorced/ Separated	Never Married
Under 21	—	—	—	40
21–39	38	—	34	24
40–64	42	—	23	36
65 and up	46	35	34	—

(As in other tables, the dashes here indicate that there were too few cases for meaningful percentages.)

This table helps clarify matters somewhat. The married are consistently more conservative than the divorced and never married (with the exception of those 65 and older), and the widowed tend to maintain their conservative stance.

With the exception of those 65 and older, those divorced, separated, and never married seem to be slightly more liberal than those married and widowed, although the differences are not dramatic.

POLREC by MARITAL2 by SEX

How about sex? Perhaps it can shed some light on this relationship. Why don't you run the tables that would result in this summary?

Percentage Who Say They Are Conservative	Married	Widowed	Divorced/ Separated	Never Married
Men	45	—	36	28
Women	38	35	21	29

As before, the married and widowed remain relatively conservative, and the divorced and never married remain relatively less conservative (except in the case of divorced/separated men).

POLREC by MARITAL2 by EDCAT

To pursue this further, you might want to consider education. Here's the summary table you should generate if you follow this avenue.

Percentage Who Say They Are Conservative	Married	Widowed	Divorced/ Separated	Never Married
Less than HS	38	36	28	39
HS graduate	38	41	24	31
Some college	42	—	24	27
College graduate	51	—	—	22
Graduate studies	38	—	44	—

Once more, we seem to have dug a dry well. Education does not seem to clarify the relationship we first observed between marital status and political philosophy. This is the point in an analysis where you sometimes wonder if you should ever have considered this line of inquiry.

POLREC by MARITAL2 by RACE

See what happens when we introduce race as a control.

Percentage Who Say They Are Conservative	Married	Widowed	Divorced/ Separated	Never Married
White	42	37	30	30
Black	31	—	26	27
Other	42	—	—	23

POLREC as Independent Variable

When we consistently fail to find a clear answer to a question—Why do people of different marital statuses differ in their political philosophies?—it is sometimes useful to reconsider the question itself. Thus far, we have been asking why marital status would affect political philosophy. Perhaps we have the question reversed. What if political philosophy affects marital status? Is that a possibility?

Perhaps those who are politically conservative are also socially conservative. Maybe it would be especially important for them to form and keep traditional families. During the 1996 presidential election, the political conservatives made "traditional family values" a centerpiece of their campaign. Let's see what the table would look like if we percentaged it in the opposite direction.

MARITAL2 * POLREC Recoded polviews Crosstabulation

| | | | POLREC Recoded polviews | | | |
			1 Liberal	2 Moderate	3 Conserva tive	Total
MARITAL2	1 married	Count	155	255	288	698
		% within POLREC Recoded polviews	39.8%	47.5%	57.5%	48.9%
	2 widowed	Count	20	58	43	121
		% within POLREC Recoded polviews	5.1%	10.8%	8.6%	8.5%
	3 divorced/separated	Count	101	92	74	267
		% within POLREC Recoded polviews	26.0%	17.1%	14.8%	18.7%
	4 never married	Count	113	132	96	341
		% within POLREC Recoded polviews	29.0%	24.6%	19.2%	23.9%
Total		Count	389	537	501	1427
		% within POLREC Recoded polviews	100.0%	100.0%	100.0%	100.0%

Look at the first row in this table. The percentage married increases steadily with increasing conservatism across the table. Divorce and singlehood, on the other hand, decrease just as steadily. Perhaps marital status is more profitably seen as a dependent variable in this context—affected to some extent by worldviews such as those that are reflected in political philosophy.

Sometimes, the direction of a relationship—which is the dependent and which is the independent variable—is clear. If we discover that voting behavior is related to gender, for instance, we can be sure that gender can affect voting, but how you vote can't change your gender. In other situations, such as the present one, the direction of a relationship is somewhat ambiguous. Ultimately, this decision must be based on theoretical reasoning. There is no way the analysis of data can determine which variable is dependent and which is independent.

If you wanted to pursue the present relationship, you might treat marital status as a dependent variable, subjecting its relationship with political philosophies to a multivariate analysis.

Political Issues

In Chapter 12, we began looking for the causes of opinions on two political issues:

> GUNLAW registration of firearms
> CAPPUN capital punishment

Now that you have the ability to undertake multivariate analysis, you can delve more deeply into the causes of public opinion. Let's think a little about capital punishment for the moment. Here are some variables that might logically affect how people feel about the death penalty.

POLREC and PARTY are obvious candidates. Liberals are generally more opposed to capital punishment than are conservatives. Similarly, Republicans have tended to support it more than have Democrats. You might check to see how these two variables work together on death penalty attitudes.

Given that capital punishment involves the taking of a human life, you might expect some religious effects. How do the different religious affiliations relate to support for or opposition to capital punishment? What about beliefs in an after-life? Do those who believe in life after death find it easier to support the taking of a life? How do religious and political factors interact in this arena?

Those opposed to capital punishment base their opposition on the view that it is wrong to take a human life. The same argument is made by those who oppose abortion. Logically, you would expect those opposed to abortion to also oppose capital punishment. Why don't you check it out? You may be surprised by what you find.

Another approach to understanding opinions about capital punishment might focus on which groups in society are most likely to be victims of it. Men are more likely to be executed than are women. Blacks are executed disproportionately often in comparison with their numbers in the population.

Conclusion

These few suggestions should launch you on an extended exploration of the nature of political orientations. Whereas people often talk pretty casually about political matters, you are now in a position to check out the facts and to dig deeply into understanding why people feel as they do about political issues.

Multivariate analysis techniques let you uncover some of the complexities that can make human behavior difficult to understand.

Main Points

- You can use your multivariate analysis skills to delve into the nature of political orientation.
- We began by exploring the relationship between political philosophy and party identification while controlling for education.
- Our findings indicate specification or a specified relationship between education and political philosophy.

- Unlike replication, specification indicates a relationship between two items that cannot be generalized to all kinds of people.
- You can test the generalizability of the relationship between two items by controlling for or holding a third variable constant.
- The direction of the relationship between variables (which is the dependent and which is the independent) is not always clear.
- In exploring the relationship between political philosophy and marital status we took turns examining both as the independent variable.
- We discovered that marital status is perhaps better seen as the dependent variable in this context.
- You can use your multivariate analysis skills to discover why people hold the opinions they do on volatile political issues such as gun control and capital punishment.

Key Terms

Epsilon (ε)   Controlling for a third variable
Specification   Constant
Replication

SPSS Commands Introduced in This Chapter

No new commands were introduced in this chapter.

Review Questions

1. What is specification?
2. How does specification differ from replication?
3. Give an example of specification.
4. Give an example of replication.
5. What does it mean to "control" for a third variable?
6. Is this the same or different from "holding a variable constant"?
7. If we wanted to instruct SPSS to create crosstabs examining the relationship between POLREC and PARTY while controlling for SEX, where in the Crosstabs window would we transfer SEX (i.e., to which field, the Row(s):, Column(s):, or third box near the bottom of the window)?
8. In examining the relationship between political philosophy and party identification, what other variables (besides sex and education) might you want to control for? Name at least two.
9. When conducting multivariate analysis, how do we ultimately know which variable is the dependent one and which is the independent one?
10. If we were performing multivariate analysis and found a relationship between RACE and voting behavior, could RACE be the dependent variable? Why or why not?
11. Name three variables from your data set which you think may logically affect or have an impact how people feel about gun control (GUNLAW) and explain why.

NAME _____

CLASS _____

INSTRUCTOR _____

DATE _____

To complete the following exercises you need to load the data file EXER.SAV. You will find answers to Questions 1–2 in Appendix A.

Use Crosstabs *to examine the relationship between RACWORK and AFFR-MACT, recode the variables to create RACWORK2 and AFFREC[3] and then label the items as follows.*

RACWORK		RACWORK2	
Old Values		**New Values**	**Labels**
1–2	→	1	Mostly White
3	→	2	Half White–Black
4–5	→	3	Mostly Black

AFFRMACT		AFFREC	
Old Values		**New Values**	**Labels**
1–2	→	1	Support
3–4	→	2	Oppose

Make sure you set the decimal places for your new variables (RACWORK2 and AFFREC) to **0**.

Now run Crosstabs *with column percentages and chi-square, designating RAC-WORK2 as the column variable and AFFREC as the row variable. Then answer the questions below.*

1. The table shows that those who work mostly with Whites are _____ [more likely/less likely/not any more or less likely] than those who work with mostly Blacks to support affirmative action.

2. The significance of chi-square is _____ [less than/more than] .05, so the relationship between AFFREC and RACWORK2 _____ [is/is not] statistically significant.

3. List three variables from the data file EXER.SAV you want to use to examine why those who work with mostly Whites are less supportive of affirmative action than those who work with mostly Blacks.
   Variable 1 _____
   Variable 2 _____
   Variable 3 _____

---

3. We recoded AFFRMACT to create AFFREC earlier as well. If you saved AFFREC you can use it for this exercise as well.

4. Justify your choice of variable 1 above (i.e., give theoretical reasons for choosing this variable).

5. Justify your choice of variable 2 above (i.e., give theoretical reasons for choosing this variable).

6. Justify your choice of variable 3 above (i.e., give theoretical reasons for choosing this variable).

7. Examine the relationship between AFFREC and RACWORK2 while controlling for variable 1 above. Run Crosstabs with chi-square. If you had to recode variable 1, make sure you explain how you did that. Then create a summary table based on the results of your Crosstab and show it below (if you need help creating a summary table, see the tables in the chapter for guidance).

8. Summarize below the major findings from your table. Explain what are, in your view, the primary observations that can be made regarding the table. Be sure to note, for instance, whether the findings supported your expectations. Use chi-square as a criterion for judging whether the differences in your table are significant (if your findings are statistically significant, you may want to go back and measure the strength of the relationship and then discuss how you did that and what you found).

NAME _____

CLASS _____

INSTRUCTOR _____

DATE _____

9. Examine the relationship between AFFREC and RACWORK2 while controlling for variable 2 above. Run Crosstabs with chi-square. If you had to recode
variable 2, make sure you explain how you did that. Then create a summary
table based on the results of your Crosstab and show it below.

10. Summarize below the major findings from your table. Explain what are, in
your view, the primary observations that can be made regarding the table. Be
sure to note, for instance, whether the findings supported your expectations.
Use chi-square as a criterion for judging whether the differences in your table
are significant (if your findings are statistically significant, you may want to go
back and measure the strength of the relationship and then discuss how you did
that and what you found).

11. Examine the relationship between AFFREC and RACWORK2 while controlling for variable 3 above. Run Crosstabs with chi-square. If you had to recode variable 3, make sure you explain how you did that. Then create a summary table based on the results of your Crosstab and show it below.

12. Summarize the major findings from your table below. Explain what are, in your view, the primary observations that can be made regarding the table. Be sure to note, for instance, whether the findings supported your expectations. Use chi-square as a criterion for judging whether the differences in your table are significant (if your findings are statistically significant, you may want to go back and measure the strength of the relationship and then discuss how you did that and what you found).

Chapter 19   A Powerful Prediction of Attitudes Toward Abortion

In previous analyses, we've seen how complex attitudes about abortion are. As we return to our analysis of this controversial topic, you have additional tools for digging deeper. Let's begin with the religious factor. Then we'll turn to politics and other variables.

Religion and Abortion

In Chapter 13, we found that both religious affiliation and measures of religiosity were related to abortion attitudes. The clearest relationships were observed in terms of the unconditional right to abortion, because only a small minority are opposed to abortion in all circumstances.

Protestants and Catholics are generally less supportive of abortion than Jews and "Nones." And on measures of religiosity, opposition to abortion increases with increasing religiosity. The most religious are the most opposed to a woman's right to choose an abortion.

With your multivariate skills, you can examine this issue more deeply. Consider the possibility, for example, that one of these relationships is an artifact of the other.

Demonstration 19.1: Religious Affiliation and Church Attendance

To explore the possibility that one of the relationships we found in Chapter 13 is merely an artifact of another association, you need to open your DEMO.SAV file and examine the relationship between religious affiliation and church attendance.[1]

---

1. The values 0 & 5–99 for the variable RELIG should be defined as missing.

CHATT * RS RELIGIOUS PREFERENCE Crosstabulation

			RS RELIGIOUS PREFERENCE				
			1 Protestant	2 Catholic	3 Jewish	4 None	Total
CHATT	1 About weekly	Count	312	131	6	7	456
		% within RS RELIGIOUS PREFERENCE	40.7%	33.2%	22.2%	3.4%	32.8%
	2 About monthly	Count	131	78	4	4	217
		% within RS RELIGIOUS PREFERENCE	17.1%	19.8%	14.8%	2.0%	15.6%
	3 Seldom	Count	238	143	12	62	455
		% within RS RELIGIOUS PREFERENCE	31.1%	36.3%	44.4%	30.5%	32.7%
	4 Never	Count	85	42	5	130	262
		% within RS RELIGIOUS PREFERENCE	11.1%	10.7%	18.5%	64.0%	18.8%
Total		Count	766	394	27	203	1390
		% within RS RELIGIOUS PREFERENCE	100.0%	100.0%	100.0%	100.0%	100.0%

As you can see, there is a pretty clear relationship between these two variables. Protestants and Catholics are the most likely to attend worship services weekly or one to three times a month. Those with no religion, of course, attend church seldom or never. If we combine the two most frequent categories, we see that 48 percent of the whole sample attends church at least one to three times a month. There are big differences among the five religious groups, however.

**Percentage Who Attend
at Least 1–3 Times a Month**

Protestants	58
Catholics	53
Jews	37
None	5

Demonstration 19.2: Religious Affiliation, Church Attendance, and Abortion

Because religious affiliation and church attendance are related to one another and each is related to abortion attitudes, there are two possibilities for us to explore. For example, perhaps church attendance seems to affect abortion attitudes only because Protestants and Catholics (relatively opposed to abortion) attend more often. Or, conversely, perhaps Protestants and Catholics seem more opposed to abortion simply because they attend church more often.

We can test for these possibilities by running a multivariate table, taking account of all three variables.

Recoding RELIG and ATTEND into Same Variables

To simplify our analysis, let's recode RELIG into two categories—"Christians" and "Others"—and recode ATTEND into two categories as well.

Because we're going to be doing several recodes in this session, let's recode the original variables this time. In other words, rather than creating a number of new variables that we may not use again, we are going to recode the original variables RELIG and ATTEND.[2]

So, let's use **Transform** → **Recode** → **Into Same Varlables....**

Make the recodes listed below, beginning with **RELIG** and then moving to **ATTEND**. Once you have recoded the items, click **Data** → **Define Variables** to label the recoded values. If you need to verify the process for recoding Into same variables, consult SPSS Command 19.1.

Recode RELIG

Old Values		New Values	Labels
1–2	→	1	Christian
3–4	→	2	Other

Recode ATTEND

Old Values		New Values Labels	
4–8	→	1	Often
0–3	→	2	Seldom

SPSS COMMAND 19.1: Recoding into Same Variables

Transform → **Recode** → **Into Same Variables...** →

Highlight the **name of the variable** you want to recode → Click the **right-pointing arrow** to move the variable to the Numeric Variables: field →

Click **Old and New Values...** →

Define Old and New Values in the Recode into Same Variables: Old and New... box →

Click **Add** to Change Old → New Values →

Click **Continue** → **OK** →

Highlight the variable in the Data Editor →

Click **Data** → **Define Variable...** → **Labels** →

Put labels on recoded variable →

Click **Continue** → **OK** →

Crosstab Recoded Variables

Now run a **Crosstab** with **column** percentages. Designate **ATTEND** as the **row** variable and **RELIG** as the **column** variable.[3]

---

2. If you save your data set after this exercise, be sure to use Save As and give it a *new name* so that you'll still be able to get back to your original, unrecoded data.

3. Be sure to designate the following numeric values as missing: RELIG— 0, 5–99; ATTEND— 9.

HOW OFTEN R ATTENDS RELIGIOUS SERVICES * RS RELIGIOUS PREFERENCE Crosstabulation

| | | | RS RELIGIOUS PREFERENCE | | |
			1 Christian	2 Other	Total
HOW OFTEN R ATTENDS RELIGIOUS SERVICES	1 LT ONCE A YEAR	Count	652	21	673
		% within RS RELIGIOUS PREFERENCE	56.2%	9.1%	48.4%
	2 ONCE A YEAR	Count	508	209	717
		% within RS RELIGIOUS PREFERENCE	43.8%	90.9%	51.6%
Total		Count	1160	230	1390
		% within RS RELIGIOUS PREFERENCE	100.0%	100.0%	100.0%

As you can see, the relationship between religious affiliation and church attendance is still obvious after categories are collapsed on both variables.

Now let's review the relationships between each variable and abortion, again using the recoded variables.

Relationship Between ABORT and Recoded Items

Simple Abortion Index * RS RELIGIOUS PREFERENCE Crosstabulation

| | | | RS RELIGIOUS PREFERENCE | | |
			1 Christian	2 Other	Total
Simple Abortion Index	0 yes/approve	Count	255	104	359
		% within RS RELIGIOUS PREFERENCE	36.3%	72.2%	42.4%
	1 conditional support	Count	277	34	311
		% within RS RELIGIOUS PREFERENCE	39.5%	23.6%	36.8%
	2 no/disapprove	Count	170	6	176
		% within RS RELIGIOUS PREFERENCE	24.2%	4.2%	20.8%
Total		Count	702	144	846
		% within RS RELIGIOUS PREFERENCE	100.0%	100.0%	100.0%

Simple Abortion Index * HOW OFTEN R ATTENDS RELIGIOUS SERVICES Crosstabulation

| | | | HOW OFTEN R ATTENDS RELIGIOUS SERVICES | | |
			1 LT ONCE A YEAR	2 ONCE A YEAR	Total
Simple Abortion Index	0 yes/approve	Count	139	233	372
		% within HOW OFTEN R ATTENDS RELIGIOUS SERVICES	32.8%	51.7%	42.5%
	1 conditional support	Count	154	166	320
		% within HOW OFTEN R ATTENDS RELIGIOUS SERVICES	36.3%	36.8%	36.6%
	2 no/disapprove	Count	131	52	183
		% within HOW OFTEN R ATTENDS RELIGIOUS SERVICES	30.9%	11.5%	20.9%
Total		Count	424	451	875
		% within HOW OFTEN R ATTENDS RELIGIOUS SERVICES	100.0%	100.0%	100.0%

Notice that the relationship between affiliation and abortion is now repre-sented by an epsilon of 36 percentage points. The relationship between church attendance and abortion has an epsilon of 19 percentage points.

Examining All Three Items at Once

Now let's look at the three-variable relationship.

Simple Abortion Index * RS RELIGIOUS PREFERENCE * ATTEND Crosstabulation

ATTEND					RS RELIGIOUS PREFERENCE		
					1 Christian	2 Other	Total
1 often	Simple Abortion Index	0 yes/approve		Count	124	8	132
				% within RS RELIGIOUS PREFERENCE	31.8%	53.3%	32.6%
		1 conditional support		Count	140	7	147
				% within RS RELIGIOUS PREFERENCE	35.9%	46.7%	36.3%
		2 no/disapprove		Count	126		126
				% within RS RELIGIOUS PREFERENCE	32.3%		31.1%
	Total			Count	390	15	405
				% within RS RELIGIOUS PREFERENCE	100.0%	100.0%	100.0%
2 seldom	Simple Abortion Index	0 yes/approve		Count	125	93	218
				% within RS RELIGIOUS PREFERENCE	41.5%	73.8%	51.1%
		1 conditional support		Count	134	27	161
				% within RS RELIGIOUS PREFERENCE	44.5%	21.4%	37.7%
		2 no/disapprove		Count	42	6	48
				% within RS RELIGIOUS PREFERENCE	14.0%	4.8%	11.2%
	Total			Count	301	126	427
				% within RS RELIGIOUS PREFERENCE	100.0%	100.0%	100.0%

To examine the results of this analysis, let's summarize the findings as follows:

Percentage Who Support Abortion Unconditionally	Christians	Others	Epsilon
Attend often	32	53	21
Attend seldom	42	74	32
Epsilon	10	21	

This multivariate analysis suggests a number of conclusions. First, neither of the possibilities we were exploring is confirmed. The opposition to abortion by Protestants and Catholics is not merely a function of their greater church atten-dance, nor is the effect of church attendance due merely to differences of affilia-tion. Each variable has an independent impact on attitudes regarding abortion.

At the same time, we can see that the impact of church attendance is less among the non-Christians, and that the impact of affiliation is less among those who attend less often. Putting the two religious variables together, we can see that the Christians who attend church often stand some distance from the other groups in their opposition to abortion. You might like to experiment some more with the religious factor, using some of the other variables included in the GSS data set. In the next section, we are going to examine the impact of political factors as a point of comparison with the religious factor.

Politics and Abortion

As we saw in Chapter 13, political philosophies have a strong impact on attitudes toward abortion. You might want to refresh your memory by rerunning this table. (You now know how. Wow!)

Simple Abortion Index * Recoded polviews Crosstabulation

			Recoded polviews			
			1 Liberal	2 Moderate	3 Conservative	Total
Simple Abortion Index	0 yes/approve	Count	160	128	74	362
		% within Recoded polviews	61.5%	42.8%	25.9%	42.8%
	1 conditional support	Count	75	116	122	313
		% within Recoded polviews	28.8%	38.8%	42.7%	37.0%
	2 no/disapprove	Count	25	55	90	170
		% within Recoded polviews	9.6%	18.4%	31.5%	20.1%
Total		Count	260	299	286	845
		% within Recoded polviews	100.0%	100.0%	100.0%	100.0%

The impact of political philosophy on unconditional support for a woman's right to choose abortion equals 36 percentage points (exactly the same as the epsilon for religious denomination). As we saw earlier, however, political party identification—despite official party differences on the issue of abortion—does not have much of an effect.

Demonstration 19.3: The Interaction of Religion and Politics on Abortion Attitudes

In a multivariate analysis, we might next want to explore the possible interaction of religion and politics on abortion attitudes. For example, in Chapter 13, we found that Protestants and Catholics were somewhat more conservative than were Jews and "Nones." Perhaps their political orientations account for the differences that the religious groups have on the issue of abortion.

With your multivariate skills, testing this new possibility is a simple matter. Take a minute to figure out the SPSS command that would provide for such a test. Then enter it and review the results.

Here's a summary table of the results you should have found if you are working with the latest recode for RELIG. Be sure you can replicate this on your own.

Percentage Who Unconditionally Support Right to Abortion	Liberal	Moderate	Conservative
Christian	52	38	23
Other	89	60	47

This table demonstrates the independent impact of religion and politics on abortion attitudes. In addition, what would you say it tells us about the religious effect observed earlier? Does it occur among all the political groups? What, if anything, do the epsilons for each political group (37, 22, 24) tell us about the religious effect?

Overall, you can see that the joint impact of politics and religion is represented by an epsilon of 66 percentage points (89 – 23), a powerful degree of prediction for these controversial opinions.

Demonstration 19.4: Constructing an Index of Ideological Traditionalism

To support our continued analysis, let's create a simple index to combine the religious and political factors. For the time being, let's just call it our "index of ideological traditionalism."

You may recall from our discussion in Chapter 9 that there are a number of steps involved in creating an index. However, all the work is worth it because in the end we will hopefully have a composite measure that captures religious and political predispositions to support abortion. In other words, we will have built an index based on our two religious items (ATTEND and RELIG) and one political item (POLREC), which allows us to predict attitudes toward abortion.

In this case our index will range from 0 (Oppose abortion) to 4 (Support abortion).

Before we begin constructing our index, it may be useful to give you a brief overview of the seven steps involved in creating our new index of ideological traditionalism, which we will call IND:

Step 1: Create new index/item "IND."

Steps 2–5: Assign points on the index based on responses to the three component variables: POLREC, RELIG, and ATTEND. As noted, our index scores will run from 0 (Opposed to abortion) to 4 (Supportive of abortion). We will assign points as follows:

Step 2: If Liberal (1) on POLREC, get 2 points on IND.

Step 3: If Moderate (2) on POLREC, get 1 point on IND.

Step 4: If Other (2) on RELIG, get 1 point on IND.

Step 5: If attend religious services seldom (2) on ATTEND, get 1 point on IND.

Step 6: Use COUNT to handle missing data.

Step 7: Define IND (i.e., missing, type...).

Now that you have reviewed the steps involved in creating our new index of ideological traditionalism IND, let's go through each of the steps one at a time.

Step 1: Create IND

To begin, select **Transform** → **Compute....**

In the Compute Variable: box, create a new Target Variable: called **IND** (for index).

We'll start by giving everyone a 0, so type **0** or use the calculator pad to move 0 into the Numeric Expression box. Your expression should now read "IND=0" as shown below.

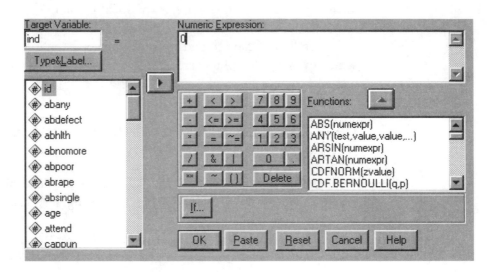

Run this instruction by selecting **OK**.

Step 2: Assign Points—If Liberal (1) on POLREC, Get 2 Points on IND

Now we are ready to begin assigning points on our index.

Open the **Compute Variable** box once again so we can start assigning points.

Let's begin by giving people 2 points if they have a 1 on POLREC (Liberal). To do this, change the Numeric Expression to **IND + 2**.

Now click **If...** and in the Compute Variable: If Cases box, select **Include if case satisfies condition:**. Then, type or click **POLREC = 1** into the rectangle box, as shown below:

Run this instruction by selecting **Continue**, **OK**, and then **OK** again to change the existing variable IND.

At this point, we have given liberals 2 points and everyone else (including those with missing data) has 0 points.

Step 3: Assign Points—If Moderate (2) on POLREC, Get 1 Point on IND

Now, let's give the "Moderates" 1 point on the index. Return to the **Compute Variable** window and make the following two changes:

- Change the Numeric Expression to **IND + 1**
- Change the If statement to **POLREC = 2**

Select **Continue**, **OK**, and **OK** to run this instruction.

Thus far, we have established an index as follows:

Liberals have 2 points.

Moderates have 1 point.

Conservatives have 0 points.

Those who are none of the above have 0 points on the index.

You may want to look at IND in the Data window or run Frequencies at any time in this process to see how the index is shaping up.

Step 4: Assign Points—If Other (2) on RELIG, Get 1 Point on IND

Now we are ready to add to the index. Go back to the **Compute Variable** window and make the following specifications.

- Leave the Numeric Expression as IND + 1
- Change the If statement to **RELIG = 2**

Run this instruction, and we've added 1 point for each non-Christian.

Step 5: Assign Points—If Seldom (2) on ATTEND, Get 1 Point on IND

Finally, return to the Compute Variable window and make these specifications:

- Leave the Numeric Expression as IND + 1
- Change the If statement to **ATTEND = 2**

Run this expression and review the logic of what we have done.

We've now created an index that presumably captures religious and political predispositions to support for a woman's right to an abortion. Scores on the index run from 0 (Opposed to abortion) to 4 (Supportive of abortion).

Step 6: Use Count to Handle Missing Data

There is one glitch in this index that we need to correct before moving on: those respondents for whom we have missing data. We don't know about the religious behavior or political orientations of those respondents for whom data were missing for ATTEND, POLREC, or RELIG. Since we can't provide an index score for respondents we don't know about, we must eliminate them from our analysis.

Let's use Count to handle this. Select **Transform** and **Count...** from the drop-down menu to open the Count Occurrences of Values Within Cases... window, and then do the following:

- Enter **MISS1** as the Target Variable:.
- Highlight **ATTEND**, **POLREC**, and **RELIG** and move them to the Variables: field by clicking the **arrow** pointing toward the Variables: field.]

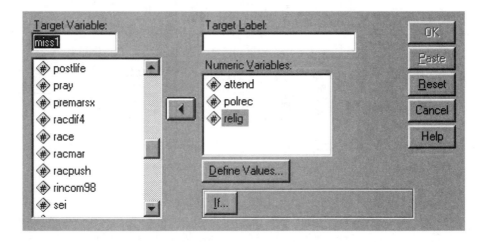

- Now Click **Define Values...**
- In the Count Values Within Cases: Values to Count window, select **System- or user-missing** and click **Add**

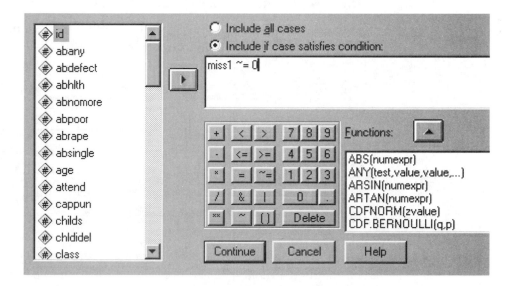

Once you have done that, click **Continue** to return to the Count screen and then select **OK** to run the Count command. Once the Count has run, MISS1 will contain the number of variables with missing data for each respondent. You can check this by creating a frequency distribution for MISS1: 0 indicates cases with no missing data, 1 indicates cases with missing data for one variable, and so on.

Now, return to the **Compute Variable** window and make this modification to the index.

- Type **–1** in the Numeric Expression field, so your expression reads IND=–1.
- Select **If…**
- In the Compute Variable: If Cases window make sure **Include if case satisfies…** is selected and then type **MISS1~= 0** in the rectangle as shown below.

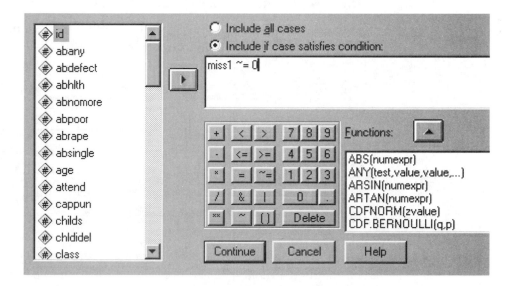

Run this instruction by selecting **Continue**, **OK**, and **OK**. Once you have done that you will have converted those with missing data from 0's to –1's in the index. We have selected –1 for the missing value code because –1 would never be a valid index score.

Step 7: Define IND

All that remains (thankfully!) is to let SPSS know what we meant by the latest modification to the index.

Select **IND** in the Data window and then click **Data** and **Define Variable...** in the drop-down menu. Select **Missing Values...** and define **–1** as a discrete missing value, then click **Continue**. While you're here, you might as well change the number of decimals to **0** in **Type...**.

Run Frequencies to Check IND

Having created such an index, it is always a good practice to check the frequencies. Run Frequencies on IND and you should get this:

IND

		Frequency	Percent	Valid Percent	Cumulative Percent
Valid	0	266	17.7	20.1	20.1
	1	394	26.3	29.8	49.9
	2	370	24.7	28.0	77.9
	3	200	13.3	15.1	93.0
	4	93	6.2	7.0	100.0
	Total	1323	88.2	100.0	
Missing	-1	177	11.8		
Total		1500	100.0		

Does IND Predict Attitudes Toward Abortion?

After all that work, let's finally see how well our index predicts abortion attitudes. To do this, run the following table.

ABORT Simple Abortion Index * IND Crosstabulation

			IND 0	IND 1	IND 2	IND 3	IND 4	Total
ABORT Simple Abortion Index	0 yes/approve	Count	28	77	105	65	57	332
		% within IND	17.4%	34.8%	47.5%	53.3%	87.7%	42.0%
	1 conditional support	Count	66	89	90	47	7	299
		% within IND	41.0%	40.3%	40.7%	38.5%	10.8%	37.8%
	2 no/disapprove	Count	67	55	26	10	1	159
		% within IND	41.6%	24.9%	11.8%	8.2%	1.5%	20.1%
Total		Count	161	221	221	122	65	790
		% within IND	100.0%	100.0%	100.0%	100.0%	100.0%	100.0%

As you can see, the index provides a very strong prediction of support for the unconditional right to an abortion: from 17 percent to 88 percent, for an epsilon of 71 percentage points. Let's see if we can improve on our ability to predict.

Sexual Attitudes and Abortion

Earlier, we discovered that attitudes about various forms of sexual behavior were also related to abortion attitudes. As you'll recall, people were asked whether they felt premarital sex and homosexuality were "Always wrong," "Almost always wrong," "Sometimes wrong," or "Not wrong at all." In addition, respondents were asked whether they had attended an X-rated movie during the past year. Each of these items was related to abortion attitudes, with those most permissive in sexual matters also being more permissive about abortion.

Demonstration 19.5: Recode PREMARSX and HOMOSEX

Because we want to pursue this phenomenon, why don't you recode HOMO-SEX and PREMARSX into *dichotomies* (only two values) of "Always or almost always wrong" versus "Only sometimes or never wrong"? That will make it easier to conduct the following analysis.

Just as when we recoded ATTEND and RELIG, we want to recode HOMO-SEX and PREMARSX "into same variables."[4] If you need to review the steps involved in doing this, see SPSS Command 19.1. In addition, the following hints may be useful to get you started.

Keep in mind that because both HOMOSEX and PREMARSX have the same values and labels, you can create the dichotomies for these two sexual attitude variables with a single command plus another to create new value labels.

Transform → Recode → Into Same Variables...

Old Values for BOTH HOMOSEX and PREMARSX	New Values	Labels
1–2	→ 1	Wrong
3–4	→ 2	Okay

As we noted earlier, if you save your data set after this session, be sure to use Save As and give it a *new name*, so that you will still be able to get back to your original, unrecoded data.

Demonstration 19.6: The Relationship Between Sexual Permissiveness and IND

Now, let's see whether the sexual behavior attitudes are related to our political-religious index that predicts abortion attitudes so powerfully. Why don't you run each of those tables now? Here's a summary of what you should find.

Percentage Who Are Permissive About	Political-Religious Index				
	0	1	2	3	4
Premarital sex	29	58	68	85	94
Homosexuality	13	27	37	59	89

4. Make sure 0, 5–9 for both HOMOSEX and PREMARSX are defined as missing.

Even though there is a great difference in the overall level of permissiveness on these issues, we can see that the political-religious index is clearly related to each one.

Why don't you also go ahead and check to see if the index predicts whether people have taken in an X-rated movie during the past year?

Demonstration 19.7: Exploring the Relationship Further

Now, let's see if the previously observed relationship between attitudes about sexual behavior and attitudes about abortion is really just a product of religious and political factors. Here's a summary of one of the tables you might look at.

Percentage Who Support Unconditional Abortion	Political-Religious Index				
	0	1	2	3	4
Premarital sex wrong	16	20	32	43	—
Premarital sex okay	24	53	55	49	92

Obviously, our index—combining religious affiliation, church attendance, and political philosophy—does not explain away the relationship between attitudes on premarital sex and attitudes on abortion. Regardless of their scores on the index, those who find premarital sex somewhat acceptable are more supportive of abortion than are those who disapprove of premarital sex.

Why don't you continue this analysis by focusing on the other sexual attitudes?

You could also consider expanding the index by including the items on sexual attitudes.

The suggestions above are just two of the many avenues you could take if you are interested in pursuing this line of inquiry further. Clearly, we have gone a long way toward accounting for people's opinions on the issue of abortion. At the same time, we've moved quickly to give you a broad view. If attitudes toward abortion interest you, there are any number of directions you could follow up on in a more focused and deliberate analysis.

Conclusion

You've had an opportunity now to see how social scientists might set out to understand people's attitudes toward abortion. We know this is a topic about which you hear a great deal in the popular media, and it may be an issue that concerns you and about which you have strong opinions. The analyses above should give you some insight into the sources of opinions on this topic.

We hope this chapter has also expanded your understanding of the possibilities for multivariate analysis. Whereas bivariate analysis allows for some simple explanations of human thoughts and behaviors, multivariate analysis permits more sophisticated investigations and discoveries.

Main Points

- You can use your multivariate analysis skills to delve more deeply into the sources of opinion on controversial issues such as abortion.

- The primary goal in this chapter was to try to predict attitudes toward abortion.

- To that end, we went through a number of items which were earlier found to have an impact on abortion attitudes: religious affiliation, measures of religiosity, political philosophy, and sexual attitudes.

- A composite measure or index, called IND, was constructed to predict support for a woman's right to have an abortion.

- IND was made up of the following component variables: ATTEND, POLREC, and RELIG.

- After working through the demonstrations in this chapter, you should have a better understanding of how a social scientist might try to begin to account for opinion on an issue such as abortion.

- With the univariate, bivariate, and multivariate analyses skills you have learned, you should now be able to design a more careful and deliberate study dealing with this or another issue/topic which interests and excites you.

Key Terms

Dichotomies

SPSS Commands Introduced in This Chapter

19.1:   Recoding into Same Variables

> **Transform → Recode → Into Same Variables... →**
>
> Highlight **the name of the variable** you want to recode → Click the **right-pointing arrow** to move the variable to the Numeric Variables: field →
>
> Click **Old and New Values... →**
>
> Define Old and New Values in the Recode into Same Variables: Old and New... box →
>
> Click **Add** to Change Old → New Values →
>
> Click **Continue → OK →**
>
> Highlight the variable in the Data Editor →
>
> Click **Data → Define Variable... → Labels →**
>
> Put labels on recoded variable →
>
> Click **Continue → OK →**

Review Questions

Answer True or False for Questions 1–6.

1. In the 1998 GSS, church attendance was related to abortion attitudes, but religious affiliation was not.

2. According to the 1998 GSS, Catholics are generally less supportive of abortion than Jews.

3. According to the 1998 GSS, opposition to abortion tends to decrease with decreasing measures of religiosity.

4. According to the 1998 GSS, religious affiliation and church attendance are related to one another, but both are not related to abortion attitudes.

5. In the 1998 GSS, political philosophy was related to abortion attitudes, but party identification was not.

6. In the 1998 GSS, those who are somewhat permissive about premarital and homosexual sex also tend to oppose abortion.

7. List the commands for instructing SPSS to recode an original variable (Into same variable).

8. If you save your data set after recoding an original variable, what should you remember to do?

9. List two findings from our multivariate analysis of the relationship between abortion, religious affiliation, and church attendance.

10. Name the three items we used to construct our index of ideological traditionalism IND.

11. Scores on IND ranged from _____ to _____.

12. Does a score of 4 on IND indicate support for or opposition to abortion?

13. How well did IND predict abortion attitudes?

14. How might you expand the index IND to include one (or more) of the variables dealing with sexual attitudes?

NAME _____

CLASS _____

INSTRUCTOR _____

DATE _____

To complete the following exercises, you need to load the data file EXER.SAV. Answers to Questions 4–6 can be found in Appendix A.

In this exercise we are going to create a simple index combining attitudes toward teen sex (PILLOK, SEXEDUC, and TEENSEX). The goal is to construct an index/composite measure called IND1 that can be used to predict attitudes toward sex and family roles. To create IND1, simply follow the steps listed below. After we set up the index initially, you will be given a chance to expand it and explore its capabilities on your own.

1. Define the following values for each item listed below as missing:

   A) PILLOK—0, 8, 9

   B) SEXEDUC—0, 3–9
   [Hint: Use Range plus one discrete missing value.]

   C) TEENSEX—0, 5–9
   [Hint: Use Range plus one discrete missing value.]

   D) FEPRESC— 0,8,9

   E) FECHLD—0,8,9

2. Recode PILLOK, TEENSEX, FEPRESCH, and FECHLD into dichotomies as shown below. Use Transform → Recode → Into Same Variables to recode the original variables. As noted earlier, if you save your data set after this exercise, be sure to use **Save As** and give the data set a *new name*, so that you are able to get back to the original, unrecoded data.

   A) PILLOK

Old Values		New Values	Labels
1–2	→	1	Okay/Agree
3–4	→	2	Wrong/Disagree

   B) TEENSEX

Old Values		New	Values Labels
1–2	→	2	Wrong
3–4	→	1	Okay

   C) FEPRESCH

Old Value		New Values	Labels
1–2	→	1	Agree
3–4	→	2	Disagree

   D) FECHLD

Old Values		New Values	Labels
1–2	→	1	Agree
3–4	→	2	Disagree

3. Create a simple index called IND1 built on the items PILLOK, SEXEDUC, and TEENSEX (which we just recoded).

   There are a number of ways to create your IND. Feel free to design your own method or follow the general steps below. You may also want to refer to our discussion in the chapter if you need to refresh your memory.

   Step 1: Create IND1

   Step 2: Assign Points for IND1 based on scores for three component items (PILLOK, SEXEDUC, TEENSEX) as follows:

   ■ If Wrong/Disagree (2) on PILLOK, give 1 point on IND1.
   ■ If Oppose (2) on SEXEDUC, give 1 point on IND1.
   ■ If Wrong (2) on TEENSEX, give 1 point on IND1.

   Our goal is to create an index (IND1) with scores ranging from 0 (least traditional attitudes toward sex and family roles—or, if you like, least conservative/ most liberal views) to 3 (most traditional attitudes toward sex and family roles— most conservative/least liberal views).

   Step 3: Missing data
   Step 4: Define IND1

   When you are done, you will have created an index (IND1) that hopefully captures predispositions to hold traditional attitudes toward sex and family roles. Again, scores on the index range from 0 (least traditional) to 3 (most traditional).

4. Run Frequencies to check IND1 and print your output.

5. See how well IND1 predicts attitudes toward sex and family roles (run tables with FEPRESCH and FECHLD). Then print both tables.

6. Does the index (IND1) provide a strong prediction of support for attitudes toward sex and family roles as measured by FEPRESCH and FECHLD? Discuss the findings of your analysis in detail below (keep in mind that FEPRESCH and FECHLD ask different questions!).

NAME _____

CLASS _____

INSTRUCTOR _____

DATE _____

7. You are now on your own! Expand IND1 to include another item of your choosing from your data file EXER.SAV (keep in mind that you may need to recode your item(s) before adding them to IND1).[5] When you have expanded the index, run Frequencies, and then see how well your new expanded index predicts attitudes toward sex and family roles. Print both your frequencies and table(s), and then discuss your findings in detail below.

8. Continue your analysis by checking to see if your new expanded index predicts FEFAM and FEHELP. Print your table(s) and discuss your findings in detail below (keep in mind that you may need to recode FEFAM and FEHELP).

_____

5. In terms of choosing a variable or variables, two possible items that may be empirically linked to the three items measuring attitudes toward teen sex, but which do not come from the same class of variables, are RACE and SEX. Because we are working with a fairly small data set and your choice of variables is somewhat limited, you may try to include either one or both of these items in your index, keeping in mind that they are demographic items and, in that sense, different from the others in IND1.

Chapter 20 Suggestions for Further Multivariate Analyses

In each of the previous analytic chapters, we have tried to leave a large number of "loose ends" for you to pursue on your own. If you are using this book in connection with a college class, you may want to follow up on some of those leads in the form of a term paper or a class project.

This chapter will build on some of those suggestions and offer some additional possibilities for your analyses. We begin with some suggestions regarding "ideal family size." We will then move to discuss other possibilities involving issues such as child training, the Protestant ethic, and prejudice. You should realize, however, that even within these fairly limited data sets, there are a number of analytic possibilities we have not considered.

Ideal Family Size and Abortion

Before leaving the topic of abortion altogether, we'd like to suggest another explanatory variable you might consider: ideal family size. We've seen previously that those who favor small families are more supportive of abortion than are those who favor large families. Now you are able to pursue this matter further. Here's the basic relationship with which you might start. Notice that you'll have to recode **CHLDIDEL** if you haven't already done that.

ABORT Simple Abortion Index * CHLDIDEL Recoded Ideal Number of Children Crosstabulation

| | | | CHLDIDEL Recoded Ideal Number of Children | | | |
			1 0 to 2	2 3 to 4	3 5 or more	Total
ABORT Simple Abortion Index	0 yes/approve	Count	118	53	22	193
		% within CHLDIDEL Recoded Ideal Number of Children	46.6%	39.6%	40.7%	43.8%
	1 conditional support	Count	91	47	9	147
		% within CHLDIDEL Recoded Ideal Number of Children	36.0%	35.1%	16.7%	33.3%
	2 no/disapprove	Count	44	34	23	101
		% within CHLDIDEL Recoded Ideal Number of Children	17.4%	25.4%	42.6%	22.9%
Total		Count	253	134	54	441
		% within CHLDIDEL Recoded Ideal Number of Children	100.0%	100.0%	100.0%	100.0%

Why don't you see whether the index of politics and religion has an impact on the ideal family sizes people reported? If it does, you should see whether the impact of ideal family size on abortion attitude is merely a matter of politics and religion or if it has an independent effect. You could substitute CHLDIDEL for the sexual attitudes in the preceding chapter.

As a somewhat more focused approach, you might review two articles that appear on-line in E-Appendix G: Renzi's "Ideal Family Size as an Intervening Variable between Religion and Attitudes towards Abortion" (1975) and D'Antonio and Stack's "Religion, Ideal Family Size, and Abortion: Extending Renzi's Hypothesis" (1980). See if you can replicate portions of the published analyses. Perhaps you can see additional variables that should be taken into account.

Child Training

In Chapter 16, we began to look into some of the factors that might affect people's views of the qualities most important to develop in children. As a reminder, the qualities were as follows:

OBEY	to obey
POPULAR	to be well-liked or popular
THNKSELF	to think for himself or herself
WORKHARD	to work hard
HELPOTH	to help others when they need help

We suggested that you start your analysis with some basic demographic variables, such as age, sex, and race. We encouraged you to consider relationships you might logically expect, such as that more educated respondents might place higher value on children's thinking for themselves.

Now you are able to explore all the possibilities in greater depth. To stay with the example of education and independence of thought in children, you could see if there are variables that shed more light on that relationship. You might check POLVIEWS, for example. Before you do, ask yourself what you would expect to find. You might also check the effect of gender while you're at it.

Earlier, we suggested you look at the impact of the sexual attitude items. Those who are permissive regarding violations of the established norms for sexual conduct often feel that they are thinking for themselves in those regards. How do such people feel about encouraging that trait in young people? With your multivariate skills, you can examine that matter with some sophistication.

Perhaps you will find it useful to combine some of the "quality" items into an index. On the face of it, OBEY and THNKSELF appear to value opposite traits. Are they negatively related to one another? Would they fit into an index of "conformity–independence," perhaps? If that seems a fruitful index to create, to which other variables does it relate?

The Protestant Ethic

One of the most famous of all books in the social sciences is Max Weber's *The Protestant Ethic and the Spirit of Capitalism* (1905/1958). In it, Weber traces the religious roots (in Calvinism) of the ethic of hard work and thrift that he found to forge the beginnings of capitalism. This ethic is something you might like to explore.

A central notion of the "Protestant ethic" is the idea of "hard work," the belief that individuals are responsible for their own economic well-being. People's wealth is taken as a sign of how hardworking and diligent they are. In its most extreme form, the Protestant ethic sees poverty as the result of slothfulness and laziness, and wealth as the product of persistence and hard work.

The GETAHEAD item in your GSS data set provides a measure of at least one dimension of the Protestant ethic that you might like to explore. To measure the degree to which people took responsibility for their own economic well-being, respondents were read this statement: "Some people say that people get ahead by their own hard work; others say that lucky breaks or help from other people are more important." Following the statement, they were asked, "Which do you think is most important?"

Why don't you begin by examining how GETAHEAD is related to other variables? It would seem logical that GETAHEAD would be related to WORKHARD. Are people who are in disadvantaged groups or have low incomes more apt to believe their fates are governed by luck rather than hard work? Or, does the belief in luck for success provide a rationalization for people who have little power to control the events that affect their lives? Because these variables are not the ratio measures that Pearson's r assumes, you can't take the results literally, but perhaps they can give you a first glimpse. Do not use this technique as a substitution for other, statistically appropriate, examinations.

If you follow these suggestions, you'll need to be prepared for some surprises—even disappointments—so it may take some hard work (not inappropriate) for you to create a measure of commitment to the Protestant ethic that you like. Then you can begin the multivariate search for the causes of this point of view. Be sure to check out the Protestants, but don't expect an easy answer.

Prejudice

In your analysis of the Protestant ethic, you may have looked at the place of the two prejudice items: RACMAR and RACPUSH. If not, you may want to do so now. Logically, the belief that people get ahead by hard work alone would seem to rule out the limits imposed by prejudice and discrimination. You can explore the relationship between some of the work ethic and prejudice items to see if this is the case.

Some beliefs about African-Americans seem to be part and parcel of a racist point of view. Prejudiced images can lead to beliefs that, when turned into action, become discrimination. As part of the 1998 GSS, respondents were read the statement, "On the average, African-Americans have worse jobs, income, and housing than white people." Then, they were asked if they thought the "differences" were because "most African-Americans just don't have the motivation or will power to pull themselves out of poverty?" Their responses are recorded in the item RACDIF4.

Demonstration 20.1: The Relationship Between RACDIF4, RACMAR, and RACPUSH

See the extent to which prejudicial beliefs are associated with the belief that African-Americans should not push themselves where they are not wanted and the belief that interracial marriage should be made illegal and the belief that African-Americans don't have the will power to pull themselves out of poverty. Be sure to define "don't know" as missing for RACDIF4, RACMAR, and RAC-PUSH before creating the following tables.

RACPUSH BLACKS SHOULDNT PUSH * RACDIF4 DIFFERENCES DUE TO LACK OF WILL Crosstabulation

			RACDIF4 DIFFERENCES DUE TO LACK OF WILL		
			1 YES	2 NO	Total
RACPUSH BLACKS SHOULDNT PUSH	1 AGREE STRONGLY	Count	33	24	57
		% within RACDIF4 DIFFERENCES DUE TO LACK OF WILL	16.8%	10.7%	13.5%
	2 AGREE SLIGHTLY	Count	67	42	109
		% within RACDIF4 DIFFERENCES DUE TO LACK OF WILL	34.2%	18.7%	25.9%
	3 DISAGREE SLIGHTLY	Count	50	51	101
		% within RACDIF4 DIFFERENCES DUE TO LACK OF WILL	25.5%	22.7%	24.0%
	4 DISAGREE STRONGLY	Count	46	108	154
		% within RACDIF4 DIFFERENCES DUE TO LACK OF WILL	23.5%	48.0%	36.6%
Total		Count	196	225	421
		% within RACDIF4 DIFFERENCES DUE TO LACK OF WILL	100.0%	100.0%	100.0%

RACMAR FAVOR LAW AGAINST RACIAL INTERMARRIAGE * RACDIF4 DIFFERENCES DUE TO LACK OF WILL Crosstabulation

			RACDIF4 DIFFERENCES DUE TO LACK OF WILL		
			1 YES	2 NO	Total
RACMAR FAVOR LAW AGAINST RACIAL INTERMARRIAGE	1 YES	Count	33	17	50
		% within RACDIF4 DIFFERENCES DUE TO LACK OF WILL	16.7%	7.2%	11.5%
	2 NO	Count	165	219	384
		% within RACDIF4 DIFFERENCES DUE TO LACK OF WILL	83.3%	92.8%	88.5%
Total		Count	198	236	434
		% within RACDIF4 DIFFERENCES DUE TO LACK OF WILL	100.0%	100.0%	100.0%

What do the tables show? Is the opinion that poverty is a result of a "lack of motivation and will" related to the view that African-Americans shouldn't push? Similarly, is RACDIF4 related to attitudes toward the legalization of interracial marriage?

Demonstration 20.2: Controlling for RACE

To test the racist quality in the first item further, let's control for RACE. If there is a racist element, we should expect to find the correlation only among whites. Let's check it out.

RACPUSH BLACKS SHOULDNT PUSH * RACDIF4 DIFFERENCES DUE TO LACK OF WILL * RACE RACE OF RESPONDENT Crosstabulation

% within RACDIF4 DIFFERENCES DUE TO LACK OF WILL

RACE RACE OF RESPONDENT			RACDIF4 DIFFERENCES DUE TO LACK OF WILL		Total
			1 YES	2 NO	
1 WHITE	RACPUSH BLACKS SHOULDNT PUSH	1 AGREE STRONGLY	16.5%	10.2%	13.3%
		2 AGREE SLIGHTLY	34.8%	21.7%	28.2%
		3 DISAGREE SLIGHTLY	27.4%	24.7%	26.1%
		4 DISAGREE STRONGLY	21.3%	43.4%	32.4%
	Total		100.0%	100.0%	100.0%
2 BLACK	RACPUSH BLACKS SHOULDNT PUSH	1 AGREE STRONGLY	26.7%	15.6%	18.3%
		2 AGREE SLIGHTLY	33.3%	6.7%	13.3%
		3 DISAGREE SLIGHTLY		20.0%	15.0%
		4 DISAGREE STRONGLY	40.0%	57.8%	53.3%
	Total		100.0%	100.0%	100.0%
3 OTHER	RACPUSH BLACKS SHOULDNT PUSH	1 AGREE STRONGLY	11.8%		6.5%
		2 AGREE SLIGHTLY	29.4%	21.4%	25.8%
		3 DISAGREE SLIGHTLY	29.4%	7.1%	19.4%
		4 DISAGREE STRONGLY	29.4%	71.4%	48.4%
	Total		100.0%	100.0%	100.0%

Looking at the table, would you say that the racist element we were looking for is evident? Is there a correlation between the opinion that poverty is a result of a "lack of motivation and will" and the belief that African-Americans shouldn't push only among whites?

Here's how you might summarize these tables in a term paper or journal article:

Percentage Who Say African Americans Shouldn't Push	Agree Strongly	Agree Slightly	Disagree Slightly	Disagree Strongly
Whites	17	35	27	21
Blacks	27	33	—	40

You may also want to look at the relationship between RACDIF4 and RAC-MAR while controlling for RACE. Is there a racist element evident here?

We've taken you through this complex multivariate analysis to demonstrate the importance of ascertaining the sometimes-hidden meanings that lie behind the responses that people give to survey questions. That's a big part of the *adventure* of social research. (We wanted to call this book *Earl, Fred, and Jeanne's Excellent Adventure*, but you know publishers.)

If you would like to continue this line of analysis, why don't you substitute POLREC for RACMAR in the above analysis? We leave that possibility in your able, multivariate hands.

Conclusion

The National Rifle Association and other proponents of extensive gun distribution (see GUNLAW) are fond of saying, "Guns don't kill people; people kill people." Well, in a more pacific spirit, we'd like to suggest that SPSS doesn't analyze data; analysts analyze data. And the good news is that you are now a bona fide, certifiable data analyst.

We've given you about all the guidance and assistance that we planned when we started this adventure. Remember, we said, "Just add you" in Chapter 1; well, it's show time. You're on your own now, although you should have a support network behind you. If you read this book in connection with a college course, you have your instructor. In any event, you can call upon SPSS for assistance, and you have us; you can reach us by calling Fred Halley at Socware, Inc., in Brockport, New York, at (716) 352-1986.

The final section of this book expands the horizons of social research even further. It suggests a number of ways that you might reach out beyond the GSS data set we have provided for your introductory experience with the adventure of social research.

Main Points

- This chapter offers suggestions for further multivariate analyses.
- If you are using this book in connection with a college course, these suggestions may be useful in helping you design a term paper or class project.
- Even within the limited data sets that accompany this text, there are numerous analytic possibilities that we have not explored or considered.
- The suggestions offered here are built on the questions and issues addressed in your data file DEMO.SAV.
- The suggestions cover issues such as ideal family size, child training, Protestant ethic, and prejudice.
- These suggestions are just a small portion of the analytic possibilities stemming from the data contained in your DEMO.SAV file.

Key Terms

No new terms were introduced in this chapter.

SPSS Commands Introduced in This Chapter

No new commands were introduced in this chapter.

Review Questions

Discuss in detail how you might apply the techniques and procedures we covered in Part V (Chapters 17–20) on multivariate analyses to examine the following topics/issues:

1. Ideal Family Size
2. Child Training
3. Protestant Work Ethic

NAME _____

CLASS _____

INSTRUCTOR _____

DATE _____

In the exercises at the end of Chapter 16 (SPSS Lab Exercise 16.1) we asked you to choose a topic or issue from the EXER.SAV data file that interests you (sex roles, law enforcement, health insurance, mass media—use and confidence, national government spending priorities, teen sex, affirmative action, or equalization). In this exercise, we are going to ask you to build on your examination of that topic/issue.

1. Write the topic/issue you are focusing on in the space below.

2. Discuss how you might apply the multivariate analyses techniques and procedures learned in that Part V to continue the univariate and bivariate analyses of this topic that you began in the exercises at the end of Chapter 16. Be as specific as possible.

3. Run the multivariate analyses you suggested in response to Question 2, print your output, and then summarize your findings below. Be as specific as possible regarding the findings of each test/procedure.

4. Access the GSSDIRS web site (www.icpsr.umich.edu/GSS99/) and identify two articles or texts that pertain to the issue/topic you are exploring. Then list the titles, authors, and other bibliographic information in the space below. Hint: One approach to identifying these articles/texts is to select "GSS Search Engine" under "Main Applications." Then search for a particular variable you are interested in by typing "Codebook Variable: and the variable name (i.e., FEHELP, FECHLD etc…)." When you access the *Codebook*, Page Down until you see "Bibliography." You can also access the *Codebook* directly at (www.icpsr.umich.edu/GSS99/Codebook.htm) and then search by subject or variable name.

5. When you have accessed and read the articles/texts, discuss what portions of the published analysis you would be interested in replicating and why. Note whether you would need access to other types of data (GSS or otherwise) to replicate portions of these studies, what types of data you would need, and so on. Also, discuss whether these articles/texts prompted you to see additional items that should be taken into account or other avenues of inquiry that you might want to pursue. In short, use the published material to help you think about other research possibilities involving this topic/issue that you may want to pursue if you continue to investigate this issue/topic in the future.

Part VI The Adventure Continues

Chapter 21 **Designing and Executing Your Own Survey**

Chapter 22 **Further Opportunities for Social Research**

In the concluding chapters, we want to explore several different ideas that may support your continued investigations into the nature of human beings and the societies they create.

It struck us that you might be interested in conducting your own survey—perhaps as a class project. Consequently, in Chapter 21, Appendix B, and E-Appendices C, D, and E (remember that some appendices are on-line at www.pineforge.com), we begin by taking a step back to look at the process of social research and the research proposal. We then focus specifically on survey research. In particular we delve into designing and administering a survey, defining and entering data in SPSS, and writing a research report.

In Chapter 22 we suggest other avenues for pursuing your social investigations. Among other things we talk about the unabridged GSS, other data sources you might explore, and other computer programs you might find useful.

We hope that by the time you finish these chapters, you will have fully realized the two purposes that lay behind our writing this book: to help you learn (a) the logic of social research and (b) how to pursue that logic through the use of SPSS. In addition, we hope you will have experienced some of the excitement and challenge that makes social research such a marvelous adventure.

Chapter 21   Designing and Executing Your Own Survey

The GSS data sets provided with this book are of special interest to researchers because they offer a window on American public opinion. We thought you might be interested in learning about the thoughts and actions of people across the country.

At the same time, it occurred to us that many of you may be interested in conducting your own survey, investigating topics, issues, and populations not addressed by the GSS or other data sets. Conducting your own survey is a good idea because data analysis in a classroom setting is sometimes more meaningful if the data are more personal. Perhaps you would like to analyze the opinions and behaviors of your own class (if it's a large one), the opinions of students elsewhere in your school, or even the attitudes of members of your community.

If you are interested in conducting a survey, this chapter, Appendix B, and E-Appendices C, D, and E are designed to help you get started developing and administering the survey, defining and entering the data in SPSS, and writing a research report (you already know how to analyze the data!). This chapter and the supporting appendices are our (albeit brief) answer to those students and readers who ask, "How can I do this myself?"

While we cannot hope to provide you with an in-depth understanding of the intricacies of survey research in such a short time, we do give you a brief overview of the steps involved in designing and implementing your own survey. When possible, we will also point you toward other resources that you may find useful as you launch your own original study.

The Social Research Process and Proposal

Before we focus on designing and executing your own survey, we want to take a step back and place survey research and data analysis, which have been the central focus of this book, in the context of the social research process as a whole.

Our primary focus in this book has been a secondary analysis of a small portion of a nationwide survey, the 1998 GSS. As you are aware, survey research is just one of many methods of data collection used by social researchers. Other methods include, but are not limited to, experimentation, participant observation, focus groups, intensive interviews, and content analysis.

Not only has our focus been limited to just one method of data collection, but it has also been limited to one (albeit crucial) step in the social research process—data analysis. We have focused on the use of one of the most popular computer software programs, SPSS, to analyze survey data. As we will discuss in the next chapter, there are other software packages that you might want to consider using as well.

Because our focus has been on the statistical analysis of survey data using SPSS, our discussions of the practice and process of social research have been necessarily limited to data analysis. Before conducting your own study, you will find it helpful to review briefly the entire social research process and to get some tips on writing a research proposal (which is often the first step in the research process) and, most importantly, to locate texts that will give you more detailed descriptions of parts of the research process not covered here.

E-Appendix C includes an excerpt from Russell K. Schutt's comprehensive research methods text, *Investigating the Social World* (1999). The excerpt focuses on the major steps involved in designing a research project and gives some guidelines for writing a research proposal. As Schutt (1999) notes, the research proposal is a crucial step in the social research process because it goes "a long way toward shaping the final research report and will make it easier to progress at later research stages" (448).

Schutt's text is just one of many comprehensive research methods texts that you may find useful. Others include Babbie: *The Practice of Social Research* (1999); Bailey: *Methods of Social Research* (1994); Judd, Smith, and Kidder: *Research Methods in the Social Sciences* (1991); and Neuman: *Social Research Methods: Qualitative and Quantitative* (1996). While this list is by no means exhaustive, it should be useful in helping to locate a text that will provide you with a comprehensive overview of social research.

Designing and Executing Your Own Survey

Like all methods of data collection, survey research has its own peculiar advantages and disadvantages, benefits and liabilities. Nevertheless, a carefully constructed and executed survey can yield results that are considered valid, reliable, and generalizable. The 1998 GSS is a good example of a carefully designed and implemented survey, yielding data from which findings can be generalized to all English speaking, noninstitutionalized American adults, eighteen years of age and older.

To design and conduct a survey that meets scientific standards, you need to pay particular attention to the steps required for survey research: research design, sampling, questionnaire construction, data collection, data processing, data analysis, and report writing.

To help you design and implement your own survey, we have included an excerpt from a guide called "SPSS Survey Tips" in E-Appendix D; this appendix discusses some of the key considerations in planning, developing, and executing a survey.[1] You should think of these tips as a general guide to designing

1. This excerpt from "SPSS Survey Tips" was used with permission of SPSS Inc. The entire guide is available at http://www. spss.com/.

and executing your own survey rather than as hard and fast rules. Keep in mind that it is unlikely that all social scientists or pollsters would agree with every recommendation. Moreover, in the "real world" the process of developing and implementing a survey is seldom as "neat" as the sequential ordering of the "tips" may suggest.

Despite these caveats, we think you will find "SPSS Survey Tips" a useful and concise overview of the steps involved in developing and implementing your own survey. In addition, you may also want to consult one of the many texts devoted to the principles and techniques of survey research. In particular, we draw your attention to Alreck and Settle: *The Survey Research Handbook* (1985); Babbie: *Survey Research Methods* (1990); and Czaja and Blair: *Designing Surveys: A Guide to Decisions and Procedures* (1996).

Sample Questionnaire

To help you collect your own data, we have included a Sample Questionnaire in E-Appendix E that asks some of the same questions found in the subset of GSS items included in your DEMO.SAV file. We've also provided the tools you may need to make any modifications that you might like in the interest of local relevance. If you wish, you can make copies of the questionnaire and use it to collect your own data.[2]

If you are more ambitious, you might choose to design a totally different questionnaire that deals with whatever variables interest you. There is no need for you to be limited to the GSS variables that we've analyzed in this book or that we've suggested in the sample questionnaire. You have learned a technology that is much more broadly usable than that. To get ideas about the kinds of things sociologists and other social scientists study, you might go to the library and thumb through the research categories in *Sociological Abstracts*.

Whatever survey you choose to conduct, the following section tells you how to get your data into a form that SPSS will accept for analysis.

Getting Ready for Data Analysis Using SPSS

Once you have designed and administered your questionnaire (or collected your data) you are ready to begin analyzing your data. Getting data ready for analysis with SPSS is really a three-step process: defining your data, editing and coding your data, and finally entering your data.

Demonstration 21.1: Step 1—Defining Your Data

The first step, often called **data definition**, involves giving each item from your questionnaire a variable name, setting the data type, describing the variable, indicating values and labels, designating missing values, setting the items level of measurement, and designating a place to store this information.

---

2. We have also included an empty data file LOCAL.SAV on the disk that came with this book. As we will discuss in more detail later in the chapter, the LOCAL.SAV file is already defined and can be used to enter data from the sample questionnaire.

This process can begin even before you have completed collecting the data if you are certain that the questionnaire itself is not going to be altered or revised.

To walk you through this process we are going to use the Sample Questionnaire provided on-line in E-Appendix E as an example. While we are not going to define each of the variables in the questionnaire, we will walk you through this process of defining the first two variables, ID and CHLDIDEL.

Example 1—Defining ID

To begin defining the variables in your survey, make sure the Data Editor is the active window. Then place your cursor at the *top of the first column* at the far left side of your Data Editor and *double-click*. Once you do that you will notice that Column 1, Row 1 becomes the **active cell**. You may also notice the Define Variable window has opened. This is the dialog box we are going to use to define our variables.

Now we will define the variable that will be situated in the first column. In the case of our Sample Questionnaire, this is the first variable ID. As you know, each column represents a variable or item. Looking at our Sample Questionnaire in E-Appendix E, you can see that the variables would be situated in the columns from left to right beginning with ID, then moving to CHLDIDEL, OBEY, POPULAR, and so on until we come to the last variable, SEX.

To begin defining our first variable ID, open the Define Variable window (if it is not open already) by selecting **Data** and **Define Variable...** from the drop-down menu.

We will begin by assigning a variable name. Then in the Change Settings box select Type... to change the data format, Labels... to assign numeric values and labels, Missing Values... to specify any missing values, Column Format... to change the column width or alignment, and finally set the level of Measurement for the item.

Variable Name: Once you are in the Define Variable window, the first step is to type the Variable Name: in the rectangle box at the top of the window. Because we already know the name of this variable is ID, simply type **ID** in the appropriate space (in doing so, you should replace the default name given by SPSS var00001).

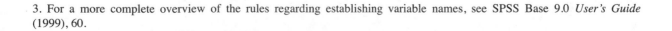

We assigned variable names to each item in our Sample Questionnaire, but if you are entering data from a questionnaire that you designed on your own, you need to know several rules that apply to selecting a variable name that SPSS will accept. The most important guidelines are that (a) the name must begin with a letter, (b) the remaining characters can be any combination of letters, numbers, or select symbols, (c) variable names cannot exceed 8 characters, and (d) each variable name must be unique (in other words, you cannot use the same variable name for two variables in one data set).[3]

---

3. For a more complete overview of the rules regarding establishing variable names, see SPSS Base 9.0 *User's Guide* (1999), 60.

Type....: Now click **Type**... to open the Define Variable Type: window.

The Define Variable Type: window allows you to specify the type of data. You will see that Numeric is already highlighted because by default SPSS assumes that all new items are numeric. In our case, ID and all the other items in our Sample Questionnaire are numeric, so we will leave Numeric highlighted. Social science data are usually numeric and occasionally string. Generally, we make infrequent use of the comma, dot, scientific, date, dollar, and currency data types.[4]

You can see that the Width: is set by default at 8 and the Decimal Places: at 2. We will leave the Width: at 8. However, because we don't require any decimal places, change the 2 to a **0** in Decimal Places: as shown below.

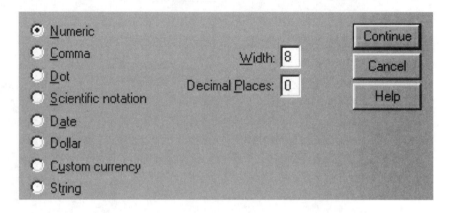

Now click **Continue** to get back to the Define Variable window.

When you are back in the Define Variable window you will notice that the change we just made is now indicated toward the top of the window in the box labeled Variable Description. Next to the subtitle Type, you should now see Numeric8.0, indicating that ID is a numeric item with a width of 8 and no decimal places.

4. For a more complete overview of data types, see SPSS Base 9.0 *User's Guide* (1999), 62 or search SPSS's extensive on-line Help option.

Variable Name: id

Variable Description
Type: Numeric8.0
Variable Label:
Missing Values: None
Alignment: Right

Change Settings

[Type...]   [Missing Values...]

[Labels..]   [Column Format...]

Measurement

◉ Scale   ○ Ordinal   ○ Nominal

[OK]   [Cancel]   [Help]

Labels…: Now click **Labels…** to open the Define Labels: window. At the top of the window you will see a rectangle space where you can insert a Variable Label:. Variable labels specify what the variable measures. While variable labels can be up to 256 characters long, short labels look better on printouts. In the case of ID, you might specify the variable label as "Identification of respondent" or **Respondent's Identification Number**, whatever is meaningful to you. Why don't you go ahead and do that now?

Variable Label: Respondent's Identification Numbe   [Continue]

Value Labels
Value: [Cancel]
Value Label: [Help]

[Add]
[Change]
[Remove]

After you have typed in the variable label, you can assign value labels for each value of the variable. The numeric value is placed in the Value: box and the value label is (not surprisingly) placed in the Value Label: box. You can then click Add.

In the case of ID, however, we do not need to assign values and labels because each respondent has a unique identification number. When we go through the example of CHLDIDEL we will give you an opportunity to practice filling in values and labels.

For now, however, just click **Continue** to get back to the Define Variable window.

Missing Values…: There are obviously "No missing values" for ID, so we do not have to open the Missing Values window in this case. However, if we did want to define missing values (as we will in the case of CHLDIDEL), all we would have to do is click Missing Values…. Then in the Missing Values box we would define the missing values as we have done previously, by choosing No missing values (the case of ID and SPSS's default setting), Discrete missing values, Range of missing values, or Range plus one discrete missing value.

If you opened the Missing Values window, you can click **Continue** to return to the Define Variable window.

Column Format…: By opening the Column Format window we can define the width of the columns in the Data Editor and specify the alignment of data values. By default, SPSS sets the column width to 8 and aligns the data on the right. Since we don't want to change either the width or text alignment, we don't need to open the Column Format window at this point.

Measurement: The last step in the process of defining your variable is indicating the variables level of measurement in the box labeled Measurement at the bottom of the Define Variable window.

You can specify the level of measurement as Scale (Interval/Ratio level data), Ordinal, or Nominal by clicking **the circle next to the appropriate level**. In the case of ID, the level of measurement is nominal, each case having its own category.

If you now look in the box in the center of your Define Variable window, you will see most of the information we specified indicated in the box titled Variable Description, under the subtitles Type:, Variable Label:, Missing Values:, and Alignment:.

Variable Name: [ID]

Variable Description
Type: Numeric8.0
Variable Label: Respondent's Identification Number
Missing Values: None
Alignment: Right

Change Settings

| Type... | Missing Values... |
| Labels.. | Column Format... |

Measurement

◯ Scale   ◯ Ordinal   ◉ Nominal

| OK | Cancel | Help |

When the variable ID has been defined, you can click **OK** to return to the Data Editor window. You will now see that ID is magically placed in the first column at the top left-hand corner of your Data Editor.

Untitled - SPSS for Windows Data Editor

File   Edit   View   Data   Transform   Analyze   Graphs   Ut

	id	var	var
1			
2			
3			
4			

Example 2 — Defining CHLDIDEL

Now that you have successfully defined the first variable from our Sample Questionnaire, why don't we go ahead and practice by defining the second item CHLDIDEL together as well. This time we will list the commands in an easy to read format.

- In your Data Editor, double-click on the **top of the second column** on the left side (directly to the right of ID). This will open the Define Variable window (if not, simply highlight the column and then click **Data** and **Define Variable…**).
- In the Define Variable window, list the variable name CHLDIDEL
- Click **Type…** .
- In the Define Variable Type window, keep the type as Numeric and the Width: at 8. However, change the Decimal Places: to **0.**
- Click **Continue** to return to the Define Variable window.
- Click **Labels…** .
- Enter the Variable Label: (for instance, "Ideal Number of Children").
- Enter **–1** in the Value box, enter **NAP** in the Value Label box, and then click **Add**. You will notice that "–1=NAP" is now specified in the box below. If you wanted to change or revise that statement for any reason, simply highlight "**–1=NAP**". When you do that you will notice that you are able to select **Remove** to delete –1=NAP. If you deleted –1=NAP, go ahead and add it again.
- Now continue entering the other Values and Labels as follows:[5]

  7 Seven+

  8 As many as want

  9 DK, NA
- Click **Continue**.
- Click **Missing Values….**
- Select **Discrete missing values**.
- Enter **–1** in the space provided.
- Click **Continue**.
- Because we are not going to alter the Column format, we can move to defining the level of measurement of our variable CHLDIDEL.
- Select the appropriate level of measurement—in this case **Scale**.
- You can now click **OK** to return to the Data Editor window.

You will see your variable CHLDIDEL in the second column in your Data Editor window.

---

5. Because the Sample Questionnaire contains questions taken from your data file DEMO.SAV, you can refer to your DEMO.SAV file or the list of variables, values, and labels contained in your DEMO.SAV data file in Chapter 4 to verify the values and labels for the variables in the Sample Questionnaire.

Untitled - SPSS for Windows Data Editor

File Edit View Data Transform Analyze Graphs U

	id	chldidel	var
1			
2			
3			
4			
5			
6			

You have now successfully defined the first two items in our Sample Questionnaire, ID and CHLDIDEL. As you can probably see, while it is not a difficult process, it can be fairly time-consuming to define all the variables from a questionnaire, even one as small as our Sample Questionnaire.

SPSS COMMAND 21.1: Defining a Variable

> Make the **Data Editor** the **active window** →
>
> **Double-click** on **column where placing variable** and the "Define Variable" window should open (if not click Data and Define Variables...) →
>
> In the "Define Variable" window enter the **Variable Name**: →
>
> Click **Type...** → In "Define Variable Type" window set **data type** → set **Width**: → set **Decimal Places**: → Click **Continue** →
>
> Click **Labels...** → In "Define Labels" window enter **Variable Label**: → enter **Value(s)** → enter **Value Label(s)** → Click **Add** → **Repeat last step** entering values, values labels and clicking **Add as many times as necessary** for each value of the variable →
>
> Click **Continue** →
>
> Click **Missing Values...** → **Designate Missing Values** in "Define Missing Values:" window →
>
> Click **Continue** →
>
> [If want to set Column Width and/or Alignment, Click Column Format... → Define Column Width → Align Text → Click Continue →]
>
> Set level of "**Measurement**" in "Define Variable Window" → Click **Continue** →
>
> **Repeat** this **process** as many times as necessary **until you have defined all the variables in your survey**.

Demonstration 21.2: Creating a Variable Template

Now that you are comfortable defining variables, we want to give you a short-cut you can use to define certain variables. It involves creating what are called *variable templates*.

As the *SPSS Base 9.0 User's Guide* (1999) explains, with variable templates you can assign the same variable definition information to multiple variables. For example, if you have a group of variables and they all use the numeric codes 1 and 2 to represent "Yes" and "No" responses and 9 to represent "Missing responses," you can create a template that contains those value labels and missing value specifications and apply the template to the entire group of variables (65).

For instance, the seven abortion variables in our Sample Questionnaire (ABDEFECT, ABNOMORE, ABHLTH, ABPOOR, ABRAPE, ABSINGLE, and ABANY) all use the numeric codes 1 and 2 to represent "Yes" and "No," 0 to represent "NAP," 8 to represent "DK," and 9 to represent "NA." Consequently, we can create a variable template for these seven variables by following the steps below.

Once again, make sure the Data Editor is the active window. Click **Data** and then choose **Templates...** from the drop-down menu to open the Template dialog box.

Now click **Define>>** in the bottom right-hand corner of the Template window. This will expand your Template window as shown below.

Now it is time to select the attributes you want to define in accordance with our previous discussion regarding defining a variable. You can define the Type..., Value Labels..., Missing Values..., and/or Column Format.... In the case of the abortion variables we will do that as follows:

- **Type... – Numeric**, Width **8**, Decimal Places **0**
- **Value Labels...**

  Values   Labels

  0   **NAP**

  1   **Yes**

  2   **No**

  8   **DK**

  9   **NA**
- **Missing Values – Discrete Missing Values 0, 8, 9**

When you have defined the template, enter a template name such as **TEST** in the space next to Name: on the left side of the window under the box labeled Template Description (to do that, you have to delete the name SPSS has given the template, DEFAULT). Then click **Add** and you will see the name of your template, TEST, appear at the top of the dialog box next to the label Template:.

Now check one or more of the variable attributes you want to apply. Do that by clicking **Type**, **Value Labels**, and **Missing Values** in the Apply box on the right side of the window as shown below.

You have now created a variable template.

Click **OK** to return to the Data Editor. The next step is to apply your new variable template TEST to the abortion variables.

SPSS COMMAND 21.2: Creating a Variable Template

Make **Data Editor** the **active window** →

Click **Data** → **Templates**... → **Define>>** →

Select the attributes you want to define (Type...; Value Labels...; Missing Values...; and/or Column Format...) →

After you have defined the template, enter a **template name** in space labeled **Name:** →

Click **Add** → Check the variable attributed you want to apply in the "Apply" box (Type, Value labels, Missing values, and/or Column format) →

Click **OK**

Demonstration 21.3: Applying a Variable Template

You can apply the variable template to items in your data set either before or after you have specified the variable name(s) and label(s) in the Data Editor. In this case, for instance, we could use the Data → Define Variable... command to specify the names, labels, and levels of measurement of each of the abortion variables before applying the template. However, because we have not already specified the names, labels, and levels of measurement of each of the abortion variables, we will apply the TEST template to the next seven columns in our Data Editor (because there are seven abortion variables), and then you can specify the names, labels, and levels of measurement for each item on your own afterwards. While we are applying the template to the next seven columns in our Data Editor, keep in mind that this would not be appropriate if we were actually defining the entire Sample Questionnaire because there are other variables that should be situated in the columns between CHLDIDEL and the first abortion variable, ABDEFECT.

For the purposes of our example, why don't you go ahead and highlight the next seven columns in your Data Editor window. You can do this by **holding down the button on the left side of your mouse as you move the cursor across the top of the seven columns** (if you had already defined the variable names, you would just highlight the names of the variables in your Data Editor).

From the menu choose **Data** and **Templates...** once again. Your template TEST may already be highlighted in the box at the top of the window labeled Template:. If not, select the template you want to apply by clicking the **down arrow** on the right side of the Template: rectangle and highlighting the name of the appropriate template (in this case TEST).

Now simply click **OK** to apply the template to the selected columns.

When you are back in the Data Editor window, you will notice that SPSS has given default names (var00001–var00007) to the seven columns we highlighted.

	id	chldidel	var00001	var00002	var00003	var00004	var00005	var00006	var00007	var
1										
2										
3										
4										

Untitled - SPSS for Windows Data Editor
File Edit View Data Transform Analyze Graphs Utilities Window Help

Now simply highlight each column in turn and use the **Data → Define Variables...** command to specify the appropriate variable name, variable label, and level of measurement for each of the abortion variables (ABDEFECT, ABNOMORE, ABHLTH, ABPOOR, ABRAPE, ABSINGLE, and ABANY), only in this case you will not have to go through all the steps discussed earlier because you already applied the template TEST to these columns, setting the Type, Variable labels, and Missing values to the appropriate specifications.

SPSS COMMAND 21.3:　Applying a Variable Template

> **Highlight column(s) or variable(s)** in the **Data Editor** →
> Click **Data → Templates...** →
> In the Template window select the **name of the template** you want to apply →
> Click **OK** →

If you have not done so already, use the Data → Define Variables command to specify the variable name(s), label(s), and level(s) of measurement for each item.

Saving Your New File

Before you end this (or any other) data definition session, remember to save the new file with a name that will remind you of its contents. If you need to refresh your memory regarding how to save a new file, see the list of SPSS commands on-line in E-Appendix F or SPSS Command 6.9 at the end of Chapter 6.

LOCAL.SAV

Now that you have mastered the commands for defining a variable as well as creating and applying a variable template, we are going to let you in on a little secret. To save you the time and trouble of having to define all the variables in the Sample Questionnaire, we have included a file named *LOCAL.SAV* on the disk that came with this book. It contains the data definition for this particular questionnaire. In short, because we know you are getting toward the end of the book and are probably anxious to begin your own adventure, we wanted to save you the time and work of having to define all the variables included in the Sample Questionnaire so we did it for you (think of it as a gift of sorts)!

For now, however, just keep the existence of LOCAL.SAV in the back of your mind. We'll show you how to use it after we discuss the next step (step 2) in the process of getting your data ready for analysis with SPSS—editing and coding your data.

Editing and Coding Your Data

The second step in the process of getting your data ready for analysis with SPSS is editing and *coding* your data. People do not always follow instructions when filling out a questionnaire. Verbal or written responses have to be transformed into a numeric code for processing with SPSS. For ease of entry, questionnaires should be edited for proper completion and coding before you attempt to key or enter them into an SPSS file.

To the extent we could, we designed the questionnaire on-line in E-Appendix E to be self-coding. By having a number next to each response for the *closed-ended* questions, the interviewer assigns a code as the respondent answers the question. Some questions we have had to leave *open-ended*, either because there would be too many responses to print on the questionnaire or because we couldn't anticipate all of the possible responses.

There are essentially four main steps involved in editing and coding your data: making sure each questionnaire has a unique ID number, coding open-ended questions, making sure the codes are easy to read, and editing each questionnaire.

Unique ID Number   Before the data for a single person can be entered into a file, the questionnaire needs to be edited. Each questionnaire should have a unique number in the ID field. We do this not because we want to identify individuals but because errors that show up later are frequently made in the coding process. For instance, we coded SEX as 1 for male and 2 for female, but in our analysis, we find a respondent with SEX coded 7. What we need to do is find the record with the erroneous code 7, look up the ID number, go back to the original questionnaire, find out what code SEX should have been, and fix it.

Coding Open-Ended Questions   Next in the editing process, we have to code the open-ended questions. All the people coding questions should be following the same written instructions for coding. For instance, at the end of E-Appendix E, we included a list of occupations and their socioeconomic statuses for coding SEI, the socioeconomic index. Other coding schemes might not be as elaborate. For instance, in a medical study, patients might be asked about the illnesses that brought them to the hospital. Coding might be as simple as classifying the illnesses as acute or chronic.

Insuring That Codes Are Easy to Read   Finally, the codes need to be written so that they are easy to read. We have designed our questionnaire to be *edge-coded*.

If you look in the right margin, you will see that we put a space for each variable's code. We included these numbers because some statistics require that variables be placed in specific "columns" across each "record." Happily, that is not a requirement of SPSS for Windows. We'll use just the numbered blanks as a convenient place to write our codes.

Editing Questionnaires Whether you are going to edit the Sample Questionnaire that we have been using as an example throughout this section or another questionnaire you designed on your own, you should get a copy of the codes used to define the file you are working with (i.e., a copy of the work you did in Step 1 when you defined your data). For this example we will access the codes used to define our LOCAL.SAV file.

When you have opened the LOCAL.SAV data file that is contained on the disk that came with this book, you will notice that the data cells are empty. Don't panic; they are supposed to be empty. This is the empty, but defined, data file LOCAL.SAV we mentioned earlier.

To display the codes for your use in coding your data, click **Utilities** followed by **File Info**. You should see the information for ID and the other variables in your Output window. To have the codes printed, simply click **File** and then **Print**.

Here is an example of the coding information you will find for the variable MARITAL, responses to Question number 4 on the questionnaire: "Are you— married, widowed, divorced, separated, or have you never been married?"

MARITAL	MARITAL STATUS

Measurement Level:	Ordinal
Column Width: Unknown	Alignment: Right
Print Format: F	
Write Format: F1	
Missing Values: 9	

Value	Label
1	MARRIED
2	WIDOWED
3	DIVORCED
4	SEPARATED
5	NEVER MARRIED
9 M	NA

For people who are married, code 1 is used. For people who are widowed, code 2 is used; divorced, code 3, and so on. Notice that code 9, no answer, has an M next to it. This means that code 9 has been designated a missing code. All missing codes are thrown out of the analysis. If respondents fail to answer a question or give two responses for one question, they should be assigned the missing value code for that variable.

After printing the coding information for each variable, you should go through each questionnaire, one at a time, to make sure the coding is correct, that there is only one code per question, and so on.

SPSS COMMAND 21.4: Accessing File Information for Coding and Editing

> Click **Utilities → File Information**
> Once you have edited and coded each of your questionnaires, you
> can move to the final step, entering data.

Entering Your Data

To enter data, either in your LOCAL.SAV file or another file for which you already defined your data, simply open the file. Once again, we are going to use our Sample Questionnaire as an example. After opening your LOCAL.SAV file, you should be looking at an empty data matrix with the variable names across the top and record numbers down the left side. You will notice that the order of the variables across the record is the same as the order of the variables on the questionnaire. We placed them in that order to make data entry easier and less error-prone.

Demonstration 21.4: Moving Through the Data Matrix

You can easily move from cell to cell in the data matrix. Pressing just the **Tab** key moves the active cell to the right, and pressing the **Shift** and **Tab** keys moves the active cell to the left. You can tell the active cell by its thick black border. Pressing the **Enter** key moves the active cell down to the next record. The directional arrows on your keyboard will also move the active cell, one cell at a time. The mouse can be used to make a cell active just by pointing and clicking. Long-distance moves can be made by pressing **Ctrl** and **Home** to move to the left-most cell on the first case and **Ctrl** and **End** to move to the rightmost cell on the last case.

SPSS COMMAND 21.5: Some Tips for Moving Through the Data Matrix

> **Tab**—to move the active cell to the right
> **Shift and Tab**—to move the active cell to the left
> **Enter**—to move the active cell down to the next record
> **Directional Arrows**—to move the active cell, one cell at a time
> **Ctrl and Home**—to move the active cell to the leftmost cell, first case
> **Ctrl and End**—to move the active cell to the rightmost cell, last case

Demonstration 21.5: Entering Data

To enter data, simply select the appropriate cell in the Data Editor, making it the active cell. When you do that, you will notice that the record number and the variable name appear in the rectangle at the top left-hand corner of the Data Editor, directly below the tool bar. You can now enter the appropriate **numeric value or code** (or your data). When you enter your data you will notice that they first appear in the *Cell Editor* at the top of the Data Editor window, just below the toolbar.

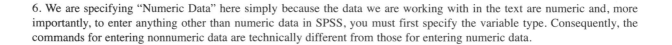

Simply press **Enter** or **move to another cell** to record your data.

SPSS COMMAND 21.6: Entering Numeric Data[6]

> Click on the **appropriate cell** to make it the active cell →
>
> Enter the **numeric value** or **code** →
>
> Press **Enter or move to another cell** to record the data in the active
>   cell

Demonstration 21.6: Revising or Deleting Data

Data may be changed at any time just by moving to the appropriate cell, keying in new values, and pressing **Enter** or moving to another cell.

If a particular case turns into a disaster, you can get rid of the entire case by clicking on the **record number** at the extreme left of a record and pressing the **Delete** key.

---

6. We are specifying "Numeric Data" here simply because the data we are working with in the text are numeric and, more importantly, to enter anything other than numeric data in SPSS, you must first specify the variable type. Consequently, the commands for entering nonnumeric data are technically different from those for entering numeric data.

SPSS COMMAND 21.7: Deleting an Entire Case

> Click on the **record number** at the far left of the Data Editor →
>   Press **Delete**

After you are done entering data, or if you want to stop entering data and continue at a later time, make sure you save your data. By clicking **File** and **Save**, you will save your data under the name that was used at the beginning of the session (in this case, for instance, LOCAL.SAV). If you wish to save it under another name, click on **File** and **Save As**. Be careful of which disk drive you save to. If the computer is in a public place, you will want to save your work on a removable disk (A: or B:) so that you can take it with you.

Writing a Research Report

After you design and execute your survey and enter and analyze the data, it is finally time to report your results. To help you through this often difficult but very crucial aspect of the research process, we have included an excerpt in Appendix B which, among other things, presents guidelines for reporting analyses that you may find useful.

In addition, many research methods texts (including some of those we referenced earlier such as Schutt, 1999) devote sections to writing research reports. Alreck and Settle (1985) and Babbie (1990) each devote a chapter specifically to reporting survey research results. You may also want to reference one of the many books devoted to writing, particularly those designed with social scientists in mind, such as Howard Becker: *Writing for Social Scientists* (1986) or Lee Cuba: *A Short Guide to Writing About Social Science* (1997).

Conclusion

Although there is a fair amount of work involved in doing your own survey, entering and analyzing your own data, and then reporting your results, there can also be a special reward or excitement about coming to an understanding about the opinions and behaviors of a group of people with whom you are directly familiar. The benefits of conducting your own study are even more evident if your survey focuses on topics and issues that are meaningful, relevant, or otherwise important to you or those in your community. In fact, the main advantage of designing and executing your own original or ***primary research*** is that you can focus specifically on those issues, topics, populations, and variables that interest you. Since you are in charge of the design, implementation, analysis, and reporting of your study, you do not have to depend on the work of other social scientists who may have approached the issue, topic, or problem differently. The downside, of course, is the fact that the time and resources involved in conducting your own study can often be tremendous. Nevertheless, we think you will find that whereas there are various advantages and disadvantages to both primary and secondary research, the rewards and excitement that come from both types of research make the time, energy, and commitment involved worth it.

Main Points

- This chapter, Appendix B, and on-line E-Appendices C, D, and E at www. pineforge.com are designed to help you construct and administer your own survey, enter the data in SPSS, and write a research report.

- E-Appendix C includes an excerpt designed to give you a sense of the steps involved in the social research process and some hints on writing a research proposal (often the first step in the research process).

- There are various considerations involved in constructing and implementing a survey that is reliable, valid, and generalizable.

- SPSS Survey Tips, which is reprinted in E-Appendix D, is included to give you an overview of how to design and execute your own survey.

- E-Appendix E contains a Sample Questionnaire with questions drawn from the 1998 GSS.

- There are three main steps involved in getting ready for data analysis using SPSS.

- Defining your data is the first step in the process.

- Variable templates are a shortcut you can use to define certain variables.

- The LOCAL.SAV file includes the data definition for the Sample Questionnaire.

- The second step in the process is editing and coding your data.

- The third step in the process is entering your data.

- The excerpt in E-Appendix C discusses one of the most important and difficult aspects of the social research process—writing a research report.

Key Terms

Data definition	Close-ended
Active cell	Open-ended
Variable templates	Edge-coded
LOCAL.SAV	Cell editor
Coding	Primary research

SPSS Commands Introduced in This Chapter

21.1:   Defining a Variable

> Make the **Data Editor** the **active window** →
>
> **Double-click** on **column where placing variable** and the "Define Variable" window should open (if not click Data and Define Variables...) →
>
> In the "Define Variable" window enter the **Variable Name**: →
>
> Click **Type...** → In "Define Variable Type" window set **data type** → set **Width**: → set **Decimal Places**: → Click **Continue** →
>
> Click **Labels...** → In "Define Labels" window enter **Variable Label**: → enter **Value(s)** → enter **Value Label(s)** → Click **Add** → **Repeat last step** entering values, values labels and clicking **Add as many times as necessary for each value** of the variable →
>
> Click **Continue** →
>
> Click **Missing Values...** → Designate Missing Values in "Define Missing Values:" window →
>
> Click **Continue** →
>
> [If want to set Column Width and/or Alignment, Click Column Format... → Define Column Width → Align Text → Click Continue →]
>
> Set level of "**Measurement**" in "Define Variable Window" → Click **Continue** →
>
> **Repeat** this **process** as many times as necessary **until you have defined all the variables in your survey**.

21.2:   Creating a Variable Template

> Make **Data Editor** the **active window** →
>
> Click **Data** → **Templates...** → **Define>>** →
>
> **Select the attributes you want to define** (Type...; Value Labels...; Missing Values...; and/or Column Format...) →
>
> After you have defined the template, enter a **template name** in space labeled **Name**: →
>
> Click **Add** → **Check** the variable attributed you want to apply in the "Apply" box (Type, Value labels, Missing values, and/or Column format)→
>
> Click **OK**

21.3:   Applying a Variable Template

> **Highlight column(s) or variable(s)** in the **Data Editor** →
> Click **Data → Templates...** →
> In the Template window select the **name of the template** you want to apply →
> Click **OK** →
> If you have not done so already, use the **Data → Define Variables** command to specify the variable name(s), label(s), and level(s) of measurement for each item

21.4:   Accessing File Information for Coding and Editing

> Click **Utilities → File Information**

21.5:   Some Tips for Moving Through the Data Matrix

> **Tab**—to move the active cell to the right
> **Shift and Tab**—to move the active cell to the left
> **Enter**—to move the active cell down to the next record
> **Directional Arrows**—to move the active cell, one cell at a time
> **Ctrl and Home**—to move the active cell to the leftmost cell, first case
> **Ctrl and End**—to move the active cell to the rightmost cell, last case

21.6:   Entering Numeric Data

> Click on the **appropriate cell** to make it the **active cell** →
> Enter the **numeric value** or **code** →
> Press **Enter or move to another** cell to record the data in the active cell

21.7:   Deleting an Entire Case

> Click on the **record number** at the far left of the Data Editor →
>   Press **Delete**

Review Questions

1. Name two methods social scientists use to collect data (besides survey research).
2. Name three decisions involved in designing a social research project.
3. Why is it important to write a research proposal?
4. Discuss at least three of the "tips" included in *SPSS's Survey Tips*.
5. List the three steps involved in getting ready for data analysis using SPSS.
6. What does "data definition" refer to?
7. Name two guidelines or rules for choosing a variable name that SPSS will accept.
8. What is a shortcut that can be used to define certain variables?
9. What SPSS command(s) would you use to create and apply a variable template?
10. What does the LOCAL.SAV file on your disk contain?
11. List two things you need to do when editing and coding your data.
12. List two ways you can move through the data matrix.
13. When you key in data, where does it appear before it is recorded (i.e., before you press Enter or move to another cell)?
14. Name two considerations involved in writing a research report.
15. Name two guidelines for reporting analyses.

NAME _____

CLASS _____

INSTRUCTOR _____

DATE _____

Our goal in this exercise is to allow you to practice defining, editing, coding, and entering your data (in short, all the steps involved in getting ready for data analysis using SPSS).

1. Print at least 8 copies of the Sample Questionnaire contained in the E-Appendix E or, better yet, make 8 copies of a questionnaire you designed on your own, and administer it to at least 8 respondents (it can be friends, family, colleagues, etc…).

2. After collecting the data, go through the three steps involved in getting data ready for analysis using SPSS:
   A) Define Your Data
   B) Edit and Code Your Data
   C) Enter Your Data

3. After you have gone through these three steps, use the Utilities → File Information command to print coding information about your new data file.

Chapter 22 Further Opportunities for Social Research

Well, we've come to the end of our introduction to SPSS. In this final chapter, we want to suggest ways in which you can expand beyond the scope of this book. In particular, we are going to focus briefly on the unabridged GSS, other data sets, and other computer programs that you may find useful as you continue your social research adventure.

The Unabridged GSS

The GSS data sets that accompany this book are limited to 41 (DEMO.SAV) and 44 (EXER.SAV) variables in order to accommodate all versions of SPSS. At the same time, you should realize that the data available through the GSS program are vastly more extensive. For instance, the 1998 data contain 879 variables and 2,832 cases. The cumulative data file that merges all the General Social Surveys conducted between 1972 and 1998 contains 3,278 variables and 38,116 cases.

Since the first General Social Survey was conducted in 1972, data have been collected on thousands of variables of interest to researchers around the country and, indeed, around the world. As we noted earlier, the National Opinion Research Center maintains an Internet site called GSSDIRS, the General Social Survey Data and Information Retrieval System. It provides an interactive cumulative index to the GSS that may be found at http://www.icpsr.umich. edu/GSS99/subject/s-index.htm. In addition to indexing variables by subject, it also lists professional and academic publications based on specific variables.

The GSSDIRS site also contains a search engine that locates abstracts of research reports produced from GSS data, an electronic edition of the complete GSS codebook, a GSS bibliography, and a data extraction system that permits downloading GSS data in a format that can be used with any version of SPSS.

Now that you are familiar with the use of GSS data through SPSS, you may be able to locate other GSS data sets through your school. In addition, GSS data may be purchased from one of the following sources:

1.   The Roper Center for Public Opinion Research
     Box 440
     University of Connecticut
     Storrs, CT 06268
     Phone: (860) 486-4440
     Fax: (860) 486-4882
     Home page: http://www.ropercenter.uconn.edu/
     E-mail: gssdata@opinion.isi.uconn.edu

2.   The Interuniversity Consortium for Political and Social Research
     (ICPSR)
     Box 1248
     University of Michigan
     Ann Arbor, MI 48106
     Phone: (313) 763-5010
     Home page: http://www.icprs.umich.edu/

3.   MicroCase Corporation
     1301 120th Avenue, NE
     Bellevue, WA 98005
     Phone: (800) 682-7367 or (206) 635-0293
     Fax: (206) 635-0953

An important reference book for your use with GSS data is the *Cumulative Codebook* published by the National Opinion Research Center at the University of Chicago (e.g., see Davis, Smith, and Marsden, 1998). Available both in book and computer forms, it may be purchased from the Roper Center. Or, if you wish, use the electronic version mentioned above.

The 1998 edition of the *Codebook* (Davis, Smith, and Marsden) contains information on all aspects of the GSS from 1972 to 1998, including exact questions, response codes, frequency counts, and so on. The table of contents for the latest edition, which is shown below, will give you an overview of the type of information included in this valuable resource:

Codebook Table of Contents[1]

Introduction

New Developments

Abbreviations and Data Identification Numbers

Index to Data Sets

Codes for the 1972–1998 Surveys—*Includes variable names, exact question text, response categories and codes, and marginal frequencies for all questions.*

1. http://www.ropercenter.uconn.edu/gss98/gsscdbk.htm

Appendices
A.   Sampling Design and Weighting
B.   Field Work and Interviewer Specifications
C.   General Coding Instructions
D.   Recodes
E.   Age and Cohort Distributions
F.   Occupational Classification Distributions
G.   Prestige Scores Distributions
H.   Industrial Classifications Distributions
I.   International Standard Classification of Occupations
J.   DOT Variables
K.   Protestant Denominations Distributions
L.   Hours Worked Distributions
M.   Abortion and ERA Distributions
N.   Changes in Question Wording, Response Categories, and Format
O.   Previous Usage
P.   Experimental Form
Q.   Rotation Design
R.   Crossnational and Topical Modules
S.   Supplemental and Related Data
T.   General Social Survey Papers
U.   Variables by Year
V.   Subject Index to Questions

Here is a sample of some of the information available to you in the main body of the *Codebook*. This selection shows how coding has been accomplished for two of the abortion items that are included in your DEMO.SAV file.

206. Please tell me whether or not <u>you</u> think it should be possible for a pregnant woman to obtain a <u>legal</u> abortion if. . .READ EACH STATEMENT, AND CIRCLE ONE CODE FOR EACH.

A.   If there is a strong chance of serious defect in the baby?

[VAR: ABDEFECT]

RESPONSE	PUNCH	YEAR COL.	780								
		1972–82	1982B	1983–87	1987B	1988–91	1993	1994	1996	1998	ALL
Yes	1	10980	236	4625	236	3,056	840	1585	1514	1415	24,487
No	2	2195	92	1210	94	707	193	341	336	385	5,553
Don't know	8	419	25	187	21	141	37	68	66	79	1,043
No answer	9	32	1	50	2	16	5	2	7	3	118
Not applicable	DK	0	0	1470	0	1,987	531	996	981	950	6,915

B.   If she is married and does not want any more children?

[VAR: ABNOMORE]

RESPONSE	PUNCH	YEAR COL.		781							
		1972–82	1982B	1983–87	1987B	1988–91	1993	1994	1996	1998	ALL
Yes	1	5920	111	2387	125	1,640	480	930	853	758	13,204
No	2	7133	216	3452	206	2,129	539	995	972	1033	16,675
Don't know	8	542	26	181	20	132	51	65	91	86	1,194
No answer	9	31	1	52	2	19	5	6	7	5	128
Not applicable	DK	0	0	1470	0	1,987	531	996	981	950	6,915

Another very valuable resource document is NORC's annual review of research uses of GSS data sets, the *Annotated Bibliography of Papers Using the General Social Survey* (e.g., see Smith, Arnold, and Lancaster, 1996).

In addition to the advantage of working with many more variables than we've included in the present file, the larger GSS data set permits you to conduct longitudinal research—to analyze changes in opinions and behaviors over the years. The initial experience of the GSS data set in connection with this book has put you in touch with a powerful research resource that we hope you'll be able to use more extensively in the future.

Other Data Sets

As if the full GSS weren't enough, there are thousands of other data sets in existence that are appropriate for analysis with SPSS.

To begin, there is a global network of data archives, or data libraries, that operate somewhat like book libraries. Instead of lending books, these archives lend or sell sets of data that have been collected previously. The National Opinion Research Center, which administers the GSS, is one such archive. Another major archive is the Roper Center for Public Opinion Research. Other data archives are maintained in the survey research centers of major universities, such as the University of California, Berkeley and Los Angeles campuses; the University of Michigan; and the University of Wisconsin.

Most of these data libraries, and in many cases the data they house, are accessible via the world wide web (www). We have already given you the web site addresses for the NORC and Roper Center. However, bear in mind that you can also access other data archives such as the Princeton University Data Library at http://www.princeton.edu/~data or the University of Michigan Documents Center at http://www.lib.umich/edu/libhome/documents.center/stats/html, just to name a few.

The data sets available for *secondary analysis* at these and other archives include, for example, studies conducted by university faculty researchers that may have been financed by federal research grants. Thus, the results of studies that may have cost hundreds of thousands of dollars to conduct can be yours now for the nominal cost of copying and shipping the data.

The Roper Center is a repository for all the data collected by the Gallup Organization, including not only American "Gallup Polls" but those conducted by Gallup in other countries. Survey research is an active enterprise in many countries. In Japan, for example, the major newspapers, such as the *Mainichi Shimbun* and *Yomiuri Shimbun*, conduct countless surveys, and it is possible for you to obtain and analyze some of those survey data through data archives in the United States.

You should realize that the U.S. government also conducts a great many surveys that produce data suitable for analysis with SPSS. The U.S. Census (http://www.census.gov/) is a chief example, and it is possible for researchers to obtain and analyze data collected in the decennial censuses. Two other examples include the Bureau of Justice Statistics and the Bureau of Labor Statistics, which can be accessed at http://www.ojp.usdoj.gov/bjs and http://stats.bls.gov/datahome.htm, respectively. For access to an almost full range of statistics produced by more than 70 U.S. federal agencies, you may want to log on to "FedStats: One Stop Shopping For Federal Statistics" at http://www.fedstats.gov/.

It is worth recalling that when Emile Durkheim set about his major analysis of suicide in Europe, he was forced to work with printed government reports of suicide rates in various countries and regions. Moreover, his reanalyses of those data needed to be done by hand.

With the advent of computers for mass data storage and analytic programs such as SPSS, the possibilities for secondary analysis have been revolutionized. You live at an enviable time in that regard.

To get a sense of the types of data sets available for secondary analysis that cover issues and topics in your discipline, you may want to search the world wide web. One site that may help you get started is "Dr. B's Wide World of Web Data," a statistical tool created at Arizona State University in the fall of 1994. Once you access the site at http://research.ed.asu.edu/siip/webdata, you will be able to link to data sets by choosing among topics that range from crime and law enforcement, demographics, and drug use and abuse to education, environment, medicine and health, and social sciences. You can also get some help locating statistical data on-line by searching: http://www.spss.com/statsweb or http://nilesonline.com/data.

This is, of course, just the tip of the iceberg. These limited recommendations don't even begin to scratch the surface of the numerous sites available to help you locate and access statistical data on the world wide web. While you should make use of the www to locate and, in some cases, access data, please bear in mind that you also have to be cautious and wary when conducting on-line searches. This is particularly true in light of the fact that anyone can post information on-line, so the accuracy of the data or other information you locate may not necessarily be conducive to sound social research. Also bear in mind that different search engines are likely to identify different sites, even when provided with the same search terms.[2]

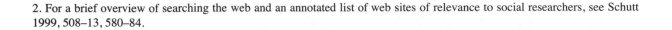

2. For a brief overview of searching the web and an annotated list of web sites of relevance to social researchers, see Schutt 1999, 508–13, 580–84.

Other Computer Programs

We have organized this book around the use of SPSS because this program is so widely used by social scientists. Quite frankly, we spent a fair amount of time considering other programs as the focus for the book, but ultimately decided it would be most useful to the greatest number of students if we used SPSS. And by the way, SPSS's popularity is due largely to its excellence as a tool for social research.

At the same time, we want you to know that there are several other excellent analytic programs available. We'll mention some of these here in the event that you may have access to them. You should realize that the commands and procedures used in other programs will differ from those of SPSS, but the logic of data analysis that we've presented in this book applies across the various programs available.

Probably the program package next most commonly used by social scientists is *SAS*. Like SPSS, it is an omnibus package of techniques that goes far beyond those to which we've introduced you in this book. Should it be useful to you, SAS functions within a broader set of programs for accounting, management, and other activities. You can learn more about SAS by accessing the SAS homepage at http://www.sas.com/.

SYSTAT is another widely used package of programs designed for social science research. Moreover, SYSTAT has an excellent and very inexpensive student version called *MYSTAT*, which you may be able to obtain through your campus bookstore, computing center, or statistics department. For an overview of SYSTAT and MYSTAT see http://www.spss.com.

MicroCase, by Cognitive Development, is another excellent program for social science data analysis. It usually comes with a large GSS data set, data on the states of the United States, data from Canadian provinces, and other data sets as well. *ShowCase*, by the same company, presents state and province data in a map format. Thus, for example, you can ask for the divorce rates in different U.S. states and see the several states shaded according to a code indicating how high or low the rates are. Unlike the command structure of SPSS, MicroCase operates primarily according to a menu system, wherein you select techniques and options from a list rather than having to remember the forms of particular commands.

Here's just a partial list of other programs that you might use for social science data analysis: ABtab, AIDA, A.STAT, BMDP, Chippendale, CRISP, DAISY, DATA-X, Dynacomp, INTER-STAT, MASS, Microquest, Microstat, Micro-SURVEY, MIDAS, Minitab, POINT FIVE, P-STAT, SAM, SNAP, SOS, Statgraf, Statpak, StatPro, STATS PLUS, Statview, Survey Mate, STAT80, STATA, SURVTAB, TECPACS.[3]

We've seen that SPSS has some capability for presenting data in a graphic form, such as histograms. Other programs, such as *Cricket* and *Harvard Graphics*, to name just two, offer powerful sets of visual techniques.

---

3. For a brief overview of a few of these statistical packages, including SAS, SPSS, STATA, S-PLUS, DBMS/COPY on UNIX, and FTP see http://www.princeton.edu/~data/software/software.html. It is important to note that this site contains information only about the various statistical packages supported by the Data and Statistical Services (DDS) at Princeton University.

Conclusion

We hope you've had some fun as you've worked through this book and that you've learned some important research techniques and some facts about the American public. We hope you have discovered that social research—although very important, especially considering the range of social problems we confront today—is also a fascinating enterprise.

Like the investigative detective, the social researcher must possess large amounts of curiosity and ingenuity. Sit beside a social researcher at work, and you'll hear him or her muttering things like, "Wait a minute. If that's the case, then I'd expect to find ..."; "Hey, that probably explains why ...; "Omigod! That means ..." Maybe you've overheard yourself practicing these social scientific incantations. If so, congratulations and welcome. If not, you have a delightful adventure waiting for you just around the corner. We'll see you there.

Main Points

- To accommodate the student version of SPSS, the data sets that accompany this text are just a small portion of the 1998 GSS.
- The unabridged 1998 GSS contains 2,832 cases and numerous variables not reflected in your DEMO.SAV and EXER.SAV files.
- Since the first GSS in 1972, more than 38,000 respondents have been asked more than 3,500 questions.
- There are many ways to access the unabridged GSS.
- The NORC web site, the GSSDIRS, is a very useful resource.
- The *Cumulative Codebook* is a valuable resource for researchers using the GSS.
- The GSS is just one of many data sets available to social researchers.
- Data sets of interest to social scientists (of which there are many) are often housed at one of the data archives, and in some cases, accessible via the world wide web.
- The federal government is an important source of statistical data of interest to social scientists.
- We focused this text on SPSS because it is so widely used by social researchers. However, it is not the only statistical package available.
- Other excellent software programs often used by social researchers include (but are not limited to): SAS, SYSTAT, MicroCase, ShowCase, and STATA, just to name a few.
- In addition, programs like Cricket and Harvard Graphics are well-known for their ability to present data graphically.

Key Terms

Secondary analysis	MicroCase
SAS	ShowCase
SYSTAT	Cricket
MYSTAT	Harvard Graphics

SPSS Commands Introduced in This Chapter

No new commands were introduced in this chapter.

Review Questions

1. How many variables and cases are contained on your DEMO.SAV file?
2. How many variables and cases are contained on your EXER.SAV file?
3. How many cases are contained in the entire 1998 GSS?
4. From 1972 to 1998, how many different questions were asked as part of the GSS?
5. How many respondents took part in the GSS from 1972 to 1998?
6. What is the GSSDIRS?
7. How can you access the GSS data?
8. What type of information does the *Codebook* contain?
9. What are data archives?
10. Name two data archives.
11. Name two specific data sets relevant to your particular discipline.
12. Besides SPSS, what statistical package is most commonly used by social scientists?
13. List two other statistical software packages used by social researchers (besides SAS and SPSS).

Appendices

You will find all the appendices except for Appendices A (Answers to Selected SPSS Lab Exercises) and B (The Research Report), which follow, on-line at <http://www.pineforge.com>. These electronic appendices are an integral part of the book so you need to make time to find and use this material on the web. Here's what you will find:

Appendix A   *Answers to Selected SPSS Lab Exercises.* Appendix A follows. We think you will find it more convenient to have this appendix in the book rather than on-line.

Appendix B   *The Research Report* also follows. This appendix contains important information on writing and presenting results, as well as some hints on writing a research report.

E-Appendix C   *The Research Proposal.* An excerpt from Russell Schutt's *Investigating the Social World* discusses the steps in the research process and writing a research proposal.

E-Appendix D   *Survey Tips.* This appendix, which is adapted with permission from the SPSS, Inc. web site, contains the steps involved in constructing and administering a survey.

E-Appendix E   *Questionnaire for Class Survey.* Students and instructors are encouraged to refer to this sample questionnaire, which was adapted from the GSS, and to use it to collect their own data.

E-Appendix F   *SPSS Commands Introduced in This Book.* This is a complete list of all the SPSS commands introduced throughout the text. We have gathered them here in one place for your convenience.

E-Appendix G   *Readings.* The following recommended readings appear in E-Appendix G.

A Theory of Involvement
Charles Y. Glock, Benjamin B. Ringer, and Earl R. Babbie
The Social Bases of Abortion Attitudes
Elizabeth Adell Cook, Ted G. Jelen, and Clyde Wilcox
Ideal Family Size as an Intervening Variable between Religion and Attitudes Towards Abortion
Mario Renzi
Religion, Ideal Family Size, and Abortion: Extending Renzi's Hypothesis
William V. D'Antonio and Steven Stack

Appendix A   Answers to Selected SPSS Lab Exercises

If you need to review the procedures for a certain question, see the references to relevant SPSS Commands included before each appropriate answer.

Chapter 5   **SPSS Lab Exercise 5.1 (Questions 1–3)**

1.   See SPSS Command 5.4 Option 1

Respondent #89	<u>3 OPPOSE PREFerences</u>
Respondent #556	<u>4 STRONGLY OPPOSE PREFerences</u>
Respondent #1065	<u>1 STRONGLY SUPPORT PREFerences</u>

2.   See SPSS Command 5.4 Option 2

Respondent #18	<u>3 OTHEr</u>
Respondent #765	<u>2 BLACk</u>
Respondent #1386	<u>1 WHITe</u>

3.   See SPSS Command 5.4 Option 3

Respondent #63	<u>2 ONLY SOMe</u>
Respondent #190	<u>3 HARDLY Any</u>
Respondent #1499	<u>1 A GREAT Deal</u>

Chapter 6   **SPSS Lab Exercise 6.1 (Questions 1–2, 5–7)**[1]

1.   See SPSS Command 6.4 or 6.5

RACE RACE OF RESPONDENT

		Frequency	Percent	Valid Percent	Cumulative Percent
Valid	1 WHITE	1177	78.5	78.5	78.5
	2 BLACK	210	14.0	14.0	92.5
	3 OTHER	113	7.5	7.5	100.0
	Total	1500	100.0	100.0	

The largest racial grouping of respondents to the 1998 GSS was <u>white</u>, with <u>79</u>%. The second largest grouping was <u>black</u> with <u>14</u>%.

---

1. Don't Know (DK) has been designated as missing for the variables used in Questions 5 and 6 (EDUC and TVHOURS). See SPSS Command 9.1 to review the procedures for defining missing values.

2.   See SPSS Command 6.4 or 6.5

HEALTH CONDITION OF HEALTH

		Frequency	Percent	Valid Percent	Cumulative Percent
Valid	1 EXCELLENT	446	29.7	29.8	29.8
	2 GOOD	719	47.9	48.1	77.9
	3 FAIR	259	17.3	17.3	95.3
	4 POOR	70	4.7	4.7	99.9
	8 DK	1	.1	.1	100.0
	Total	1495	99.7	100.0	
Missing	9 NA	5	.3		
Total		1500	100.0		

Most respondents to the 1998 GSS reported that they are in <u>good</u> health, with <u>48%</u> of the sample. This was followed by <u>30%</u> of respondents who reported being in <u>excellent</u> health. Only <u>5%</u> of respondents reported being in poor health.

5.   See SPSS Command 6.6

Descriptive Statistics

	N	Minimum	Maximum	Mean	Std. Deviation
EDUC HIGHEST YEAR OF SCHOOL COMPLETED	1492	0	20	13.30	2.90
Valid N (listwise)	1492				

The mean education of respondents to the 1998 GSS is <u>13.30</u>, and two-thirds of them have between <u>10.40</u> and <u>16.20</u> years of education.

6.   See SPSS Command 6.6

Descriptive Statistics

	N	Minimum	Maximum	Mean	Std. Deviation
TVHOURS HOURS PER DAY WATCHING TV	1246	0	20	2.82	2.12
Valid N (listwise)	1246				

Respondents to the 1998 GSS reported watching an average of <u>2.82</u> hours of television a day, and two-thirds of them watched between <u>.7</u> and <u>4.94</u> hours of television per day.

7.   See SPSS Command 6.8

EDUCREC Recoded Education

		Frequency	Percent	Valid Percent	Cumulative Percent
Valid	1 less than HS graduate	255	17.0	17.1	17.1
	2 HS graduate	468	31.2	31.4	48.5
	3 some college	385	25.7	25.8	74.3
	4 college graduate	384	25.6	25.7	100.0
	Total	1492	99.5	100.0	
Missing	System	8	.5		
Total		1500	100.0		

Chapter 7   **SPSS Lab Exercise 7.1 (Questions 1–4)[2]**

1.   See SPSS Command 7.1

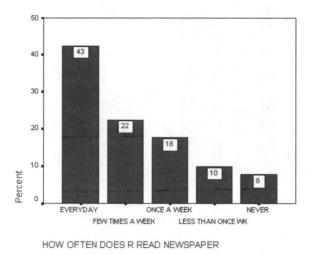

HOW OFTEN DOES R READ NEWSPAPER

<u>Bar</u>

About <u>43</u>% of respondents read a newspaper every day, whereas approximately <u>8</u>% said they never read a newspaper.

2.   See SPSS Command 7.2

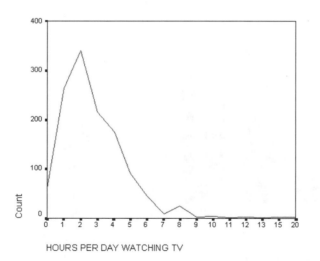

HOURS PER DAY WATCHING TV

<u>Line</u>

Most respondents reported watching about <u>2</u> hours of television each day. The lowest point(s) on the chart, indicating the least common number of hours of television watching by respondents, was <u>11 and 13</u>. The number of hours respondents spend watching television every day drops off considerably after approximately <u>2</u> hours.

---

2. Don't Know (DK) has been declared missing for the variables used in Questions 1 and 2. See SPSS Command 9.1 to review the procedures for defining missing values.

3.   See SPSS Command 7.1

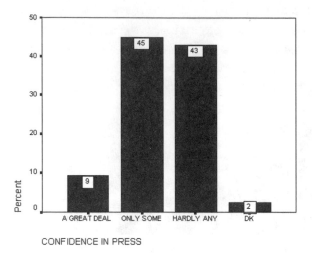

CONFIDENCE IN PRESS

<u>Bar</u>
<u>Example: Only about 9% of the sample said they have a "Great deal" of confidence in the press, whereas more than 80% of respondents reported having "Only some" (approximately 45%) or "Hardly any" (approximately 43%) confidence in the press.</u>

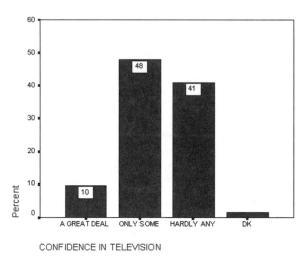

CONFIDENCE IN TELEVISION

4.   See SPSS Command 7.1

<u>Bar</u>
<u>Example: Most respondents said they have "Only some" confidence in television at just under 50%. This was followed closely by just over 40% of the respondents who reported having "Hardly any" confidence in television. Only 10% of the sample expressed a "Great deal" of confidence in television.</u>

Chapter 8   **SPSS Lab Exercise 8.1 (Questions 1–14)**

1.   SPSS Command 5.4

Support/oppose police officer striking a citizen if...

    A. <u>POLABUSE</u>   <u>Citizen said vulgar or obscene things</u>

    B. <u>POLATTAK</u>   <u>Citizen attacking policeman with fists</u>

    C. <u>POLESCAP</u>   <u>Citizen attempting to escape custody</u>

    D. <u>POLMURDR</u>   <u>Citizen questioned as a murder suspect</u>

    E. <u>POLHITOK</u>   <u>Ever approve of police striking citizen</u>

2–7.   SPSS Command 8.2 Option 1

2.   <u>67%</u> of respondents who answered the question said they can imagine a situation in which they would approve of a police officer striking a citizen. [POLHITOK— valid percent]

3.   <u>29%</u> of respondents who answered the question reported they would not approve of a police officer striking a citizen under any circumstances. [POLHITOK—valid percent]

4.   A. <u>POLATTAK 91%</u> [valid percent]

    B. <u>POLESCAP 67%</u> [valid percent]

5.   A. <u>POLABUSE 7%</u> [valid percent]

    B. <u>POLMURDR 6%</u> [valid percent]

6.   A. <u>POLATTAK 91%</u>

    B. <u>POLESCAP 67%</u>

    C. <u>POLABUSE 7%</u>

    D. <u>POLMURDR 6%</u>

7.   <u>Example: The table indicates that there is a great deal of agreement among respondents in terms of situations in which they would and would not support a police officer striking a citizen. Moreover, the table indicates the complexity of the American public's opinion in this area and their ability to walk a fine line, or strike a balance, between two competing "rights": the general public's right to safety and security and an individual's civil rights. For instance, 91% of respondents said they would support an officer striking a citizen if the officer was being attacked and more than two-thirds said they would support an officer striking a citizen if the citizen was attempting to escape custody. At the same time, the vast majority made a distinction between those situations and situations in which the officer and the public were not in serious, immediate, or potential physical danger. In those situations, the vast majority of respondents said they would not approve of an officer</u>

striking a citizen simply, for instance, if the citizen said vulgar or obscene things or if the citizen was being questioned as a murder suspect.

8–13.   SPSS Command 8.3

POLATTAK CITIZEN ATTACKING POLICEMAN WITH FISTS * POLABUSE CITIZEN SAID VULGAR OR OBSCENE THINGS Crosstabulation

Count

		POLABUSE CITIZEN SAID VULGAR OR OBSCENE THINGS			Total
		1 YES	2 NO	8 DK	
POLATTAK CITIZEN ATTACKING POLICEMAN WITH FISTS	1 YES	72	826	15	913
	2 NO	1	77	1	79
	8 DK		12	2	14
Total		73	915	18	1006

8.   <u>72</u> respondents said they would support a police officer striking a citizen in both cases.

9.   <u>826</u> respondents said they would support a police officer striking a citizen if the citizen attacked the officer with his fists but not if the citizen said vulgar and obscene things.

10.   <u>77</u> respondents said they would not support a police officer striking a citizen in either situation.

11.   Only <u>1</u> respondent said he/she would support an officer striking a citizen if the citizen said vulgar and obscene things but not if the citizen attacked the officer with his fists.

12.   <u>898</u> of those with an opinion said they would approve of a police officer striking a citizen if the citizen attacked the officer with his fists, whereas <u>78</u> said they would not.

13.   <u>73</u> of those with an opinion said they would approve of a police officer striking a citizen if the citizen said vulgar and obscene things, whereas <u>903</u> said they would not.

14.   SPSS Command 8.3

POLESCAP CITIZEN ATTEMPTING TO ESCAPE CUSTODY * POLMURDR CITIZEN QUESTIONED AS MURDER SUSPECT Crosstabulation

Count

		POLMURDR CITIZEN QUESTIONED AS MURDER SUSPECT			Total
		1 YES	2 NO	8 DK	
POLESCAP CITIZEN ATTEMPTING TO ESCAPE CUSTODY	1 YES	51	614	11	676
	2 NO	8	268	2	278
	8 DK		49	4	53
Total		59	931	17	1007

Example: The table indicates that a large number of respondents make fine distinctions between those situations in which they would and would not support an officer striking a citizen. While only 51 respondents said they would support an officer striking a citizen in both cases and 268 said they would not support an officer striking a citizen in either situation, 614 respondents distinguished between the two situations, indicating they would support an officer if the citizen was attempting to escape custody but not if he was being questioned as a murder suspect. Only 8 respondents said they would support an officer striking a citizen if the citizen was being questioned as a murder suspect but not if the citizen was attempting to escape from custody.

Chapter 9   **SPSS Lab Exercise 9.1[3] (Questions 1–18)**

1–3.   SPSS Command 5.4

              Would you support a police officer striking an adult male citizen if...

1.   Citizen said vulgar or obscene things

2.   Citizen attacked the police officer with his fists

3.
Value	Label
0	NAP
1	Yes
2	No
8	DK
9	NA

4–6.   SPSS Command 9.1

5.   The value of DK for the variables listed in Question 4 is 8.

6.   See SPSS Command 9.1

7.   The lower the index score...

8.   The higher the index score...

9–10.   SPSS Command 9.2

11.   SPSS Command 6.4

---

3. Make sure Don't Know (DK) is designated as missing for each of the variables used in SPSS Lab Exercises 9.1–19.1. See SPSS Command 9.1 to review the procedures for defining missing values.

11.

POLIN

		Frequency	Percent	Valid Percent	Cumulative Percent
Valid	0	72	4.8	7.4	7.4
	1	827	55.1	84.7	92.1
	2	77	5.1	7.9	100.0
	Total	976	65.1	100.0	
Missing	-1	524	34.9		
Total		1500	100.0		

12.   7% received a score of 0 on the index.

         85% received a score of 1 on the index.

         8% received a score of 2 on the index.

13.   SPSS Command 9.3

14.   90% of those with a score of 0 on the index...

         76% of those with a score of 1 on the index...

         9% of those with a score of 2 on the index...

15.   30% of those with a score of 0 on the index...

         4% of those with a score of 1 on the index...

         9% of those with a score of 2 on the index...

16.   85% of those with a score of 0 on the index...

         74% of those with a score of 1 on the index...

         18% of those with a score of 2 on the index...

17.   Example: The POLIN index was validated because it accurately predicts differences in responses to each of the other "Police striking" variables. In each case, those with a lower score on the index are more likely to support a police officer striking a citizen under the conditions specified than are those with a higher score on the index.

18.   SPSS Command 9.4

POLFORCE disapproval of police violence

		Frequency	Percent	Valid Percent	Cumulative Percent
Valid	0	18	1.2	2.0	2.0
	1	77	5.1	8.4	10.3
	2	565	37.7	61.3	71.6
	3	198	13.2	21.5	93.1
	4	64	4.3	6.9	100.0
	Total	922	61.5	100.0	
Missing	-1	578	38.5		
Total		1500	100.0		

POLHITOK EVER APPROVE OF POLICE STRIKING CITIZEN * POLFORCE disapproval of police violence Crosstabulation

			POLFORCE disapproval of police violence					Total
			0	1	2	3	4	
POLHITOK EVER APPROVE OF POLICE STRIKING CITIZEN	1 YES	Count	13	60	446	106	9	634
		% within POLFORCE disapproval of police violence	86.7%	82.2%	80.5%	55.8%	14.8%	71.0%
	2 NO	Count	2	13	108	84	52	259
		% within POLFORCE disapproval of police violence	13.3%	17.8%	19.5%	44.2%	85.2%	29.0%
Total		Count	15	73	554	190	61	893
		% within POLFORCE disapproval of police violence	100.0%	100.0%	100.0%	100.0%	100.0%	100.0%

Chapter 11   SPSS Lab Exercise 11.1 (Questions 1–8)

1. <u>Example: Whites are more likely than Blacks to believe that working women have a detrimental impact on their children.</u>

2. <u>Independent variable: race [RACE]</u>
    <u>Dependent variable: attitudes toward working women [FECHLD]</u>

3–8.   SPSS Command 11.1

3. <u>FECHLD</u>

4. <u>RACE</u>

5.

FECHLD MOTHER WORKING DOESNT HURT CHILDREN * RACE RACE OF RESPONDENT Crosstabulation

			RACE RACE OF RESPONDENT			Total
			1 WHITE	2 BLACK	3 OTHER	
FECHLD MOTHER WORKING DOESNT HURT CHILDREN	1 STRONGLY AGREE	Count	167	32	13	212
		% within RACE RACE OF RESPONDENT	21.6%	22.7%	16.5%	21.4%
	2 AGREE	Count	351	73	39	463
		% within RACE RACE OF RESPONDENT	45.5%	51.8%	49.4%	46.7%
	3 DISAGREE	Count	197	28	21	246
		% within RACE RACE OF RESPONDENT	25.5%	19.9%	26.6%	24.8%
	4 STRONGLY DISAGREE	Count	57	8	6	71
		% within RACE RACE OF RESPONDENT	7.4%	5.7%	7.6%	7.2%
Total		Count	772	141	79	992
		% within RACE RACE OF RESPONDENT	100.0%	100.0%	100.0%	100.0%

FECHLD by RACE

LINE A	White	Black	Other
LINE B	<u>67%</u>	<u>75%</u>	<u>66%</u>

6. <u>Example: Blacks are somewhat more likely than Whites to agree with the statement that a working mother does not have a detrimental impact on her children.</u>

7. $\underline{75 - 67 = 8}$

8.   Example: While we have found evidence of a relationship between race and atti-
            tudes toward the impact of working women on their children, we have not
            proven our hypothesis because while there seems to be an association between
            these two variables, it may not necessarily be a causal relationship.
            Consequently, these findings are probably best looked at as evidence of, not
            proof of, a causal relationship.

Chapter 12   SPSS Lab Exercise 12.1 (Question 1–2)

1–2.   SPSS Command 11.1

1.

NATHEAL IMPROVING & PROTECTING NATIONS HEALTH * HEALTH CONDITION OF HEALTH Crosstabulation

			HEALTH CONDITION OF HEALTH				
			1 EXCELLENT	2 GOOD	3 FAIR	4 POOR	Total
NATHEAL IMPROVING & PROTECTING NATIONS HEALTH	1 TOO LITTLE	Count	141	229	90	25	485
		% within HEALTH CONDITION OF HEALTH	67.8%	64.3%	73.2%	65.8%	66.9%
	2 ABOUT RIGHT	Count	56	109	27	11	203
		% within HEALTH CONDITION OF HEALTH	26.9%	30.6%	22.0%	28.9%	28.0%
	3 TOO MUCH	Count	11	18	6	2	37
		% within HEALTH CONDITION OF HEALTH	5.3%	5.1%	4.9%	5.3%	5.1%
Total		Count	208	356	123	38	725
		% within HEALTH CONDITION OF HEALTH	100.0%	100.0%	100.0%	100.0%	100.0%

NATHEAL by HEALTH

LINE A   <u>Excellent   Good   Fair   Poor</u>

LINE B   <u>68%</u>   <u>64%</u>   <u>73%</u>   <u>66%</u>

2.   Example: There does not appear to be a relationship between the variables repre-
            sented in the table above, NATHEAL and HEALTH. The dependent variable
            (NATHEAL) does not appear to change with changes in the independent variable
            (HEALTH).

Chapter 13   SPSS Lab Exercise 13.1 (Questions 1–9)

1–2.   SPSS Command 5.4

1.   A. PILLOK   Agree/disagree that birth control should be available to teens ages
                         14–16 even if their parents do not approve.

B. SEXEDUC   Favor/oppose sex education in public schools.

C. TEENSEX   Whether or not premarital sex is okay for 14–16 year olds.

2.   A. PILLOK   Value   Label

0   NAP

1   Strongly agree

2   Agree

3   Disagree

4   Strongly disagree

8   DK

9   NA

B. SEXEDUC   0   NAP

1   Favor

2   Oppose

3   Depends

8   DK

9   NA

C. TEENSEX   0   NAP

1   Always wrong

2   Almost always wrong

3   Sometimes wrong

4   Not wrong at all

5   Other

8   DK

9   NA

3.   SPSS Command 6.8

4–9.   SPSS Command 11.1

4.

	Men	Women
PILLREC	56%	55%
SEXEDUC	86%	87%
TEENREC	15%	7%

5.   Example: The table shows that there is very little difference between men and women on these three items. For the first two, PILLREC and SEXEDUC, the percents permissive are within 1% of each other. For TEENREC, about twice the percentage of men were permissive than were women (15% to 7%), but both sexes were overwhelmingly not permissive.

6.

	Strng. A.	Agr.	Disagr.	Strng. D.
PILLREC	39%	44%	59%	70%
SEXEDUC	60%	76%	93%	97%
TEENREC	3%	5%	13%	17%

7.   Example: This table shows that people who disagree with traditional domestic sex roles are also more likely to be permissive in their attitudes toward sex.

8.

	Strng. A.	Agr.	Disagr.	Strng. D.
PILLREC	42%	46%	62%	68%
SEXEDUC	64%	81%	93%	97%
TEENREC	7%	7%	13%	13%

9.   Example: This table shows that the more people believe kids do not suffer when their mother works, the more permissive they tend to be in their attitudes toward sex.

Chapter 14   SPSS Lab Exercise 14.1 (Questions 1–7, 13–21, 29–38)

1–7.   SPSS Command 14.1

1.   Nominal

2.   Nominal

3.   Lambda

4.

	White	Black	Other
Yes	75%	50%	54%

5. <u>Example: Whites are more likely than Blacks or those of "Other" races to say that there are situations in which they would approve of a police officer striking a citizen.</u>

6. The strength/value of <u>lambda</u> is <u>.003</u>.

7. <u>Example: The value of lambda for RACE and POLHITOK is .003, so this is a weak and uninteresting relationship.</u>

13–21. SPSS Command 14.2

13. <u>Ordinal</u>

14. <u>Ordinal</u>

15. <u>Gamma</u>

16.

	All White	Mstly. Wt.	Half-Half	Mstly. Blk	All Black
Very Lkly.	23%	19%	20%	21%	14%
Somewhat Lkly.	53%	46%	45%	42%	29%

17. <u>Example: Those respondents who work with all or mostly Whites are more likely to say that it is either somewhat or very likely that Whites are hurt by affirmative action. Conversely, respondents who work with all or mostly Blacks are less likely to suggest that it is either somewhat or very likely that Whites are hurt by affirmative action.</u>

18. The strength/value of <u>gamma</u> is <u>.127</u>.

19. <u>No</u>

20. <u>The relationship between these two variables as indicated by the value of gamma at .127 is weak to somewhat moderate, suggesting that this is a relationship that, while not particularly strong, may be worth noting.</u>

21. <u>Because neither of these items are numeric, there is no direction of association.</u>

29–32. SPSS Command 14.3

29.

Correlations

		AGE AGE OF RESPONDENT	SEI RESPONDENT SOCIOECONOMIC INDEX
AGE AGE OF RESPONDENT	Pearson Correlation	1.000	-.007
	Sig. (2-tailed)	.	.798
	N	1500	1426
SEI RESPONDENT SOCIOECONOMIC INDEX	Pearson Correlation	-.007	1.000
	Sig. (2-tailed)	.798	.
	N	1426	1426

<u>I/R</u>

30.   I/R

31.   Pearson's *r* for AGE and SEI is <u>−.007</u>.

32.   <u>Example: Pearson's *r* for AGE and SEI is −.007. This indicates a weak, uninter-
             esting relationship that is not worth noting</u>.

33–37.   SPSS Command 14.5

33.
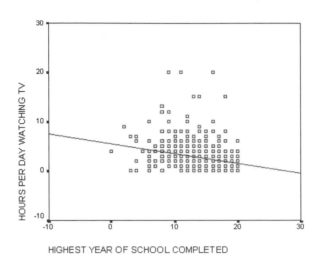

HIGHEST YEAR OF SCHOOL COMPLETED

             <u>I/R</u>

34.   <u>I/R</u>

35.   <u>Negative</u>

36.   <u>Decrease somewhat</u>

37.   <u>Example: The direction of the relationship between the variables is negative. As
             years of education increases, the number of hours of television watched per day
             decreases somewhat. Judging from the spread of the dots (cases) around the regres-
             sion line, the relationship seems to be moderate.</u>

38.   SPSS Command 14.3

             <u>Example: Pearson's *r* for EDUC and TVHOURS is −.269. This indicates a moder-
             ate to somewhat strong relationship that is fairly interesting and worth noting</u>

.

Chapter 15   SPSS Lab Exercise 15.1 (Questions 2–15, 17–19)

2–8.   SPSS Command 15.1

2.

	White	Black	Other	Chi Sq. Asymp. Sig.
Support	9%	43%	23%	.000

	Male	Female	
Support	12%	17%	.038

3. <u>Example: This table suggests that Whites are much less likely than Blacks or those of other races to support affirmative action.</u>

4. <u>.000</u>
<u>Less than .05</u>

5. <u>Example: The significance of chi square is .000, so the relationship between RACE and AFFREC is statistically significant.</u>

6. <u>Example: Women at 17% are slightly more likely than men at 12% to express support for affirmative action.</u>

7. <u>.038</u>
<u>Less than .05</u>

8. <u>Example: The significance of chi square is .038, less than .05, so the relationship between SEX and AFFREC is statistically significant.</u>

9–15. SPSS Command 15.2

9.

Group Statistics

	RACE RACE OF RESPONDENT	N	Mean	Std. Deviation	Std. Error Mean
AGE AGE OF RESPONDENT	1 WHITE	1177	47.36	17.41	.51
	2 BLACK	210	42.38	15.78	1.09
EDUC HIGHEST YEAR OF SCHOOL COMPLETED	1 WHITE	1170	13.45	2.94	8.60E-02
	2 BLACK	209	12.49	2.78	.19
SEI RESPONDENT SOCIOECONOMIC INDEX	1 WHITE	1125	50.369	19.389	.578
	2 BLACK	194	43.757	18.044	1.295

Independent Samples Test

| | | Levene's Test for Equality of Variances | | t-test for Equality of Means | | | | | | |
| | | F | Sig. | t | df | Sig. (2-tailed) | Mean Difference | Std. Error Difference | 95% Confidence Interval of the Difference | |
									Lower	Upper
AGE AGE OF RESPONDENT	Equal variances assumed	6.546	.011	3.868	1385	.000	4.98	1.29	2.45	7.50
	Equal variances not assumed			4.142	307.062	.000	4.98	1.20	2.61	7.34
EDUC HIGHEST YEAR OF SCHOOL COMPLETED	Equal variances assumed	8.746	.003	4.386	1377	.000	.96	.22	.53	1.39
	Equal variances not assumed			4.557	297.076	.000	.96	.21	.55	1.38
SEI RESPONDENT SOCIOECONOMIC INDEX	Equal variances assumed	10.027	.002	4.430	1317	.000	6.612	1.492	3.684	9.540
	Equal variances not assumed			4.661	275.630	.000	6.612	1.419	3.819	9.405

	White	*Black*
AGE		
Mean	47.36	42.38
Sig.	.000	
EDUC		
Mean	13.45	12.49
Sig.	.000	
SEI		
Mean	50.369	43.757
Sig.	.000	

10.   Higher
       $47.36 - 42.38 = 4.98$

11.   Example: The mean age of Whites is higher than that of Blacks, and the difference is significant.

12.   Higher
       $13.45 - 12.49 = .96$

13.   Example: The mean education of Whites is slightly higher than that of Blacks, and the difference is significant.

14.   Higher
       $50.369 - 43.757 = 6.612$

15.   Example: The mean SEI of Whites is higher than that of Blacks, and the difference is significant.

17–19.   SPSS Command 15.3

17.

Tests of Between-Subjects Effects

Dependent Variable: EDUC HIGHEST YEAR OF SCHOOL COMPLETED

Source	Type III Sum of Squares	df	Mean Square	F	Sig.
Corrected Model	1279.551ª	4	319.888	42.097	.000
Intercept	4107.452	1	4107.452	540.537	.000
CLASS	1279.551	4	319.888	42.097	.000
Error	11261.472	1482	7.599		
Total	275494.0	1487			
Corrected Total	12541.024	1486			

a. R Squared = .102 (Adjusted R Squared = .100)

.000

18.   Example: The findings are statistically significant. If EDUC and CLASS were
unrelated to each other in the population, we might expect samples that would generate this kind of explained variance less than once in 1,000 samples.

19.

Tests of Between-Subjects Effects

Dependent Variable: AGE AGE OF RESPONDENT

Source	Type III Sum of Squares	df	Mean Square	F	Sig.
Corrected Model	12573.160ª	4	3143.290	10.888	.000
Intercept	65611.883	1	65611.883	227.273	.000
CLASS	12573.160	4	3143.290	10.888	.000
Error	430151.4	1490	288.692		
Total	3573935	1495			
Corrected Total	442724.6	1494			

a. R Squared = .028 (Adjusted R Squared = .026)

Chapter 17   SPSS Lab Exercise 17.1 (Questions 1–3, 5–7, 18–23)

1–8.   SPSS Command 17.1

1.

	Lower	Working	Middle	Upper
White	70%	67%	56%	54%
Black	75%	85%	72%	80%

2.   For whites:... decreases

3.   For blacks:... stays about the same

5.

	Lower	Working	Middle	Upper	Chi Sqr.	Sig.
Male	33%	17%	11%	12%	10.452	.107
Female	26%	16%	16%	7%	7.985	.239

6.   For males:… <u>decreases</u>… <u>is not</u>

7.   For females:… <u>decreases</u>… <u>is not</u>

18–23.   SPSS Commands 17.2 and 17.3

18.

Coefficients[a]

Model		Unstandardized Coefficients		Standardized Coefficients	t	Sig.
		B	Std. Error	Beta		
1	(Constant)	5.475	.276		19.850	.000
	EDUC HIGHEST YEAR OF SCHOOL COMPLETED	-.199	.020	-.269	-9.835	.000
2	(Constant)	5.715	.289		19.785	.000
	EDUC HIGHEST YEAR OF SCHOOL COMPLETED	-.194	.020	-.263	-9.594	.000
	RACE2 Dummy Race	-.386	.142	-.075	-2.729	.006
3	(Constant)	5.336	.343		15.565	.000
	EDUC HIGHEST YEAR OF SCHOOL COMPLETED	-.187	.020	-.253	-9.104	.000
	RACE2 Dummy Race	-.443	.144	-.086	-3.076	.002
	AGE AGE OF RESPONDENT	7.133E-03	.003	.058	2.049	.041

a. Dependent Variable: TVHOURS HOURS PER DAY WATCHING TV

19.   <u>5.475</u>

20.   <u>–.199</u>

21.   TVHOURS = <u>5.475</u> + (EDUC × <u>–.199</u>)

22.   TVHOURS = <u>5.475</u> + (10 × <u>–.199</u>) = <u>3.485</u>

23.   TVHOURS = <u>5.715</u> + (EDUC × <u>–.194</u>) + (WHITE × <u>–.386</u>)

Chapter 18   SPSS Lab Exercise 18.1 (Questions 1–2)

1–2.   SPSS Command 15.1

1.   <u>Less likely</u>

2.   <u>Less than   is</u>

Chapter 19   SPSS Lab Exercise 19.1 (Questions 1–5)

1.   SPSS Command 9.1

2.   SPSS Command 19.1

3.   SPSS Command 9.2

4.

IND1

		Frequency	Percent	Valid Percent	Cumulative Percent
Valid	0 very liberal	83	5.5	8.8	8.8
	1 liberal	434	28.9	46.3	55.1
	2 conservative	321	21.4	34.2	89.3
	3 very conservative	100	6.7	10.7	100.0
	Total	938	62.5	100.0	
Missing	-1 missing	562	37.5		
Total		1500	100.0		

5.

FEPRESCH PRESCHOOL KIDS SUFFER IF MOTHER WORKS * IND1 Crosstabulation

			IND1				Total
			0 very liberal	1 liberal	2 conservative	3 very conservative	
FEPRESCH PRESCHOOL KIDS SUFFER IF MOTHER WORKS	1 agree	Count	19	148	146	71	384
		% within IND1	23.5%	35.0%	46.5%	73.2%	42.0%
	2 disagree	Count	62	275	168	26	531
		% within IND1	76.5%	65.0%	53.5%	26.8%	58.0%
Total		Count	81	423	314	97	915
		% within IND1	100.0%	100.0%	100.0%	100.0%	100.0%

FECHLD MOTHER WORKING DOESNT HURT CHILDREN * IND1 Crosstabulation

			IND1				Total
			0 very liberal	1 liberal	2 conservative	3 very conservative	
FECHLD MOTHER WORKING DOESNT HURT CHILDREN	1 agree	Count	68	316	209	40	633
		% within IND1	81.9%	73.3%	66.8%	40.8%	68.4%
	2 disagree	Count	15	115	104	58	292
		% within IND1	18.1%	26.7%	33.2%	59.2%	31.6%
Total		Count	83	431	313	98	925
		% within IND1	100.0%	100.0%	100.0%	100.0%	100.0%

Appendix B   The Research Report

This book has considered the variety of activities that compose the analysis of social research. In this appendix, we turn to an often neglected subject: reporting your analyses of data to others. Unless the research is properly communicated, all the efforts devoted to the previously discussed procedures will go for naught.

Before proceeding further on this topic, we should suggest one absolutely basic guideline. Good social scientific reporting requires good English (unless you are writing in a foreign language). Whenever we ask the figures to speak for themselves, they tend to remain mute. Whenever we use unduly complex terminology or construction, communication is reduced. Every researcher should read and reread (at approximately three-month intervals) an excellent small book by William Strunk, Jr., and E. B. White, *The Elements of Style*.[1] If you do this faithfully, and if even 10 percent of the contents rub off, you stand a rather good chance of making yourself understood and your findings perhaps appreciated.

Scientific reporting has several functions, and it is a good idea to keep these in mind. First, the report communicates to an audience a body of specific data and ideas. The report should provide those specifics clearly and with sufficient detail to permit an informed evaluation. Second, the scientific report should be viewed as a contribution to the general body of professional knowledge. While remaining appropriately humble, you should always regard your research report as an addition to what we know about social research. Finally, the report should serve the function of stimulating and directing further inquiry.

Some Basic Considerations

Despite these general guidelines, different reports serve different purposes. A report that is appropriate for one purpose might be wholly inappropriate for another. This section of this appendix deals with some of the basic considerations in this regard.

Audience

Before drafting your report, you must ask yourself who you hope will read it. Normally, you should make a distinction between professional colleagues and general readers. If your report is written for the former, you may make certain assumptions about their existing knowledge and may perhaps summarize certain points rather than explaining them in detail. Similarly, you may use more technical language than would be appropriate for a general audience.

At the same time, you should always remain aware that any science or profession is composed of factions or cults. Terms and assumptions acceptable to your immediate colleagues may confuse other professionals. The possibility of confusion applies with regard to substance as well as techniques. The family sociologist who is writing for a general audience, for example, should explain previous findings in more detail than would be necessary if he or she were addressing an audience of sociologists specializing in the family area.

Form and Length of the Report

We should begin this subsection by saying that our comments apply to both written and oral reports. These two forms, however, will affect the nature of the report.

It is useful to think about the variety of reports that might result from a research project. To begin, you may wish to prepare a short *research note* for publication in an academic or technical journal. Such reports should be approximately one to five pages in length (typed, double-spaced) and should be concise and direct. In such a small amount of space, you will not be able to present the state of the field in any detail, and your methodological notes must be somewhat abbreviated as well. Basically, you should tell the reader why you feel a brief note is justified by your findings, and then tell what those findings are.

Often, researchers must prepare reports for the sponsors of their research. These may vary greatly in length, of course. In preparing such a report, however, you should bear in mind the audience for the report—scientific or lay persons—and their reasons for sponsoring the project in the first place. It is both bad politics and bad manners to bore the sponsors with research findings in which they have no interest or which have no value to them. At the same time, it may be useful to summarize the ways in which the research has advanced basic scientific knowledge (if it has).

Working papers or monographs are another form of research reporting. Especially for a large and complex project, it will be useful to obtain comments on your analysis and the interpretation of your data. A working paper constitutes a tentative presentation with an implicit request for comments. Working papers can also vary in length, and they may present all of the research findings of the project or only a portion of them. Because your professional reputation is not at stake in a working paper, you should feel free to present tentative interpretations that you cannot altogether justify—identifying them as such and asking for evaluations.

Many research projects result in papers delivered at professional meetings. Often, these serve the same purpose as working papers. You can present findings and ideas of possible interest to your colleagues and ask for their comments. Although the length of professional papers may vary depending on the organization of the meetings, we encourage you to say too little rather than too much. Although a working paper may ramble somewhat through a variety of tentative conclusions, conference participants should not be forced to sit through an oral unveiling of the same. Interested listeners can always ask for more details later, and uninterested ones can gratefully escape.

Probably the most popular research report is the article published in an academic journal. Again, lengths vary, and you should examine the lengths of articles previously published by the journal in question. As a rough guide, however, 20 typed pages is as good as any. A subsequent section on the organization of the report is based primarily on the structure of a journal article, so we shall say no more at this point, except to indicate that student term papers should be written on this model. As a general rule, a term paper that would make a good journal article will also make a good term paper.

A book, of course, represents the most prestigious form of research report. It has all the advantages of the working paper—length and detail—but it should be a more polished document. Because the publication of research findings as a book gives those findings an appearance of greater substance and worth, you have a special obligation to your audience. Although you will still hope to receive comments from colleagues, possibly leading you to revise your ideas, you must realize that other readers may be led to accept your findings uncritically.

Aim of the Report

Some reports may focus primarily on the *exploration* of a topic of interest. Inherent in this aim is the tentativeness and incompleteness of the conclusions. You should clearly indicate to your audience the exploratory aim of the study and point to the shortcomings of the particular project. An important aspect of an exploratory report is to point the way to more refined research on the topic.

Many studies have a *descriptive* purpose, and the research reports from such studies will have a descriptive element. You should carefully distinguish for the reader those descriptions that apply only to the sample and those that are inferred to the population. Whenever inferential descriptions are to be made, you should give your audience some indication of the probable range of error in those descriptions.

Many reports have an *explanatory* aim; the writer wishes to point to causal relationships among variables. Depending on the probable audience for your report, you should carefully delineate the rules of explanation that lie behind your computations and conclusions, and, as in the case of description, you must give your readers some guide to the relative certainty of your conclusions.

Finally, some research reports may have the aim of *proposing action*. For example, the researcher of prejudice may wish to suggest ways in which prejudice may be reduced, on the basis of the research findings. This aim often presents knotty problems, however, because your own values and orientations may interfere with your proposals. Although it is perfectly legitimate for your proposals to be motivated by personal values, you must ensure that the specific actions you propose are warranted by your data. Thus you should be especially careful to spell out the logic by which you move from empirical data to proposed action.

Organization of the Report

Although the organization of reports differs somewhat on the basis of form and purpose, it is possible to suggest a general format for presenting research data. The following comments apply most directly to a journal article, but with some modification they apply to most forms of research reports.

Purpose and Overview

It is always helpful to the reader if you begin with a brief statement of the purpose of the study and the main findings of the analysis. In a journal article, such an overview is sometimes given in the form of an *abstract* or *synopsis*.

Some researchers find this difficult to do. For example, your analysis may have involved considerable detective work, with important findings revealing themselves only as a result of imaginative deduction and data manipulation. You may wish, therefore, to lead the reader through the same exciting process with a degree of suspense and surprise. To the extent that this form of reporting gives an accurate picture of the research process, we feel it has considerable instructional value. Nevertheless, many readers may not be interested in following your entire research account, and not knowing the purpose and general conclusions in advance may make it difficult for them to understand the significance of the study.

An old forensic dictum says: Tell them what you're going to tell them; tell them; and then tell them what you told them. You would do well to follow this dictum in the preparation of research reports.

Review of the Literature

Because every research report should be placed in the context of the general body of scientific knowledge, it is important to indicate where your report fits in that picture. Having presented the general purpose of your study, you should then bring the reader up to date on the previous research in the area, pointing to general agreements and disagreements among the previous researchers.

In some cases, you may wish to challenge previously accepted ideas. You should carefully review the studies that led to the acceptance of those ideas and then indicate the factors that have not previously been considered or the logical fallacies present in the previous research.

When you are concerned with resolving a disagreement among previous researchers, you should organize your review of the literature around the opposing points of view. You should summarize the research supporting one view, then summarize the research supporting the other, and finally suggest the reasons for the disagreement.

To an extent, your review of the literature serves a bibliographic function for readers, indexing the previous research on a given topic. This can be overdone, however, and you should avoid an opening paragraph that runs three pages, mentioning every previous study in the field. The comprehensive bibliographic function can best be served by a bibliography at the end of the report, and the review of the literature should focus on only those studies that have direct relevance to the present study.

Avoiding Plagiarism

Whenever you are reporting on the work of others, it is important that you be clear about who said what. It is essential that you avoid *plagiarism*, the theft of another's words and/or ideas—whether intentional or accidental—and the presentation of those words and ideas as your own. Because this is a common and sometimes unclear problem for college students, let's take a minute to examine it in some detail. Here are the main ground rules regarding plagiarism:

- You cannot use another writer's exact words without using quotation marks (or setting off the quote as an extract) and giving a complete citation, which indicates the source of the quotation such that your reader could locate that quotation in its original context. As a rule of thumb, taking a passage of eight or more words without citation is a violation of federal copyright laws.

- It is also not acceptable to edit or paraphrase another's words and present the revised version as your own work.

- Finally, it is not acceptable even to present another's ideas as your own, even if you use totally different words to express those ideas.

The following examples should clarify what is and is not acceptable in the use of another's work.

The Original Work

Laws of Growth

Systems are like babies: once you get one, you have it. They don't go away. On the contrary, they display the most remarkable persistence. They not only persist; they grow. And as they grow, they encroach. The growth potential of systems was explored in a tentative, preliminary way by Parkinson, who concluded that administrative systems maintain average growth of 5 to 6 percent per annum regardless of the work to be done. Parkinson was right so far as he goes, and we must give him full honors for initiating the serious study of this important topic. But what Parkinson failed to perceive, we now enunciate the general systems analog of Parkinson's Law.

The System Itself Tends to Grow At 5 to 6 Percent Per Annum

Again, this Law is but the preliminary to the most general possible formulation, the Big-Bang Theorem of Systems Cosmology.

Systems Tend to Expand to Fill the Known Universe[2]

Now let's look at some of the *acceptable* ways you might make use of Gall's work in a term paper.

Acceptable: John Gall, in his work titled *Systemantics*, draws a humorous parallel between systems and infants: "Systems are like babies: once you get one, you have it. They don't go away. On the contrary, they display the most remarkable persistence. They not only persist; they grow."[3]

Acceptable: John Gall warns that systems are like babies. Create a system and it sticks around. Worse yet, Gall notes, systems keep growing larger and larger.[4]

Acceptable: It has also been suggested that systems have a natural tendency to persist, even grow and encroach (Gall 1975, p. 12). [Note: This format requires that you give a complete citation in your bibliography or reference section.]

Here now are some *unacceptable* uses of the same material, reflecting some common errors.

Unacceptable: In this paper, I want to look at some of the characteristics of the social systems we create in our organizations. First, systems are like babies: once you get one, you have it. They don't go away. On the contrary, they display the most remarkable persistence. They not only persist; they grow. [It is unacceptable to quote someone else's material directly without using quotation marks and giving a full citation.]

Unacceptable: In this paper, I want to look at some of the characteristics of the social systems we create in our organizations. First, systems are a lot like children: once you get one, it's yours. They don't go away; they persist. They not only persist, in fact: They grow. [It is unacceptable to edit another's work and present it as your own.]

Unacceptable: In this paper, I want to look at some of the characteristics of the social systems we create in our organizations. One thing I've noticed is that once you create a system, it never seems to go away. Just the opposite, in fact: They have tendency to grow. You might say systems are a lot like children in that respect. [It is unacceptable to paraphrase someone else's ideas and present them as your own.]

All of the preceding unacceptable examples show instances of plagiarism, and they represent a serious offense. Admittedly, there are some gray areas. Some ideas are more or less in the public domain, not belonging to any one person. Or you may reach an idea on your own that someone else has already put in writing. If you have a question about a specific situation, discuss it with your instructor in advance.

We have discussed this topic in some detail because it is important that you place your research in the context of what others have done and said, and yet the improper use of others' material is a serious offense. Mastering this matter, however, is a part of your coming of age as a scholar.

Study Design and Execution

A research report containing interesting findings and conclusions can be very frustrating when the reader is unable to determine the methodological design and execution of the study. The worth of all scientific findings depends heavily on the manner in which the data were collected and analyzed.

In reporting the design and execution of a survey, for example, you should always include the following: the population, the sampling frame, the sampling method, the sample size, the data collection method, the completion rate, and the methods of data processing and analysis. Comparable details should be given if other methods are used. The experienced researcher is able to report these details in a rather short space, without omitting anything required for the reader's evaluation of the study.

Analysis and Interpretation

Having set the study in the perspective of previous research, and having described the design and execution of it, you should then present your data. The following major section will provide further guidelines in this regard. For now, a few general comments are in order.

The presentation of data, the manipulations of those data, and your interpretations should be integrated into a logical whole. It is frustrating to the reader to discover a collection of seemingly unrelated analyses and findings with a promise that all the loose ends will be tied together later in the report. Every step in the analysis should make sense—at the time it is taken. You should present your rationale for a particular analysis, present the data relevant to it, interpret the results, and then indicate where that result leads next.

Summary and Conclusions

Following the forensic dictum mentioned earlier, we believe it is essential to summarize the research report. You should avoid reviewing every specific finding, but you should review all of the significant ones, pointing once more to their general significance.

The report should conclude with a statement of what you have discovered about your subject matter and where future research might be directed. A quick review of recent journal articles will probably indicate a very high frequency of the concluding statement, "It is clear that much more research is needed." This is probably always a true conclusion, but it is of little value unless you can offer pertinent suggestions about the nature of that future research. You should review the particular shortcomings of your own study and suggest ways in which those shortcomings might be avoided by future researchers. You should also draw implications for social welfare policy and program development, social work practice, and, if appropriate, social work education. Make sure that the implications that you develop are supported by your findings; do not use this section of the report as a license to make unsupported editorial pronouncements.

Guidelines for Reporting Analyses

The presentation of data analyses should provide a maximum of detail without being cluttered. You can accomplish that best by continually examining your report to see whether it achieves the following aims.

Quantitative data should be presented in such a way as to permit recomputations by the reader. In the case of percentage tables, for example, the reader should be able to collapse categories and recompute the percentages. Readers should be given sufficient information to permit them to compute percentages in the table in the opposite direction from your own presentation.

All aspects of the analysis should be described in sufficient detail to permit a secondary analyst to replicate the analysis from the same body of data. This means that he or she should be able to create the same indexes and scales, produce the same tables, arrive at the same regression equations, obtain the same factors and factor loadings, and so forth. That will seldom be done, of course, but if the report is presented in such a manner as to make it possible, the reader will be far better equipped to evaluate the report.

A final guide to the reporting of methodological details is that the reader should be in a position to replicate the entire study independently. Recall from our earlier discussions in this book that replicability is an essential norm of science generally. A single study does not prove a point; only a series of studies can begin to do so. Unless studies can be replicated, there can be no meaningful series of studies.

We previously mentioned the importance of integrating data, analysis, and interpretations in the report. A more specific guideline can be offered in this regard. Tables, charts, and figures, if any, should be integrated into the text of the report—appearing near that portion of the text discussing them. Sometimes students describe their analyses in the body of the report and place all the tables in an appendix at the end. This procedure greatly impedes the reader. As a general rule, it is best to (a) describe the purpose for presenting the table, (b) present it, and (c) review and interpret it.

Be explicit in drawing conclusions. Although research is typically conducted for the purpose of drawing general conclusions, you should carefully note the specific basis for such conclusions. Otherwise you may lead your reader into accepting unwarranted conclusions.

Point to any qualifications or conditions warranted in the evaluation of conclusions. Typically, you are in the best position to know the shortcomings and tentativeness of your conclusions, and you should give the reader the advantage of that knowledge. Failure to do so can misdirect future research and result in a waste of research funds.

We will conclude with a point made at the outset of this appendix, as it is extremely important. Research reports should be written in the best possible literary style. Writing lucidly is easier for some people than for others, and it is always harder than writing poorly. You are again referred to Strunk and White's *Elements of Style*. Every researcher would do well to follow this procedure: Write. Read Strunk and White. Revise. Reread Strunk and White. Revise again. That will be a difficult and time-consuming endeavor, but so is science.

A perfectly designed, carefully executed, and brilliantly analyzed study will be altogether worthless unless you are able to communicate your findings to others. This appendix has attempted to provide some general and specific guidelines toward that end. The best guides are logic, clarity, and honesty. Ultimately, there is no substitute for practice.

Notes

1. William Strunk, Jr., and E. B. White, *The Elements of Style*, 3rd ed. (New York: Macmillan, 1979). Another useful reference about writing is H. W. Fowler, *A Dictionary of Modern English Usage* (New York: Oxford University Press, 1965).

2. John Gall, *Systemantics: How Systems Work and Especially How They Fail* (New York: Quadrangle, 1975), 12–14. Note that in the original work Gall previously gave a full citation for Parkinson.

3. John Gall, *Systemantics: How Systems Work and Especially How They Fail* (New York: Quadrangle, 1975), 12.

4. John Gall, *Systemantics: How Systems Work and Especially How They Fail* (New York: Quadrangle, 1975), 12.

References

Alreck, Pamela A., & Settle, Robert B., 1985. *The Survey Research Handbook*. Homewood, IL: Irwin.

Alwin, Duane F. 1989. "Changes in Qualities Valued in Children in the United States, 1964 to 1984." *Social Science Research*, 18:195–236.

Babbie, Earl. 1990. *Survey Research Methods*, 2nd Ed. Belmont, CA: Wadsworth.

——. 1998. *The Practice of Social Research*, 8th Ed. Belmont, CA: Wadsworth.

Bailey, Kenneth D. 1994. *Methods of Social Research*, 4th Ed. New York: Free Press.

Becker, Howard S. 1986. *Writing for Social Scientists*. Chicago: University of Chicago Press.

Blake, Judith. 1989. *Family Size and Achievement*. Berkeley: University of California Press.

Carmines, Edward G., & Champagne, Richard A. Jr. 1990. "The Changing Content of American Racial Attitudes: A Fifty Year Portrait." *Research in Micropolitics*, 3:187–208.

Cook, Elizabeth Addell, Jelen, Ted G., & Wilcox, Clyde. 1992. *Between Two Absolutes: Public Opinion and the Politics of Abortion*. Boulder, CO: Westview.

Cuba, Lee. 1997. *A Short Guide to Writing About Social Science*, 3rd Ed. New York: Longman.

Czaja, Ronald, & Blair, Johnny. 1996. *Designing Surveys: A Guide to Decisions and Procedures*. Thousand Oaks, CA: Pine Forge Press.

D'Antonio, William V., & Stack, Steven. 1980. "Religion, Ideal Family Size, and Abortion: Extending Renzi's Hypothesis." *Journal for the Scientific Study of Religion*, 19:397–408.

Davis, James A., & Smith, Tom W. 1992. *The NORC General Social Survey: A User's Guide*. Newbury Park, CA: Sage.

—— 1996. *General Social Surveys, 1972–1996: Cumulative Codebook*. Chicago: National Opinion Research Center.

Davis, James A., Smith, Tom W. & Marsden, Peter V. 1999. *General Social Surveys, 1972–1998 Cumulative Codebook*. Chicago: National Opinion Research Center.

Frankfort-Nachmias, Chava. 1997. *Social Statistics for a Diverse Society*. Thousand Oaks, CA: Pine Forge Press.

—— (forthcoming). *Introduction to Social Statistics*. Thousand Oaks, CA: Pine Forge Press.

Freedman, David, Pisani, Robert, & Purves, Roger. 1998. *Statistics*, 3rd Ed. Belmont, CA: Wadsworth.

Freeman, Linton. 1968. *Elementary Applied Statistics*. New York: John Wiley & Sons.

Glock, Charles Y., Ringer, Benjamin B., & Babbie, Earl R. 1967. *To Comfort and to Challenge*. Berkeley: University of California Press.

Grisby, Jill S. 1992. "Women Change Places." *American Demographics,* 14:46–50.

Healey, Joseph. 1996. *Statistics: A Tool for Social Research*, 4th Ed. Belmont, CA: Wadsworth.

Healey, Joseph, Boli, John, Babbie, Earl, & Halley, Fred. 1999. *Exploring Social Issues Using SPSS for Windows*. Thousand Oaks, CA: Pine Forge Press.

Judd, Charles M., Kidder, Louise H., & Smith, Eliot R. 1991. *Research Methods in the Social Relations*. Fort Worth: Holt, Rinehart & Winston.

Levin, Jack, & Fox, James Alan. 2000. *Elementary Statistics in Social Research*, 7th Ed. New York: Longman.

Loether, Herman J. 1993. *Descriptive and Inferential Statistics: An Introduction*. Boston: Allyn and Bacon.

Moore, David S., and McCabe, George P. 1993. *Introduction to the Practice of Statistics,* 2nd Ed. New York: W. H. Freeman.

Nakao, Keiko, & Treas, Judith. 1994. "Updating Occupational Prestige and Socioeconomic Scores: How the New Measures Measure Up." *Sociological Methodology*, 24:1–72.

Neuman, William Lawrence. 1999. *Social Research Methods: Qualitative and Quantitative Approaches*. Boston: Allyn and Bacon.

Renzi, Mario. 1975. "Ideal Family Size as an Intervening Variable Between Religion and Attitudes Towards Abortion." *Journal for the Scientific Study of Religion*, 14:23–27.

Rubin, Allen, & Babbie, Earl. 1997. *Research Methods for Social Work*, 3rd Ed. Belmont, CA: Wadsworth.

Schuman, Howard, Steeh, Charlotte, & Bobo, Lawrence. 1985. *Racial Attitudes in America: Trends and Interpretations*. Cambridge, MA: Harvard University Press.

Schutt, Russell K. 1999. *Investigating the Social World: The Process and Practice of Research*, 2nd Ed. Thousand Oaks, CA: Pine Forge Press.

Siegel, Sidney, & Catsellan, N. John Jr. 1988. *Nonparametric Statistics for the Behavioral Sciences*, 2nd Ed. New York: McGraw Hill.

Smith, Tom W., & Arnold, Bradley J. 1990. "The Polls: A Report: The Sexual Revolution?" *Public Opinion Quarterly*, 54:415–35.

———. 1996. *Annotated Bibliography of Papers Using the General Social Survey*, 11th ed. Chicago: National Opinion Research Center.

SPSS. 1999. *SPSS Base 9.0 User's Guide*. Chicago: SPSS Inc.

Weber, Max. 1958. *The Protestant Ethic and the Spirit of Capitalism*. Translated by Talcott Parsons. Reprint. New York: Scribners.

Wellings, Kaye, Field, Julia, & Whitaker, Luke. 1994. "Sexual Attitudes" in *Sexual Attitudes and Lifestyles*. Oxford: Blackwell Scientific Publications, 225–58.

Witte, Robert S. 1997. *Statistics*, 5th Ed. Fort Worth: Harcourt Brace College Publishers.

Index/Glossary

A

Abortion, 12, 28, 126–129
Abortion attitudes, 12–13, 123, 126–129
    age, 213–214
    causes, 126–129, 211, 232
    education, 219
    family, 219
    family size, 127, 132, 171–172
    gender, 211–213
    generational differences, 213
    politics, 216–218
    predicting, 126–129, 155, 160, 231
    race, 219
    religion, 214–216
    sexual attitudes, 173, 218–219
    social class differences, 130–133
active cell—The cell in the SPSS data editor with heavy black lines around it which can be moved in numerous ways.
Active cell, 62
Age:
    abortion attitudes, 213–214
    as continuous variable, 81
    gender, religiosity and, 309–311
    politics, 197–199
    religiosity, 10, 186–188
algorithm—A detailed sequence of actions or steps to perform in order to accomplish a task.
Algorithm, 147
analysis of variance (ANOVA)—An analytical technique aimed at determining whether variables are related to each other. It is based on a comparison of the differences (income, for example) between 3 or more subgroups and the variance on the same variable within each of the subgroups. For example, how does the difference in average income compare with income differences among Whites, Blacks, and Asians?
analysis of variance (ANOVA), 288–290
Attributes. *See* **category/categories**
Average. *See* Mean

B

Babbie, E.R., 10, 181, 186
bar chart—A graph that displays the frequency or percentage of various categories of a variable. Categories of the variable are displayed along the horizontal axis, while frequencies or percentages are displayed along the vertical axis. The height of the bar indicates the frequency or percentage of cases in each category. Particularly useful in displaying variables with a relatively small number of categories, such as discrete/categorical data and data at the nominal or ordinal levels of measurement.
Bar chart, 106–110, 116–117
bivariate analysis—A mode of data analysis in which two variables are examined simultaneously for the purpose of discovering whether they are related to each other, or independent of one another. An example would be the analysis of

gender and attitudes toward abortion. It is the beginning foundation for causal analysis.
Bivariate analysis, 123, 181, 185. *See also* Abortion; Child training; Family size, desired; Measures of association; Political orientations; Poverty explanations; Prejudice; Religiosity; Sexual behavior attitudes; Tests of significance
    versus multivariate analysis, 309
Bivariate distribution. *See* Crosstabulation

C

Capital punishment, 12, 206
Case. *See* Respondent
categorical variables—Categorical or discrete variables are those whose attributes or values are completely separate from one another; such as gender, with the attributes male and female. Distinguished from continuous variables.
Categorical variables, 182
category/categories—The specific attributes that make up a variable. For example, the categories or attributes of the variable SEX (gender) are 'male' and 'female.' While the categories or attributes of the variable MARITAL (marital status) are 'married,' 'widowed,' 'divorced,' 'separated' and 'never married.' It is sometimes easy to confuse the categories or attributes of a variable with the variable itself.
Category/categories, 1
ceiling effect—A term used to refer to situations in which, for example, the overall percentage of respondents agreeing to something approaches one-hundred percent, making it impossible for there to be much variation among subgroups.
Ceiling effect, 216
cell editor—The small window just below the Tool bar in the SPSS Data Editor. When entering data in SPSS you will notice that it appears in the Cell Editor before being recorded in the Data Matrix.
Cell editor, 393
Child training, 172
Children, 28
chi-square—A test of statistical significance appropriate for two nominal variables.
Chi-square
    calculating, 280–283
    contingency table logic, 277–280
close-ended question—Questionnaire items in which the respondent is provided with preformulated responses to choose from. For example, Have you ever been divorced or legally separated?_1.Yes_2.No_3.Don't Know
Close-ended question, 391
Code. *See* Value
Coding, 241
coding—Along with editing the questionnaire, this is the second step in the process of getting ready for data analysis. Coding involves transforming the raw data collected into a fixed form which can easily be entered into the computer.